MW00560070

CONSTITUTIONAL LAW

TWELFTH EDITION

STEVEN L. EMANUEL

Founder and Editor-in-Chief, the *CrunchTime* series,
Emanuel Law Outlines, and *Emanuel Bar Review*

Harvard Law School, J.D. 1976
Member, NY, CT, MD and VA bars

The Emanuel CrunchTime® Series

Copyright © 2013 CCH Incorporated.

Published by Wolters Kluwer Law & Business in New York.

Wolters Kluwer Law & Business serves customers worldwide with CCH, Aspen Publishers, and Kluwer Law International products. (www.wolterskluwerlb.com)

No part of this publication may be reproduced or transmitted in any form or by any means, electronic or mechanical, including photocopy, recording, or utilized by any information storage or retrieval system, without written permission from the publisher. For information about permissions or to request permissions online, visit us at www.wolterskluwerlb.com, or a written request may be faxed to our permissions department at 212-771-0803.

To contact Customer Service, e-mail customer.service@wolterskluwer.com, call 1-800-234-1660, fax 1-800-901-9075, or mail correspondence to:

Wolters Kluwer Law & Business
Attn: Order Department
PO Box 990
Frederick, MD 21705

Printed in the United States of America.

1 2 3 4 5 6 7 8 9 0

ISBN 978-1-4548-2486-2

This book is intended as a general review of a legal subject. It is not intended as a source of advice for the solution of legal matters or problems. For advice on legal matters, the reader should consult an attorney.

Certified Chain of Custody
Product Line Contains At Least
20% Certified Forest Content
www.sfiprogram.org
SFI-00756

About Wolters Kluwer Law & Business

Wolters Kluwer Law & Business is a leading global provider of intelligent information and digital solutions for legal and business professionals in key specialty areas, and respected educational resources for professors and law students. Wolters Kluwer Law & Business connects legal and business professionals as well as those in the education market with timely, specialized authoritative content and information-enabled solutions to support success through productivity, accuracy and mobility.

Serving customers worldwide, Wolters Kluwer Law & Business products include those under the Aspen Publishers, CCH, Kluwer Law International, Loislaw, ftwilliam.com and MediRegs family of products.

CCH products have been a trusted resource since 1913, and are highly regarded resources for legal, securities, antitrust and trade regulation, government contracting, banking, pension, payroll, employment and labor, and healthcare reimbursement and compliance professionals.

Aspen Publishers products provide essential information to attorneys, business professionals and law students. Written by preeminent authorities, the product line offers analytical and practical information in a range of specialty practice areas from securities law and intellectual property to mergers and acquisitions and pension/benefits. Aspen's trusted legal education resources provide professors and students with high-quality, up-to-date and effective resources for successful instruction and study in all areas of the law.

Kluwer Law International products provide the global business community with reliable international legal information in English. Legal practitioners, corporate counsel and business executives around the world rely on Kluwer Law journals, looseleafs, books, and electronic products for comprehensive information in many areas of international legal practice.

Loislaw is a comprehensive online legal research product providing legal content to law firm practitioners of various specializations. Loislaw provides attorneys with the ability to quickly and efficiently find the necessary legal information they need, when and where they need it, by facilitating access to primary law as well as state-specific law, records, forms and treatises.

ftwilliam.com offers employee benefits professionals the highest quality plan documents (retirement, welfare and non-qualified) and government forms (5500/PBGC, 1099 and IRS) software at highly competitive prices.

MediRegs products provide integrated health care compliance content and software solutions for professionals in healthcare, higher education and life sciences, including professionals in accounting, law and consulting.

Wolters Kluwer Law &Business, a division of Wolters Kluwer, is headquartered in New York. Wolters Kluwer is a market-leading global information services company focused on professionals.

TABLE OF CONTENTS

Preface

Thank you for buying this book.

The *CrunchTime* Series is intended for people who want Emanuel quality, but don't have the time or money to buy and use the full-length *Emanuel Law Outline* on a subject. I've designed the Series to be used in the last few weeks (or even less) before your final exams. This edition covers all Supreme Court developments through the end of the Court's 2012-2013 term, including:

❏ *U.S. v. Windsor*, in which the Court invalidated the federal Defense of Marriage Act's ban on federal recognition of state-sanctioned **same-sex marriages;**

❏ *Fisher v. Univ. of Texas*, where the Court said that **race-conscious admissions systems** at public universities **violate Equal Protection** unless the university proves that there are **"no workable race-neutral alternative methods"**; and

❏ *Shelby County v. Holder*, where the Court invalidated a key part of **the Voting Rights Act of 1965**, by holding that the Act's **"preclearance"** requirement — compelling certain states to get advance federal approval for even small changes to their voting methods — went beyond Congress' Fifteenth Amendment enforcement powers.

This book includes the following features, most of which have been extracted from the corresponding *Emanuel Law Outline*:

▓ **Flow Charts** — I've reduced many of the principles of *Constitutional Law* to a series of 10 Flow Charts, created specially for this book and never published elsewhere. I think these will be especially useful on open-book exams. A list of all the Flow Charts is printed on p. 2.

▓ **Capsule Summary** — This is a 140-page summary of the subject. I've carefully crafted it to cover the things you're most likely to be asked on an exam. The Capsule Summary starts on p. 41.

▓ **Exam Tips** — My team and I compiled these by reviewing dozens of actual past essay and multiple-choice questions asked in past law-school and bar exams, and extracting the issues and fine distinctions that surface most often on exams. The Exam Tips start on p. 185.

▓ **Short-Answer** questions — These questions are generally in a Yes/No format, with a "mini-essay" explaining each one. The questions start on p. 251.

▓ **Multiple-Choice** questions — These are in a Multistate-Bar-Exam style, and were adapted from *The Finz Multistate Method*, which is also published by Wolters Kluwer Law & Business. The questions start on p. 319.

■ *Essay* questions — These questions are actual ones asked on law school or bar exams. They start on p. 347. Sample answers are provided.

My deepest thanks go to two of my colleages at Wolters Kluwer, Barbara Lasoff and Barbara Roth, who have helped greatly to assure the reliability and readability of this and my other books for many years.

Good luck in your ConLaw course. If you'd like any other Wolters Kluwer publication, you can find it at your bookstore or at **www.aspenlaw.com**. If you'd like to contact me, you can email me at **semanuel@westnet.com**.

Steve Emanuel
Larchmont, NY
September 2013

FLOW CHARTS

TABLE OF CONTENTS
to
FLOW CHARTS

Note: The "Ch.xx"-style cross-references in the Flow Charts' footnotes (e.g., "See Ch.6, V(B)") are to the full-length *Emanuel Law Outline* on Constitutional Law (31st Ed., © 2013, Wolters Kluwer Law & Business). For a description of other citation styles used in the Flow Charts, see footnote 1 to Flow Chart 1-1.

Figure 1-1
How to Analyze Any Con Law Problem

Use this chart to figure out which provisions of the Constitution are likely to be implicated in any fact pattern. Not every Con Law issue is dealt with, but many of the most common types are. The footnotes will direct you to additional sources.[1]

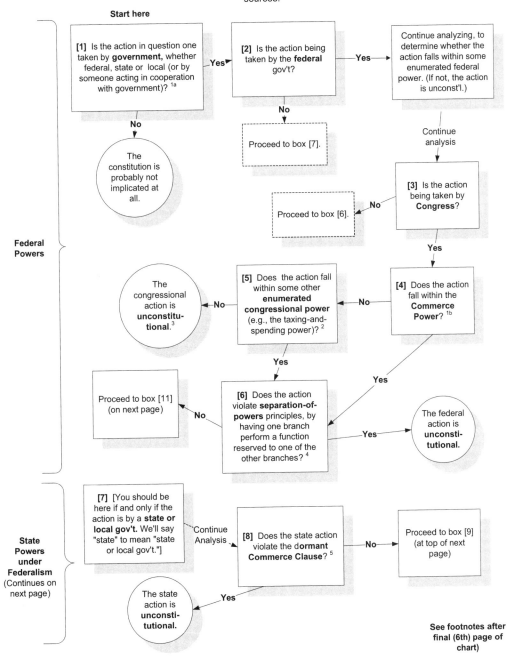

Start here

[1] Is the action in question one taken by **government,** whether federal, state or local (or by someone acting in cooperation with government)? [1a]

[2] Is the action being taken by the **federal gov't?**

Continue analyzing, to determine whether the action falls within some enumerated federal power. (If not, the action is unconst'l.)

No — The constitution is probably not implicated at all.

No — Proceed to box [7].

Continue analysis

[3] Is the action being taken by **Congress?**

No — Proceed to box [6].

Yes

Federal Powers

The congressional action is **unconstitutional.** [3]

[5] Does the action fall within some other **enumerated congressional power** (e.g., the taxing-and-spending power)? [2]

[4] Does the action fall within the **Commerce Power?** [1b]

No ← No

Yes

Yes

Proceed to box [11] (on next page)

[6] Does the action violate **separation-of-powers** principles, by having one branch perform a function reserved to one of the other branches? [4]

No

Yes — The federal action is **unconstitutional.**

State Powers under Federalism (Continues on next page)

[7] [You should be here if and only if the action is by a **state or local gov't.** We'll say "state" to mean "state or local gov't."]

Continue Analysis

[8] Does the state action violate the **dormant Commerce Clause?** [5]

No — Proceed to box [9] (at top of next page)

The state action is **unconstitutional.**

Yes

See footnotes after final (6th) page of chart

Figure 1-1
How to Analyze Any Con Law Problem
(p.2)

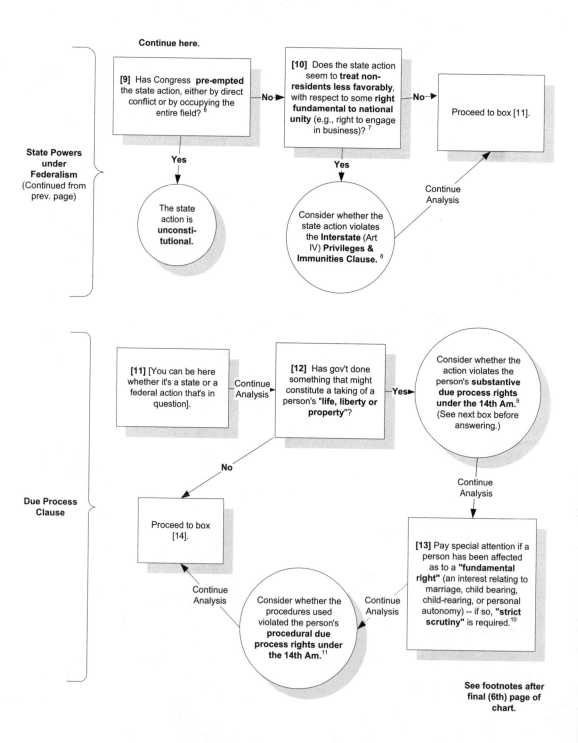

Continue here.

State Powers under Federalism
(Continued from prev. page)

[9] Has Congress **pre-empted** the state action, either by direct conflict or by occupying the entire field? [6]

—No►

[10] Does the state action seem to **treat non-residents less favorably**, with respect to some **right fundamental to national unity** (e.g., right to engage in business)? [7]

—No►

Proceed to box [11].

Yes
▼
The state action is **unconstitutional.**

Yes
▼
Consider whether the state action violates the **Interstate** (Art IV) **Privileges & Immunities Clause.** [8]

Continue Analysis

Due Process Clause

[11] [You can be here whether it's a state or a federal action that's in question].

Continue Analysis ►

[12] Has gov't done something that might constitute a taking of a person's **"life, liberty or property"**?

—Yes►

Consider whether the action violates the person's **substantive due process rights under the 14th Am.** [9] (See next box before answering.)

No
▼
Proceed to box [14].

Continue Analysis

Consider whether the procedures used violated the person's **procedural due process rights under the 14th Am.** [11]

Continue Analysis

Continue Analysis
▼
[13] Pay special attention if a person has been affected as to a **"fundamental right"** (an interest relating to marriage, child bearing, child-rearing, or personal autonomy) -- if so, **"strict scrutiny"** is required. [10]

See footnotes after final (6th) page of chart.

Figure 1-1
How to Analyze Any Con Law Problem
(p. 3)

Continue here.

[14] [You can be here whether it's a state or a federal action that's in question.]

Cont. Anal.

[14a] Has gov't made a **classification**, under which different groups are intentionally treated differently?

Yes →

No → Proceed to box [18].

Consider whether the classification violates the affected person's **Equal Protection rights under the 14th Am.**[12] (See boxes [15]-[17] before answering.)

Continue Analysis

Equal Protection Clause

[17] Pay special attention if the classification is based on **gender** or **illegitimacy** -- if so, **"middle-level review"** is required. [15]

←Continue Analysis---

[16] Pay special attention if the classification affects a **"fundamental right"** (voting, ballot access, court access, right to change state of residence) -- if so, **"strict scrutiny"** may be required. [14]

←Continue Analysis---

[15] Pay special attention if the classification is a **"suspect"** one (**race, national origin** or **alienage**) -- if so, **"strict scrutiny"** is required. [13]

Continue Analysis

14th Am. Privileges or Immunities Clause

[18] [You should only be here if it's a state (not a federal) action that's in question. If not, proceed to box [21].]

Cont. Anal.

[19] Has gov't treated **newly-arrived residents** less favorably than those who have been in-state longer?

No ►

[20] Has gov't interfered with a person's **right to vote** in **national elections**?

Yes →

Yes →

No →

Consider whether the state has violated the **Privileges or Immunities Cl.** of the **14th Am.**[16]

Continue Analysis

Proceed to box [21].

Taking Clause

No

No

[21] [You can be here whether it's a state or a federal action that's in question.]

Cont. Anal.

[22] Has gov't **deprived a person of his property** for **"public use"** (eminent domain)?

Yes →

Consider whether gov't has paid **"just compensation"** for the taking. If not, the action probably violates the 5th Am's **Taking Clause.** [17]

Cont. Anal.

Proceed to box [23] at top of next page.

See footnotes after final (6th) page of chart.

Figure 1-1
How to Analyze Any Con Law Problem
(p. 4)

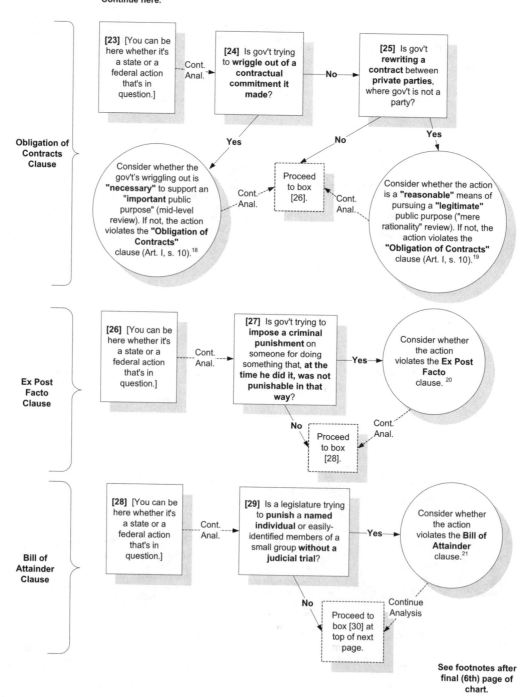

Figure 1-1
How to Analyze Any Con Law Problem
(p. 5)

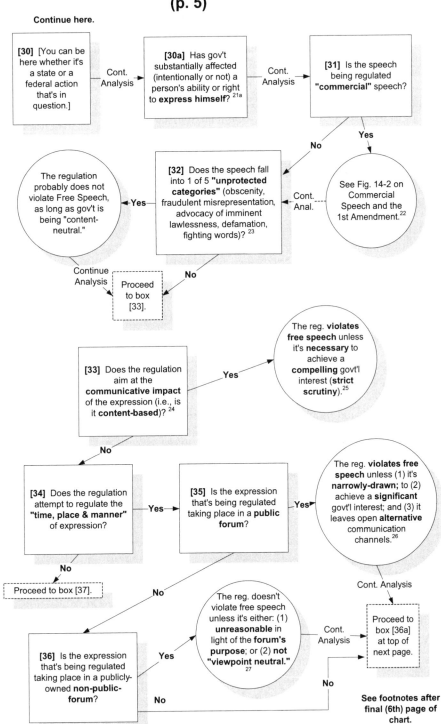

Figure 1-1
How to Analyze Any Con Law Problem
(p. 6)

Continue here.

[36a] [You can be here whether it's a state or a federal action that's in question.]

Continue Analysis →

[37] Does the gov't regulation have a substantial relationship to a **religious body** or a **religious topic**?

Yes →

Consider whether the gov't action violates the **Establishment** clause.[28] (Read box [38] before answering.)

No ↓

Proceed to box 42.

Continue Analysis ↓

[38] The action will violate the Establ. Cl. unless it meets all 3 of these tests: (1) it has a **secular** legislative **purpose**; (2) it does **not** have a **primary effect** of advancing religion; and (3) it does not foster an **excessive governmental entanglement** with religion.

Freedom of Religion Clause of 1st Am.

Consider whether the gov't action violates the **Free Exercise** clause. [Read boxes [40] & [41] before answering.]

← **Yes**

[39] Does the action represent govt'l coercion (intentional or unintentional) of a person that **significantly interferes** with the person's **free exercise of his religious principles** or **practices?**[29]

← Cont. Anal.

No ↓

Proceed to box 42. ←

Cont. Analysis

Continue Analysis ↓

[40] If the interference is **intentional**, it will violate the Free Exercise clause unless it is: (1) **necessary** to achieve (2) a **compelling** gov't objective (i.e., **strict scrutiny**)[30] . . .

Continue Analysis →

[41] But if the interference is **unintentional**, the review is **less strict**. (Example: If gov't makes a particular conduct a crime for everyone, that criminalization is not a Free Exercise violation no matter how great the burden is on a person's exercise of religious practice.) [31]

---

[42] [If the controversy is taking place in **federal court**, analyze its const'l procedural aspects here. If the case is in state court, your analysis is over.]

Cont. Anal. →

[43] Is the plaintiff asking for an **"advisory opinion,"** because no one is before the court who has suffered or is soon likely to suffer a legal harm? [32]

→ **No** →

[44] Does the plaintiff lack **"standing,"** because she herself has not been injured (nor is likely to be injured) by the defendant's complained-of act? [33]

Justicia-bility

[48] Does the suit **seek damages from a state** on behalf of a private citizen, in violation of the **Eleventh Am.?** [37]

Yes →

The suit **may not be const'ly heard** in federal court.

← **Yes**

[45] Is the action not yet **"ripe"** because it has not yet become sufficiently concrete to be easily adjudicated? [34]

Yes (from [42]) · **Yes** (from [43]) · **Yes** (from [44] No ↓)

No ↓

No ↓   **No** ↓

The suit **may constitutionally be heard** in federal court.

← **No**   **Yes** ↓   **Yes** →

[46] Is the suit now **"moot"** because events occurring after the suit was filed have deprived P of an ongoing stake in the controversy? [35]

[47] Does the suit raise an unjusticiable **"political question"?** [36]

← **No**

See footnotes on next page.

Notes to
Figure 1-1 (How to Analyze Any Con Law Problem)

[1] References to Figures (e.g., "Fig. 4-1") are to flow charts. References to a "Part" in a Figure are to a curly-braced section-marking at the left-side of a page of the flow chart. Thus "Fig. 6-1, Part I ('Dormant Commerce Clause Analysis')" refers to the section of flow chart 6-1 that is indicated by a curly-brace and the label "Dormant Commerce Clause Analysis" (which happens to be the section that takes up the first 2/3s of the first page of Figure 6-1).

References of the form "Ch.xx..." are to places in the main Emanuel Constitutional Law outline, 27th Edition, © 2009. Thus a reference to "Ch.10(II)(E)(1)(a)" would mean Chap. 10 of the main Con Law outline, roman-numeral II, paragraph (E)(1)(a).

[1a] Except for certain conduct relating to slavery, the Constitution only limits the power of governments, not the powers of non-governmental private actors.

However, before you conclude that a particular action carried out principally by a non-governmental-actor is purely private and thus has no constitutional implications, remember that under "state action" analysis, sometimes a private person's conduct will be so closely linked to government that the conduct will be treated as if it were by government. See Ch.12 on State Action.

[1b] See Fig. 4-2, "Federal Commerce Power." See also Ch.4, "The Federal Commerce Power."

[2] See Fig. 4-1, "Powers of the U.S. Congress."

Remember that unless a particular congressional action falls within a specific power that is enumerated somewhere in the Constitution, the action is beyond the scope of Congress' power. For instance, Congress has no power to legislate for the "general welfare" (as a state does). See Ch.5 ("Other National Powers"), especially Ch.5(IV).

[3] In using this flow chart, if you reach the conclusion that a particular action is unconstitutional, you should continue your analysis anyway, since that will lead to a more thorough analysis. (For instance, a provision may violate more than one constitutional provision -- and that's something that is good to show your professor that you know.) Therefore, when you reach an "action is unconstitutional" circle like this one, continue

your analysis as if the answer to the most recent question had been the opposite -- that should get you to the appropriate next area of the flow chart.

[4] See Ch.8, "Separation of Powers."

[5] See Fig. 6-1 ("The Dormant Commerce Clause & Congressional Action"), Part I ("Federal Powers"). See also Ch.6(I).

Note that if the state is acting as a "market participant" (not as a regulator), the Dormant Commerce Clause does not apply. See footnote 5 to Fig. 6-1.

[6] See Fig. 6-1 ("The Dormant Commerce Clause & Congressional Action"), Part II ("Federal Preemption Analysis").

[7] See Ch.7(IV). The rights that meet this "fundamental to national unity" standard are all related to commerce, such as the right to be employed, the right to practice one's profession, and the right to engage in business.

[8] Once a state interferes with a "right fundamental to national unity," there is a violation of the P&I clause unless it is the case that both: (1) non-residents are a peculiar source of the evil which the law is enacted to remedy; and (2) there is a "substantial relationship" between the statutory discrimination against non-residents and the problem the state is attempting to solve by discriminating. (Example: Alaska gives state residents an absolute preference for jobs on the Alaska pipeline. Held, even though there is high in-state employment, the preference flunks both tests, so it violates the P&I clause. [Hicklin v. Orbeck])

Note that there's no "market participant" exception to the P&I clause, as there is to the dormant Commerce Clause (see footnote 5 above).

[9] See Fig. 9-1 ("Substantive Due Process"). See also Ch.9(II)-(IV).

[10] See Ch.9(IV). If strict scrutiny is applied, the governmental action will be invalid unless it is the case that both: (1) the government's objective is "compelling" (not just "legitimate"); and (2) the fit between the means chosen and the objective is so tight that the means chosen are "necessary" to achieve the objective.

**Footnotes continue on
next page.**

Page 2 of Notes to
Figure 1-1 (How to Analyze Any Con Law Problem)

[11] See Ch.9(V). Remember that the requirement of procedural fairness applies only when gov't is taking a person's life, liberty or property. If gov't is taking an action that does not affect a person's life, liberty or property, gov't may act as arbitrarily as it wants.

Example: City decides that it will award a gov't contract to the mayor's best friend, instead of to P, the most-qualified and lowest-priced bidder. (Assume there's no state or city law specifying how government contracts shall be awarded.) Even though City may have acted with arbitrary or unfair procedures, P has no procedural-due-process claim, because he had no property or liberty interest in being awarded the project.

[12] See Fig. 10-1 ("Equal Protection").

[13] See Fig. 10-1, Part I ("Suspect Classifications / 'Strict Scrutiny' Review"). As with substantive due process (see footnote 10 above), strict scrutiny means that the use of the suspect classification must be necessary to achieve a compelling gov'tl objective.

[14] See Fig. 10-1, Part II ("Fundamental Rights / 'Strict Scrutiny' Review").

[15] See Fig. 10-1, Part III ("Mid-Level Review"). Mid-level review means that the classification will be struck down unless the government is pursuing an "important" objective, and the gender- or illegitimacy-based classification is "substantially related" to achievement of that important objective.

Note that mid-level review will be applied even where gov't is acting in a gender-based way with an objective of remedying past gender-based discrimination. That is, gender-based affirmative action (e.g., trying to eradicate past discrimination against women) still has to pass mid-level review. See Ch.10(IV)(B).

[16] See Ch.11(I).

[17] See Ch.11(II).

[18] See Ch.11(III)(B).

[19] See Ch.11(III)(C) and (D).

[20] See Ch.11(IV).

[21] See Ch.11(V).

[21a] See Fig. 14-1 ("Freedom of Expression"), especially footnote 2. See also Ch.14(I)(E).

[22] As Fig. 14-2 makes clear, content-based regulations of commercial speech are scrutinized less strictly than such restrictions on other forms of speech, such as core political speech.

[23] See Fig. 14-1, Part I ("Unprotected Categories"). See also Ch.14(II) (advocacy of imminent lawlessness); Ch.14(VI) (defamation); Ch.14(VII) (obscenity); Ch.14(IV)(H) (fighting words).

[24] See Fig. 14-1, Part II (" 'Content-based' / Strict Scrutiny Review"), especially footnote 11.

[25] See Fig. 14-1, especially footnotes 12 and 13.

[26] See Fig. 14-1, Parts III ("Time/Place/Manner Analysis for Content-Neutral Regulations of Expression in True Public Forums") and IV ("Time/Place/Manner Analysis for Content-Neutral Regulations of Expression in Semi-Public Forums").

[27] See Fig. 14-1, Part V ("Time/Place/Manner Analysis for Content-Neutral Regulations of Expression in Non-Public Forums").

[28] See Fig. 15-1, Part I ("Establishment Clause"). See also Ch.15(II).

[29] See Fig. 15-1, Part II ("Free Exercise Clause"). See also Ch.15(III).

[30] See Ch.15(III)(B).

[31] See Ch.15(III)(C)-(E); Emp. Div. v. Smith.

[32] See Ch.16(II).

[33] See Ch.16(III).

[34] See Ch.16(V).

[35] See Ch.16(IV).

[36] See Ch.16(VII).

[37] See Ch.16(VI).

Figure 4-1
Powers of the U.S. Congress

Use this chart to help you figure out whether a particular congressional statute
falls within constitutional limits. Note that the chart is not absolutely complete,
but it covers the most important sources of congressional power. All powers
mentioned in this chart are listed in Art. I, §8 unless otherwise noted.

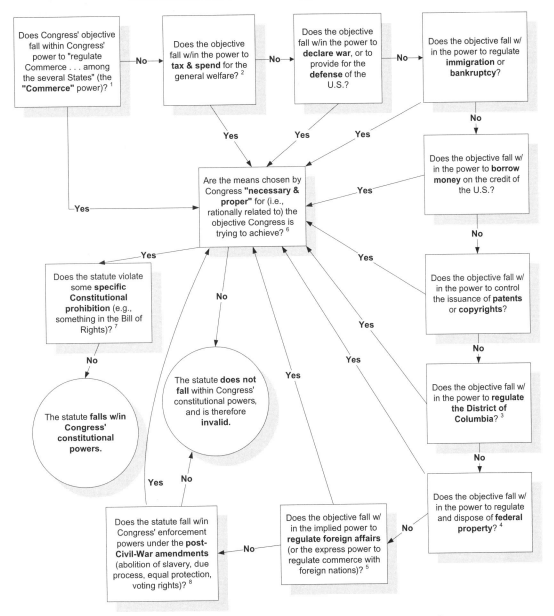

See footnotes on next page.

Notes to
Figure 4-1 (Powers of the U.S. Congress)

[1] See the detailed discussion in Ch.4, "The Federal Commerce Power."

[2] Note that in Art. I, §8, the phrase "provide . . . for the general welfare" modifies the phrase "lay and collect Taxes. . ." In other words, there's no *general* congressional power to "provide for the general welfare" -- there's only the power to tax and then to spend the resulting revenues for the general welfare. This is a key limitation compared with any state's "police powers" -- a state can do anything not specifically forbidden by the Constitution, whereas Congress (like the other two branches) can only do what's specifically allowed, and passing laws that aid the "general welfare" (other than as part of the taxing-and-spending power) is not something that's allowed. In other words, general regulation -- not tied to taxing-and-spending -- is not allowed if it doesn't fall within some other enumerated power (e.g., the Commerce power).

[3] Congress has full police powers within the District of Columbia. Therefore, it can enact (and has done so) a complete criminal code and can regulate civil conduct just the way a state can (e.g., zoning laws, or education policy).

[4] Examples: Congress can construct, sell or close a Post Office. Congress can regulate conduct on an Army base or other federal enclave. Congress can pass laws making certain conduct criminal in a national park.

[5] The constitution nowhere mentions a power to regulate foreign affairs. The power to regulate foreign commerce is given in Art. I, §8, in the same clause as the Commerce power relating to commerce among the states.

[6] The "Necessary and Proper" Clause is the last clause in Art. I, §8.

Keep in mind that the Necessary and Proper Clause is interpreted so as to give Congress very broad authority: all that's required is that the means chosen be rationally related to carrying out some enumerated federal power.

Example: Congress wants to civilly commit sexually-dangerous federal prisoners at the end of their prison sentences. Held, the Necessary and Proper Clause gives Congress the authority to do this: Congress has the power to define and punish federal crimes, and detaining dangerous federal prisoners at the end of their sentences is a means that is rationally related to the carrying out of this power. [*U.S. v. Comstock*]

But the means must be "incidental" to the enumerated power, rather than creating a "substantial expansion" of federal authority.

Example: Congress orders that most Americans without health insurance must buy it or pay a penalty to the IRS. Held, this "individual mandate" is not a Necessary and Proper means of carrying out Congress' Commerce powers, because the Commerce power itself does not cover requiring someone who is not presently in a market to enter that market by buying a product, and what Congress is doing here is not "incidental" to (but rather, a "substantial expansion" of) Congress' actual Commerce powers. [*N.F.I.B. v. Sebelius*]

[7] Example: Suppose Congress passes a law saying, "Any business operating in interstate commerce may not hire more than two persons who are of African descent." This is an exercise of the Commerce power, but since it violates another explicit constitutional provision (the Equal Protection clause of the 14th Amendment), it's invalid.

Example based on state sovereignty: The Tenth Amendment prevents Congress from either (1) compelling a state to enact or enforce a particular law or type of law; or (2) compelling state/local officials to perform federally-specified administrative tasks. See *N.Y. v. U.S.* and *Printz v. U.S.*, both discussed in Ch.4(V)(E).

[8] See Ch.13.

Figure 4-2
Federal Commerce Power

Use this chart to help you figure out whether a particular federal statute or
regulation is authorized by the federal Commerce power. Note that around the
edges, your analysis will inevitably be somewhat imprecise -- for instance,
deciding that the federal action in question does or doesn't "substantially affect"
commerce may be difficult. "I/C" means "interstate commerce."

Start here.

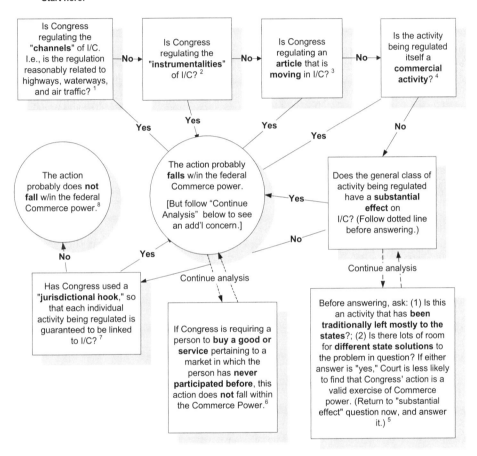

Notes

[1] If the answer is yes, Congress may regulate even an activity that is itself entirely intrastate (e.g., a boat travelling the Columbia River from one point in Washington State to another).

[2] "Instrumentalities" are the things that are used as a means of carrying out interstate commerce. (Example: Congress could probably regulate each car, since cars are commonly used as means of carrying out I/C.

This is true even though a particular car being regulated was never used except intrastate, and only for pleasure.)

[3] Example: Congress can regulate the interstate exchange of motor-vehicle-operator information (e.g., names & addresses of drivers), because this information is itself sold, and moves, in interstate commerce. [*Reno v. Condon*]

Footnotes continue on next page.

Notes (cont.) to
Figure 4-2 (Federal Commerce Power)

[4] If the answer is "yes," Congress can probably regulate even if the particular instance of the activity is entirely intrastate. (Example: D raises corn, and sells his entire small crop to his neighbors within the same state. Congress may regulate, even though the particular activity is entirely intrastate, because it's a "commercial" activity.)

[5] For question (1), examples of activities traditionally left to the states are education, family law, and general criminal law. For question (2), an example of a "yes" answer would be the educational curriculum (lots of reasonable choices in what and how to teach); by contrast, legalization of the possession of addictive drugs would be a "no" (a uniform national standard would work better).

[6] Example: In order to control health-care costs and expand access to health insurance, Congress says that many people without health insurance must buy it or pay a penalty to the IRS (the "individual mandate"). Held, the individual mandate exceeds Congress' Commerce powers. Even if the collective decision of millions of people to not buy health insurance substantially affects the interstate market for such insurance (by raising prices), it is not within Congress' Commerce-regulating power to force someone not in the market for a good or service to enter the market to buy it. That's because there must be some pre-existing "activity" to regulate, and people who have chosen not to buy insurance are not engaging in a pre-existing activity. [*N.F.I.B. v. Sebelius.*]

[7] Example: Suppose Congress says, "Anyone who possesses in a school a gun that has moved in I/C is guilty of a federal crime." Even though Congress can't criminalize all in-school gun possession (that's the holding of *U.S. v. Lopez*), the "jurisdiction hook" here -- only guns that have actually moved in I/C are covered -- probably narrows the statute enough to save it.

[8] Examples: (1) Congress makes it a crime to possess a gun in a school -- since education has nothing to do with I/C, and since a gun doesn't necessarily have much to do with I/C, the statute does not fall w/in the Commerce power (this is the holding of *U.S. v. Lopez*).

(2) Congress makes it a crime to burn down a private house. This probably has too little connection with commerce.

Figure 6-1

The Dormant Commerce Clause
& Congressional Action

Use this chart to figure out whether a state regulation is (1) violating the
Commerce Clause or (2) preempted by federal action.

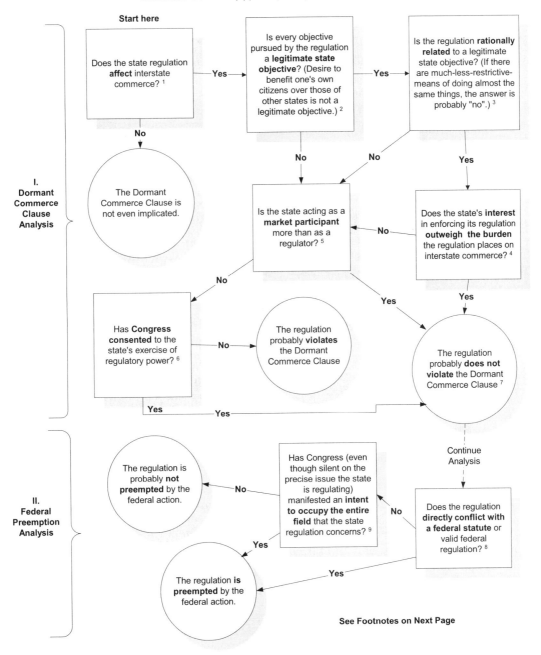

See Footnotes on Next Page

Notes to
Figure 6-1 (Dormant Commerce Clause)

[1] Even a relatively small impact on interstate commerce will be enough for a "yes" answer, in which case you'll have to continue with the Dormant Commerce Clause analysis.

[2] Examples of objectives that are probably legitimate: State honestly wants to guard the health, safety or general welfare of its citizens (and isn't using this as a smokescreen for pursuing the pure economic interests of its citizens). Example of illegitimate objective: State is really trying to further the economic interests of its own citizens at the expense of the interests of out-of-staters. A "no" answer to this question is the most common way that a state will violate the Dormant Commerce Clause.

Some common scenarios where forbidden economic-discrimination is likely to be found: (1) State tries to protect in-state producers against competition from out-of-state producers; (2) State tries to keep its valuable in-state products (e.g., oil) from being sent out-of-state; (3) State tries to keep out "bad stuff" from out-of-state, while allowing the same bad stuff to be produced in-state (e.g., state bans landfills from taking out-of-state garbage but not in-state garbage).

[3] This is a quite easy-to-satisfy test: the means chosen just has to be a plausible way of attacking the problem that the state's trying to solve, not the "best" or a "very good" way. Also, the Court will give great deference to any findings of "fact" that the state legislature purports to have made when it chose these particular means to solve this particular problem.

On the other hand, if there is a much less restrictive alternative method of regulation that the state could have selected, which would have solved the problem as well or almost as well, the court is likely to say that there is no rational relation between means and end.

[4] This is a rough balancing test. The state will be deemed to have flunked this test only if the burden on interstate commerce is clearly excessive compared to the local benefits. Example: If the state requires every truck passing through to have a $10,000 set of mud flaps that would prevent 1 non-fatal accident in the state each year, the burden would be clearly excessive compared to the benefit.

[5] The state is a "market participant" when it's acting as a purchaser, seller, or buyer of the good or service in question. In that event, it's exempt from Dormant Commerce Clause scrutiny. (Example: A state-owned oil company favors in-state customers in times of shortage.) (But check out the Art. IV Priv. & Immun. clause in Ch.7, because there's no market-participant exception under that clause.)

[6] Congress is always free to specifically consent to a particular form of state discrimination against out-of-staters. Example: Congress has authorized states to regulate insurance companies in such a way that a state can treat in-state insurers more favorably than out-of-state insurers. (But such discrimination may violate the Equal Protection clause: see *Metropolitan Life Ins. v. Ward.*)

[7] Even if you've gotten to this circle (no Dorm. Comm. Cl. problem), you must continue the analysis to make sure that Congress hasn't preempted the state regulation.

[8] There are two main types of "direct conflict": (1) It's impossible to obey both the state and the federal regulations simultaneously; or (2) (more common) The objectives behind the state and federal regulations are inconsistent (e.g., the state is trying to squelch all development of mobile-phone technology, and the federal gov't is trying to encourage it).

[9] This is a matter of Congressional intent: Did Congress intend to occupy the field completely, with no or minimal state regulation? Some clues to an intent to occupy a field: (1) It's a matter traditionally left to federal control (e.g., immigration or bankruptcy); (2) There's a very broad pattern of federal regulation already in place (e.g., nuclear energy); (3) Congress has set up an agency with broad powers (e.g., the FCC). Clue to an intent not to occupy the field: The subject matter is traditionally left to the states (e.g., education, insurance, most safety matters).

Figure 9-1
Substantive Due Process

Use this chart to figure out whether a state or federal attempt to regulate primary conduct and rights (as opposed to the procedures for vindicating rights) violates the 14th (or in the case of federal action, the 5th) Amendment's Due Process Clause.

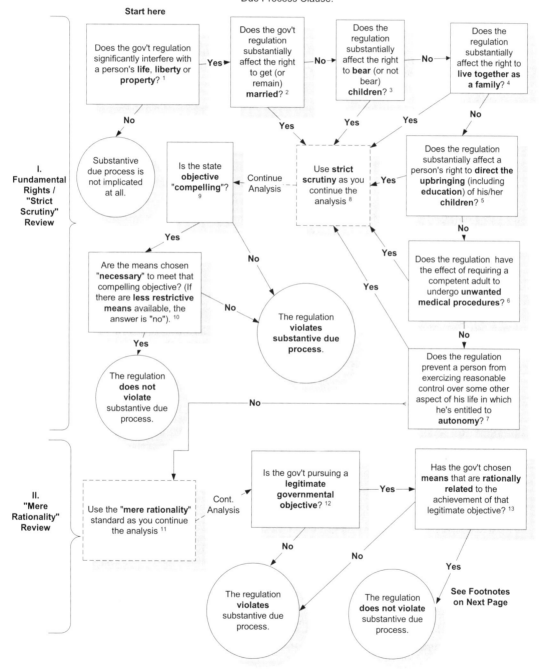

Notes to
Figure 9-1 (Substantive Due Process)

1 If the regulation does not interfere with the plaintiff's life, liberty or property, there's no room for the due process clause to apply. (Remember, the 14th amendment doesn't say that that the state must not deprive a person of due process in the abstract -- it says that a state shall not "deprive any person of *life, liberty or property*, without due process of law.")

2 Classic example: Court strictly scrutinizes (and strikes down) state law saying, "People who are behind on child support payments may not remarry." [*Zablocki v. Redhail.*] Other possible examples: State bars ex-felons, or persons presently in prison, from marrying.

3 Key example: Strict scrutiny for any law substantially burdening a woman's right to abort (*Roe v. Wade*; *Planned Parenthood v. Casey*). Other examples: (1) laws burdening contraception (e.g., *Griswold v. Ct.*); (2) laws forcibly sterilizing the mentally incompetent.

4 Examples: (1) Local zoning ordinance that prevents members of an extended family from living together (*Moore v. East Cleveland*); (2) law that takes away physical custody of a child from a natural parent who has been raising that child. (Statutes falling within (2) might pass muster, but the point is that they'd have to survive strict scrutiny.)

5 Examples: (1) Laws requiring all parents to send their children to public rather than private schools (*Pierce v. Soc. of Sisters*), or prohibiting all home-schooling; (2) law forbidding a parent from administering any corporal punishment to a child.

6 Example: Patient is competent, adult, Christian Scientist who declines dialysis (which would save his life); a law authorizing the state to forcibly require him to undergo the treatment would get strict scrutiny (and probably fall). (Cf. *Cruzan v. Mo. Dept. of Hlth*). (But a law making it a crime to assist someone, even a terminally-ill person, in committing suicide does not get strict scrutiny. *Wash. v. Glucksberg*.)

7 Possible examples: (1) statute makes it a crime to dress or wear one's hair a certain way; (2) statute makes it a crime to practice law; (3) statute makes it a crime to be unemployed when one could obtain a job. (But there seem to be no recent Sup. Ct. cases falling within this whole category; it's not clear whether the Court would apply strict scrutiny to this group of "autonomy" situations.)

Note that the right of adults to engage in various kinds of sex considered deviant by some (e.g., gay "sodomy") has been found not to trigger strict scrutiny. See *Bowers v. Hardwick* (not overruled on this point by *Lawrence v. Texas*). The same is probably true of adultery and fornication. (But such restrictions on adult consensual sex may nonetheless violate substantive due process because they flunk even the easy "rational-relation" test — see n. 12 below.)

8 If you use strict scrutiny, you should apply a strong presumption that the regulation fails that scrutiny, and is invalid. (Conversely, if you find that the regulation does not trigger strict scrutiny, you should apply a pretty strong presumption that it will be upheld.)

9 It's not clear what "compelling" means, beyond the concept of "very, very important." Usually, this is less the problem than is the means-end-fit part of the strict scrutiny test (next box).

10 This part of the test is very hard for the government to meet -- even if the only alternative is just a little less restrictive, and considerably less good at achieving the compelling objective, the Court is still likely to conclude that the means-end fit is not tight enough. Example: It's probably a compelling state interest to reduce teen-age out-of-wedlock sex and thus sexually-transmitted diseases, but an outright ban on contraceptive sales to minors is not a "necessary" means of achieving that objective, since a public-education campaign might do the job almost as well, with less interference with the protected right to procreate.

11 If you've gotten to this box, you should now apply a strong presumption in favor of constitutionality. You should be at this box if the regulation involves most types of economic regulation, and many types of health and safety regulation.

12 It is rare for a state objective to flunk this easy-to-satisfy test. Anything falling within the state's "police power" (defined broadly to include virtually any health, safety or "general welfare" goal) will suffice.

Footnotes Cont. on Next Page

Page 2 of Notes to
Figure 9-1 (Substantive Due Process)

But one state objective that may be invalid is the majority's "moral disapproval" of some adult consensual sexual practice or lifestyle arrangement, especially when practiced by an unpopular minority (e.g., gay people).

Example 1: When a state forbids "sodomy" (defined as contact between one person's mouth or anus and another's genitalia), and the state's sole objective is to express moral disapproval of homosexuality, the state's objective is illegitimate, and the ban flunks rational-relation review. [*Lawrence v. Texas*]

Example 2: Congress refuses to recognize, for any federal purpose, a same-sex marriage valid in the state where it occurred. Held, this refusal was motivated solely by moral disapproval of and hostility to gays. Such disapproval cannot be a "legitimate state interest." Therefore, the lack of recognition violates the constitutional rights of gay people married under state law. (The decision seems to find a violation of both substantive due process and equal protection, though the Court's language is ambiguous about which interest has been violated.) [*U.S. v. Windsor*]

Figure 10-1
Equal Protection

Use this chart to figure out whether a state or federal[1] classification among
people violates the 14th Amendment's Equal Protection Clause.

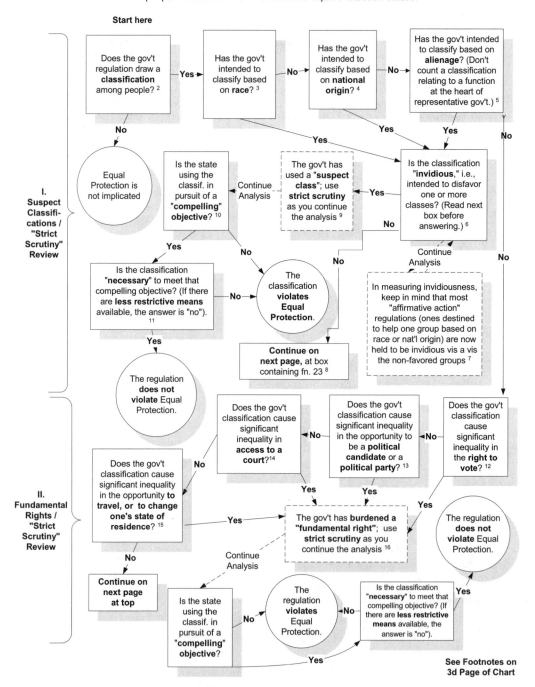

See Footnotes on
3d Page of Chart

Figure 10-1
Equal Protection (Cont.)

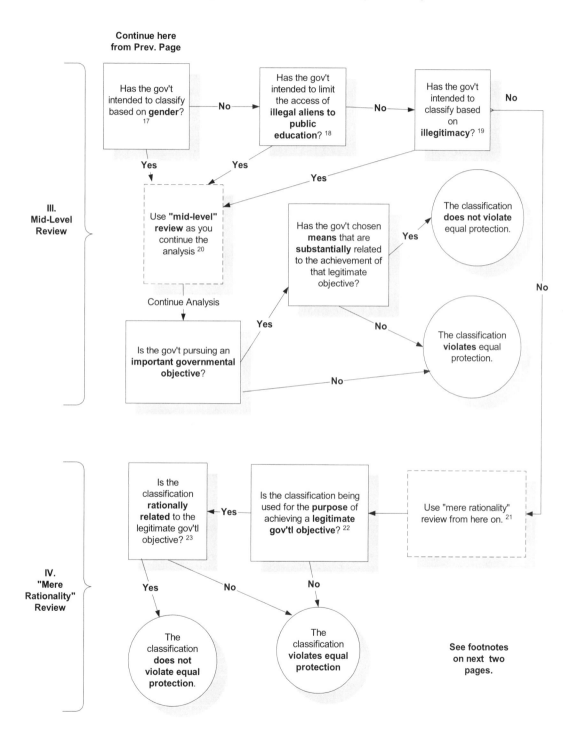

**Continue here
from Prev. Page**

Has the gov't intended to classify based on **gender**? [17]

— No → Has the gov't intended to limit the access of **illegal aliens to public education**? [18]

— No → Has the gov't intended to classify based on **illegitimacy**? [19]

— No →

**III.
Mid-Level
Review**

Yes ↓ (gender) | Yes (illegal aliens) | Yes (illegitimacy)

Use **"mid-level" review** as you continue the analysis [20]

Continue Analysis ↓

Is the gov't pursuing an **important governmental objective**?

— Yes → Has the gov't chosen **means** that are **substantially** related to the achievement of that legitimate objective?

— Yes → The classification **does not violate** equal protection.

— No → The classification **violates** equal protection.

— No → The classification **violates** equal protection.

No →

**IV.
"Mere
Rationality"
Review**

Is the classification **rationally related** to the legitimate gov'tl objective? [23]

— Yes ← Is the classification being used for the **purpose** of achieving a **legitimate gov'tl objective**? [22]

— No ← Use "mere rationality" review from here on. [21]

Yes ↓ | No → | No →

The classification **does not violate equal protection**.

The classification **violates equal protection**

**See footnotes
on next two
pages.**

Notes to
Figure 10-1 (Equal Protection)

[1] The Equal Protection clause is part of the 14th Amendment, and by its terms applies only to state and local governments. But the Fifth Amendment's Due Process clause has been interpreted as requiring the federal government to avoid classifications that, if taken by a state, would violate the Equal Prot. clause.

[2] The Equal Prot. clause applies only when government makes a classification, i.e., a legislative distinction that treats two similarly-situated groups differently (or, occasionally, that treats two differently-situated groups the same). See Ch.10 I(B)(2) & (3). (Example: Gov't passes a statute that says that those under 21 may not buy liquor. This is a classification, because it treats minors differently than non-minors.)

Classifications may occur either in the act of legislation (statute- and rule-drafting) or the act of administration (carrying out the law); the former is more common. But it's not a classification if the gov't merely decides which pre-defined class someone fits into (that's typically a due process matter instead.)

[3] Note that it's not enough that a classification somehow "involves" race: it must be the case that the government has intended to treat members of one race differently than members of another. In other words, a government classification that merely has a differential *effect* on members of one race as opposed to another doesn't qualify under this (or any other) branch of equal protection analysis. (But intent may be proved by circumstantial evidence.)

Note that a classification intended to disadvantage whites (or any other racial group that has not been the victim of systematic societal prejudice in the past) still counts as a race-based classification. (See footnote 7 below).

[4] Examples: (1) Discrimination against persons who were born in Latin America; (2) discrimination against people who are descended from Italians (i.e., Italian-Americans).

But note that discrimination based solely on lack of U.S. citizenship does not fall within this "national origin" prong -- see the "alienage" box, footnote 5, instead.

[5] "Alienage" means "not a U.S. citizen." Example: A state says that non-citizens may not work as lawyers -- that's an alienage-based classification, and will be strictly scrutinized. (*In re Griffiths*.)

But the standard alienage analysis does not apply where the classification is used to limit the right of non-citizens to perform "functions that go to the heart of representative government." (*Sugarman v. Dougall*.) Instead, mere-rationality review applies here (go to the box accompanying footnote 21 below). Examples of jobs that go to the heart of representative gov't: public school teachers; probation officers.

[6] Example of non-invidious classification: A state orders that funds be supplied to test any African American (but not caucasians) for sickle-cell anemia. Since medical evidence indicates that only African Americans are likely to have sickle cell disorder, no group (neither blacks nor whites) is intended to be disfavored.

But note that where gov't intentionally classifies by race, the Court is extremely skeptical of assertions that the discrimination is not invidious. Examples: (1) School separation on a "separate but equal" basis that is supposedly not intended to treat one race worse than the other is in fact invidious, and invalid. [*Brown v. Bd. of Ed.*] (2) A law banning intermarriage is invidious discrimination, and invalid. [*Loving v. Va.*]

[7] As the box indicates most (maybe all) "affirmative action" programs are now held to be invidious, and therefore subjected to strict scrutiny. [*Richmond v. Croson.*] Examples: (1) A state gives extra "points" to blacks and hispanics in deciding whom to admit to a state university; (2) Congress says that 10% of all federal-gov't dollars spent on private contractors must reserved for businesses owned by minority groups. [*Adarand Constr. v. Pena*]

[8] If the classification -- although it involves race, national origin or alienage -- is not invidious, it is probably analyzable under the "mere rationality" standard (see box accompanying footnote 21 below). However, this is not completely clear.

[9] Since you are applying strict scrutiny on account of the suspect classification, you should apply a strong presumption that the classification is invalid. (No suspect classification has been upheld since the 1940s.)

**Footnotes continue on
next page**

Page 2 of Notes to
Figure 10-1 (Equal Protection)

[10] There are only a few objectives that will probably be found compelling and that might be invoked in support of a suspect classification.

One example of compelling state interest: Protecting safety and welfare of minors. (But the bigger obstacle is the means-end fit, described in the next box.)

Where race-conscious measures are used (as in affirmative action cases), only two objectives have been found compelling: (1) the eradication of the effects of past discrimination by the governmental body taking the race-conscious measures; and (2) the pursuit of diversity in a university's student body.

[11] It is extremely rare that the fit between even a compelling objective and a suspect classification is found to be tight enough to meet the "necessary" requirement.

Example (fit not tight enough): In a child custody case, a state can't disfavor the parent who re-marries a person of another race. The goal of shielding the child from private prejudice (prejudice directed at the custodial parent and her new spouse, plus incidentally at the child) may be compelling. But the means chosen -- catering to private prejudice -- is not the only possible means of achieving that objective, so it's not a "necessary" means. [Palmore v. Sidoti]

In race-conscious public-school and university admissions, the fit may or may not be tight enough, depending on the means chosen and the end being pursued (as the next 3 Examples show).

Example (fit not tight enough): To pursue student-body diversity, University gives an automatic 20-point "diversity bonus" to any minority applicant, out of 100 points needed for admissions. Because this automatic scheme is tantamount to a quota (and isn't based on individual evaluation of how the applicant will contribute to diversity), the scheme isn't "necessary" to achieve the compelling interest in diversity, so the scheme violates the equal protection rights of white applicants. [Gratz v. Bollinger]

Example (fit not tight enough): City classifies each student as white or non-white, and then permits transfers only if the student would lessen the racial imbalance at the school. Because (in part) of the crudeness of the white/non-white distinction, the transfer scheme is not a necessary means of combatting the evil of racially-isolated schools, and violates the equal protection rights of those not permitted to transfer because of their race. [Parents Involved v. Seattle]

Example (fit tight enough): To pursue student-body diversity, Law School treats minority status as one "plus factor" among many, while individually evaluating every applicant. Because this scheme is a "holistic" one rather than a "quota," it is closely tied to the compelling interest in having a diverse law school, and therefore does not violate the equal protection rights of white applicants. [Grutter v. Bollinger]

[12] Strict scrutiny is not used if the classification or requirement is reasonably related to determining a voter's qualifications (only mid-level review is used). But strict scrutiny is used if the classification or requirement is not reasonably related to determining a voter's qualifications.

Examples – reasonably related to voter qualifications: (1) requirement that voter present a government-issued photo ID [Crawford v. Marion County]; (2) denial of vote to felons; (3) vote restricted to bona fide residents of the jurisdiction. So these get mid-level review, and are valid as long as they're closely tied to achieving an important governmental interest (which these 3 examples probably are).

Examples – not reasonably related to voter qualifications: (1) poll taxes; (2) vote restricted to persons with a "special interest" such as property owners; (3) vote restricted to those who have lived in the state for more than 1 year. These get strict scrutiny, and are generally invalid. [Harper v. Va. Bd.]

[13] Example: A regulation making it very difficult for a newly-formed political party, even a very popular one, to get its candidates on the ballot. [Williams v. Rhodes.]

[14] Example: A $50 fee for getting a divorce. [Boddie v. Ct.]

[15] Example: A state law denying welfare benefits to anyone who hasn't lived in the state for at least a year. [Shapiro v. Thompson.]

**Footnotes continue
on next page.**

Page 3 of Notes to
Figure 10-1 (Equal Protection)

[16] The scrutiny in this "fundamental rights" scenario is pretty much the same as in the "suspect class" scenario.

[17] Examples: (1) A state lets women drink at a younger age than men. [*Craig v. Boren*] (2) A state military college refuses to admit women. [*U.S. v. Va.*]

Note that affirmative action statutes (ones designed to remedy prior societal discrimination against women) are also subjected to mid-level review.

[18] Example: A state charges illegal aliens a fee to attend public school. [*Plyler v. Doe*]

[19] Example: A state bars any illegitimate child from inheriting from a parent who dies intestate, without ever giving the child a chance to prove that the decedent was his parent. [*Clark v. Jeter*]

[20] Where mid-level review is used, the classification sometimes survives, and sometimes falls, in roughly equal proportions. The tightness of the means-end fit (are the means "substantially related" to the important governmental objective?) seems to be the most important factor in whether the classification survives.

Note that mid-level review will be applied even where gov't is acting in a gender-based way with an objective of remedying past gender-based discrimination. That is, gender-based affirmative action (e.g., trying to eradicate past discrimination against women) still has to pass mid-level review. See Ch.10(IV)(B).

[21] Most economic regulation, and probably most regulatory attempts to safeguard health and safety, fall into this category.

It is very rare for a classification subjected to "mere rationality" review to be invalidated. Therefore, you should apply a strong presumption that such a classification is valid. Only if the means chosen strike you as completely arbitrary and capricious should you conclude that the classification might be struck down. (But see note 23 below, final two paragraphs.)

[22] Courts give extreme deference to the legislature's choice of objectives. Also, courts will often hypothesize about objectives that the legislature might have been trying to achieve (even if there's no evidence that this was what in fact motivated the legislature).

[23] Again, this is an extremely easy-to-satisfy test: even a very loose link between means and end will suffice, as long as the means chosen aren't completely irrational. For instance, the fact that the legislature has attacked only one aspect of a problem (i.e., has chosen to "take one step at a time") won't be enough to make the means-end fit too loose. Example: A ban on all on-vehicle advertising except ads for the vehicle's owner isn't irrational, even though the distraction and visual blight from an ad for the vehicle's owner isn't any less than from an ad for a third-party advertiser -- the state may choose to eradicate some evils of a particular type without having to simultaneously eradicate them all. [*Railway Express v. N.Y.*]

But keep in mind that if government is singling out an unpopular minority for worse treatment, then even though mere-rationality review is supposedly used, the courts are likely to apply it with special rigor. That's most dramatically true of regulations that disfavor gay people.

Example: Congress enacts a statute (Defense of Marriage Act, or "DOMA") that says same-sex couples may not be recognized as married for purposes of federal law, even if the couple is married under state law. *A*, a woman validly married under state law to *B* (also a woman), wants to take the estate tax marital deduction when *B* dies, but is blocked by DOMA. Held (by the Supreme Court) for *A*. DOMA was enacted for the sole purpose of harming gays, an unpopular minority. Causing such harm is not a legitimate governmental objective. Therefore, DOMA violates *A*'s equal protection rights. (The case does not explicitly say whether the Court was using mere rationality, but that appears to be the standard the Court used.) [*U.S. v. Windsor*]

Figure 11-1
The "Taking" Clause

Use this chart to determine whether government action constitutes a Fifth/
Fourteenth Amendment "taking" of private property, for which "just
compensation" must be paid. "O" is the owner of the property.

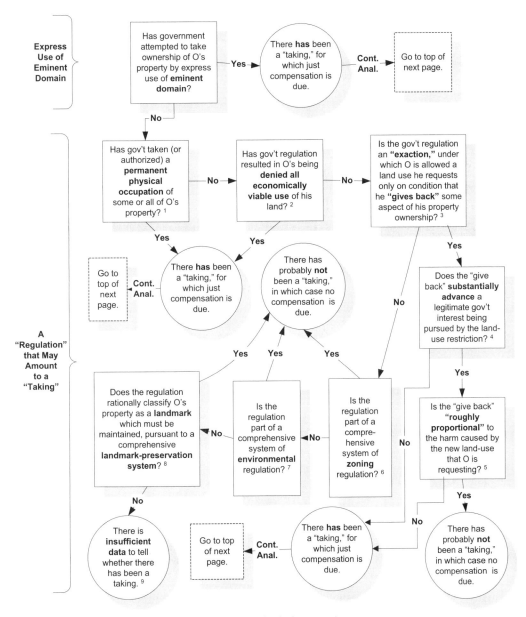

See footnotes beginning on next page.

Figure 11-1
The "Taking" Clause (cont.)

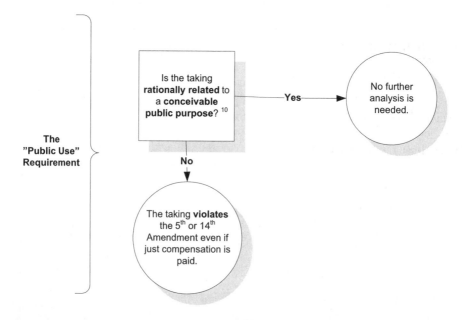

Notes

¹ Example: City passes an ordinance that requires landlords to permit cable TV companies to install their cable facilities in rental apartments, and limits to $1 what landlords can charge the cable companies. This ordinance brings about a permanent physical occupation of the landlord's property, so City must pay just compensation. [Cf. Loretto v. Teleprompter Manhattan CATV Corp.]

² Example: City classifies beachfront property owned by O as in danger of erosion, and permanently bars O from building any permanent habitable structure on the premises. Held, if this restriction prevents O from making any economically viable use of his property (which it seems to be doing), it is a taking for which compensation must be paid. [Lucas v. South Carolina Coastal Council.]

³ For an explanation of how the "substantially advances" and "roughly proportionate" requirements (see notes 4 and 5 below) apply only to exaction cases, not to general land-use-regulation cases, see Lingle v. Chevron USA. Example: O has a house on the beach, which

O wants to rebuild bigger. Local government forbids O from rebuilding unless O gives the public an easement to walk parallel to the ocean from the north of O's property to the south of it. Held, this "give back" requirement (i.e., this "exaction") is a compensable taking unless the give back substantially advances a legitimate governmental interest. (See next box for whether the give back meets this test.) [Nollan v. Calif. Coastal Comm.]

⁴ Example: Same facts as prior footnote. Held, the give back or exaction (easement to walk along ocean is required to be given to public) does not substantially advance the governmental interest which is being pursued. That's because the harms feared by the government (mainly, that O's bigger house would block views of the beach) would not be substantially advanced by the easement here (which would be usable only by people already on the public beaches north or south of O's property whose views would not be blocked by the bigger house anyway, and not usable by people on the street whose views would be blocked by the bigger house). [Nollan, supra, n. 3.]

Footnotes continue on next page.

Page 2 of Notes to
Figure 11-1 (The "Taking" Clause)

[5] Example: O wants to expand her building supply store. City gives her permission to do so, but only on condition that O convey 10% of her property to City for a public-use bicycle path. *Held*, City's demand for the conveyance is not "roughly proportional" to the harm (extra traffic) that would be caused by O's expansion. Therefore, the demand constituted a taking of O's property. [*Dolan v. City of Tigard*]

Note: Suppose that government denies the permit outright, and then merely suggests (without imposing a formal condition) that if the land owner were to make some specified dedication, or pay some specified sum of money to be used on another parcel, the permit denial might be reversed. The "substantially advances" and "roughly proportional" rules apply to this "no condition but denial with suggestions for a cure" scenario, too. [*Koontz v. St. John's River Water Mgmt. Dist.* (2013)]

[6] As long as the taking is part of a comprehensive zoning scheme (as opposed to "spot zoning" that singles out O's parcel for special negative treatment), and as long as the regulation leaves O with at least some economically viable use of his property, it is very unlikely that a taking will be found.

Example: O's land has historically been used for farming, and still is. As part of a comprehensive zoning scheme, Town zones all presently-operating farms, including O's, as an "agricultural zone," and disallows any use other than farming (and disallows the building of any structures not appurtenant to a farming use). As long as farming on O's parcel remains economically viable, the prohibition on non-farming uses is very unlikely to be held to be a taking.

[7] Example: City prevents O from operating a dump on his land, on the theory that the dump attracts rodents, causes odors, and is therefore environmentally unsound. So long as City's action vis-a-vis O is part of a comprehensive system of environmental regulation, that action is very unlikely to constitute a taking.

[8] Example: O owns Grand Central Terminal in City. Under a general landmark preservation statute applicable throughout City, the Terminal has been classified as a landmark whose facade cannot be destroyed or materially altered. *Held*, because the landmark preservation designation here was part of a comprehensive system of landmark preservation, City has not committed a taking of O's property. [*Penn Central Transport. Co. v. New York City*]

[9] If you got to this box because the regulation purported to be a zoning, environmental or landmark-preservation regulation, but failed to do so in a comprehensive manner, there is a possibility that the regulation will be held to be a taking because of the combination of its diminution of the value of O's property and its lack of comprehensiveness. However, there are no modern-era Supreme Court cases involving such a scenario, so we cannot give any guidance about how the Court would analyze this type of "non-comprehensive-regulation" scenario.

[10] This "rationally related to a conceivable public purpose" test comes from the 2005 case of *Kelo v. New London*, and will presumably be extremely easy to satisfy. *Kelo* establishes that all the requirement that the taking be for a "public use" *means* is merely that the use be rationally related to some conceivable public purpose, a requirement so loose as to be almost meaningless. For instance, in *Kelo* itself, the Court found that taking property for "economic development" purposes (by turning the property over to a for-profit developer so as to create jobs and tax revenues) met the "public use" requirement.

However, if a taking were clearly shown to have been made solely for the purpose of turning the property over to a politically powerful private party, with the alleged public benefit being merely a sham, then the Court might find that the public-use requirement was not met. There should be very few such cases, however, so you will ordinarily answer "yes" to this box.

Figure 14-1
Freedom of Expression

Use this chart to analyze any problem in which government (state or federal)
seems to be limiting someone's legal right or practical ability to express herself
on any subject.

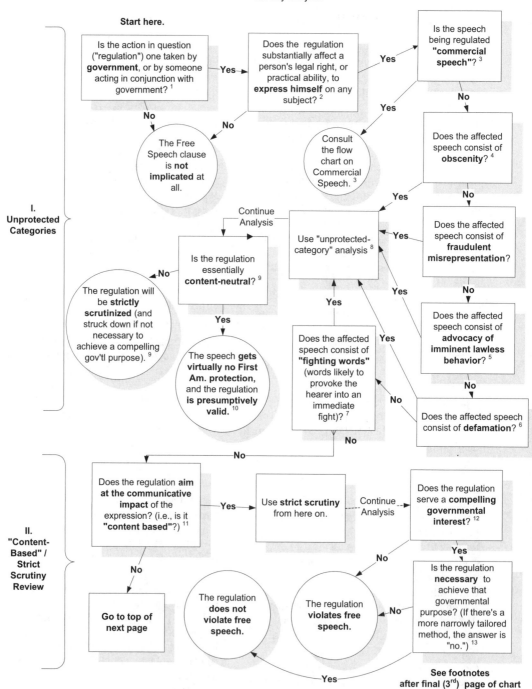

Figure 14-1
Freedom of Expression
(p. 2)

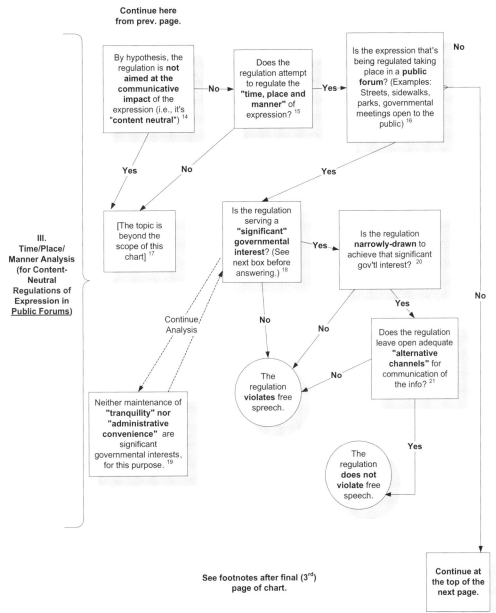

See footnotes after final (3rd)
page of chart.

Figure 14-1
Freedom of Expression
(p. 3)

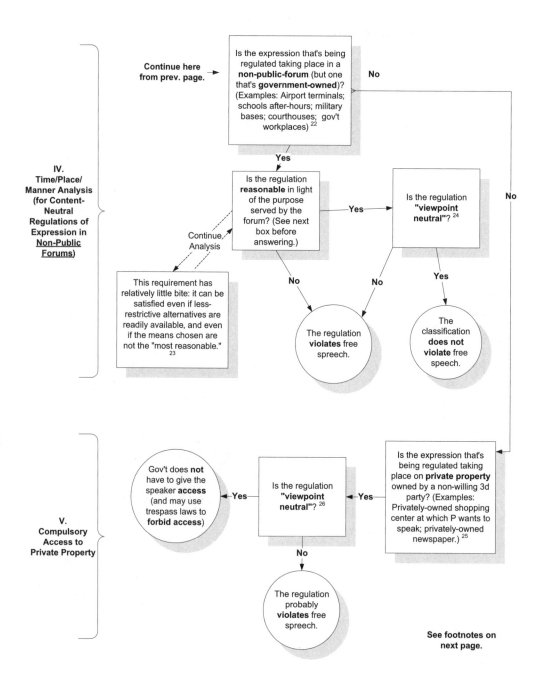

See footnotes on
next page.

Notes to
Figure 14-1 (Free Expression)

[1] The First Amendment's guarantee of free speech only applies to restrictions imposed by government (state or federal), or by private persons acting in conjunction with government, not those imposed by private persons acting alone.

Example: A private employer says to its employees, "If you criticize the company, you'll be fired." The employer has not violated the employees' free speech rights, because by hypothesis the employer is not a government actor.

[2] Answer "yes" as long as what's being regulated has a meaningful expressive component, even if the activity is "conduct" rather than pure expression.

Sometimes what's being regulated is obviously pure expression, so it's clear that it's covered by the First Amendment. (Example: A restriction on advertising.) But usually in interesting Con Law problems, what's being regulated is conduct. The fact that it's conduct that's being regulated doesn't mean that there are no First Amendment implications -- lots of conduct has an expressive component, and where this is so the conduct qualifies for First Amendment protection just the same as "pure expression" does. Example: A statute limits the circumstances under which people can march through the streets of a downtown area. Even though a march is "conduct", it's clearly got a significant expressive component, so it gets First Amendment protection.

[3] See "Commercial Speech under the 1st Amendment," Fig. 14-2.

[4] Material is "obscene" (and thus largely unprotected by the First Amendment) if "to the average person, applying contemporary community standards, the dominant theme of the material taken as whole appeals to prurient interest." [*Roth v. U.S.*]. Example: Pictures showing people having sex are obscene under this definition; publication and distribution of such pictures may therefore be outlawed as long as the gov't acts in a viewpoint-neutral way (see footnote14).

[5] Answer "yes" only if the advocacy meets both of these tests: (1) it's intended to incite or produce "imminent lawless action"; and (2) viewed as of the moment of the speech, it's likely to incite or produce that imminent lawless action. [*Brandenburg v. Ohio*] Example of advocacy that qualifies: A speaker to an angry mob says, "Burn down the courthouse." (But a speech saying, "If our treatment by the justice system doesn't improve soon, we should burn down the courthouse" would not qualify, because it's not an intent to incite imminent lawless action.)

[6] When the question arises, it's almost always in a scenario where a plaintiff sues a defendant for defamation (slander or libel), and the question is whether the state may allow the plaintiff to recover. If the plaintiff is a "public figure" who's complaining about the defendant's speech concerning the plaintiff's official conduct, the government can allow a recovery (and you should answer "yes" to the question in the box) only if: (1) the statement was false; and (2) the speaker acted with "actual malice," i.e., either with knowledge that the statement was false, or with reckless disregard of whether the statement was true or false. [*N.Y. Times v. Sullivan*]

If the plaintiff is not a public figure, it's easier for her to recover; but still, the state can't allow recovery (and you should answer "no" to the question in the box) unless: (1) the statement was false; and (2) the defendant was at least negligent in making the statement. [*Gertz v. Robert Welch*]

[7] Answer "yes" only if the speaker's words are likely to provoke immediate violence against the speaker. Example: Speaker, who is a member of the American Nazi party, says in a speech where black people are present, "Right now, I'll beat the crap out of any N____ in the audience who comes forward and tells me he deserves equal rights with the white people who founded this country." These are fighting words (and thus only minimally protected) if you find that they would tend to incite an immediate fight or breach of the peace. [*Chaplinsky v. N.H.*]

[8] The basic idea is that if the speech falls into one of these 5 unprotected categories (obscenity, fraudulent misrepresentation, advocacy of imminent lawlessness, defamation or fighting words), it's so lacking in social value that it may be completely prohibited so long as the state acts in a content-neutral way. (For the meaning of "content-neutral," see footnotes 9 and 11.)

**Footnotes continue on
next page.**

Page 2 of Notes to
Figure 14-1 (Free Expression)

[9] Answer "yes" only if it appears that the state is not regulating based on the precise "message" being conveyed by the speaker, and is, instead, banning all speech falling within the broad unprotected category. Example: The state is free to ban all defamation. And if it does so, it's acting in a content-neutral way: it's treating all messages falling into the broad "defamation" category the same. But if the state bans only defamations directed against, say, public officials, or members of minority groups, that would be non-content-neutral (since within the broad category of defamations some are allowed and others not, based on the communicative content of the message), and would be strictly scrutinized (and probably struck down). [R.A.V. v. City of St. Paul]

[10] The presumption that content-neutral regulation of unprotected categories is valid means that: (1) the state may completely proscribe materials falling into the proscribed categories (e.g., the state may forbid all distribution of obscene materials); and (2) if the state doesn't want to completely forbid the entire category, it may impose much greater "time, place and manner" regulation than if the expression did not fall within an unprotected category. (The limits on "time, place and manner" regulation of speech outside the unprotected categories are covered in all of the boxes below from footnote 15 on.)

[11] "Content based" regulation is regulation that takes into account the meaning of the speaker's message. It's regulation that is directed at the "communicative impact" of the speaker's message.

Examples of content-based regulation: (1) State forbids drugstores from advertising prescription drug prices because it thinks consumers will shop on price and get poor service [Va. Pharmacy]; (2) State lets P recover civilly where D speaks "outrageously" and intentionally causes P emotional distress (e.g., D carries signs at P's son's funeral saying the son died in war because God was punishing the U.S. for its pro-gay policies) [Snyder v. Phelps]; (3) Congress makes it a crime to lie about having received a military medal, even if the lie is oral and causes no discernible harm [U.S. v. Alvarez]. In these three cases, strict scrutiny would be used.

Examples of content-neutral (i.e., non-content-based) regulation: (1) State prohibits sound

trucks that broadcast messages at greater than a certain decibel level; (2) City forbids distribution of leaflets, because it fears littering. In these two cases, the easier-to-satisfy rules on "time, place and manner" regulation (see footnote 15 et. seq.) would apply.

[12] The "compelling interest" prong is the less-interesting of the two prongs: most cases are decided not on the basis that the governmental interest was not compelling, but on the basis that content-based regulation of speech wasn't a necessary way to combat the evil.

[13] The most important thing to remember about the "necessary to achieve a compelling governmental interest" test is that content-based regulation of speech is almost never found to be a "necessary" means of achieving even a compelling governmental evil. That is, once the speech is outside of the five unprotected categories (obscenity, defamation, etc.), it's simply not open to government to argue that the message contained in the speech is so dangerous that the message can be limited on content-based grounds.

Thus, (1) if more speech could at least partially eliminate the evil feared by gov't (which it usually can), the Court will probably find that the content-based means chosen isn't "necessary"; (2) the gov't can't claim that the content of the expression has been or will be adequate articulated by other speakers; (3) the gov't can't claim that the speaker can make his point just as well in some other place, at some other time, or in some other manner -- once the gov't is found to be objected to a message based on its contents, not even a "trifling" or "minor" interference with that message will be tolerated. See Ch.14(I)(C)(3)(a).

This strict scrutiny applies not only where gov't tries to regulate the precise viewpoint being expressed, but also where it tries to put off-limits an entire category of expression without regard to particular viewpoint. Example: A state university makes its facilities generally available for registered student groups, but doesn't allow any student groups to use the facilities "for purposes of religious teaching or worship." Held, this is content-based regulation, and must be strictly

**Footnotes continue on
next page.**

Page 3 of Notes to
Figure 14-1 (Free Expression)

scrutinized (and in fact invalidated). [*Widmar v. Vincent*] (See footnote 14 for more on this point.)

Therefore, once you find that gov't has regulated in a content-based way towards a protected category (not one of the 5 unprotected categories listed in footnote 8), you should apply a heavy presumption that the regulation is invalid.

[14] See footnote 11 for two examples of content-neutral regulation.

The requirement of content-neutrality means that the regulation must be "viewpoint neutral" and "category neutral." In other words, gov't can't allow some types of messages but ban or regulate others, based on the viewpoint or category that the messages fall into. Example: Gov't can't say that charitable solicitations are allowed in public forums but political-campaign solicitations are not. And, it can't say that people may discuss politics in a public forum but not religious topics.

[15] The organization of this flow chart reflects the somewhat simplistic view that any regulation that is not content-based must be a "time, place and manner" regulation. (See footnote 17 for further details about this simplifying assumption.)

Examples of "time, place and manner" regulation: (1) City bans the handing out of any printed materials to any passers-by in the downtown area, as an anti-littering measure; (2) City bans loudspeakers operating at more than 10 decibels in public; (3) State requires a permit for any assemblage of more than 10 persons, as a general crowd-control measure.

[16] A place falls into this "public forum" class if either: (1) it has been traditionally used for public discussion, such as streets and sidewalks (a "traditional" public forum); or (2) government has decided to open it up to a broad variety of expressive conduct, such as a school made available after hours to a variety of public uses, or a governmental meeting open to the public (a "designated" public forum).

[17] Any regulation that is neither content-based nor "time, place and manner" is beyond the scope of this flowchart. Example: Limits on free association are not really handled by this flow chart, since they don't necessarily fall neatly into either "content-based" or "time, place & manner" categories.

[18] Note that once you're in this portion of the flow chart (time-place-manner regulation of expression in a true public forum), you should apply what is essentially mid-level review of the regulation: it will be sustained if it's narrowly drawn to achieve a significant gov'tl interest (and leaves alternative channels open). This level of review often (but by no means always) leads to the regulation's being upheld.

Examples of regulations that serve a significant gov'tl interest (and that also satisfy the other two tests, "narrowly-drawn" and "alternative channels"): (1) When less-intrusive measures haven't worked, a judge may enjoin protesters from blocking public access to the place they're protesting [*Madsen v. Women's Health Ctr.*]; (2) A city may completely ban posting of signs on public property in order to combat "visual blight." [*L.A. v. Taxpayers for Vincent*]

[19] Example of "administrative convenience" not being a significant gov'tl interest: When a city bans all leafleting, the city's desire not to have to pick up litter is not a significant gov'tl interest. [*Schneider v. State.*] Example of maintaining "tranquility" not being a significant gov'tl interest: Gov't of a small town bans any public speech to 10 or more people in a city park after 5:00 PM on the grounds that it will disturb neighbors' peace and quiet; the interest in maintaining tranquility is probably not "significant."

[20] This requirement does not mean that the state must choose the absolutely least-restrictive or least-intrusive means of achieving its objective. Instead, the state must merely avoid choosing means that are "substantially broader than necessary" to achieve the governmental objective. [*Ward v. Rock Ag. Racism*] Example: A city that wants to keep sound volumes low may require all music performers in city parks to use city-provided sound equipment, instead of the slightly-less-intrusive means of monitoring the sound levels on the performers' own equipment during the concert. [*Ward, supra.*]

When you consider the "narrowly-drawn" requirement, keep in mind the doctrine of overbreadth, used in First Amendment cases: If *A* is complaining about the regulation, he can do so by showing that the regulation

**Footnotes continue on
next page.**

Page 4 of Notes to
Figure 14-1 (Free Expression)

imposes significant and unconstitutional burdens on *B* (even if it doesn't unconstitutionally burden *A*, and even if *B* is hypothetical). So if *A* can show that the regulation is so broadly-drawn that it is prohibiting lawful expression by *B*, *A* will win. Ch.14(III)(A).

[21] Example: A city entirely bans the display of "signs" on residential property, and interprets this to mean that P can't post a sign in the window of her home urging the end to a pending war. *Held*, the ban on signs fails to leave open adequate alternative channels for private citizens of limited means to express their opinions on public matters. [*City of Ladue v. Gilleo*]

[22] What we call here a "non-public forum" is sometimes called a "limited public forum." The two terms refer to the same thing: government-owned property whose use is not tightly linked to expression.

Other examples of non-public forums: Post offices; jails; school mail systems; publicly-operated buses; utility poles. The basic idea is that even when properly is publicly-owned, if it has no significant historical links to expression (and isn't commonly used for expression today), it falls into this non-public forums category, which can be regulated as long as the regulation is merely "reasonable" and "viewpoint-neutral."

[23] Example: A city can ban all face-to-face solicitation of money within airport terminals it operates. This ban is "reasonable" because of the risks of deception and fraud, and because the solicitation may slow the flow of passenger traffic.

[24] This is an aspect of the requirement of content-neutrality: The gov't can restrict speech across

the board in a non-public-forum, but it can't choose to allow some viewpoints while denying the express of other ones. Examples: (1) A school district can't let non-religious community groups use its classrooms after hours but refuse access to religious groups who want to conduct programs (including prayers) for elementary-school students [*Good News Club v. Milford*]; (2) A university can't fund non-religiously-oriented student activities but refuse to fund activities relating to religion. [*Rosenberger v. U. Va.*]

Probably the viewpoint-neutrality rule means that government also cannot put whole "categories" of expression off-limits in a non-public forum, as long as the expression belongs to the same basic type of activity that is allowed in the forum. Thus as *Good News* and *Rosenberger* illustrate, if government allows community groups to use schools for after-school "activities," groups that want to put on activities that include a large religious-worship component may not be excluded.

[25] Examples: (1) P wants to distribute political literature in a shopping center owned by D, who doesn't want to let him do so. (2) P wants to buy political advertising in a privately-owned newspaper that doesn't want to run the ad. The issue in both cases is whether gov't may pass a law letting the owner of the private property say "no". As long as the law is viewpoint-neutral, the answer (as shown in the circle at the left) is "yes" -- gov't may enforce private-property rights in this way.

[26] Example: Gov't probably can't say, "No person may engage in political speech in a shopping center over the owner's objection, but a person has a right to engage in religious speech in the shopping center even if the owner objects."

Figure 14-2
Commercial Speech
under the 1st Amendment

Use this chart when government may have singled out some form of
commercial speech for special regulation.

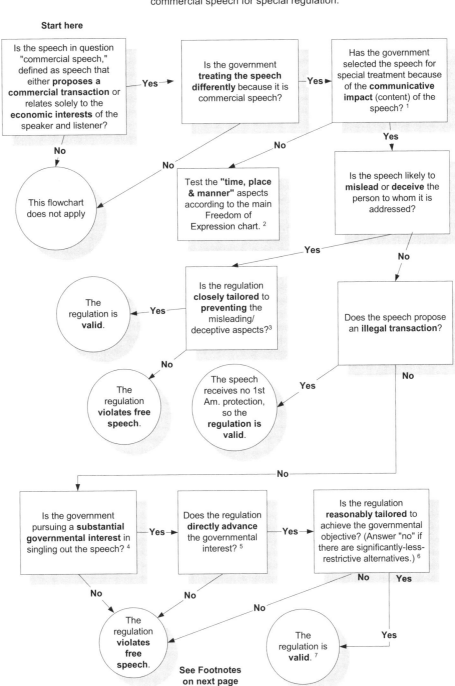

Start here

Is the speech in question "commercial speech," defined as speech that either **proposes a commercial transaction** or relates solely to the **economic interests** of the speaker and listener?

— Yes → Is the government **treating the speech differently** because it is commercial speech?

— Yes ► Has the government selected the speech for special treatment because of the **communicative impact** (content) of the speech? [1]

No ↓ This flowchart does not apply

No → Test the **"time, place & manner"** aspects according to the main Freedom of Expression chart. [2]

Yes ↓ Is the speech likely to **mislead** or **deceive** the person to whom it is addressed?

Yes → Is the regulation **closely tailored** to **preventing** the misleading/ deceptive aspects? [3]

— Yes → The regulation is **valid**.

No → The regulation **violates free speech**.

The speech receives no 1st Am. protection, so the **regulation is valid**.

No ↓ Does the speech propose an **illegal transaction**?

— Yes → (The speech receives no 1st Am. protection, so the regulation is valid.)

— No —

Is the government pursuing a **substantial governmental interest** in singling out the speech? [4]

— Yes → Does the regulation **directly advance** the governmental interest? [5]

— Yes → Is the regulation **reasonably tailored** to achieve the governmental objective? (Answer "no" if there are significantly-less-restrictive alternatives.) [6]

No / **Yes**

No ↓ **No** ↓ **No** →

The regulation **violates free speech**.

The regulation is **valid**. [7]

— Yes ←

See Footnotes on next page

Notes to
Figure 14-2 (Commercial Speech)

[1] Example: A state says that lawyers may not take out newspaper advertisements listing their services. This is content-based regulation: it is the communicative impact of the message ("Use our services") that the state is regulating.

[2] See footnotes 15 - 24 of Fig. 14-1 ("Freedom of Expression"). However, it seems likely that the state has somewhat broader authority to regulate time, place & manner in the case of commercial speech than in the case of, say, core political speech. For instance, the means-end fit can probably be somewhat looser in the commercial-speech area. But there are no Supreme Court cases on point.

[3] Example: Suppose the speech might or might not be misleading, depending on the context and the listener's degree of sophistication. The state must choose a regulation that limits the misleading tendency without also needlessly curtailing aspects of the message that wouldn't be likely to be misleading.

[4] Most governmental interests will probably qualify. For instance, preventing consumer confusion and deception will often qualify -- the fight is usually over the other two tests ("directly advance" and "reasonably tailored"). [See *Central Hudson Gas*, establishing a three-part test, of which "substantial gov'tl interest" is one part.]

[5] Example: A state forbids the advertising of cigarette prices, on the theory that price advertising will lead to lower prices, and lower prices will lead to more consumption, which is bad. The ban would probably flunk the "directly advance" test, since it's far from certain that suppressing price information materially decreases consumption. [Cf. *44 Liquormart v. R.I.*]

[6] Example: Same facts as in prior footnote. The ban on prices flunks the "reasonably tailored" test as well as the "directly advance" test, since there are less-intrusive alternatives available that will work as well or almost as well. For instance, the state could spend more money advertising the dangers of smoking.

Also, note that it now seems that even if gov't could <u>completely ban</u> a product, that fact <u>doesn't</u> give gov't the power to broadly <u>regulate</u> advertising so as to reduce demand for the product. So the fact that gov't could (or might be able to) make cigarettes completely illegal doesn't mean that gov't can ban cigarette advertising. [Cf. *44 Liquormart.*]

[7] Also, keep in mind that the fact that the speech being regulated is commercial rather than, say, political, means that gov't has some other extra-broad powers. For instance: (1) The <u>overbreadth</u> doctrine doesn't apply (so business *A* can't argue that a regulation should be struck down because it violates the free-speech rights of business *B*); (2) Gov't probably has somewhat greater right to regulate the <u>time, place & manner</u> of the speech; and (3) The heavy presumption against <u>prior restraints</u> doesn't apply (so gov't can probably require, say, that ads by utilities must be submitted to regulatory agencies before being run).

Figure 15-1
Freedom of Religion
under the 1st Amendment

Use this chart when government has taken any action that seems to concern religion.

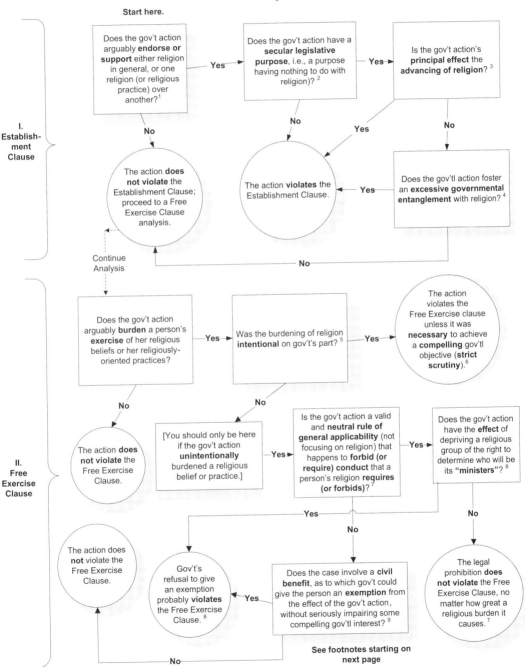

See footnotes starting on next page

Notes to
Figure 15-1 (Freedom of Religion)

[1] Examples of endorsement or support: (1) Gov't treats people who attend religious services more favorably than those who don't; (2) Gov't endorses religion by making a religious service part of a gov't-provided service (e.g., school prayer); (3) Gov't prefers one religious group over another (e.g., by giving tax breaks to one group but not another).

[2] The test in this box, and the tests in the next two boxes, make up the 3-part test of *Lemon v. Kurtzman*. Note that the gov't action is invalid if there's an unfavorable (pro-religious) answer to any of the 3 tests.

If the gov't action has multiple purposes, at least one of which is a secular one, the action apparently satisfies this test.

[3] Note that secondary effects that facilitate religion are not fatal.

Example: A state gives vouchers for $2000 in tuition assistance to any parents living in City who want to send their child to private school. 95% of the parents who participate use the money to send their children to parochial school, where the children are schooled in religious doctrine. *Held*, even though the tuition program has an effect of advancing religion, the program does not violate the "principal effect" test, and therefore does not violate the Establishment Clause. [*Zelman*]

In general, where any effect of advancing religion takes place through the individual choices made by private citizens (e.g., the parents in *Zelman*), there's no violation of the "primary effect" prong.

[4] This test is triggered mainly in two types of situations: (1) where the gov't would have to do a lot of scrutiny and bookkeeping to determine whether a program was valid; or (2) where a religious body would gain quasi-governmental powers. Example of type (2): State says that no tavern may locate w/in 500 feet of a church if the church objects -- this gives churches too much power in governmental affairs. [*Larkin v. Grendel's Den*]

[5] Example: The governing body of City doesn't like the practice of the Santeria religion, whose adherents are considered low-class. City therefore outlaws animal sacrifices, for the purpose of making observance of Santeria more difficult. [*Church of the Lukumi Babalu Aye*]

Note: Probably you should answer "yes" to this "Was the burdening intentional?" box only where the government is trying to "sanction" (punish) the religious practice, not where the government is merely non-punitively withholding some generally-applicable benefit from use in connection with a religious activity.

Example: State gives merit scholarships for college to high-achieving students, but excludes anyone who wants to study for the ministry. *Held*, *Lukumi* doesn't apply, and there's no Free Exercise violation, because the "no ministry" rule doesn't involve a criminal or civil "sanction," merely a refusal to grant an affirmative benefit to subsidize an essentially religious endeavor. [*Locke v. Davey*]

[6] Example: Gov't, acting for anti-religious purposes, bans animal sacrifices, and says it's doing so for public-health reasons (since sacrificial remains are often not properly disposed of). Because the ban is underinclusive (it doesn't deal with other similar sources of public-health concerns like disposal of animals killed by hunters), the means chosen are not "necessary" to achieve the gov'tl public-health purpose, so the ban flunks strict scrutiny. [*Church of the Lukumi Babalu Aye*]

[7] For instance, if gov't makes something a crime (and in doing so gov't is not acting with religious or anti-religious motives), the legal prohibition won't violate the Free Exercise Clause, no matter how great the religious burden or how little the gov't benefit.

Example: Gov't makes it a crime to smoke peyote. This makes it impossible for certain Native Americans to conduct a time-honored religious ritual. Gov't refuses to give an exemption to the Native Americans. *Held*, there is no Free Ex. violation, because the ban was a valid and neutral rule of general applicability, so gov't does not have to give an exemption, no matter how severely the ban affects the Native Americans' religious practices. [*Employment Div. v. Smith*]

[8] Example: A church/school fires X, a teacher who acts as a "minister" of the church. The firing would ordinarily violate the federal Americans with Disabilities Act. *Held*, the church's Free Exercise rights (and Establishment Clause rights) entitle it to an exemption from the ADA, because without an exemption, government would be interfering

Footnotes continue on next page.

Page 2 of Notes to
Figure 15-1 (Freedom of Religion)

with the internal decision-making of the church regarding its core faith and mission. [*Hosanna-Tabor v. EEOC*]

[9] There are few situations that will qualify for this box, because *Employment Div. v. Smith* (see note 7) will take care of the vast majority of unintentional-effect cases. The only cases that may qualify are those in which P is seeking a government benefit that is available only if P violates a religious tenet (and even those are not certain to qualify). The case in the following example is a pre-*Smith* case, so its continued validity is unknown.

Example: A state says that P can't receive unemployment benefits if there's an available job that she could hold but that she refuses to take because she would have to work on her Sabbath day. Held, this rule violates Free Exercise, because gov't has refused to give an exemption from its blanket rule where it could do so without seriously undermining any compelling gov't objective. [*Sherbert v. Verner* (1963)] (It's not clear whether the case would be decided the same way today, after 1990's *Employment Div. v. Smith* decision.)

CAPSULE SUMMARY

TABLE OF CONTENTS
OF CAPSULE SUMMARY

CAPSULE SUMMARY

Chapter 1

Chapter 1

INTRODUCTION

I. THREE STANDARDS OF REVIEW

A. Three standards: There are three key *standards of review* which reappear constantly throughout Constitutional Law. When a court reviews the constitutionality of government action, it is likely to be choosing from among one of these three standards of review: (1) the *mere-rationality* standard; (2) the *strict scrutiny* standard; and (3) the *middle-level review* standard.

  1. Mere rationality: Of the three standards, the easiest one to satisfy is the *"mere rationality"* standard. When the court applies this "mere-rationality" standard, the court will **uphold** the governmental action so long as two requirements are met:

   a. Legitimate state objective: First, the government must be pursuing a *legitimate governmental objective*. This is a very broad concept — practically any type of health, safety or "general welfare" goal will be found to be "legitimate."

   b. Rational relation: Second, there has to be a *"minimally rational relation"* between the means chosen by the government and the state objective. This requirement, too, is extremely easy to satisfy: only if the government has acted in a completely *"arbitrary and irrational"* way will this rational link between means and end not be found.

  2. Strict scrutiny: At the other end of the spectrum, the standard that is hardest to satisfy is the *"strict scrutiny"* standard of review. This standard will only be satisfied if the governmental act satisfies two very tough requirements:

   a. Compelling objective: First, the *objective* being pursued by the government must be *"compelling"* (not just "legitimate," as for the "mere-rationality" standard); and

   b. Necessary means: Second, the *means* chosen by the government must be *"necessary"* to achieve that compelling end. In other words, the "fit" between the means and the end must be extremely tight. (It's not enough that there's a "rational relation" between the means and the end, which is enough under the "mere-rationality" standard.)

    i. No less restrictive alternatives: In practice, this requirement that the means be "necessary" means that there must not be any *less restrictive* means that would accomplish the government's objective just as well.

3. **Middle-level review:**   In between these two review standards is so-called *"middle-level"* review.

    a. **"Important" objective:**   Here, the governmental objective has to be *"important"* (half way between "legitimate" and "compelling").

    b. **"Substantially related" means:**   And, the means chosen by the government must be *"substantially related"* to the important government objective. (This "substantially related" standard is half way between "rationally related" and "necessary.")

B. **Consequences of choice:**   The court's choice of one of these standards of review has two important consequences:

  1. **Burden of persuasion:**   First, the choice will make a big difference as to who has the *burden of persuasion*.

    a. **Mere rationality:**   Where the governmental action is subject to the "mere-rationality" standard, the *individual* who is attacking the government action will generally bear the burden of persuading the court that the action is unconstitutional.

    b. **Strict scrutiny:**   By contrast, if the court applies "strict scrutiny," then the *governmental body* whose act is being attacked has the burden of persuading the court that its action is constitutional.

    c. **Middle-level review:**   Where "middle level" scrutiny is used, it's not certain how the court will assign the burden of persuasion, but the burden will usually be placed on the government.

  2. **Effect on outcome:**   Second, the choice of review standard has a very powerful effect on the *actual outcome*. Where the "mere-rationality" standard is applied, the governmental action will *almost always be upheld*. Where "strict scrutiny" is used, the governmental action will *almost always be struck down*. (For instance, the Supreme Court applies strict scrutiny to any classification based on race, and has upheld only one such strictly scrutinized racial classification in the last 50 years.) Where middle-level scrutiny is used, there's roughly a 50-50 chance that the governmental action will be struck down.

    a. **Exam Tip:**   So when you're writing an exam answer, you've got to concentrate exceptionally hard on choosing the correct standard of review. Once you've determined that a particular standard would be applied, then you might as well go further and make a prediction about the outcome: if you've decided that "mere rationality" applies, you might write something like, "Therefore, the court will almost certainly uphold the governmental action." If you've chosen strict scrutiny, you should write something like, "Therefore, the governmental action is very likely to be struck down."

C. **When used:**   Here is a quick overview of the entire body of Constitutional Law, to see where each of these review standards gets used:

  1. **Mere rationality:**   Here are the main places where the "mere-rationality" standard gets applied (and therefore, the places where it's very hard for the

person attacking the governmental action to get it struck down on constitutional grounds):

a. **Dormant Commerce Clause:** First, the "mere-rationality" test is the main test to determine whether a state regulation that affects interstate commerce violates the ***"dormant Commerce Clause."*** The state regulation has to pursue a legitimate state end, and be rationally related to that end. (But there's a second test which we'll review in greater detail later: the state's interest in enforcing its regulation must also outweigh any ***burden*** imposed on interstate commerce, and any discrimination against interstate commerce.)

b. **Substantive due process:** Next comes ***substantive due process***. So long as no "fundamental right" is affected, the test for determining whether a governmental act violates substantive due process is, again, "mere rationality." In other words, if the state is pursuing a legitimate objective, and using means that are rationally related to that objective, the state will not be found to have violated the substantive Due Process Clause. So the vast bulk of ***economic regulations*** (since these don't affect fundamental rights) will be tested by the mere-rationality standard and almost certainly upheld.

c. **Equal protection:** Then, we move on to the ***equal protection*** area. Here, "mere-rationality" review is used so long as: (1) ***no suspect*** or ***quasi-suspect classification*** is being used; and (2) ***no fundamental right*** is being impaired. This still leaves us with a large number of classifications which will be judged based on the mere-rationality standard, including: (1) almost all economic regulations; (2) some classifications based on alienage; and (3) rights that are not "fundamental" even though they are very important, such as food, housing, and free public education. In all of these areas, the classification will be reviewed under the "mere-rationality" standard, and will therefore almost certainly be upheld.

d. **Contracts Clause:** Lastly, we find "mere-rationality" review in some aspects of the ***"Obligation of Contracts"*** Clause.

2. **Strict scrutiny:** Here are the various contexts in which the court applies *strict scrutiny*:

a. **Substantive due process/fundamental rights:** First, where a governmental action affects *fundamental rights*, and the plaintiff claims that his ***substantive due process*** rights are being violated, the court will use strict scrutiny. So when the state impairs rights falling in the ***"privacy"*** cluster of marriage, child-bearing, and child-rearing, the court will use strict scrutiny (and will therefore probably invalidate the governmental restriction). For instance, government restrictions that impair the right to use contraceptives receive this kind of strict scrutiny.

b. **Equal protection review:** Next, the court uses strict scrutiny to review a claim that a classification violates the plaintiff's ***equal protection*** rights, if the classification relates either to a ***suspect classification*** or a ***fundamental right***. "Suspect classifications" include ***race, national ori-***

gin, and (sometimes) ***alienage***. "Fundamental rights" for this purpose include the right to ***vote***, to be a ***candidate***, to have access to the ***courts***, and to ***travel interstate***. So classifications that either involve any of these suspect classifications or impair any of these fundamental rights will be strictly scrutinized and will probably be struck down.

c. **Freedom of expression:** Next, we move to the area of ***freedom of expression***. If the government is impairing free expression in a ***content-based way***, then the court will use strict scrutiny and will almost certainly strike down the regulation. In other words, if the government is restricting some speech but not others, based on the ***content of the messages***, then this suppression of expression will only be allowed if necessary to achieve a compelling purpose (a standard which is rarely found to be satisfied in the First Amendment area). Similarly, any interference with the right of ***free association*** will be strictly scrutinized.

d. **Freedom of religion/Free Exercise Clause:** Lastly, the court will use strict scrutiny to evaluate any impairment with a person's ***free exercise*** of religion. Even if the government does ***not intend*** to impair a person's free exercise of his religion, if it substantially burdens his exercise of religion the government will have to give him an ***exemption*** from the otherwise-applicable regulation unless denial of an exemption is necessary to achieve a compelling governmental interest.

3. **Middle-level review:** Finally, here are the relatively small number of contexts in which the court uses middle-level review:

a. **Equal protection/semi-suspect:** First, middle-level review will be used to judge an ***equal protection*** claim, where the classification being challenged involves a ***semi-suspect*** trait. The two traits which are considered semi-suspect for this purpose are: (1) ***gender***; and (2) ***illegitimacy***. So any government classification based on gender or illegitimacy will have to be "substantially related" to the achievement of some "important" governmental interest.

b. **Contracts Clause:** Second, certain conduct attacked under the Obligation of Contracts Clause will be judged by the middle-level standard of review.

c. **Free expression/non-content-based:** Finally, in the First Amendment area we use a standard similar (though not identical) to the middle-level review standard to judge government action that impairs expression, but does so in a ***non-content-based*** manner. This is true, for instance, of any content-neutral ***"time, place and manner"*** regulation.

CHAPTER 2

THE SUPREME COURT'S AUTHORITY AND THE FEDERAL JUDICIAL POWER

I. THE SUPREME COURT'S AUTHORITY AND THE FEDERAL JUDICIAL POWER

A. *Marbury* **principle:** Under *Marbury v. Madison*, it is the Supreme Court, not Congress, which has the authority and duty to declare a congressional statute unconstitutional if the Court thinks it violates the Constitution.

B. Supreme Court review of state court decision: The Supreme Court may review state court opinions, but only to the extent that the decision was decided *based on federal law.*

   1. "Independent and adequate state grounds": Even if there is a federal question in the state court case, the Supreme Court may not review the case if there is an "*independent and adequate*" state ground for the state court's decision. That is, if the same result would be reached even had the state court made a different decision on the federal question, the Supreme Court may not decide the case. This is because its opinion would in effect be an "advisory" one.

      a. Violations of state and federal constitutions: If a state action violates the *same clause* of both state and federal constitutions (e.g., the Equal Protection Clause of each), the state court decision may or may not be based on an "independent" state ground. If the state court is saying, "This state action would violate our state constitution whether or not it violated the federal constitution," that's "independent." But if the state court is saying, "Based on our reading of the constitutional provision (which we think has the same meaning under both the state and federal constitutions), this state action violates both constitutions," this is *not* "independent," so the Supreme Court may review the state court decision.

   2. Review limited to decisions of highest state court: Federal statutes limit Supreme Court review to decisions of the *highest state court available*. But this does not mean that the top-ranking state court must have ruled on the *merits* of the case in order for the Supreme Court to review it. All that is required is that the case be heard by the highest state court *available* to the petitioner. (*Example:* A state trial court finds a particular state statute to be valid under the federal Equal Protection Clause. An intermediate appellate court in the state affirms; the highest state court refuses to hear an appeal from the affirmance. As a matter of both the federal judicial power and federal statutes, the Supreme Court may hear this case, because the intermediate appellate court was the highest court "available" to the petitioner.)

C. Federal judicial power: Article III, Section 2 sets out the federal judicial power. This includes, among other things: (a) cases arising under the *Constitution* or the *"laws of the U.S."* (i.e., cases posing a "federal question"); (b) cases of *admiralty*; (c) cases between *two or more states*; (d) cases between *citizens of different states*; and (e) cases between a state or its citizens and a *foreign country or foreign citizen*. Note that this does *not* include cases where both parties are citizens (i.e., residents) of the same state, and no federal question is raised.

II. CONGRESS' CONTROL OF FEDERAL JUDICIAL POWER

A. Congress' power to decide: *Congress* has the general power to *decide what types of cases the Supreme Court may hear*, so long as it doesn't expand the Supreme Court's jurisdiction beyond the federal judicial power (as listed in the prior paragraph). [*Ex parte McCardle*]

B. Lower courts: Congress also may decide what *lower federal courts* there should be, and what cases they may hear. Again, the outer bound of this power is that Congress can't allow the federal courts to hear a case that is not within the federal judicial power.

> **Example 1:** Congress may cut back the jurisdiction of the lower federal courts pretty much whenever and however it wishes. Thus Congress could constitutionally eliminate diversity jurisdiction (i.e., suits between citizens of different states), even though such suits are clearly listed in the Constitution as being within the federal judicial power.

> **Example 2:** But Congress could not give the lower federal courts jurisdiction over cases between two citizens of the same state, where no federal issue is posed. The handling of such a case by the federal courts would simply go beyond the federal judicial power as recited in the Constitution.

CHAPTER 3

FEDERALISM AND FEDERAL POWER GENERALLY

I. THE CONCEPT OF FEDERALISM

A. The federalist system: We have a *"federalist"* system. In other words, the national government and the state governments co-exist. Therefore, you always have to watch whether some power being asserted by the federal government is in fact allowed under the Constitution, and you must also watch whether some power asserted by the states is limited in favor of federal power.

B. Federal government has limited powers: The most important principle in this whole area is that the federal government is one of *limited, enumerated powers*. In other words, the three federal branches (Congress, the executive branch, and the federal courts) can only assert powers *specifically granted* to them by the United States Constitution. So any time Congress passes a statute, or the President issues, say, an Executive Order, or the federal courts decide a case, you've got to ask: What is the enumerated, specified power in the U.S. Constitution that gives the federal branch the right to do what it has just done? (This is very different from what our Constitution says about the powers of *state* governments: state governments can do whatever they want as far as the U.S. Constitution is concerned, unless what they are doing is *expressly forbidden* by the Constitution.)

1. **No general police power:** The most dramatic illustration of this state/federal difference is the general *"police power."* Each state has a general police power, i.e., the ability to regulate solely on the basis that the regulation would enhance the welfare of the citizenry. But there is *no general federal police power*, i.e., no right of the federal government to regulate for the health, safety or general welfare of the citizenry. Instead, each act of federal legislation or regulation must come within one of the very specific, enumerated powers (e.g., the Commerce Clause, the power to tax and spend, etc.).

   a. **Tax and spend for general welfare:** Congress *does* have the right to "lay and collect taxes ... to pay the debts and provide for the ... general welfare of the United States. ... " (Article I, Section 8.) But the phrase "provide for the ... general welfare" in this sentence modifies "lay and collect taxes ... to pay the debts. ... " In other words, the power to tax and spend is subject to the requirement that the general welfare be served; there is no *independent* federal power to provide for the general welfare.

C. **"Necessary and Proper" Clause:** In addition to the very specific powers given to Congress by the Constitution, Congress is given the power to "make all laws which shall be *necessary and proper* for carrying into execution" the specific powers.

   1. **Rational-relation test:** The "Necessary and Proper" Clause is easy for Congress to satisfy: if Congress is seeking an *objective* that is within the specifically enumerated powers, then Congress can use *any means* that is: (1) *rationally related* to the objective Congress is trying to achieve; and (2) is not specifically forbidden by the Constitution.

      a. **Broad reading given to Clause:** Congress gives a very *broad and deferential reading* to Congress' powers under the Clause.

      Example: Congress passes a statute to civilly commit certain sexually-dangerous federal prisoners at the end of their prison sentences. The prisoners attack the statute as being beyond Congress' powers.

      Held: Congress acted properly. The "Necessary and Proper" Clause grants Congress broad authority. Congress is entitled to large discretion in choosing the particular means to carry out a given enumerated power — all that's required is that Congress chooses a means that's *rationally related* to the implementation of some constitutionally-enumerated power. Here, Congress has the power to define federal crimes, and to run a prison system housing those who commit such crimes. Allowing the Federal Bureau of Prisons to maintain custody of prisoners who would be dangerous to others if released is a rational method of carrying out the federal power to incarcerate those who commit federal crimes. [*U.S. v. Comstock*]

D. Can't violate specific constitutional provision: Even where congressional action appears to fall within a specific grant of power, the federal action may not, of course, violate some *other* specific constitutional guarantee. In other words, congressional (or other federal) action must satisfy *two* tests to be constitutional: (1) it must fall within some specific grant of power under the Constitution; and (2) it must not violate any specific constitutional provision.

CHAPTERS 4, 5 AND 8

POWERS OF THE FEDERAL GOVERNMENT; THE SEPARATION OF POWERS

I. POWERS OF THE THREE FEDERAL BRANCHES

A. Powers of the three branches: Here is a summary of the powers of the *three branches* of the federal government:

1. **Congress:** Here are the main powers given to Congress :

    a. **Interstate commerce:** Congress has the power to *regulate interstate commerce*, as well as foreign commerce.

    b. **Taxing and spending:** Congress has the power to *tax* and the power to *spend*.

    c. **DC:** Congress can regulate the *District of Columbia*.

    d. **Federal property:** Congress has power to regulate and dispose of *federal property.*

    e. **War and defense:** Congress can *declare war*, and can establish and fund the armed forces.

    f. **Enforcement of Civil War amendments:** Congress can *enforce* the *post-Civil War amendments*. (For instance, under its power to enforce the Thirteenth Amendment's abolition of slavery, Congress can ban even private intrastate non-commercial conduct.)

2. **President:** Here are the main powers of the President:

    a. **Execution of laws:** The President holds the *"executive power."* That is, he *carries out* the laws made by Congress. It is his obligation to make sure the laws are "faithfully executed."

    b. **Commander in Chief:** He is *Commander in Chief* of the armed forces. So he directs and leads our armed forces (but he cannot declare war — only Congress can do this).

    c. **Treaty and foreign affairs:** The President can make *treaties* with foreign nations (but only if two-thirds of the Senate approves). He appoints *ambassadors.* Also, he effectively controls our *foreign policy* — some of this power over foreign policy stems from his right to appoint ambassadors, but much is simply *implied* from the nation's need to speak with a single voice in foreign affairs (so that congressional involvement in the details of foreign affairs will generally not be appropriate).

   d. **Appointment of federal officers:** The President appoints all *federal officers*. These include *cabinet members*, *federal judges* and *ambassadors*. (But the Senate must approve all such federal officers by majority vote.) As to "*inferior* [federal] officers," it's up to Congress to decide whether these should be appointed by the President, by the judicial branch, or by the "heads of departments" (i.e., cabinet members). (But Congress can't make these lower-level appointments itself; it may merely decide who *can* make these appointments.)

   e. **Pardons:** The President can issue *pardons*, but only for federal offenses. (Also, he can't pardon anyone who has been impeached and convicted.)

   f. **Veto:** The President may *veto* any law passed by both houses (though this veto may be *overridden* by a 2-3's majority of each house). If the President doesn't veto the bill within 10 days after receiving it, it becomes law (unless Congress has adjourned by the 10th day after it sent him the bill — this is the so-called "pocket veto").

3. **Judiciary:** The federal *judiciary* may decide "cases" or "controversies" that fall within the federal judicial power. See the section on "Federal Judicial Power" in the chapter called "The Supreme Court's Authority and the Federal Judicial Power," above.

II. THE FEDERAL COMMERCE POWER

  A. **Summary:** Probably Congress' most important power is the power to "*regulate Commerce* ... among the several states." (Art. I, §8.) This is the "Commerce power."

> **Exam Tip:** Any time you have a test question in which Congress is doing something, first ask yourself, "Can what Congress is doing be justified as an exercise of the Commerce power?" Most of the time the answer will be "yes."

  B. **Summary of modern view:** There seem to be *four broad categories* of activities which Congress can constitutionally regulate under the Commerce power:

   1. **Channels:** First, Congress can regulate the use of the *"channels"* of interstate commerce. Thus Congress can regulate in a way that is reasonably related to highways, waterways, and air traffic. Presumably Congress can do so even though the activity in question in the particular case is completely intrastate.

   2. **Instrumentalities:** Second, Congress can regulate the *"instrumentalities"* of interstate commerce, even though the particular activities being regulated are completely intrastate. This category refers to people, machines, and other "things" used in carrying out commerce.

Example: Probably Congress could say that every truck must have a specific safety device, even if the particular truck in question was made and used exclusively within a single state.

3. **Articles moving in interstate commerce:** Third, Congress can regulate *articles moving* in interstate commerce.

   Example: The states and private parties keep information about the identities of drivers. Since this information gets exchanged across state lines (e.g., from states to companies that want to sell cars), the information is an article in interstate commerce and Congress may regulate how it's used. [*Reno v. Condon*]

4. **"Substantially affecting" commerce:** Finally, the biggest (and most interesting) category is that Congress may regulate those activities having a *"substantial effect"* on interstate commerce. [*U.S. v. Lopez.*] As to this category, the following rules now seem to apply:

   a. **Activity is commercial:** If the activity itself is arguably *"commercial,"* then it doesn't seem to matter whether the *particular instance* of the activity directly affects interstate commerce, as long as the instance is part of a general class of activities that, *collectively*, substantially affect interstate commerce. So even purely intrastate activities can be regulated if they're directly "commercial." This is especially true where Congress regulates the intrastate commercial activities as part of a *broad scheme* to regulate interstate commerce in the same activity.

      Example: In the federal Controlled Substances Act (CSA), Congress outlaws all distribution and possession of marijuana. California then makes it legal under state law for a Californian to cultivate marijuana for her own personal medicinal use. The U.S. seeks to prevent P, a Californian, from taking advantage of this state-law loophole. P asserts that the application of the CSA to bar P from personally cultivating marijuana for her own personal medical use is beyond Congress' Commerce powers.

      Held, Congress' Commerce powers extend to this regulation of P's own cultivation and use. Marijuana is a commercial commodity, and the CSA is regulating interstate commerce in that commodity. Congress reasonably feared that if it exempted personal — and thus "intrastate" — cultivation and use of marijuana for medical purposes, some of the marijuana so cultivated would be illegally drawn into the interstate market, jeopardizing Congress' overall scheme of banning the drug. So the private cultivation of marijuana by people like P, even though purely an intrastate activity, falls within Congress' Commerce power. [*Gonzales v. Raich*]

   b. **Activity is not commercial:** But if the activity itself is *not "commercial,"* then there will apparently have to be a *pretty obvious connection* between the activity and interstate commerce.

      Example 1: Congress makes it a federal crime to possess a firearm in or near a school. The act applies even if the particular gun never moved in (or affected) interstate commerce. *Held*, in enacting this statute Congress went beyond its Commerce power. To fall within the Commerce power, the activity being regulated must have a "substantial effect" on interstate commerce. The link between gun-possession in a school and interstate commerce is too tenuous to qualify as a "substantial effect," because if it did, there would be essentially no limit to Congress' Commerce power. [*U.S. v. Lopez*]

Example 2: Congress says that any woman who is the victim of a violent gender-based crime may bring a civil suit against the perpetrator in federal court. *Held*, Congress went beyond its Commerce power. Although it may be true that some women's fear of gender-based violence dissuades them from working or traveling interstate, gender-based violence is not itself a commercial activity, and the connection between gender-based violence and interstate commerce is too attenuated for the violence to have a "substantial effect" on commerce. [*U.S. v. Morrison*]

    i. Jurisdictional hook: But where the congressional act applies only to particular activities each of which has a direct link to interstate commerce, then the act will probably be within the Commerce power. Thus the use of a ***"jurisdictional hook"*** will probably suffice. (*Example*: Suppose the statute in *Lopez* by its terms applied only to in-school gun possession if the particular gun had previously moved in interstate commerce. This would be enough of a connection to interstate commerce to qualify.)

  c. Little deference to Congress: The Court ***won't*** give much ***deference*** (as it used to) to the fact that Congress ***believed*** that the activity has the requisite "substantial effect" on interstate commerce. The Court will basically decide this issue for itself, from scratch. It certainly will no longer be enough that Congress had a ***"rational basis"*** for believing that the requisite effect existed — the effect must *in fact* exist to the Court's own independent satisfaction. [*Lopez.*]

  d. Traditional domain of states: If what's being regulated is an activity the regulation of which has ***traditionally*** been the ***domain of the states***, and as to which the states have expertise, the Court is less likely to find that Congress is acting within its Commerce power. Thus ***education***, ***family law*** and ***general criminal law*** are areas where the court is likely to be especially suspicious of congressional "interference."

    i. National solution: However, the fact that the activity has traditionally fallen within the states' domain can be ***outweighed*** by a showing that a ***national solution*** is needed. This would be so, for instance, where one state's choice heavily affects other states. Regulation of the ***environment*** is an example, since air and water pollution migrate across state boundaries. The same would be true of regulation of ***drug trafficking*** (e.g., Congress can regulate forbid cultivation of marijuana, because otherwise, Congress' national ban on the drug might be undermined; see *Gonzales v. Raich*).

e.   Forcing someone to buy or sell a product: Congress may not use its Commerce powers to require that a person *not presently in the market-place* for a particular type of product *buy that product*. That's true even if many individuals' combined failure to purchase the product significantly affects interstate commerce in the product. [*N.F.I.B. v. Sebelius* (2012)]

   i.   Health insurance: So, for instance, Congress can't use its Commerce powers to require otherwise-uninsured citizens to either *purchase health insurance* or pay a penalty, even though the uninsureds' failure to have insurance has a substantial effect on the interstate health-insurance market by increasing everyone else's insurance costs. [*N.F.I.B. v. Sebelius, supra.*]

   Example: Congress, in an attempt to greatly broaden the availability of health-care insurance, enacts the 2010 Affordable Care Act ("ACA"). Because pre-ACA there have been millions of uninsured individuals, and these individuals have been receiving government-mandated emergency health care paid for by higher taxes and higher insurance premiums charged to everyone else, the ACA imposes an "individual mandate." Under the individual mandate, most uninsured individuals are required to buy a specified level of health insurance. If an individual doesn't buy qualifying insurance, he is required to make a "shared-responsibility payment" to the Internal Revenue Service, which the ACA refers to as a "penalty." (The payment to the IRS is typically much less than the cost of qualifying insurance.) In Congress' view, the individual mandate and the shared-responsibility payment system fall within the Commerce power, because these measures are simply a means of regulating how and when people will pay (via insurance) for a product (health care) that they would inevitably consume even without regulation. Twenty-six states claim that the mandate goes beyond the Commerce power.

   Held, 5-4, for the state plaintiffs on this point: the individual mandate is not authorized by the Commerce power. The Commerce Clause allows Congress to regulate "*existing commercial activity.*" But it does not allow Congress to "compel[] individuals to *become* active in commerce by purchasing a product, on the ground that their failure to do so affects interstate commerce." Allowing Congress to regulate based on the effect of *inaction* on commerce "would bring countless decisions an individual could potentially make within the scope of federal regulation[.]" For instance, many Americans do not eat a balanced diet, and therefore become obese. Obese people have higher health costs, which are borne in part by other Americans. Under Congress' theory, therefore, "Congress could address the diet problem by ordering everyone to buy vegetables." But giving Congress the power to "regulate what we do not do [would] fundamentally chang[e] the relation between the citizen and the Federal Government," in a way the drafters of the Commerce power never intended.

Four dissenters claim that the individual mandate falls within the Commerce power, because virtually all uninsured persons will eventually consume health care, and 90% will do so within any 5-year period. Therefore, all Congress is doing is regulating the terms by which individuals *pay* for an interstate good they already consume: "Persons subject to the mandate must now pay for medical care *in advance* (instead of at the point of service) and *through insurance* (instead of out-of-pocket). ... Establishing payment terms for goods in or affecting interstate commerce is *quintessential economic regulation*." [*N.F.I.B. v. Sebelius, supra*]

Note: But by a different 5-4 majority, the Court in *N.F.I.B.* sustained the individual mandate as an exercise of Congress' **taxing** power. See *infra*, pp. 58-59.

C. **The Tenth Amendment as a limit on Congress' power:** The **Tenth Amendment** provides that "the powers not delegated to the United States by the Constitution, nor prohibited by it to the States, are reserved to the States respectively, or to the People." This Amendment today seems to place a small but possibly significant limit on Congress' ability to use its Commerce power to **regulate the states**.

1. **Generally-applicable law:** If Congress passes a **generally applicable law**, the fact that the regulation **affects the states** has virtually no practical significance, and the Tenth Amendment never comes into play. If the regulation would be valid if applied to a private party, it is also valid as to the state.

   Example: Congress passes minimum-wage and overtime provisions, which are made applicable to all businesses of a certain size. The statute contains no exemption for employees of state-owned mass transit systems. *Held*, the regulation even of state employees here is a constitutional exercise of the commerce power, and is not forbidden by the Tenth Amendment. [*Garcia v. San Antonio Metropolitan Transit Authority*]

2. **Use of state's law-making mechanisms:** But the Tenth Amendment *does* prevent Congress from interfering in certain ways with a state's **law-making processes**. Congress may not simply "commandeer the legislative processes of the states by directly **compelling them to enact and enforce a federal regulatory program.**" [*New York v. United States*]

   Example: Congress provides that each state must arrange for the disposal of toxic waste generated within its borders, or else be deemed to "take title" to the waste and thereby become liable for tort damages stemming from it. *Held*, the congressional scheme violates the Tenth Amendment. Congress may not force a state to enact and enforce a federal regulatory program, and this is in effect what Congress has tried to do here. *New York v. United States, supra*.

a. **Administrative actions:** Similarly, Congress may not compel a state or local government's *executive branch* to perform functions, even ones that are easy-to-do and involve no discretion.

Example: Congress can't order local sheriffs to perform background checks on applicants for handgun permits. [*Printz v. U.S.*]

III. THE TAXING AND SPENDING POWERS

A. **Taxing power:** Congress has the power to *"lay and collect taxes."* (Art. I, §8.) This is an independent source of congressional power, so it can be used to reach conduct that might be beyond the other sources of congressional power, like the Commerce Clause.

1. **Regulation:** Congress can probably *regulate* under the guise of taxing, so long as there's some real revenue produced.

2. **Limits on taxing power:** There are a few *limits* which the Constitution places upon the taxing power:

   a. **Direct taxes:** "Direct taxes" must be allocated among the states in proportion to population. This provision is of little practical importance today.

   b. **Customs duties and excise taxes must be uniform:** All *customs duties* and *excise taxes* must be *uniform* throughout the United States. (*Example:* Congress may not place a $.10 per-gallon federal excise tax on gasoline sales that take place in New Jersey, and a $.15 per-gallon tax on those that take place in Oklahoma.)

   c. **No export taxes:** Congress may not tax any *exports* from any state. (*Example:* Congress may not place a tax on all computers which are exported from any state to foreign countries.)

3. **Effect of calling a measure a "penalty":** The fact that Congress labels a measure as a *"penalty"* does *not* prevent the measure from being upheld as a valid tax, as long as the measure actually functions in a way that resembles a tax. [*N.F.I.B. v. Sebelius* (2012)]

   Example: In the 2010 Affordable Care Act ("ACA"), Congress requires most individuals to purchase health insurance, even if they have previously chosen to "self-insure." (This requirement is called the "individual mandate.") If a covered person doesn't make the required insurance purchase, she must pay the IRS at tax-filing time a *"shared-responsibility payment,"* which the Act repeatedly characterizes as a *"penalty"* rather than as a tax. If a person doesn't make the shared-responsibility payment, the IRS can use some of its standard tax-collection methods, but cannot bring a *criminal prosecution*.

   Held, by a 5-4 vote, the individual mandate and shared-responsibility payment scheme is a valid exercise of Congress' taxing power. If a federal statute would be unconstitutional unless found to be a valid tax, the Court will treat it as a tax as long as that interpretation is a "fairly possible" one. The process here "yields the essential feature of any tax: it *pro-*

duces at least some revenue for the Government." And the fact that Congress called this a "penalty" rather than a "tax" is not dispositive, because the Court will look at the reality of how the scheme operates, not the label used by Congress. Here, the payment to the IRS would typically be far less than the price of insurance, making it look more like a tax (which a rational person might voluntarily choose to pay instead of buying insurance) than a penalty for unlawful conduct. Also, by prohibiting criminal prosecutions for non-payment (and by not referring to the failure to buy insurance as "unlawful"), Congress has again made the payment seem more like a tax than a penalty for wrongdoing.

The four dissenters would hold that where Congress designates a payment as a "penalty" rather than a "tax," that should by itself be enough to prevent the scheme from being authorized by the tax-and-spend power. [*N.F.I.B. v. Sebelius, supra.*]

B. Spending power: Congress also has the power to "pay the debts and provide for the common defense and general welfare of the United States." (Art. I, §8.) This is the "***spending***" power.

1. Independent power: This is an independent power, just like the Commerce power. So Congress could spend to achieve a purely local benefit, even one that it couldn't achieve by regulating under the Commerce power.

2. Use of conditions: Congress may generally place ***conditions*** upon use of its spending power, even if the congressional purpose is in effect to regulate. Conditions placed upon the doling out of federal funds are usually justified under the "Necessary and Proper" Clause (which lets Congress use any means to seek an objective falling within the specifically-enumerated powers, as long as the means is rationally related to the objective, and is not specifically forbidden by the Constitution).

Example: Suppose Congress makes available to the states certain funds that are to be used for improving the states' highway systems. Congress provides, however, that a state will lose 5% of these funds unless the state passes a statute imposing a speed limit of no higher than 55 mph on all state roads. Even without reference to the Commerce Clause, this is a valid use of congressional power. That's because by the combination of the spending power and the "Necessary and Proper" Clause, Congress is permitted to impose conditions (even ones motivated solely by regulatory objectives) on the use of federal funds. [*South Dakota v. Dole*]

a. Conditions can't amount to "coercion": But there is a ***limit*** to how much pressure Congress can bring to bear on the states when it sets conditions on a new program that relies on the spending power. Pressure that amounts to ***"coercion"*** will cause the new program to go beyond the spending power.

i. Loss of pre-existing federal funding: So far, this "coercion" problem has arisen only where Congress tells the states that if they don't agree to participate in a new federally-funded program, they will lose ***major federal funding*** associated with an independent ***pre-existing***

program. In this situation, the Court will ask whether Congress has left the states ***"no real option but to acquiesce"*** in the new program and its conditions. If the answer is "yes," the Court will conclude that Congress has ***coerced*** the states, and that this coercion ***goes beyond the scope of Congress' spending power.*** (Only one case — set forth in the following Example — has found that Congress used such unconstitutional coercion.)

Example: Every state has for decades participated in Medicaid, a federal-state program under which the states provide health care for certain classes of poor people, and Congress pays most of the costs. In the 2010 Affordable Care Act (ACA), Congress dramatically expands the Medicaid program by means of the "Medicaid Expansion." Under the Medicaid Expansion, each participating state must now give Medicaid coverage to *every adult under 65* with income up to 133% of the federal poverty level (whereas far fewer people have been covered by most states under the pre-Expansion version of Medicaid). Congress promises to pay all or nearly all of the costs (depending on the year) of the Expansion. If a state declines to participate in the Expansion, it will lose ***all*** Medicaid funding, not just the "extra" funding to cover the newly-eligible recipients. An average state that declines to agree to the Expansion will lose, in addition to the funds to cover the Expansion itself, more than 10% of its total budget. Twenty-six states claim that the threatened loss of all existing Medicaid funding is so coercive that the Medicaid Expansion goes beyond Congress' spending power.

Held (by a 7-2 vote), for the plaintiff states. Congress is entitled to impose conditions on the use of money it provides to states. But the Court will give closer scrutiny to those situations in which Congress, in connection with *one* federally-financed program, imposes conditions that take the form of threats to terminate a state's participation in *another* significant federally-funded program. Here, Congress has held "a gun to the head" of the states: a state that rejects the Medicaid Expansion (essentially a new program) will lose all funding for "old" Medicaid, typically over 10% of the state's overall budget. This is "economic dragooning that leaves the states with *no real option but to acquiesce*" in the Medicaid Expansion. Such compulsion goes beyond Congress' spending power.[1] [*N.F.I.B. v. Sebelius* (2012)] (other aspects of which are discussed *supra*, pp. 56 and 58-59).

C. **"General Welfare" Clause:** Although, as noted above, Congress can "provide for the common defense and general welfare of the United States," the reference to "general welfare" does ***not*** confer any independent source of congressional power. In other words, no statute is valid solely because Congress is trying to

---

1. But the Court held that the rest of the ACA could be ***severed*** from the unconstitutional condition. So each state got to choose to either participate in the Medicaid Expansion, or instead to keep its pre-existing Medicaid rights and funding.

bring about the "general welfare." Instead, the phrase "for the general welfare" describes the circumstances under which Congress may use its "taxing and spending" power. So if Congress is *regulating* (rather than taxing and spending), it must find a specific grant of power (like the Commerce Clause), and it's not enough that the regulation will promote the general welfare.

IV. THE SEPARATION OF POWERS

A. **Separation of powers generally:** Let's now review some of the major practical consequences that come from the fact that each federal branch gets its own set of powers. These practical consequences are collectively referred to as *"separation of powers"* problems.

1. **President can't make the laws:** The most important single separation of powers principle to remember is that the *President cannot make the laws*. All he can do is to *carry out the laws* made by Congress.

   Example: During the Korean War, Pres. Truman wants to avert a strike in the nation's steel mills. He therefore issues an "executive order" directing the Secretary of Commerce to seize the mills and operate them under federal direction. The President does not ask Congress to approve the seizure. *Held*, the seizure order is an unconstitutional exercise of the lawmaking authority reserved to Congress. [*Youngstown Sheet & Tube v. Sawyer*]

   a. **Line Item Veto:** The principle that the President can't make the laws means that the President can't be given a *"line item veto."* That is, if Congress tries to give the President the right to veto individual portions of a statute (e.g., particular expenditures), this will violate the Presentment Clause. (The Presentment Clause says that bills are enacted into law by being passed by both Houses, then being presented to the President and signed by him.) [*Clinton v. City of New York*]

   b. **Congress' acquiescence:** But the scope of the President's powers may be at least somewhat expanded by *Congress' acquiescence* to his exercise of the power. This congressional acquiescence will never be *dispositive*, but in a close case, the fact that Congress acquiesced in the President's conduct may be enough to tip the balance, and to convince the Court that the President is merely carrying out the laws rather than making them.

   c. **Implied powers:** Recall that Congress' powers are somewhat expanded by the "Necessary & Proper" clause — Congress can pass any laws reasonably related to the exercise of any enumerated power. There's no comparable "Necessary & Proper" clause for the President. But the effect is the same, because of the inherent vagueness of the phrase "shall take care that the laws be faithfully executed..." The Constitution does specifically enumerate some of the President's powers (e.g., the pardon power, the commander-in-chief power, etc.), but this specific list is not supposed to be exclusive. Instead of giving a complete list of the President's powers (as is done for Congress), the Constitution gives the President this general "executive" or "law carrying out" power.

   i. **Consequence:** Consequently, so long as the President's act seems reasonably related to carrying out the laws made by Congress, the Court won't strike that act merely because it doesn't fall within any narrow, enumerated Presidential power. (*Example:* Nothing in the Constitution expressly gives the President prosecutorial discretion (the power to decide whom to prosecute), yet he clearly has this power, because it's part of the broader job of "carrying out the law.")

  d. **Delegation:** Congress may *delegate* some of its power to the President or the executive branch. This is how federal agencies (which are usually part of the executive branch) get the right to formulate *regulations* for interpreting and enforcing congressional statutes. If Congress delegates *excessively* to federal agencies (by not giving appropriate standards), the delegation can be struck down — but this is very rare.

 2. **War powers:** Be alert for separation-of-powers issues when the President's *war-related powers* are at stake.

  a. **Can't declare war:** The President is the Commander-in-Chief of the armed forces. But *only Congress, not the President, can declare war.* The President can commit our armed forces to repel a sudden attack, but he cannot fight a long-term engagement without a congressional declaration of war.

  b. **Habeas corpus:** The constitutional right of prisoners — including foreign prisoners of war — to make a *habeas corpus petition* reflects separation-of-powers principles. Under the *"Suspension Clause"* of Art. I, § 9, cl. 2, the government (i.e., the executive branch) may not suspend habeas corpus — the right of a state or federal prisoner to prove to a federal judge that the prisoner is being held in violation of the constitution or federal law — except "when in Cases of Rebellion or Invasion the public Safety may require it."

   Example: At the President's urging after 9/11, Congress passes a law that foreigners held by the military as enemy combatants at the U.S. base in Guantanamo Bay, Cuba may not use a habeas corpus petition to a federal district judge to contest the legality of their imprisonment. (Instead, such prisoners are required to appeal to the federal Court of Appeals for the D.C. Circuit, but that court is limited to reviewing the record of the military tribunal that made the enemy-combatant classification, and can't examine newly-discovered evidence.) The Ps, foreigners captured abroad, held at Guantanamo and classified as enemy combatants, seek a ruling that the law unconstitutionally takes away their right to show by habeas petition that they were misclassified as an enemy combatant.

   Held, for the Ps. The law violates the Suspension Clause, because the appeal procedure in the law is not an adequate substitute for habeas corpus, and even foreigners imprisoned by the U.S. have habeas rights. Separation-of-powers principles make it vital that the judicial branch keep the power to hear habeas challenges to the executive branch's authority to imprison a person. [*Boumediene v. Bush*]

3. **Treaties and executive agreements:** As noted, the President has the power to enter into a ***treaty*** with foreign nations, but only if two-thirds of the Senate approves. Additionally, the Court has held that the Constitution implicitly gives the President, as an adjunct of his foreign affairs power, the right to enter into an ***"executive agreement"*** with a foreign nation, without first getting express congressional consent.

4. **Appointment and removal of executive personnel:** The President, not Congress, is given the power to ***appoint federal executive officers***. This is the ***"Appointments" Clause***.

   a. **Text of Clause:** The Clause (Article II, §2) says that the President shall "***nominate***, and by and with the ***Advice and Consent of the Senate***, shall appoint ***Ambassadors … Judges*** of the Supreme Court, and all other ***Officers of the United States***. …" The Clause then goes on to provide that "the Congress may by Law vest the Appointment of such ***inferior Officers***, as they think proper, in the President alone, in the Courts of Law, or in the Heads of Departments."

   b. **Interpretation:** The Clause means, in the most general sense, that ***Congress may not appoint executive-branch or judicial-branch federal officials***.

   c. **Top-level ("principal") officers:** In the case of ***"principal"*** officers of the United States (i.e., ***top-level*** officers), the President nominates a candidate, and the Senate must, as a constitutional matter, decide whether to approve the nomination. As to such officers, Congress ***may not take away or limit*** the President's right of appointment.

      i. **Cabinet members:** "Principal" executive-branch officers are people who have ***no boss*** except for the President. ***Members of the Cabinet*** and ***ambassadors*** are the main examples of such officers.

      Example: Congress may not appoint a Secretary of Defense — it must wait for the President to nominate the Secretary, at which point the Senate can choose to consent or reject the nomination.

   d. **Lower-level ("inferior") officers:** In the case of ***lower-level*** federal officials (the ones the Appointments Clause calls ***"inferior*** officers"), Congress ***does*** have the right to limit the President's right of appointment (because the final sentence of the Clause says that "Congress may by Law vest the Appointment of such ***inferior*** Officers, as they think proper, in the ***President alone***, in the ***Courts of Law***, or in the ***Heads of Departments***)."

      i. **Three possible appointers:** So although Congress cannot itself *make* appointments of inferior officers, it has the right to choose, on a position-by-position basis, to confer the power of appointment on ***any*** of the following: (1) the ***President***; (2) the ***federal judiciary***; or (3) the ***"heads of departments"*** (e.g., Cabinet members).

      Example 1: Congress creates the post of Deputy Secretary of State, and says that the person occupying this post must be appointed by the

Secretary of State. There is no Appointments Clause problem with this statute, since (1) the Secretary of State is a cabinet member and is thus automatically a "head of [a] department"; and (2) the Deputy Secretary is an "inferior" federal officer, the power to appoint whom Congress may therefore confer (by authority of Article II, § 2, final sentence) on the head of the department in which the Deputy will serve.

Example 2: Congress creates the post of *Assistant* Deputy Secretary of State, and gives the power of appointment for this post to the Deputy Secretary of State. This statute *is* a violation of the final portion (the "inferior officers" part) of the Appointments Clause, assuming that the post is senior enough that the person who holds it exercises "significant authority." (Significant authority is required for a person to be an inferior federal officer at all, as opposed to a rank-and-file federal employee who is not even an inferior officer.)

Why is this a violation? Because although Congress can limit the President's power to make appointment of an inferior federal officer, Congress must give this appointment power either to the President, the judiciary, or a "head of department" (typically, a Cabinet member). The Deputy Secretary of State does not fall into any of these three categories, so Congress can't constitutionally grant her the power to appoint an inferior federal officer.

e. **Congress can't appoint federal executives:** The most important single thing to remember about the appointment of federal officers is that *Congress has no power to directly appoint federal executive officers,* whether they're *top-level* (i.e. "principal" officers) or *lower-level* ("inferior" officers).

Example: Congress establishes the Federal Election Commission, which enforces federal campaign laws. The Commission has power to bring civil actions against violators. The statute establishing the Commission allows Congress to appoint a majority of the Commission's members. *Held,* the tasks performed by the Commission are primarily executive, and its members are "officers of the United States." Therefore, the members must be appointed by the President, not Congress. [*Buckley v. Valeo*]

f. **Removal of federal officers:** The power to *remove* federal officers similarly rests mainly with the *President*.

i. **General rule:** The general rule (subject to exceptions discussed below) is that the President *may remove* any presidential or executive-branch appointee *without cause*.

ii. **High-level ("principal") federal officers:** Thus Congress may not limit in any way the President's right to remove a *high-level* ("principal") purely-executive-branch appointee, such as a *Cabinet member* or *ambassador*.

Example: The President may remove the Secretary of State at any time, without cause. Congress may not limit this right by saying, for instance, "The President may remove the Secretary of State only for good cause."

iii. **Lower-level and independent:** But Congress has more freedom to limit the way that both high-level and lower-level officers at *"independent"* federal agencies, and *lower-level* (*"inferior"*) executive-branch officers, may be removed. In general, Congress may say that these officers may be removed by the President or his subordinate *only for cause*.

(1) **Independent agency-heads:** Thus suppose an appointee performs a *judicial* or *quasi-judicial* function, such as the head of an independent agency created by Congress. Congress may, in order to guard against interference from the Executive Branch, say that the officer shall be removed only for cause.

Example: Congress creates the Federal Reserve. This agency is an "independent" quasi-legislative agency rather than a purely-executive-branch agency (i.e., it doesn't exist just to carry out the law; by means of the rule-making authority delegated to it by Congress, it also "makes" the law). Therefore, Congress may say that (i) the Chairman (who is a "principal federal officer," i.e., someone who has no boss) shall serve a fixed term of 6 years; and (ii) the President may not remove a sitting Chairman except for cause.

(2) **Lower-level ("inferior") officers:** Similarly, in the case of an *"inferior"* federal officer (i.e., one who has a boss, such as someone who reports to the head of a cabinent department), Congress may say that the officer shall serve a fixed term, and may be removed only for cause. And that's true even if the officer is a pure executive-branch employee.

Example: Congress may say that a Special Prosecutor who is to investigate possible executive-branch wrongdoing — an "inferior" executive officer — may only be removed by the executive branch for "good cause" or other inability to perform his duties. [*Morrison v. Olson*])

Note: But Congress *can't* confer *two levels* of good-cause protection, even for the benefit of officers who work in independent agencies. So Congress can say that the Chairman of the Federal Election Commission may be removed by the President only for cause, but Congress can't then say, "there shall be a Deputy FEC Commissioner, who may be removed by the Chairman only for cause." Such a provision would unduly limit the President's ability to discharge his power to appoint federal officers. [Cf. *Free Enterprise Fund v. Public Co. Accounting Oversight Bd.*]

      iv. Impeachment: Separately, Congress may remove any federal executive officer by *impeachment*, discussed immediately below.

    g. Impeachment: Congress can remove any "officer" of the U.S. (President, Vice President, Cabinet members, federal judges, etc.) by *impeachment*. The House must vote by a *majority* to impeach (which is like an indictment). Then, the Senate conducts the trial; a two-thirds vote of the Senators present is required to convict. Conviction can be for treason, bribery, and other "high crimes and misdemeanors." Probably only serious crimes, and serious non-criminal abuses of power, fall within the phrase "high crimes and misdemeanors."

5. Removal of federal judges: Federal *judges* cannot be removed by *either* Congress or the President. Article III provides that federal judges shall hold their office during "good behavior." This has been held to mean that so long as a judge does not act improperly, she may not be removed from office. The only way to remove a sitting federal judge is by formal *impeachment* proceedings, as noted above.

    a. Non-Article III judges: However, the above "life tenure" rule applies only to garden-variety federal judges who hold their positions directly under Article III. Congress is always free to establish what are essentially *administrative* judgeships, and as to these, lifetime tenure is not constitutionally required.

B. Legislative and executive immunity:

1. Speech and Debate Clause: Members of Congress are given a quite broad immunity by the "Speech and Debate" Clause: "For any speech or debate in either house, [members of Congress] shall not be questioned in any other place." This clause shields members of Congress from: (1) civil or criminal suits relating to their legislative actions; and (2) grand jury investigations relating to those actions.

2. Executive immunity: There's no executive branch immunity expressly written into the Constitution. But courts have recognized an implied executive immunity based on separation of powers concepts.

    a. Absolute for President: The President has *absolute* immunity from civil liability for his *official* acts. [*Nixon v. Fitzgerald*] (There's *no* immunity for the President's *unofficial* acts, including those he committed before taking office. [*Clinton v. Jones*])

    b. Qualified for others: But all other federal officials, including presidential aides, receive only *qualified* immunity for their official acts. (They lose this immunity if they violate a "clearly established" right, whether intentionally or negligently.) [*Harlow v. Fitzgerald*]

3. Executive privilege: Presidents have a qualified right to refuse to disclose confidential information relating to their performance of their duties. This is called "*executive privilege*."

    a. Outweighed: Since the privilege is qualified, it may be outweighed by other compelling governmental interests. For instance, the need for the

President's evidence in a ***criminal trial*** will generally outweigh the President's vague need to keep information confidential. [*U.S. v. Nixon*]

CHAPTER 6

TWO LIMITS ON STATE POWER: THE DORMANT COMMERCE CLAUSE AND CONGRESSIONAL ACTION

I.   THE DORMANT COMMERCE CLAUSE

A.   Dormant Commerce Clause generally: The ***mere existence*** of the federal commerce power ***restricts the states*** from ***discriminating against***, or ***unduly burdening***, interstate commerce. This restriction is called the ***"dormant Commerce Clause."***

  1.   Three part test: A state regulation which affects interstate commerce must satisfy ***each*** of the following three requirements in order to avoid violating the dormant Commerce Clause:

  [1]   The regulation must pursue a ***legitimate state end***;

  [2]   The regulation must be ***rationally related*** to that legitimate state end; and

  [3]   The regulatory ***burden*** imposed by the state on interstate commerce must be ***outweighed*** by the state's interest in enforcing its regulation.

  a.   Summary: So to summarize this test, it's both a ***"mere-rationality"*** test (in that the regulation must be rationally related to fulfilling a legitimate state end) plus a separate ***balancing test*** (in that the benefits to the state from the regulation must outweigh the burdens on interstate commerce).

  2.   Discrimination against out-of-staters: Above all else, be on the lookout for ***intentional discrimination against out-of-staters***. If the state is promoting its residents' ***own economic interests***, this will not be a legitimate state objective, so the regulation will virtually automatically violate the Commerce Clause.

  Example: New York refuses to let a Massachusetts wholesaler set up a receiving station in New York, from which he can buy New York milk to sell it to Massachusetts residents. New York is worried that this will deprive New Yorkers of enough milk. *Held*, this restriction violates the dormant Commerce Clause — New York is protecting its own citizens' economic interests at the expense of out-of-staters, and this is an illegitimate objective. [*H.P. Hood & Sons v. DuMond*]

  3.   Health/safety/welfare regulations: Regulations that are truly addressed to the state's ***health, safety and welfare*** objectives are usually "legitimate." (But again, this cannot be used as a smokescreen for protecting residents' own economic interests at the expense of out-of-staters.)

4. **Balancing test:** When you perform the balancing part of the test (to see whether the benefits to the state from its regulation outweigh the unintentional burdens to commerce), pay special attention to whether there are *less restrictive means* available to the state: if the state could accomplish its objective as well (or even almost as well) while burdening commerce less, then it probably has to do so.

   Example: Wisconsin can't ban all out of state milk, even to promote the legitimate objective of avoiding adulterated milk — this is because the less restrictive means of conducting regular health inspections would accomplish the state's safety goal just as well. [*Dean Milk Co. v. Madison*]

   a. **Lack of uniformity:** A measure that leads to a *lack of uniformity* is likely to constitute a big burden on interstate commerce. For instance, if various states' regulations are *in conflict*, the Court will probably strike the minority regulation, on the grounds that it creates a lack of uniformity that substantially burdens commerce without a sufficiently great corresponding benefit to the state.

5. **Some contexts:** The most standard illustrations of forbidden protectionism are where the state says, *"You can't bring your goods into our state,"* or *"You can't take goods out of our state into your state."* Here are some other contexts where dormant Commerce Clause analysis may be important:

   a. **Embargo of natural resources:** Laws that prevent *scarce natural resources* from moving out of the state where they are found are closely scrutinized. Often, this is just protectionism (e.g., a state charges higher taxes on oil destined for out-of-state than for in-state use). But even if the state's interest is *conservation* or *ecology*, the measure will probably be struck down if *less-discriminatory alternatives* are available.

   b. **Environmental regulations:** Similarly, the states may not *protect their environment* at the expense of their neighbors, unless there is no less-discriminatory way to achieve the same result. (*Example:* New Jersey prohibits the importing of most solid or liquid waste into the state. *Held*, this violates the Commerce Clause. Even if the state's purpose was to protect the state's environment or its inhabitants' health and safety, the state may not accomplish these objectives by discriminating against out-of-staters. [*Philadelphia v. New Jersey*])

   c. **"Do the work in our state":** Statutes that pressure out-of-state businesses to *perform certain operations* within the state are likely to be found violative of the dormant Commerce Clause. Such statutes will probably be found to unduly burden interstate commerce.

6. **Discrimination by city against out-of-towners:** The dormant Commerce Clause also prevents a *city or county* from protecting its own local economic interests by discriminating against both out-of-state and out-of-town (but in-state) producers. (*Example:* Michigan allows each county to decide that it will not allow solid wastes generated outside the county to be disposed of in the county. County X responds by barring both non-Michigan waste and waste generated in Michigan by counties other than X. *Held*, this scheme

violates the dormant Commerce Clause because it is an attempt to protect local interests against non-local interests. The regulation is not saved merely because it discriminates against in-state but out-of-county waste producers as well as out-of-state producers. [*Fort Gratiot Sanitary Landfill v. Mich. Dept. of Nat. Res.*]

7. **Market participant exception:** But there is one key *exception* to the dormant Commerce Clause rules: if the state acts as a *market participant*, it *may* favor local over out-of-state interests. (*Example:* South Dakota owns a cement plant. It favors in-state customers during shortages. *Held*, this does not violate the Commerce Clause, because the state is acting as a market participant. [*Reeves v. Stake*])

B. **State taxation of interstate commerce:** Just as state regulation may be found to unduly burden (or discriminate against) interstate commerce, so state *taxation* may be found to unduly burden or discriminate against interstate commerce, and thus violate the Commerce Clause. To strike a state tax as violative of the Commerce Clause, the challenger must generally show either:

1. **Discrimination:** That the state is *discriminating* against interstate commerce, by taxing in a way that unjustifiably benefits local commerce at the expense of out-of-state commerce.

2. **Burdensome:** Or, that the state's taxing scheme (perhaps taken in conjunction with other states' taxing schemes) unfairly *burdens* interstate commerce even though it doesn't discriminate on its face. One way this can happen is if the tax leads to *unfair cumulative taxation*. The test is whether, if every state applied the same tax, commerce would be unduly burdened.

   Example: North Dakota requires every out-of-state mail order vendor who sends mail into the state to collect N.D. use tax on any sales made to N.D. buyers, even if the vendor has no in-state employees. *Held*, this taxing scheme violates the Commerce Clause, because it unduly burdens interstate commerce. If this scheme were allowable, all 6,000 taxing jurisdictions in the U.S. could impose local-tax-collection requirements on all out-of-state vendors, making compliance virtually impossible. [*Quill Corp. v. North Dakota*]

II. CONGRESSIONAL ACTION — PREEMPTION AND CONSENT

A. **Federal preemption generally:** The discussion above relates only to the "dormant" Commerce Clause, i.e., the situation in which Congress has not attempted to *exercise* its Commerce power in a particular area. Now, we consider what happens when Congress *does* take action in a particular area of commerce.

1. **Supremacy Clause:** If there is a *conflict* between *federal law and state law*, the *state law is simply invalid*. The *Supremacy Clause* of the Constitution (Article VI Clause 2) says that "This Constitution, and the Laws of the United States which shall be made in Pursuance thereof … shall be the supreme Law of the Land. … " So if federal and state law conflict, the

Supremacy Clause means that *state law must yield to federal law*. In that event, federal law is said to have "*preempted*" state law.

2. Express vs implied preemption: Federal preemption of state law falls into two main categories: "*express*" preemption and "*implied*" preemption:

❑ *Express* preemption occurs when a federal law *specifically* (i.e., "expressly") says that it preempts state or local law.

❑ *Implied* preemption occurs when Congress does *not* expressly state that it intends to preempt state or local law, but *manifests an intent* to do so.

B. Express preemption: Congress sometimes, in enacting a statute, takes the trouble to state explicitly that the statute is intended to preempt some area of state or local law. That is, Congress says, "In the area of [X], the only governing law shall be federal law." This is "*express preemption.*" As long as the federal statute is validly enacted (e.g., it falls within one of Congress' enumerated powers, such as the Commerce power), any state or local law that falls *within the zone* intended by Congress to be *exclusively federal* will be *invalid* under the Supremacy Clause.

> **Example:** The federal Employee Retirement Income Security Act (ERISA) says that it "supersede[s] any and all State laws insofar as they ... relate to any employee benefit plan[.]" If a state purports to regulate some aspect of an employee benefit plan, the state regulation will be valid as a violation of the Supremacy Cause. That's true even though the state regulation may be perfectly consistent with ERISA.

C. Implied preemption: Most preemption cases involve "*implied preemption*," i.e., situations in which Congress has not explicitly said that it intends to preempt state or local law, but in which the *structure or purpose* of the congressional action suggests that Congress intended to displace non-federal law.

There are *two main types* of implied preemption:

❑ "*field* preemption" and

❑ "*conflicts* preemption"

[*Gade v. National Solid Wastes Management*]

1. "Field preemption": "*Field preemption*" occurs "where the scheme of federal regulation is *so pervasive* as to make reasonable the inference that Congress *left no room* for the states to supplement it." *Gade, supra.* In other words, field preemption occurs where Congress has indicated that it intends to "*occupy the entire field*" in question.

> **Example:** In 1940, Congress passes the Alien Registration Act, which requires aliens 14 and over to register with the federal Immigration and Naturalization Service, be finger-printed, and obey other restrictions. The prior year, Pennsylvania passed a state alien registration act which required all aliens to register with a state agency, and to receive and carry a state-issued alien identification card.
>
> *Held*, the state alien registration law is preempted by the federal one. The federal government's special role in immigration and foreign

relations, and Congress' decision to enact a single integrated system for alien registration, make it clear that Congress intended to displace any state requirements that aliens register. [*Hines v. Davidowitz*]

   a. **Congressional intent is paramount:** In field preemption, as with other preemption categories, the issue is always one of *congressional intent.*

      i. **Broad federal coverage of area:** Where the existing federal regulatory scheme is *broad*, and *covers most of the subject area*, the Court is much more likely to find federal field-preemption than where the federal scheme is less comprehensive.

      ii. **Field traditionally left to states:** Subject matter areas *traditionally left to the states* are *less likely* to be found to be the subject of federal field-preemption. This means that if the subject area is usually viewed as "*local*" rather than "national," preemption is unlikely to be found. This is especially true in cases involving *health* and *safety* regulations.

      iii. **National matters:** Conversely, areas *traditionally left to federal control*, such as foreign relations, bankruptcy, patent and trademark, admiralty, immigration, etc., will normally be found to be federally preempted. Registration of aliens, at issue in *Hines, supra*, is an illustration.

2. **"Conflicts preemption":** *"Conflicts preemption"* applies to two situations: first, where compliance with both federal and state regulations is a *physical impossibility*; and second, where state law is inconsistent with the *purposes and objectives* of federal law.

   a. **Direct physical conflict:** Occasionally, federal and state regulations are drafted in such a way that it is *physically impossible for a person to obey the federal and state regulations simultaneously.* When this happens, the state regulation is of course invalid. *Labelling regulations* sometimes fall into this category.

      Example: Wisconsin's syrup-labeling rules are written in such a way that if out-of-state syrup is labeled so as to comply with the federal Food and Drug Act, the syrup will be mislabeled under Wisconsin law. *Held*, the Wisconsin regulations are invalid under the Supremacy Clause. [*McDermott v. Wisconsin*]

   b. **Conflict in purposes:** Alternatively, a regulatory scheme imposed by a state may be inconsistent with the *purposes* of a federal regulation. Here, too, the issue is always: what was the *intent* of Congress?

      Example: California passes a law conditioning the construction of any new nuclear plant in the state upon a finding by a state agency that there would be "adequate storage facilities and means of disposal" for that waste. Does the state scheme conflict with the purposes of the federal nuclear-power regulatory system, in which Congress showed a desire to promote adoption of nuclear power?

Held, "no" — the California waste-disposal requirement does *not* conflict with federal purposes. While it is true that Congress showed a desire to promote the spread of nuclear power, the history of the legislation demonstrates that Congress only wanted to do this if and where nuclear power could be used safely. Therefore, allowing states to require adequate storage and disposal of hazardous waste does not conflict with the purposes behind the federal regulatory scheme, so California's regulation is not preempted. [*Pacific Gas & Electric Co. v. State Energy Comm'n*]

D. Federal consent to state laws: May Congress affirmatively **consent** to state action which would otherwise be an unconstitutional violation of the Commerce Clause?

1. **Generally allowable:** The answer is "**yes**": Congress **may affirmatively consent to state interference with interstate commerce**.

2. **Discrimination against out-of-state corporations:** For instance, the Court has allowed Congress to authorize a state to discriminate overtly against out-of-state corporations.

> **Example:** Congress passes a statute that reserves to the states the power to regulate insurance, and that provides that no federal statute shall be construed to invalidate any state insurance law or tax, unless the federal statute specifically relates to insurance. A New Jersey insurance company sues to overturn a South Carolina tax of 3% on premiums received from all South Carolina insurance underwriting; the tax does not apply to South Carolina insurance firms.
>
> *Held*, even though the tax is "discriminatory" and would thus be invalid under ordinary Commerce Clause analysis, the tax is valid under the federal statute. Congress itself would have the power to discriminate against interstate commerce and in favor of local trade; there is no reason why such discrimination cannot be conducted by Congress in conjunction with the states. [*Prudential Insurance Co. v. Benjamin*]

CHAPTER 7

INTERGOVERNMENTAL IMMUNITIES; INTERSTATE RELATIONS

I. TAX AND REGULATORY IMMUNITIES

A. Several types of immunities: There are several kinds of *immunities* produced by our federalist system:

1. **Federal immunity from state taxation:** The federal government is immune from being *taxed by the states*.

a. **"Legal incidence" standard:** This immunity applies only if the *"legal incidence"* of the tax — not just the practical burden — falls on the federal government.

Example: Suppose a private contractor doing work for the federal government under a cost-plus contract is required to pay a state tax. The fact that the burden of this tax will be passed on to the federal goverment under the contract won't be enough to trigger the immunity. This is so because on these facts, the "legal incidence" of the tax is not on the U.S.

2. **State immunity from federal taxation:** The *states* have *partial immunity* from federal taxation. What this means is that the federal government can't tax property used in or income from a state's performance of its *basic governmental functions.* (*Example:* The federal government probably can't put a property tax on a state's public parks.)

3. **Federal immunity from state regulation:** The federal government is essentially free from *state regulatory interference*. (*Example:* A state cannot set the laws for conduct on a military post located within the state, unless Congress consents.)

   a. **Federal contractors:** State regulation of a federal *contractor* (one performing a contract on behalf of the federal government) may also violate the federal immunity from state regulation. However, as in the state taxation context, the states have greater leeway to regulate federal contractors than to regulate the federal government directly. In general, a state may regulate federal contractors as long as the regulation does not interfere with *federal purposes* or *policies*. For instance, a state regulation that has the effect of *increasing the cost* borne by the federal government under the contract might be invalid as a violation of this immunity.

4. **State immunity from federal regulation:** The converse immunity, immunity of the *states* from *federal* regulation, exists only in a very theoretical way. In general, federal regulation of the states is valid. However, if a federal regulatory scheme had the effect of preventing the states from exercising their *core functions*, this might be found to be a violation of the Tenth Amendment.

II. THE INTERSTATE PRIVILEGES AND IMMUNITIES CLAUSE

A. **Interstate Privileges and Immunities:** Article IV of the Constitution says that "the Citizens of each State shall be entitled to all Privileges and Immunities of Citizens in the several States." This is the *"interstate" Privileges and Immunities Clause.* (Be sure you distinguish this from the Privileges or Immunities Clause of the Fourteenth Amendment, which prevents a state from denying certain rights of "national citizenship" (like the right to travel).)

   1. **Standard:** The interstate Privileges and Immunities Clause prevents a state from *discriminating against non-residents*. But it only operates with respect to rights that are *fundamental* to *national unity*.

a. **What rights are fundamental:** The rights that are "fundamental in the national unity" are all related to ***commerce***. Thus the right to ***be employed***, the right to ***practice one's profession***, and the right to ***engage in business*** are all fundamental, and are therefore protected by the interstate Privileges and Immunities Clause.

Example: Alaska requires that Alaskan residents be given an absolute preference over non-residents for all jobs on the Alaska oil pipeline. *Held*, since access to employment is a right fundamental to national unity, Alaska's decision to prefer its own citizens over out-of-staters impairs the out-of-staters' rights under the interstate Privileges and Immunities Clause, and is invalid. [*Hicklin v. Orbeck*, the "Alaska Hire" case]

2. **Two-prong test:** Even if a state does impair an out-of-stater's exercise of a right fundamental to national unity, the state impairment is not necessarily invalid. But the state will lose unless it satisfies a two-pronged test:

a. **"Peculiar source of evil":** First, the state must show that out-of-staters are a *"peculiar source of the evil"* the statute was enacted to rectify.

b. **Substantial relation to state objective:** Second, the state must show that its solution (the discriminatory statute) is *"substantially related"* to this "peculiar evil" the out-of-staters represent. Generally, to meet this prong the state must show that there are no ***less discriminatory alternatives*** that would adequately address the problem. (For instance, in *Alaska Hire*, had Alaska been able to show that there was no other way to combat unemployment than to absolutely prefer in-staters, it would have met this prong.)

3. **No "market participant" exception:** Recall that a state is immune from Commerce Clause violations if it's acting as a ***market participant***. But there's ***no*** such market participant exception for the Privileges & Immunties Clause. (Thus even if, in the *Alaska Hire* case, Alaska had been hiring the workers itself, its absolute preference for residents would have violated the clause.)

4. **Distinguished from Equal Protection:** When a non-resident is discriminated against, he may also have an Equal Protection claim. But there are two key differences:

a. **Aliens and corporations:** The Equal Protection Clause can apply to ***corporations*** and to ***aliens***; the Privileges & Immunities Clause can't.

b. **Strict scrutiny:** Conversely, the level of scrutiny given to the state's action is much tougher under Privileges & Immunities Clause than under Equal Protection Clause. Under Equal Protection, non-residency isn't a suspect classification, and therefore the discrimination must just meet a standard of "mere rationality." Under the Privileges & Immunities Clause, by contrast, the statute must survive what amounts to ***strict scrutiny*** — the non-residents must be a "peculiar source of the evil," and there must not be less-discriminatory alternatives available.

    c. **Tactical tip:** Wherever possible, couch the attack as Privileges & Immunities, rather than Equal Protection, since the level of scrutiny usually makes a dispositive difference.

CHAPTER 9

THE DUE PROCESS CLAUSE

I. INTRODUCTION

A. Two major principles: For the rest of this outline, we'll be talking about rights guaranteed to individuals by the Constitution. Before we get into the individual rights, there are two general principles that are crucial to remember:

    1. **Protected against the government:** First, practically all of the individual rights conferred by the Constitution upon individuals *protect only against government action*. They do *not* protect a person against acts by other private individuals. (*Example:* Suppose P is a woman who's two months pregnant, and none of the private hospitals in her state will perform an abortion. P's substantive due process right to an abortion has not been violated, because the government has not interfered with that right.)

        Note: The only exception to the "government action only" rule is the Thirteenth Amendment's ban on slavery, which *does* apply to private conduct.

    2. **Not directly applicable to states:** The other general principle to remember is the central role of the Fourteenth Amendment's *Due Process* Clause. Many of the important individual guarantees are given by the Bill of Rights (the first ten amendments). For instance, the First Amendment rights of free expression and freedom of religion fall into this category. But the Bill of Rights does *not directly* apply to the states. However, the Fourteenth Amendment's Due Process Clause (which does apply to the states) has been interpreted to make nearly all of the Bill of Rights guarantees applicable to the states — these individual guarantees are "incorporated" into the Bill of Rights. "Incorporation" is discussed further below.

II. THE 14TH AMENDMENT GENERALLY

A. Text of 14th Amendment: Section 1 of the 14th Amendment provides, in full, that: "All persons born or naturalized in the United States, and subject to the jurisdiction hereof, are citizens of the United States and of the State wherein they reside. No State shall make or enforce any law which shall abridge the privileges or immunities of citizens of the United States; nor shall any State deprive any person of life, liberty, or property, without due process of law; nor deny to any person within its jurisdiction the equal protection of the laws."

1. **Three rights:** So in one sentence we have three major rights: (1) the right to due process; (2) the right to equal protection; and (3) the right to the privileges or immunities of national citizenship.

B. **The Bill of Rights and the states:** One of the major functions of the 14th Amendment's Due Process Clause is to make the ***Bill of Rights*** — that is, the first 10 amendments — applicable to the states.

1. **Not directly applicable to states:** The Bill of Rights is not ***directly*** applicable to the States. The Supreme Court held early on (in 1833) that the Bill of Rights limited only the federal government, not state or municipal governments.

2. **Effect of due process clause:** But enactment of the 14th Amendment in 1868 effectively changed this. The 14th Amendment directly imposes on the states (and local governments as well) the requirement that they not deprive anyone of "life, liberty or property" without due process. Nearly all the guarantees of the Bill of Rights have been interpreted by the Supreme Court as being so important that if a state denies these rights, it has in effect taken away an aspect of "liberty."

3. **Application of Bill of Rights to states:** The Supreme Court has never said that due process requires the states to honor the Bill of Rights as a whole. Instead, the Court uses an approach called ***"selective incorporation."*** Under this approach, each right in the Bill of Rights is examined to see whether it is of ***"fundamental"*** importance. If so, that right is "selectively incorporated" into the meaning of "due process" under the 14th Amendment, and is thus made binding on the states.

4. **Nearly all rights incorporated:** By now, nearly ***all rights contained in the Bill of Rights*** have been incorporated, one by one, into the meaning of "due process" (and thus made applicable to the states). The only major Bill of Rights guarantees ***not*** incorporated are:

   a. **Grand jury:** The 5th Amendment's right not to be subject to a criminal trial without a ***grand jury indictment*** (so that a state may begin proceedings by an "information," as some states do); and

   b. **Right to jury in civil cases:** The 7th Amendment's right to a ***jury trial*** in ***civil*** cases.

   c. **Excessive fines:** The 8th Amendment's prohibition on ***excessive fines***. (But that Amendment's prohibition on excessive ***bail does*** apply to the states.)

5. **"Jot-for-jot" incorporation:** Once a given Bill of Rights guarantee is made applicable to the states, the ***scope*** of that guarantee is interpreted the ***same way*** for the states as for the federal government. The Court has rejected "the notion that the 14th Amendment applies to the states only a 'watered-down' ... version of the individual guarantees of the Bill of Rights." [*Malloy v. Hogan*]

   Example: The 4th Amendment right not to be subject to an unreasonable search or seizure is interpreted the same way whether the case involves federal or state police — thus if on a given set of facts the FBI would be found to have violated the 4th Amendment, so would local police.

C. **The federal Due Process Clause:** We'll generally be discussing the *14th* Amendment's due process clause, which binds the states. But keep in mind that there is also a due process clause in the *5th* Amendment, that is binding on the *federal* government. Both clauses have been interpreted the same way, so that any state action that would be forbidden by the 14th Amendment Due Process Clause is also forbidden to the federal government via the 5th Amendment Due Process Clause. (For instance, exactly the same limits apply to federal and state regulations that impair the right to have an abortion.)

III. SUBSTANTIVE DUE PROCESS — ECONOMIC AND SOCIAL WELFARE REGULATION

A. **Substantive due process generally:** There are two quite different functions that the Due Process Clause serves. Most obviously, it imposes certain *procedural* requirements on governments when they impair life, liberty, or property. (We'll be talking about this "procedural due process" area below.) But the Due Process Clause also limits the *substantive power* of the states to regulate certain areas of human life. This "substantive" component of the Due Process Clause derives mainly from the interpretation of the term *"liberty"* — certain types of state limits on human conduct have been held to so unreasonably interfere with important human rights that they amount to an unreasonable (and unconstitutional) denial of "liberty".

> **Exam Tip:** Any time your fact pattern suggests that a state or federal government is *taking away* some thing or value that could be considered "life," "liberty," or "property," then entirely apart from the issue of whether the government has used proper procedures, you must ask the question: Has the government by carrying out this taking violated the individual's *substantive* interest in life, liberty, or property?

1. **Non-fundamental rights:** There's an absolutely critical distinction that you must make right at the outset, when you're analyzing a substantive due process problem. That's the distinction between *fundamental* and *non-fundamental* rights. If a right or value is found to be "non-fundamental," then the state action that impairs that right only has to meet the easy *"mere-rationality"* test. In other words, it just has to be the case that the state is pursuing a *legitimate governmental objective*, and is doing so with a means that is *rationally related* to that objective.

   a. **Economic regulation:** Nearly all *economic* regulation (and most *"social welfare"* regulation) will turn out to implicate only non-fundamental rights, and will almost certainly be upheld under this easy-to-satisfy mere-rationality standard. So anytime you can't find a fundamental right being impaired, you should presume that the measure does not violate substantive due process.

2. **Fundamental rights:** But if a state or federal government is impairing a *"fundamental"* right, then it's a different ball game entirely: here, the court uses ***strict scrutiny.*** Only if the governmental action is *"necessary"* to achieve a *"compelling"* governmental objective, will the government avoid violating substantive due process.

3. **Significance of distinction:** So 95% of the battle in analyzing a substantive due process problem is deciding whether the right in question is "fundamental" or not. Once you know that, you pretty much know how the case will come out — if the right is not "fundamental," there's almost certainly no substantive due process problem; if the right *is* fundamental, then strict scrutiny will almost certainly result in the measure being invalidated. So as you prepare for your exam, it's worth devoting some significant mental effort to remembering which rights are fundamental.

B. **Economic and social-welfare regulation:** It is very easy for state *economic regulation* to survive substantive due process attacks. *Since 1937, the Court has not struck down an economic regulation for violating substantive due process.*

1. **Two requirements:** Today, an economic statute has to meet only two easily-satisfied requirements to be in conformity with substantive due process:

   a. **Legitimate state objective:** The state must be pursuing a *legitimate state objective*. But virtually any health, safety or "general welfare" goal comes within the state's *"police power"* and is thus "legitimate".

   b. **Minimally rationally related:** Second, there must be a *"minimally rational relation"* between the means chosen by the legislature and the state objective. To put it another way, the Court will presume that the statute is constitutional unless the legislature has acted in a completely *"arbitrary and irrational"* way.

2. **Other (non-economic) non-fundamental rights:** Outside the economic area, the same rule applies as long as no *fundamental right* is being affected: the state must merely be pursuing a legitimate state objective by rational means. So most *"social welfare"* legislation merely has to meet this very easy standard. We discuss below what rights are "fundamental" — in summary, these rights relate to sex, opposite-sex marriage, child-bearing and child-rearing, all components of the general "right to privacy." (By contrast, practically no economic rights are "fundamental" — the sole exception may be the right to practice a profession or calling, and even this is not certain.)

   a. **General rule:** For now, the important thing to remember is that if the right does *not* fall within this grouping of "fundamental" rights, the state must merely act rationally in pursuit of some health, safety or other "general welfare" goal.

   Example: New York sets up a prescription drug reporting scheme, whereby the names and addresses of all patients who receive prescriptions for certain drugs must be reported by doctors, and are placed on a central computer. Some individuals claim that this regulation infringes on their right to avoid government collection of private matters. *Held,* the statute does infringe on a patient's right to keep prescription information secret. But this right is not "fundamental." Therefore, the statute will be sustained as long as the state is acting in pursuit of a legitimate state objective, and has chosen a rational means. Here, these requirements are satisfied. [*Whalen v. Roe*].

b.   **Regulation struck down though right is non-fundamental:** Where the right being regulated is non-fundamental, and the review is therefore mere-rationality, the regulation will usually, ***but not always***, be sustained. Some regulations — especially those found to be motivated by ***public hostility to unpopular minorities*** — are found to be so irrational that they cannot pass even mere-rationality review.

i.   **Sexual expression:** For instance, regulations that ***interfere with sexual expression***, though given mere-rationality review, may be ***struck down*** as totally irrational.

Example: Laws criminalizing sodomy, enforced principally against gays, have been struck down as failing the rational-relation test, on the theory that they demean homosexuals and interfere with their autonomy, in a way that the Court has deemed "illegitimate." [*Lawrence v. Texas*]

ii.   **Gay marriage:**   State bans on ***gay marriage*** may turn out to fall into this category of impairments of a non-fundamental right that nonetheless flunks mere-rationality review.

(1)   ***Windsor* invalidates DOMA:**   The Court's 2013 decision in *U.S. v. Windsor* (*infra*, p. 110) suggests that the Court will likely eventually recognize ***a general constitutional right of gay people to enter into marriage.*** In *Windsor*, the majority said that Congress had acted unconstitutionally by providing in the Defense of Marriage Act (DOMA) that the federal government may not recognize same-sex marriages ***validly performed under state law***. The Court seems to have held in *Windsor* that Congress was motivated in DOMA by a "***bare congressional desire to harm a politically unpopular group***," and that this was not a legitimate objective under either substantive due process or equal protection. So the Court may well eventually find that *state laws* preventing same-sex marriages cannot survive even mere-rationality substantive due process review any more than the federal DOMA could.

IV. SUBSTANTIVE DUE PROCESS — REGULATIONS AFFECTING FUNDAMENTAL RIGHTS

A.   **Fundamental rights generally:**   The rest of our discussion of substantive due process will be solely about fundamental rights.

1.   **Strict scrutiny:**   If a state or federal regulation is impairing a fundamental right, the court ***strictly scrutinizes*** the regulation. Here is what it means in practical terms for the Court to apply strict scrutiny to a state or federal regu-

lation that impairs a fundamental right: (1) the objective being pursued by the state must be *"compelling"* (not just "legitimate" as for a non-fundamental right); and (2) the means chosen by the state must be *"necessary"* to achieve that compelling end. In other words, there must not be any *less restrictive means* that would do the job just as well (if there were, then the means actually chosen wouldn't be "necessary").

   a. **Burden of proof:** When strict scrutiny is used, there is an important impact on *who bears the burden of persuasion*. In the usual case in which strict scrutiny is not being used, the person attacking the statute has the burden of showing that the state is pursuing an illegitimate objective, or that the state has chosen a means that is not rationally related to its objective. But if strict scrutiny is used because a "fundamental" right is involved, the burden of proof shifts: now, it's up to the state to show that it's pursuing a compelling objective, and that the means it chose are "necessary" to achieve that objective.

2. **Rights governed:** The only rights that have been recognized as "fundamental" for substantive due process purposes are ones related to the loose category *"right to privacy."* Sometimes this area is said to involve the "right to *autonomy*" — what we're really talking about is usually a person's right to *make his own decisions* about *highly personal matters*. This right of privacy or autonomy derives indirectly from several Bill of Rights guarantees, which collectively create a *"penumbra"* or *"zone"* of privacy.

   a. **List:** The list of rights or interests falling within this "right to privacy" or "right to autonomy" include actually just a few related areas: *opposite-sex marriage*, *child-bearing*, and *child-rearing*. So anytime you're looking at a particularly narrow interest and you have to decide whether it's "fundamental," first ask yourself, "Does it fall within the areas of marriage, child-bearing, or child-rearing?" If not, it's probably not "fundamental."

      i. **Illustrations:** So the right to *use birth control*, to *live together with your family*, to *direct the upbringing* and *education* of your children, to *marry* — these are some (probably most) of the specific interests that are "fundamental."

      ii. **Non-illustrations:** By contrast, an interest that does not fall within one of these areas probably is not fundamental — for instance, an adult's interest in having consensual sex outside of marriage seems not to be "fundamental." (The right to *abortion* used to be "fundamental," but now seems to be only "quasi-fundamental" after *Planned Parenthood v. Casey.*)

B. **Birth control:** Individuals' interest in *using birth control* is "fundamental." So whether a person is married or single, he or she has a fundamental interest in contraception, and the state cannot impair that interest without satisfying strict scrutiny. (*Example:* Planned Parenthood cannot be prohibited from supplying condoms or diaphragms to single or married adults who want them. [*Griswold v. Connecticut*])

1. **Minors:** We still don't know whether *minors* have a fundamental right to contraception. If this comes up on your exam, just say that there is plausible logic behind viewing a minor's interest in contraception as being either "fundamental" or "non-fundamental."

C. **Abortion:** The right of *abortion* is the primary example of a right protected by substantive due process. But the right of abortion as it stood under *Roe v. Wade* has been largely overhauled — and *cut back* — by *Planned Parenthood of Southeastern Pennsylvania v. Casey*.

   1. **The right today:** Here is what seems to be the status of abortion: A woman has a constitutionally-protected privacy interest in choosing to have an abortion *before viability*. However, the state has a somewhat countervailing interest in *protecting "potential life,"* even before viability. This conflict seems to yield the following results:

      a. **No right to ban:** The state does not have the right to *ban* all pre-viability abortions. Also, the state may not even forbid all pre-viability abortions except those necessary to save the life or health of the mother.

      b. **Regulation:** However, the state has a far greater ability to *regulate* the abortion process than it did before *Casey*. The state may regulate only if it does not place an *"undue burden"* on the woman's right to choose a pre-viability abortion. A regulation will constitute an "undue burden" if the regulation "has the purpose or effect of placing a *substantial obstacle* in the path of a woman" seeking a pre-viability abortion.

      c. **Not a fundamental right that will be strictly scrutinized:** Abortion is *not a fundamental right*, and restrictions on it will not *be strictly scrutinized*. This represents a huge departure from the law as it stood under *Roe v. Wade*.

   2. **What constitutes "undue burden":** Most state regulation will apparently *not* constitute an "undue burden," and will thus be sustained.

      Example 1 (informed consent): The state may impose an elaborate "informed consent" provision, whereby at least 24 hours before performing an abortion, the physician must inform the woman of the nature of the procedure, the health risks of both abortion and childbirth, the probable gestational age of the fetus, the availability of state-printed materials, etc. *Casey*.

      Example 2 (partial-birth procedure): The federal government may outlaw the "partial birth" abortion method, without giving an exception for cases in which the physician believes that the procedure may be needed to safeguard the woman's health. The ban on this procedure is not an undue burden, because Congress has made a credible finding of fact that the partial-birth method is never necessary for the woman's health. [*Gonzales v. Carhart*]

   3. **Consent:** Even after *Casey*, the state is limited in the extent to which it can require the *consent* of third parties before an abortion is performed.

      a. **Spousal consent:** The state may *not* give a pregnant woman's *spouse* a *veto right* over the woman's abortion decision. [*Planned Parenthood v. Danforth*] In fact, the state may not even require that the woman *notify* her spouse of her intent to get an abortion, even if the state exempts cases of spousal sexual assault or threatened bodily injury. [*Casey*]

b. Parental consent: The state *may* require that an *unemancipated* woman under the age of 18 obtain *parental* consent. The state may also require that this parental consent be "informed," even if this requires an in-person visit by the parent to the facility, and even if it involves a 24-hour waiting period.

   i. Court hearing: But if the state does require parental consent, it must give the girl an opportunity to persuade a judge that an abortion is in her best interests. This is a *"judicial bypass."*

   ii. Emancipation or maturity: The state must also allow an individualized judicial hearing at which the girl may persuade the court that she is in fact sufficiently *mature* or *emancipated* that she is able to make this decision for herself. If the girl proves this, the abortion must be allowed even if the judge believes that the abortion is not in the girl's best interest.

4. Public funding: States may refuse to give *public funding* (e.g., Medicaid) for abortions even though they give such funding for other types of operations. Also, states may prohibit public hospitals from performing abortions.

5. Abortion counseling: The government may, as a *condition of funding* family-planning clinics, insist that the doctor or other professional *not recommend abortion*, and not refer clinic patients to an abortion provider. [*Rust v. Sullivan*]

6. Types of abortion: The state has substantial freedom to place regulations on the *types* of abortions that may be performed.

Example: The federal government may completely outlaw the "partial birth" abortion method, without giving an exception for cases in which the physician believes that the procedure may be needed to safeguard the woman's health. The ban on this procedure is rationally related to the achievement of several state goals, including safeguarding unborn life and making it less likely that a woman will later have profound regret over the particular abortion method she selected. Also, the ban does not constitute an undue burden on the woman's right to abort, because Congress has made a credible finding of fact that the partial-birth method is never necessary for the woman's health. [*Gonzales v. Carhart* (2007).]

D. Family relations: Whenever the state interferes with a person's decision about how to live his *family life* and *raise his children*, you should be on the lookout to see whether a fundamental right is being interfered with.

1. Right to live together: For instance, *relatives* have a fundamental right to *live together*.

Example: A city may not enact a zoning ordinance that prevents first cousins from living together, because the right of members of a family — even a non-nuclear family — to live together is "fundamental," and any state interference with that right will be strictly scrutinized. [*Moore v. East Cleveland*]

Note: What the Court was protecting in *Moore* was clearly the right of *families* to live together, not the more general right to live with whomever one wants outside of ties of blood and marriage. Thus the Court had previously held [*Belle Terre v. Borass*] that unrelated people had no "fundamental right" to live together, and in *Moore* the Court pointed out that families' rights to live together were different, and much stronger.

2. **Upbringing and education:** Similarly, a parent's right to direct the *upbringing* and *education* of his children is "fundamental."

   Example 1: The state may not require parents to send their children to public schools. Parents have a fundamental right to determine how their children will be educated. [*Pierce v. Soc. of Sisters*]

   Example 2: A parent has a fundamental interest in deciding who will spend time with the child. Therefore, the state may not award visitation rights to a child's grandparents over the objection of the child's fit custodial parent, unless the state first gives "special weight" to the parent's wishes. [*Troxel v. Granville*]

   a. **Right to continue parenting:** There's also probably a fundamental right to *continue parenting* — so the state can't take away your child just because it thinks a foster home would be "better" for the child. (Even if there's child abuse, the parent still has a fundamental right to parent, but here the state's interest in protecting the child would be "compelling," so putting the child in foster care would probably satisfy strict scrutiny.)

   b. **No relationship:** If a parent has *never married* the other parent, and has never *developed a relationship* with the child (e.g., they have never lived together), then there is probably *not* a fundamental right to continue to be a parent. (So the state may, for instance, deny the non-custodial unwed parent who has never participated in the child's upbringing the right to block an adoption of the child. [*Quilloin v. Walcott*]

3. **Right to marry:** The *right to marry* — at least marry a person of the opposite sex — is also fundamental, so again the state can only interfere with this right by passing strict scrutiny. (*Example:* A state may not forbid anyone from remarrying unless he is not current on all support payments from his prior marriage. [*Zablocki v. Redhail*])

   a. **Same-sex marriage:** Although conventional marriage is "fundamental," as *Zablocki* shows, the right of persons of the *same sex* to marry, or to enter some other socially-recognized ceremony of commitment, has so far *not* been classified by the Court as fundamental. However, in *U.S. v. Windsor* (2013) (*infra*, p. 110) the Court struck down Congress' refusal to recognize for federal-law purposes same-sex marriages that had been validly performed under state law. For more about what *Windsor* means for the status of same-sex marriage, see Par. (E)(1)(b) *infra*, p. 84.

E. **Adult sex:** There is no general fundamental right to engage in *adult consensual sexual activity*. Therefore, the Court will generally review restrictions on adult consensual sexual activity under the *mere-rationality* test.

1. **Rational-relation review "with bite":**   However, although the Court purports to use the mere-rationality standard to review restrictions on adult sexual activity, the Court will sometimes ***strike down*** the regulation on the grounds that it interferes with people's sexual autonomy. In doing so, the Court has seemed to use mere-rationality review ***"with bite"*** — i.e., without the usual amount of ***deference*** to the legislature — especially in cases involving ***gay rights.***

    a. **Homosexual sodomy:** Thus the Court has ***struck down*** all state laws that ***criminalize homosexual sodomy***, on the grounds that such laws ***"demean the lives of homosexual persons***," and thereby violate their substantive due process rights. [*Lawrence v. Texas*] In *Lawrence*, the Court said that gays have "the full right to engage in their [homosexual] conduct without intervention of the government."

        i. **Not a "fundamental" right:** But the Court in *Lawrence* stopped short of calling the adult sex a "fundamental right" for substantive due process purposes; the Court purported to use mere-rationality review, but did so "with bite," i.e., with unusual rigor.

    b. **Same-sex marriage:** Related to the "homosexual sodomy" issue is the issue of ***same-sex marriage.*** The Court decided in *U.S. v. Windsor* (*infra*, p. 110) that Congress could not constitutionally refuse to ***recognize same-sex marriages that have been validly performed under state law.*** *Windsor* seems to have been based in part on substantive due process theory (as well as on equal protection theory). The decision also seems to have given Congress much less than the usual ***deference*** paid to the legislature in cases of mere-rationality review (i.e., cases where there is no "fundamental" substantive due process right at issue).

        i. **Significance:** Therefore, although *Windsor* does not recognize a *general* right to same-sex marriage, fundamental or otherwise (it merely forces the federal government to recognize state-consecrated same-sex marriages), the case seems like a large step towards the Court's eventual recognition of such a right. But as in *Lawrence*, the Court may ultimately find such a state-law due process right to same-sex marriage not by calling the right "fundamental," but by applying unusual demanding mere-rationality review.

F. **The "right to die," and the right to decline unwanted medical procedures:**

    The law of "right to die" and "right to pull the plug" is developing. Here's what we know already:

    1. **Can't be forced to undergo unwanted procedures:** A competent adult has a 14th Amendment liberty interest in ***not being forced to undergo unwanted medical procedures***, including artificial life-sustaining measures. It's not clear whether this is a "fundamental" interest. (*Example:* P, dying of stomach cancer, has a liberty interest in refusing to let the hospital feed him through a feeding tube.)

    2. **State's interest in preserving life:** The state has an important ***countervailing interest in preserving life.***

3. **"Clear and convincing evidence" standard:** In the case of a now-incompetent patient, the state's interest in preserving life entitles it to say that it won't allow the "plug" to be "pulled" unless there is ***"clear and convincing evidence"*** that the patient would have voluntarily declined the life-sustaining measures. [*Cruzan v. Missouri*]

   Example: P is comatose, hospitalized, being fed through a tube, and kept breathing through a respirator. P's parents want the hospital to discontinue the tube-feeding and respirator. *Held,* the state may insist that if the parents can't show "clear and convincing evidence" that during her conscious life P showed a desire not to be kept alive by such artificial measures, the measures must be continued. [*Cruzan, supra*]

   a. **Living wills and health-care proxies:** But probably the states must honor a *"living will"* and a *"health-care proxy."* In a living will, the signer gives direct instructions. In a health-care proxy, the signer appoints someone else to make health-care decisions.

4. **No "right to commit suicide":** Terminally-ill patients do ***not*** have a general liberty interest in ***"committing suicide."*** Nor do they have the constitutional right to ***recruit a third person*** to help them commit suicide. [*Washington v. Glucksberg*]

   Example: A state may make it a felony for a physician to knowingly prescribe a fatal dose of drugs for the purpose of helping the patient commit suicide.

G. **Other possible places:** Here are a couple of other areas where there might be a fundamental right.

   1. **Reading:** You probably have a fundamental right to ***read what you want***. (*Example*: A state cannot forbid you from reading pornography in the privacy of your own home, even though it can make it criminal for someone to sell you that pornography.) [*Stanley v. Georgia*]

   2. **Physical appearance:** You may have a fundamental right to control your ***personal appearance***. (*Example:* If the public school which you are required to attend forces you to cut your hair to a length of no more two inches for boys and four inches for girls, this might violate a "fundamental right." But this is not clear.)

H. **Final word:** Deciding whether the right in question is "fundamental" is, as noted, the key to substantive due process analysis. But it's not the end of the story. Even if you decide that the right is "fundamental" you've still got to carry out the strict scrutiny analysis: it might turn out that the state's countervailing interest is indeed "compelling" and the means chosen is "necessary" to achieve that interest. (*Example:* A state has a compelling interest in taking a child away from an abusive parent and putting him into foster care.)

   1. **Non-fundamental:** Conversely, even if the right is not "fundamental," you've still got to apply the "mere rationality" standard, and you might decide that the state is being so completely irrational that the state action is a violation of substantive due process anyway.

V. PROCEDURAL DUE PROCESS

A. Introduction: We turn now to the other main aspect of the 14th Amendment's Due Process Clause: this is the requirement that the state act with adequate or fair *procedures* when it deprives a person of life, liberty or property. Here, the emphasis is on the particular case presented by the particular person — has the government handled his particular situation fairly? Our discussion is divided into two main questions: (1) has the individual's life, liberty or property been "taken"?; and, if so, (2) what process was "due" him prior to this taking?

   1. Life, liberty or property: The most important single thing to remember about procedural due process is that there cannot be a procedural due process problem unless government is taking a person's *life*, *liberty* or *property*. In other words, there is *no general interest in having the government behave with fair procedures.* (*Example:* A city hires for an opening on its police force. The city can be as arbitrary and random as it wants, because as we'll see, an applicant for a job has no liberty or property interest in obtaining the job. Therefore, the city doesn't have to give the applicant a hearing, a statement of reasons why she didn't get the job, a systematic test of her credentials, or any other aspect of procedural fairness.)

   2. Distinction between substance and procedure: Always distinguish between "substantive" due process and "procedural" due process. Procedural due process applies only where *individual determinations* are being made.

   Example: Suppose a state passes a law that says that no person with child support may marry. This statute raises an issue of substantive due process — unless this means of enforcing child support payments is necessary to achieve a compelling state interest, the state may not use that method at all, against anyone. Separately, even if this "ban on marriage" could pass this substantive due process hurdle (which it apparently can't, based on past Supreme Court cases like *Zablocki v. Redhail*) the state still must use *adequate procedures* before enforcing the ban *against a particular person.* For instance, the state must probably provide a person with *notice* that the ban will be applied, and a *hearing* at which he can show that the ban shouldn't apply to him because (for instance) he's fully paid up. The obligation to use fair procedures always applies *"one case at a time,"* and governs the application of government action to a particular person in a particular situation.

B. Liberty: Remember that *"liberty"* is one of the things the government cannot take without procedural due process. What *is* "liberty" for due process purposes?

   1. Physical liberty: First, we have the interest in *"physical"* liberty. This liberty interest is violated if you are *imprisoned*, or even if you are placed in some other situation where you do not have physical freedom of movement (e.g., juvenile and/or civil commitment).

   2. Intangible rights: Also, a person has a liberty interest in being able to do certain intangible things not related to physical freedom of movement. There's no complete catalog of what interests fall within this "intangible" aspect of liberty. Here are some examples, however: (1) the right to drive; (2) the right to practice one's profession; (3) the right to raise one's family. But one's interest in having a ***good reputation*** is not "liberty" (so the state can call you a crook without giving you due process — see *Paul v. Davis*).

C. **Property:** The government also can't take ***"property"*** without procedural due process. Here are the things that may be "property" for procedural due process purposes:

1. **Conventional property:** First, of course, we have "conventional" property (i.e., personal and real property). Thus the government cannot impose a monetary fine against a person, or declare a person's car forfeited, without complying with procedural due process.

   a. **Debt collection:** Certain kinds of ***debt collection*** devices involve "property." For instance, if the state lets private creditors ***attach*** a person's bank account prior to trial (which means that the owner can't get at the funds), even that temporary blockage is a "taking" of property. Similarly, if the state lets a private creditor ***garnish*** a person's wages, that's a taking of property. On the other hand, if the state simply passes a law that lets creditors use ***self-help*** to repossess goods, there's no governmental taking of property when the creditor repossesses. (The due process requirement applies only where it is *government* that does, or at least is involved in, the taking of liberty or property.)

2. **Government benefits:** ***Government benefits*** may or may not constitute "property" rights. Generally, if one is just ***applying*** for benefits and hasn't yet been receiving them, one does ***not*** have a property interest in those benefits. (*Example:* If P applies for welfare, and has never gotten it before, the government does not have to comply with procedural due process when it turns P down. Therefore, the government doesn't have to give P a statement of reasons, a hearing, etc.)

   a. **Already getting benefits:** But if a person has ***already been getting the benefits***, it's probably the case that he's got a property interest in ***continuing*** to get them, so that the government cannot ***terminate*** those benefits without giving him procedural due process. [*Goldberg v. Kelly*] (But state law can change even this — for instance, if the state statute governing welfare benefits says that "benefits may be cut off at any time," you probably don't have a property interest in continuing to get those benefits, so you have no claim to due process.)

3. **Government employment:** A government ***job*** is similar to government benefits.

   a. **Applicant:** If you're just ***applying*** for the job, you clearly do ***not*** have a property interest in it.

   b. **Already have job:** If you already have the job, then the court looks to *state law* to determine whether you had a property interest in the job.

      i. **Ordinarily at-will:** Ordinarily, under state law a job is ***terminable at will***; if so, the jobholder has no property right to it, so he may be fired without due process.

ii. **Legitimate claim of entitlement:** If either a statute or the public employer's *practices* give a person a *"legitimate claim of entitlement"* to keep the job, then she's got a property interest. (*Example*: If a public university follows the publicized custom of never firing anybody from a non-tenured position without cause except on one year's notice, then a non-tenured teacher has a property right to hold his non-tenured job for a year following notice. [*Perry v. Sindermann*])

D. **Process required:** If a person's interest in property or liberty is being impaired, then she is entitled to due process. But *what procedures* does the person get? There is no simple answer.

1. **Traditional civil litigation:** When a person's property is at stake in a traditional *civil lawsuit*, the range of procedural protections required by due process is broad. The litigant probably has a due process right to a *hearing*, the right to *call witnesses*, the right to *counsel*, and the right to a *fair and objective trial*.

   a. **Punitive damages:** In some circumstances the award of *punitive damages* may violate the defendant's due process rights.

      i. **Ratio of actual to punitive:** A punitive damages award will violate due process if it is *"grossly excessive."* [*BMW of North America v. Gore.*] One of the most important factors in whether an award of punitive damages is grossly excessive is the *ratio* of the *punitive damages* to the *actual damages.* A punitive award that is *more than nine times* the compensatory award probably won't satisfy due process. [*State Farm Mut. Automobile Insur. Co. v. Campbell*].

      ii. **Reprehensibility:** Another of the key factors in the due process analysis is the *reprehensibility* of the defendant's conduct — the more reprehensible the conduct, the higher the amount of punitive damages that may be awarded without violating due process.

      iii. **Conduct vis a vis strangers to the litigation:** Only the defendant's conduct *towards the plaintiff,* not its conduct towards *strangers to the litigation,* may be taken into account by the jury in setting the amount of punitive damages. [*Philip Morris USA v. Williams*].

   b. **Judicial bias:** A litigant also has a procedural due process right to be free of a *large risk of bias on the part of the judge hearing the case*.

      i. **Standard:** Removal of the judge is required where "a person with a personal stake in a particular case had a *significant and disproportionate influence in placing the judge on the case* by *raising funds or directing the judge's election campaign* when the case was pending or imminent." [*Caperton v. A.T. Massey Coal Co.*]

      ii. **Campaign contributions:** So in states that *elect judges, large judicial campaign contributions* by one party in a pending case can give the other party a procedural due process right to have the judge in question *removed from the case*. [*Caperton, supra*]

2. **Criminal defendants and prisoners:** *Criminal defendants* receive the broadest procedural due process protections during the course of their trial (e.g., right to counsel, right to present witnesses, right to confront opposing witnesses, etc.).

   a. **Convicted prisoners:** Once the criminal defendant has been *convicted*, he gets dramatically *less* procedural due process protection. Thus prison officials who give extra punishment to a prisoner or change his terms of confinement won't commit a substantive due process violation, and don't need to observe procedural due process protections during their decision-making process, so long as their action doesn't "impose[] *atypical and significant hardship* on the inmate in relation to the *ordinary incidents of prison life*." [*Sandin v. Conner*]

      Example: A prisoner who is charged with disobeying prison regulations is not entitled by due process to *present witnesses* during the disciplinary hearing, even if the hearing leads to his being put in solitary confinement for 30 days. [*Sandin*]

      i. **Access to DNA testing:** A prisoner has no independent liberty interest in being given access to *DNA evidence to prove his innocence*. [*District Attorney's Office for the Third Judicial District v. Osborne*] So as long as the state's overall procedures for allowing a prisoner to use newly-discovered evidence to show his innocence are not "fundamentally unfair" (which they will rarely be), the prisoner has no due process post-conviction right to test the prosecution's crime-scene samples, even at his own expense, to see if the samples match his DNA. [*Osborne, supra*]

3. **Non-judicial proceeding:** Where the property or liberty interest is being impaired in something *other* than a judicial proceeding, the state does *not* have to give the individual the full range of procedural safeguards that would be needed for a court proceeding. Instead, for any particular procedural safeguard that the plaintiff says she should get (e.g., the right to a hearing), the court conducts a *balancing* test. The strength of the plaintiff's interest in receiving the procedural safeguard is weighed against the government's interest in avoiding extra burdens.

   Examples: If A has been receiving welfare benefits, these benefits may not be terminated without giving A an evidentiary hearing, because a wrongful termination of welfare benefits, even temporarily, is likely to lead to extreme hardship, without a large countervailing benefit to the government. [*Goldberg v. Kelly*] By contrast, a tenured employee who is being fired from a government job gets fewer procedural safeguards — he gets notice of the charges and an opportunity to present some evidence, but not a full adversarial evidentiary hearing with right to counsel; this is because the government's interest in being able to fire unsatisfactory employees quickly is factored into the balance. [*Cleveland Board of Ed. v. Loudermill*]

a. **School suspensions:** Where a *public-school student* is *suspended* for disciplinary reasons for more than a trivial period, due process requires that he be given at least *oral notice* of the charges against him and, if he denies them, an *explanation of the evidence* the authorities have and an *opportunity to present his side of the story.* [*Goss v. Lopez*] But the student is *not* constitutionally entitled to *written notice, a formal hearing,* the right to have *counsel present,* or the right to *call and examine witnesses.*

CHAPTER 10

EQUAL PROTECTION

I. EQUAL PROTECTION GENERALLY

A. **Text of clause:** The Equal Protection Clause is part of the 14th Amendment. It provides that "[n]o state shall make or enforce any law which shall ... deny to any person within its jurisdiction the equal protection of the laws."

    1. **General usage:** The Clause, like all parts of the 13th, 14th and 15th Amendments, was enacted shortly after the Civil War, and its primary goal was to attain free and equal treatment for ex-slaves. But it has always been interpreted as imposing a *general* restraint on the governmental use of classifications, not just classifications based on race but also those based on sex, alienage, illegitimacy, wealth, or any other characteristic.

    2. **State and federal:** The direct text of the Clause, of course, applies only to state governments. But the federal government is also bound by the same rules of equal protection — this happens by the indirect means of the Fifth Amendment's Due Process Clause. So if a given action would be a violation of Equal Protection for a state, that same action would be unconstitutional if done by the federal government (though in this situation, if you wanted to be scrupulously correct, you would call it a violation of the Fifth Amendment's Due Process Clause).

        a. **Government action only:** The Equal Protection Clause, and the Fifth Amendment's Due Process Clause, apply *only to government action*, not to action by private citizens. This is commonly referred to as the requirement of *"state action,"* and is discussed further below.

        Example: D, a large private university, refuses to admit African American students. No government participates in this decision. The university's conduct cannot be a violation of the Equal Protection Clause, because there is no "state action."

    3. **Making of classes:** The Equal Protection Clause is only implicated where the government *makes a classification*. It's not implicated where the government merely decides which of two classes a particular person falls into. (For instance, if Congress says that you don't receive Social Security if you work more than 1,000 hours per year, then it's made a classification that distin-

guishes between those who work more than 1,000 hours and those who work less — this classification can be attacked under the Equal Protection Clause. But an administrative determination that a particular person did or did not work 1,000 hours is not a classification, and cannot be attacked under the Equal Protection Clause, only the Due Process Clause.)

4. **"As applied" vs. "facial":** Here is some nomenclature: If P attacks a classification that is clearly written into the statute or regulation, he is claiming that Equal Protection is violated by the statute or regulation ***"on its face."*** If P's claim is that the statute does not make a classification on its face, but is being ***administered*** in a purposefully discriminatory way, then he is claiming that the statute or regulation is a violation of equal protection ***"as applied."*** (*Example:* A statute that says "you must be a citizen to vote" creates a classification scheme "on its face" — citizens vs. non-citizens. But if P claims that in actual administration, blacks are required to prove citizenship but whites are not, then his equal protection claim would be on the statute "as applied.")

   a. **Same standards for both:** Either kind of attack — facial or "as applied," — may be made. Both follow essentially the same principles. For instance, if no suspect classification or fundamental right is involved, the classification scheme will violate the Equal Protection Clause if it's not rationally related to a legitimate state objective, whether the scheme is on the face of the statute or merely in the way the statute is applied.

5. **What the Clause guarantees:** The Clause in essence guarantees that ***people who are similarly situated will be treated similarly.***

   Example: Consider racial segregation in the public schools. Such segregation gives a different treatment to two groups that are similarly situated, African Americans and whites. Therefore, it violates the Equal Protection rights of African Americans. (Of course, this reflects a judgment that there are no meaningful differences between blacks and whites that relate to public education. If the issue were, say, compulsory medical screening for sickle cell anemia, blacks and whites might not be similarly situated.)

   a. **Dissimilar:** The Equal Protection Clause also guarantees that people who are *not* similarly situated will not be treated similarly. But this aspect is rarely of practical importance, because courts are rarely convinced that differences in situation require differences in treatment by the government.

6. **Three levels of review:** Recall that in our discussion of substantive due process, we saw that depending on the circumstances, one of two sharply different standards of review of governmental action was used, the easy "rational relation" test or the very demanding "strict scrutiny" standard. In the Equal Protection context, we have two tests that are virtually the same as these two, plus a third "middle level" of scrutiny. Let's consider each of the three types of review:

   a. **Ordinary "mere-rationality" review:** The easiest-to-satisfy standard of review applies to statutes that: (1) are ***not based on a "suspect classification"***; (2) do not involve a ***"quasi-suspect"*** category that the Court has implicitly recognized (principally gender and illegitimacy); and (3) don't impair a *"fundamental right."* This is the so-called *"mere-rationality"* standard. Almost every **economic regulation** will be reviewed under this easy-to-satisfy standard. (This is similar to the ease with which economic regulation passes muster under the substantive due process clause.) Under this easiest "mere-rationality" standard, the Court asks only "whether it is conceivable that the classification bears a rational relationship to an end of government which is not prohibited by the Constitution."

   i. **Standard summarized:** So where "mere-rationality" review is applied, the classification must satisfy two easy tests: (1) government must be pursuing a *legitimate governmental objective*; and (2) there must be a *rational relation* between the classification and that objective. Furthermore, it's not necessary that the court believe that these two requirements are satisfied; it's enough that the court concludes that it's *"conceivable"* that they're satisfied.

b. **Strict scrutiny:** At the other end of the spectrum, the Court will give *"strict scrutiny"* to any statute which is based on a *"suspect classification"* or which impairs a *"fundamental right."* (We'll be discussing below the meaning of these two terms, "suspect classification" and "fundamental right.") A classification based on *race* is a classic example of a "suspect class"; the right to *vote* is an example of a fundamental right.

   i. **Standard:** Where strict scrutiny is invoked, the classification will be upheld only if it is *necessary* to promote a *compelling* governmental interest. Thus not only must the objective be an extremely important one, but the "fit" between the means and the end must be extremely tight. This strict scrutiny test is the same as for substantive due process when a "fundamental right" (e.g., the right to privacy) is involved.

c. **Middle-level review:** In a few contexts, the Court uses a *middle level* of scrutiny, more probing than "mere rationality" but less demanding than "strict scrutiny." This middle level is mainly used for cases involving classifications based on *gender* and *illegitimacy*.

   i. **Standard:** This middle-level test is usually stated as follows: the means chosen by the legislature (i.e., the classification) must be *substantially related* to an *important governmental objective*. So the legislative objective must be *"important"* (but not necessarily "compelling," as for strict scrutiny), and means and end must be *"substantially related"* (easier to satisfy than the almost perfect "necessary" fit between means and end in strict scrutiny situations).

7. **Importance:** Constitutional Law essay exams very frequently test the Equal Protection Clause because: (1) it's open-ended, so it applies to a lot of different situations; (2) there are often no clear right or wrong answers under it, so it gives the student a good chance to show how well she can articulate arguments on either side; and (3) it's one of the two or three most important single limitations on what government can do to individuals.

a. **Test tip:** Therefore, any time you're asked to give an opinion about whether a particular governmental action is constitutional, make sure to check for an equal protection violation.

II. ECONOMIC AND SOCIAL LAWS — THE "MERE-RATIONALITY" STANDARD OF REVIEW

A. **Non-suspect, non-fundamental rights (economic and social legislation):** First, let's examine the treatment of classifications that do *not* involve either a *suspect class* or a *fundamental right*. Most *economic* and *social-welfare* legislation falls into this category.

1. **Mere rationality:** Here, as noted, courts use the "mere-rationality" standard. In other words, as long as there is some *rational relation* between the classification drawn by the legislature and some *legitimate legislative objective*, the classification scheme will not violate the Equal Protection Clause.

   Example: Suppose the Muni City Council, in order to cope with a budget deficit, increases the fares on all city-operated buses from $1 to $2. Statistical evidence shows that 80% of people who ride the Muni bus system on a typical day have incomes below the city-wide median. At the same time the City Council increases the bus fares, it refuses to raise the annual automobile inspection fee; car owners on average have higher-than-median incomes. P, a bus passenger, sues Muni, arguing that it is a violation of his equal protection rights for the city to increase bus fares for the poor while not increasing inspection fees for the affluent.

   A court would apply the "mere-rationality" standard to this regulation, because poverty is not a suspect class, and no fundamental right is at issue here. Since the City Council could rationally have believed that Muni's deficit would be better handled by raising bus fares, and because the Council could rationally have decided to tackle its deficit problem one phase at a time, the constitutional challenge will almost certainly lose.

   a. **Need not be actual objective:** One thing this "mere-rationality" standard means is that the "legitimate government objective" part of the test is satisfied even if the statute's defenders come up with merely a *"hypothetical"* objective that the legislature "might have" been pursuing. The government does not have to show that the objective it's pointing to was the one that *actually motivated* the legislature.

   b. **No empirical link:** Also, there does not have to in fact be even a "rational relation" between the means chosen and the end — all that's required is that the legislature *"could have rationally believed"* that there was a link between the means and the end.

   c. **Loose fit:** Finally, a very *loose fit* between means and end will still be O.K.

2. **Conclusion:** Therefore, if you decide that a particular government classification does not involve a suspect category or a fundamental right, and should thus be subjected to "mere-rationality" review, you should almost always

conclude that the classification survives equal protection attack. (But see the discussion of "mere rationality with bite" immediately below, for an important exception to this rule.)

3. **Review "with bite" for laws motived by "animus":** But if the Court finds that a law has been motivated solely by ***"animus"*** or ***"hostility"*** towards a ***politically-unpopular group***, the Court has generally been willing to **strike down** such legislation even though only "mere-rationality" review is supposedly being used. In so doing, the Court has said that the **desire to harm an unpopular group** cannot be a ***"legitimate governmental objective."*** These cases are frequently described as involving mere-rationality review ***"with bite,"*** i.e., review without the customary ***extreme deference*** to the legislature that made the challenged classification.

   a. **"Hippies"** For instance, where the Court found that a federal statute was motivated solely by congressional animus against "hippies," it invalidated the statute. [*U.S. Dep't of Agric. v. Moreno*]

      Example: Congress changes the Food Stamp program to exclude any household that had two or more unrelated members. The Supreme Court later concludes that the change "was intended to ***prevent so-called 'hippies' and 'hippie communes' from participating"*** in the program.

      Held, this change did not even satisfy mere-rationality review. If equal protection means anything, "it must at the very least mean that ***a bare congressional desire to harm a politically unpopular group cannot constitute a legitimate governmental interest."*** Therefore, the change here flunks mere-rationality review because it does not meet the requirement of a legitimate governmental interest. [*Moreno, supra.*]

   b. **Gays and same-sex marriage:** Similarly, the Court has been quick to find that legislation disadvantaging **gays** and/or **same-sex marriage** was motivated solely by "animus," and to strike down such legislation even while purporting to use mere-rationality review.

      Example: Colorado amends its constitution to prohibit any state or local law that protects homosexuals against discrimination on the basis of their sexual orientation or conduct. *Held*, this amendment violates gays' equal protection rights — it's not even minimally rational, and is motivated solely by animus towards gays. [*Romer v. Evans*]

      i. ***Windsor* and DOMA:** Similarly, the Court has invalidated a federal statute (the Defense of Marriage Act, or DOMA), in which Congress defined ***marriage*** in such a way as to refuse to recognize same-sex marriages entered into under state law. [*U.S. v. Windsor, infra*, p. 110.] The Court seems to have concluded in *Windsor* that Congress was motivated solely by animus towards gays and same-sex marriage. The case also seems to hold that DOMA did not satisfy even mere-rationality review, though the Court's review of the statute seems to have been conducted "with bite," i.e., with much less than the deference to the legislature that is usually applied in mere-rationality cases.

4. **Non-suspect classes:** Here is a partial list of classifications that have been held *not* to involve a suspect or quasi-suspect class:

a. **Age:** Classifications based on *age*.

Example: Suppose that a state requires all state troopers over 50 to retire, in order preserve a physically fit police force. Because age is not a suspect or quasi-suspect classification, the "mere-rationality" test will be used. Because there is some slight overall relation between age and fitness, this requirement is satisfied, so the retirement rule does not violate equal protection. [*Mass. Board of Retirement v. Murgia*]

b. **Wealth:** Classifications based upon *wealth*.

Example: Suppose that a state provides that no low-income housing project may be built in any community unless a majority of the voters approve it in a popular referendum. A resident who would like to live in the low-income housing that would be built if allowed challenges the statute on equal protection grounds. Even if P shows that the statute was motivated by a desire to discriminate against the poor, P's constitutional challenge will probably fail. Because wealth is not a suspect or quasi-suspect class, the court will use "mere-rationality" review, and will uphold the statute if it finds that the legislature could reasonably have believed that its statute might help achieve some legitimate state objective, perhaps letting communities avoid the greater governmental cost that arguably accompanies concentrations of low-income residents.

c. **Mental condition:** Classifications based upon *mental illness* or *mental retardation*.

Example: A city makes it harder for group homes for the mentally retarded to achieve zoning permission than for other group living arrangements to do so. This classification, based upon mental status, will not be treated as suspect or quasi-suspect, and will thus be subject only to "mere-rationality" review. (However, such a zoning procedure was found to violate even "mere rationality," in [*City of Cleburne v. Cleburne Living Center*].)

d. **Sexual orientation:** Classifications based on *sexual orientation*. Thus governments, at least historically, have faced only mere-rationality review when they have treated *homosexuals* differently from heterosexuals. (But as noted *supra*, the Court now seems to apply mere-rationality review *"with bite"* to what it perceives as anti-gay legislation, even though gays still don't have suspect or semi-suspect status.)

III. SUSPECT CLASSIFICATIONS, ESPECIALLY RACE

A. **Suspect classifications:** At the other end of the spectrum, we apply *strict scrutiny* for any classification that involves a *"suspect class."*

1. **Race and national origin:** There are only three suspect classes generally recognized by the Supreme Court: (1) *race*; (2) *national origin*; and (3) for

some purposes, *alienage*. So be on the lookout for a classification based on race, national origin, or alienage. For other classifications, you can safely assume that these are not suspect.

2. **Purposeful:** One of the most important things to remember about strict scrutiny of suspect classifications is that this strict scrutiny will only be applied where the differential treatment of the class is *intentional* on the part of the government. If the government enacts a statute or regulation that merely has the unintended incidental *effect* of burdening, say, African Americans worse than whites, the court will *not* use strict scrutiny. [*Washington v. Davis*] *This is probably the most frequently-tested aspect of suspect classifications.*

    Example: Suppose a city gives a standardized test to all applicants for the local police force. The city and the test designers do not intend to make it harder for African Americans than for whites to pass the test. But it turns out that a lot fewer African Americans pass than whites, even though the applicant pools otherwise seem identical. This differential will not trigger strict scrutiny, because the government did not intend to treat African Americans differently from whites.

    a. **Circumstantial evidence:** However, remember that an intent to classify based on a suspect class can be proven by *circumstantial*, not just direct, evidence. For instance, if a particular police force picks new officers based on a personal interview conducted by the police chief, and over five years it turns out that only 1% of African American applicants receive jobs but 25% of whites do (and there is no apparent objective difference in the black versus white applicant pools), this statistical disparity could furnish circumstantial evidence of purposeful discrimination, which would then allow a court to apply strict scrutiny to the selection procedures.

3. **Invidious:** In addition to the requirement that the discrimination be "purposeful," it must also be *"invidious,"* i.e., based on prejudice or tending to denigrate the disfavored class. This requirement is what has caused race, national origin, and (for some purposes) alienage to be the only suspect classes — these involve the only minorities against whom *popular prejudice is sufficiently deep.*

    a. **Rationale:** Why do we give especially close scrutiny to governmental action that disadvantages very unpopular minorities? Because ordinarily, groups will protect themselves through use of the *political process*, but: (1) these particular groups don't usually have very much political power, because the past discrimination against them has included keeping them out of the voting system; and (2) even if the minority votes in proportion to its numbers, the majority is very likely to vote as a block against it, because of the minority's extreme unpopularity.

    b. **"Discrete and insular" minority:** A famous phrase to express this concept, from a footnote in a Supreme Court opinion, is *"discrete and insular minorities"* — discrete and insular minorities are ones that are so disfavored and out of the political mainstream that the courts must make extra efforts to protect them, because the political system won't.

   c. **Traits showing suspectness:** Here are some traits which probably make it more likely that a court will find that a particular class is suspect:

      i. **Immutability:** If the class is based on an *immutable* or unchangeable trait, this makes a finding of suspectness more likely. Race and national origin qualify; wealth does not. The idea seems to be that if you can't change the trait, it's especially unfair to have it be the basis of discrimination.

      ii. **Stereotypes:** If the class or trait is one as to which there's a prevalence of false and disparaging *stereotypes*, this makes a finding of suspectness more likely. Again, race, national origin and alienage seem to qualify, at least somewhat better than, say, wealth.

      iii. **Political powerlessness:** If the class is *politically powerless*, or has been subjected to *widespread discrimination* (especially official discrimination) historically, this makes it more likely to be suspect.

   d. **"Separate but equal" as invidious:** Even if a classification involves a group that has frequently been discriminated against, the classification's defenders may argue that their particular use of the classification is not "invidious" because it's not intended to disadvantage the class. *Affirmative action* is one example where this argument might be raised. Another context in which the requirement that the discrimination be "invidious" arises is the *"separate but equal"* situation; in this context, the defenders of the classification claim that although both classes are treated differently, the unpopular class is being treated no "worse." In general, the Court now seems to hold that discrimination based on race or national origin is *"per se" invidious*; for instance, the argument that the races are being treated "separately but equally" will almost never serve as a successful defense to an Equal Protection problem.

      Example: Virginia forbids interracial marriage. It claims that blacks aren't disfavored, because whites are blocked from marrying blacks just as much as blacks are blocked from marrying whites. *Held*, the statute's legislative history shows that it was enacted to protect the "racial purity" of whites, so the classification is invidious and violates Equal Protection. [*Loving v. Virginia*]

4. **Strict equals fatal:** Once the court does decide that a suspect classification is involved, and that strict scrutiny must be used, that scrutiny is almost always *fatal* to the classification scheme. For instance, no purposeful racial or ethnic classification has survived strict scrutiny since 1944.

   a. **"Necessary" prong:** Sometimes, this is because the state cannot show that it is pursuing a "compelling" objective. But more often, it's because the means chosen is not shown to be *"necessary"* to achieve that compelling objective. A means is only "necessary" for achieving the particular objective if there are *no less discriminatory alternatives* that will accomplish the goal as well, or almost as well.

Example: Suppose Pearl Harbor occurred today, and the U.S. government once again put any citizen of Japanese ancestry into an internment camp. Presumably this would not be a "necessary" means of dealing with the danger of treason and sabotage, because less discriminatory alternatives like frequent document inspections and/or loyalty oaths would be almost as effective as virtual imprisonment.

5. **Some examples:** Here are two contexts in which claims have been made (and in most instances accepted) that a suspect class has been intentionally discriminated against in violation of Equal Protection:

    a. **Child custody and adoption:** Some notion of "racial compatibility" or "racial purity" may motivate state officials to differentiate based on race in *child custody* and *adoption* proceedings. In general, the practical rule is that the state may not impose flat rules that handle child custody and adoption differently based solely on the race of the child and parents.

    Example: Mother and Father are divorced, and Mother is given custody of Child. All are white. Mother then marries Husband, who is African American. The family court transfers custody to Father, on the grounds that Child will be socially stigmatized if she grows up in an interracial family. *Held*, this custody decision can't survive strict scrutiny — government may not bow to private racial prejudices. [*Palmore v. Sidoti*]

    b. **Political process:** Actions taken by government that relate to the *political process*, and that are intended to disadvantage racial or ethnic minorities, often run afoul of Equal Protection.

    Example: A state requires that in every election, each candidate's race must appear on the ballot. *Held*, this violates Equal Protection because it was motivated by a desire to keep African Americans out of office. [*Anderson v. Martin*]

6. **Segregation:** The clearest example of a classification involving a suspect class and thus requiring strict scrutiny is *segregation*, the maintenance of physical separation between the races.

    a. **General rule:** Official, intentional segregation based on race or national origin is a violation of the Equal Protection Clause. As the result of *Brown v. Board of Education*, even if the government were to maintain truly "separate but equal" facilities (in the sense that, say, a school for blacks had as nice a building, as qualified teachers, etc., as a school for whites), the intentional maintenance of separate facilities *per se* violates the Equal Protection Clause.

    b. **Education and housing:** The two areas where official segregation is most often found are *education* and *housing.*

       i. **Education:** Thus if a school board establishes attendance zones for the purpose of making one school heavily African American and/or Hispanic, and another school heavily white, this would violate Equal Protection.

ii. **Housing:** Similarly, government may not intentionally segregate in housing. For example, it's a violation of Equal Protection for a city to do its *zoning* in such a way that all *government-subsidized housing* is built in the heavily black part of town, if the intent of this zoning practice is to maintain racial segregation.

c. **Must be *de jure*:** But it's critical to remember that there is a violation of equal protection only where the segregation is the result of *intentional government action*. In other words, the segregation must be *"de jure,"* not merely *"de facto."*

Example: School district lines are drawn by officials who have no desire to separate students based on race. Over time, due to housing choices made by private individuals, one district becomes fully African American, and the other all-white. Even though the schools are no longer racially balanced, there has been no equal protection violation, because there was no act of intentional separation on the part of the government. *Cf. Bd. of Ed. v. Dowell.*

d. **Wide remedies:** If a court finds that there has been intentional segregation, it has a wide range of *remedies* to choose from. For instance, it can bus students to a non-neighborhood school, or order the redrawing of district boundaries. But whatever remedy the court chooses, the remedy must *stop* once the effects of the original intentional discrimination have been eradicated. (Then, if because of housing patterns or other non-government action, the schools become resegregated, the court may *not* reinstitute its remedies.)

IV. RACE-CONSCIOUS AFFIRMATIVE ACTION

A. **Race-conscious affirmative action:** You're more likely to get an exam question about race-conscious *affirmative action* than about official discrimination against racial minorities. If you see a question in which government is trying to help racial or ethnic minorities by giving them some sort of preference, you should immediately think "equal protection" and you should think "strict scrutiny."

1. **Public entity:** Be sure to remember that there can only be a violation of equal protection if there's *state action*, that is, action by the federal government or by a state or municipality. In general, the use of affirmative action by private entities does *not* raise any constitutional issue (except perhaps where a judge orders a private employer to implement a race-conscious plan). But any time you have a fact pattern in which a police department, school district, public university, or other governmental entity seems to be intentionally preferring one racial group over another, that's when you know you have a potential equal protection problem.

2. **Strict scrutiny:** It is now the case that *any affirmative action program that classifies on the basis of race will be strictly scrutinized.* [*Richmond v. Croson*] So a race-conscious affirmative action plan, whether it's in the area of employment, college admissions, voting rights or anywhere else, must be

adopted for the purpose of furthering some "compelling" governmental interest, and the racial classification must be "necessary" to achieve that compelling governmental interest.

   a. Past discrimination: Since a race-conscious affirmative action plan will have to be in pursuit of a "compelling" governmental interest, probably the only interest that could ever qualify is the government's interest in *redressing past discrimination*. So if the government is merely trying to get a *balanced work force*, to get *racial diversity* in a university, to make African Americans more economically successful, or any other objective that is not closely tied to undoing clear past discrimination, you should immediately be able to say, "The government interest is not compelling, and the measure flunks the strict scrutiny test."

   b. Clear evidence: Even if the government's trying to redress past discrimination, there's got to be *clear evidence* that this discrimination in fact occurred.

      i. Societal discrimination: Redressing past discrimination "*by society as a whole*" will *not* suffice. There must be past discrimination closely related to the problem, typically *by government*.

   c. Quotas: One device that is especially vulnerable to Equal Protection attack is the racially-based *quota*. A racially-based quota is an inflexible number of admissions slots, dollar amounts, or other "goodies" set aside for minorities. For instance, it's a quota if the state says that 1/2 of all new hires in the police department must be African American, or if it says that 20% of all seats in the public university's law school class will be set aside for African Americans and Hispanics. Probably *virtually all racially-based quotas will be struck down even where the government is trying to eradicate the effects of past discrimination* — the Court will probably say that a quota is not "necessary" to remedy discrimination, because more flexible "goals" can do the job.

   d. Congress: It doesn't make any (or at least much) difference that the affirmation action program was enacted by *Congress* rather than by a state or local government. Here, too, the Court will apply strict scrutiny if the program is race-conscious. [*Adarand Constructors, Inc. v. Pena*].

      i. Possibly greater deference: However, the Court might give slightly greater *deference* to a congressional finding that official discrimination had existed in a particular domain, or that a particular race-conscious remedy was required, than it would to a comparable finding by a state or local government. (We don't know yet whether this greater deference would occur.)

B. Preferential admissions in higher education: Any scheme which gives a preference to one racial group for *admission* to a *public university* must be *strictly scrutinized*. However, such preferences will not necessarily be *invalidated* as the result of this strict scrutiny.

   1. Main principles: Here are what seem to be the main principles governing affirmative action in public-university admissions, as the result of two 2003 cases involving the University of Michigan and one 2013 case involving the University of Texas:

[a] Race-conscious admissions measures will *receive strict scrutiny*, and thus must be narrowly-tailored to achieve a compelling objective.

[b] The pursuit of *"educational diversity" in the student body* can be a *compelling objective*. (But mere *"racial balancing,"* in which the sole object is to make the student body reflect the percentage of racial or ethnic minorities in some other population, like the state's body of just-graduating high school seniors, is *not* a compelling objective.)

[c] A *one-student-at-a-time evaluation* in which the student's race is merely one factor among various ones considered may well be *sufficiently narrowly-tailored* to achieving the goal of having an "educationally diverse" student body.

[d] Mechanical approaches resembling *quotas*, such as automatically awarding an applicant a fixed number of *points* towards admission based on his race, are *not narrowly-tailored* and therefore violate equal protection.

[e] Even where a race-conscious method is not quota-like, the court may find the method to be sufficiently narrowly-tailored to the achievement of educational diversity *only* if the university carries the burden of showing that *"no workable race-neutral alternatives"* would achieve the educational benefits of diversity *as well or "about as well"* as the race-conscious method actually chosen.

[f] When the court is deciding whether the university has carried its burden of showing that its race-conscious admissions scheme is narrowly tailored (in [e] above), the university is *not entitled to any judicial deference* to its conclusion that there were "no workable race-neutral alternatives." That is, the court must examine *from scratch* what plausible race-neutral methods of selecting a class existed for that university, and whether these methods would have been administratively workable (e.g., cost-effective) and would have achieved the same, or almost the same, "educational diversity."

2. **Three key cases:** Here is a brief summary of the three key Supreme Court cases on race-conscious university admissions policies, and of how each illustrates one or more of the above six principles.

   a. **Illustration of valid plan:** The following case illustrates principles [a], [b] and [c] above (plan is *upheld* despite strict scrutiny, because it pursues the compelling goal of educational diversity, and does so in a sufficiently narrowly-tailored way):

   Example (valid plan): The University of Michigan Law School evaluates each applicant's entire file, weighing such variables as undergraduate GPA, LSAT scores, and the contribution the applicant will make to diversity in the student body. The school treats as a major "plus" factor an applicant's membership in one of three historically-discriminated-against groups, blacks, Hispanics and Native Americans. The school does so to create a "critical mass" of these minority students, so that they will participate without feeling isolated.

Held (by a 5-4 vote), this form of affirmative-action is constitutional. The interest in a diverse student body is a compelling one, and the approach here — in that it relies on an individualized, non-mechanical evaluation of each applicant — is narrowly tailored to achieve that interest. [*Grutter v. Bollinger*]

Note: It's not certain that *Grutter* would be decided the same way today, now that Justice O'Connor (who voted with the majority there) has been replaced by Alito (who is far more hostile to race-conscious government action in the name of affirmative action). At the least, *Fisher v. Univ. of Texas*, discussed *infra* in Par. (c), shows that if the plan upheld in *Grutter* were before the present Court, the University of Michigan Law School would bear a heavy burden of showing that there were "no workable race-neutral alternatives" available to it, a burden which the *Grutter* Court recited but seems not to have rigorously applied.

b. **Illustration of invalid plan:** The following case illustrates principles [a], [b], and [d] above (plan is *invalidated* after strict scrutiny; although it pursues the compelling goal of educational diversity, it does not do so in a sufficiently narrowly-tailored way, because it is a mechanical approach resembling a quota):

Example (invalid plan): The University of Michigan undergraduate college awards pre-measured "points" to applicants for various attributes (e.g., up to 5 points for being an outstanding artist or student leader). Every black or Hispanic applicant automatically gets 20 points for diversity. 100 points are needed for admission. The extra 20 points for minority-group status has the effect that virtually every minimally-qualified black or Hispanic applicant is admitted, whereas many well-qualified non-minority applicants are rejected.

Held (by 6-3), this form of affirmative action is unconstitutional, because it is not narrowly-tailored to the achievement of the compelling interest in student-body diversity. The scheme here is a mechanical one that is equivalent to a quota, not an individualized-evaluation scheme like the one approved in *Grutter, supra*. And the fact that "near-misses" can be flagged for individualized review does not save the scheme. [*Gratz v. Bollinger*]

c. **Illustration of narrow-tailoring requirement:** The following case (which is more recent than the above two) illustrates principles [a], [b], [e] and [f] (plan *remanded* for strict scrutiny to be applied again to it; although the plan pursues the compelling goal of educational diversity, the university must show that there were "no workable race-neutral alternatives," and the university will not be entitled to any deference from the court on the issue of whether such alternatives existed):

Example: The University of Texas reserves about 75% of its admissions slots for a race-neutral "Top Ten Percent" program, under which any student who finishes in the top 10% of her in-state public high school class is guaranteed admission. The remaining 25% of slots are then filled by the use of a "holistic review" method, which has recently been modified so that race and ethnicity (particularly being black or Hispanic) will be expressly considered as a plus factor, but is just one factor among many. The University decides to use add race-consciousness to its pre-existing holistic method because "seminar" classes at the school (i.e., those containing between five and 24 students) rarely contain a "critical mass" of black and Hispanic students. P, who is white, narrowly misses qualifying under either program. She sues the University, claiming that its use of race in the holistic method prevented her from gaining admission under that method and violated her equal protection rights. The lower courts reject her claim, while giving great deference to the University's conclusion that the plan's race-conscious aspect is the only feasible way to bring about the compelling goal of educational diversity in the entering case.

Held, case remanded for the lower courts to re-apply strict scrutiny. The University must bear the burden of proving that race-consciousness is *"necessary"* for achieving the educational diversity that's being sought. Strict scrutiny "require[s the] court to examine with care, and *not defer to*, a university's 'serious, good faith consideration of *workable race-neutral alternatives.*'" If a race-neutral approach could promote the interest in diversity even "about as well" as the selected race-conscious method, and would do so "at tolerable administrative expense," then the university may not consider race. [*Fisher v. Univ. of Texas* (2013)]

Note: Fisher seems to mean that courts' determination of whether the means-end fit is sufficiently tight in admissions cases will be very *context-specific* — the same race-conscious plan might pass muster in one university, program or state and not in another. For instance, on remand in *Fisher* itself, the apparent-workability of the Top Ten Percent plan in filling 75% of the U. Texas class (workable mainly because of Texas' heavily racially-segregated public high schools) would likely work *against* the University, whereas such a race-neutral plan might be found *not* "workable" in another context (e.g., in an undergraduate program in a state with less-segregated public high schools, or in a graduate or professional program).

C. Other affirmative action contexts:

1. **Admissions to public schools by race-conscious means:** *No individual student's race may be considered in making that student's public high-school or elementary school assignment,* if the district is not combating prior official segregation. [*Parents Involved in Community Schools v. Seattle School District No. 1* (2007).]

Example: The Seattle school system adopts a "tiebreaker" plan for allocating spaces to incoming ninth graders who want to attend certain racially-imbalanced oversubscribed high schools. One of the tiebreakers is that as between a white and non-white student seeking admission to the same oversubscribed high school, the one who will lessen the target school's degree of racial imbalance (compared with district-wide percentages) will get the slot. Thus a black student will be selected over a white student if the target school already has a materially higher percentage of white students in it than the overall district white percentage. Seattle has never been found to have officially practiced school segregation; racial imbalance in the target schools schools is due to racially-imbalanced residential housing patterns.

Held, the race-conscious plan here must be strictly scrutinized, and will be struck down. Five members of the Court believe that it is not narrowly-tailored to meet any governmental objective. The decisive fifth member of the Court (Kennedy) believes that reducing school-by-school racial imbalance and increasing diversity in the student population are compelling governmental interests, but that the plan here — based on labelling each student as "white" or "non-white" — is not necessary to achieve those interests, because the district has not shown that methods not involving the "crude" binary racial classification of each student (e.g., race-conscious drawing of school-attendance zones) cannot adequately achieve these same objectives. [*Parents Involved in Community Schools v. Seattle School District No. 1, supra.*]

2. **Minority set-asides:** *Minority set-asides*, by which some percentage of publicly-funded contracts are reserved for minority-owned businesses, will be subjected to scrutiny and generally struck down. That's true whether the set-aside is enacted by Congress or by a state/local government.

3. **Employment:** Anytime a public *employer* gives an intentional preference to one racial group, strict scrutiny will probably be called for.

   a. **Layoffs:** If the employer intentionally prefers blacks over whites when it administers *layoffs*, that preference will almost certainly be unconstitutional. [*Wygant v. Jackson Bd. of Ed.*]

   b. **Hiring:** A racial preference in *hiring* is almost as hard to justify (though it might pass muster if that particular public employer had clearly discriminated against African Americans in the past, and there seemed to be no way short of a racial preference in hiring to redress that past discrimination).

   c. **Promotions:** A race-based scheme of awarding *promotions* to cure past discrimination (so that African Americans eventually get promoted to the levels that they would have been at had there not been any discrimination in the first place) is the easiest to justify, since it damages the expectations of whites the least. But even this will have to satisfy strict scrutiny.

4. **Drawing of election districts:** A *voter* who thinks she has been disadvantaged by the drawing of *electoral districts* in a race-conscious (or other "group conscious") way may bring an equal protection suit against the government body that drew the district lines. But the plaintiff must show either: (1) that the lines were drawn with the *purpose* and *effect* of *disadvantaging the group* of which P is a part; or (2) that *race* was the *"predominant factor"* in how the district lines were drawn.

a. **"Partisan gerrymander" claims almost impossible to win:**   The first of these types of claims — "my group has been systematically disadvantaged" — is used to attack *"partisan gerrymanders,"* gerrymanders based on political factors rather than racial factors. These claims are *almost impossible to win.* [*Vieth v. Jubelirer*]

   i. **Lack of political power over many elections:** For one thing, the mere fact that in one or two election cycles the plaintiff group does not get nearly the same percentage of seats as it has of the total electorate can never by itself suffice to win an Equal Protection challenge to a partisan gerrymander. At the very least, the Ps must show that they lack political power, and have been *fenced out of the political process*, over *many elections.*

   ii. **Never successful:** *No partisan-gerrymander claim has ever succeeded.* See, e.g., *League of United Latin Amer. Citizens v. Perry,* where a congressional-district gerrymander was upheld even though the lower court found (and the Supreme Court agreed) that "the single-minded purpose of the [party ruling the state legislature] in enacting the [gerrymander] was to *gain partisan advantage.*"

b. **Race as predominant factor:** But the second type of attack — "race was the predominant factor in drawing district lines" — has a *much better chance of success.* If the court concludes that *race* was the *predominate factor* in how the electoral district lines were drawn, the court will *strictly scrutinize* the lines, and probably strike them down. Legislatures may "take account" of race in drawing district lines (just as they take account of ethnic groups, precinct lines, and many other factors), but they may not make race the predominant factor, unless they can show that using race in this way is necessary to achieve a compelling governmental interest (e.g., eradication of prior official voting-rights discrimination). The desire to create the maximum number of "majority black" districts will not by itself be a "compelling" interest. [*Miller v. Johnson*]

5. **Law enforcement and other operational areas:** Even   where   government's own *operational needs* are arguably aided by a race-conscious policy, the Court will strictly scrutinize this use of race. Thus race-conscious government decisions in such operational areas as *law enforcement, prison administration* and the *military* will be strictly scrutinized.

   Example: A state prison system racially segregates new prisoners in cell assignments, believing that this cuts down on gang-related violence. *Held*, the race-conscious policy must be strictly scrutinized, even though the state believes that its policy does not prefer one race over another. [*Johnson v. California*]

V. MIDDLE-LEVEL REVIEW (GENDER, ILLEGITIMACY AND ALIENAGE)

A. **Middle-level review generally:** A few types of classifications are subjected to "middle-level" review, easier to satisfy than strict scrutiny but tougher than "mere rationality."

1. **Standard:** Where we apply the middle-level standard, the government objective must be *"important,"* and the means must be *"substantially related"* to that objective.

   a. **No hypothetical objective:** One important respect in which mid-level review differs from "mere-rationality" review concerns the state *objectives* that the Court will consider. Recall that in the case of the easy "mere-rationality" review, the Court will consider virtually *any objective that might have conceivably motivated* the legislature, regardless of whether there's any evidence that that objective was in fact in the legislature's mind. But with "intermediate-level" review, the Court will *not* hypothesize objectives; it will consider only those objectives that are shown to have *actually motivated the legislature.*

2. **What classes:** There are two main types of classifications that get middle-level review: (1) *gender*; and (2) *illegitimacy.* We also consider *alienage* here, because it has aspects of both strict scrutiny and mere rationality, so it's kind of a hybrid.

B. **Gender:** The most important single rule to remember in the entire area of middle-level scrutiny is that *sex-based classifications get middle-level review.* [*Craig v. Boren*] So if government intentionally classifies on the basis of sex, it's got to show that it's pursuing an important objective, and that the sex-based classification scheme is substantially related to that objective.

   Example: City sets the mandatory retirement age for male public school teachers at 65, and for female teachers at 62. Because this classification is based upon gender, it must satisfy middle-level review: City must show that its sex-based classification is substantially related to the achievement of an important governmental objective. In this case, it is unlikely that City can make this showing.

1. **Benign as well as invidious:** The same standard of review is used whether the sex-based classification is *"invidious"* (intended to harm women) or *"benign"* (intended to help women, or even intended to redress past discrimination against them).

2. **Male or female plaintiff:** This means that where government classifies based on sex, the scheme can be attacked either by a *male* or by a *female*, and either gender will get the benefit of mid-level review.

   Example: Oklahoma forbids the sale of low-alcohol beer to males under the age of 21, and to females under the age of 18. *Held*, this statute violates the equal protection rights of males aged 18 to 20, because it is not substantially related to the achievement of important governmental objectives. [*Craig v. Boren*]

3. **Purpose:** Sex-based classifications will only be subjected to middle-level review if the legislature has *intentionally* discriminated against one sex in favor of the other. (This is similar to the requirement for strict scrutiny in race-based cases.) If, as the result of some governmental act, one sex happens

to suffer an ***unintended burden*** greater than the other sex suffers, that's not enough for mid-level review.

Example: Massachusetts gives an absolute preference to veterans for civil service jobs. It happens that 98% of veterans are male. *Held*, this preference does not have to satisfy mid-level review because the unfavorable impact on women was not intended by the legislature. Therefore, the preference does not violate equal protection, since it satisfies the easier "mere-rationality" standard. [*Personnel Admin. of Mass. v. Feeney*]

4. **Stereotypes:** Be on the lookout for *stereotypes*: if the legislature has made a sex-based classification that seems to reinforce stereotypes about the "proper place" of women, it probably cannot survive middle-level review. (*Example:* Virginia maintains Virginia Military Institute as an all-male college, because of the state's view that only men can handle the school's harsh, militaristic method of producing "citizen soldiers." *Held*, this sex-based scheme does not satisfy mid-level review, because it stems from traditional ways of thinking about gender roles; there are clearly *some* women who are qualified for and would benefit from the VMI approach, and these women may not be deprived of the opportunity to attend VMI. [*U.S. v. Virginia*])

5. **"Exceedingly persuasive justification":** Although the Supreme Court still gives gender-based classifications only mid-level, not strict, scrutiny, the Court now applies that scrutiny in a very tough way. The Court now says that it will require an ***"exceedingly persuasive justification"*** for any gender-based classification, and will review it with ***"skeptical scrutiny."*** [*U.S. v. Virginia, supra.*]

C. **Illegitimacy:** Classifications disadvantaging ***illegitimate children*** are "semi-suspect" and therefore get middle-level review.

1. **Claims can't be flatly barred:** Therefore, the state can't simply bar unacknowledged illegitimate children from bringing wrongful death actions, from having any chance to inherit, etc. Such children must be given at least ***some reasonable opportunity*** to obtain a ***judicial declaration of paternity*** (e.g., in a suit brought by their mother). Once they obtain such a declaration, they must be ***treated equivalently to children born legitimate.***

Example: Pennsylvania passes a statute of limitations saying that no action for child support may be brought on behalf of an out-of-wedlock child unless the action is brought before the child turns 6. *Held*, the statute violates the child's equal protection rights. Since the classification is based on out-of-wedlock status, it will be upheld only if it is substantially related to an important governmental objective. Concededly, Pennsylvania has an interest in avoiding the litigation of stale or fraudulent claims. But the 6-year statute of limitations is not "substantially related" to the achievement of that interest. [*Clark v. Jeter*]

D. **Alienage:** Alienage might be thought of as a "semi-suspect" category. In fact, though, alienage classifications, depending on the circumstances, will be subjected either to ***strict scrutiny*** or to ***mere-rationality*** review (so there's only middle-level review as a kind of "average").

1. **Distinguished from national origin:** Be careful to distinguish "alienage" from "national origin": if a person is discriminated against because he is *not yet a United States citizen,* that's "alienage" discrimination. If, on the other hand, he's discriminated against because he is a naturalized citizen who originally came from Mexico (or whose ancestors came from Mexico), that's discrimination based on "national origin." Remember that national origin always triggers strict scrutiny, whereas alienage does not necessarily do so.

2. **General rule:** Subject to one large exception covered below, discrimination against aliens is subject to ***strict scrutiny.***

   Example 1: A state cannot deny welfare benefits to aliens, because such a classification based on alienage cannot be shown to be necessary to the achievement of a compelling state interest. [*Graham v. Richardson*]

   Example 2: A state cannot prevent resident aliens from practicing law, because such a classification cannot survive strict scrutiny. [*In re Griffiths*]

3. **"Representative government" exception:** But the major exception is that strict scrutiny does not apply where the discrimination against aliens relates to a ***"function at the heart of representative government."*** Basically, this means that if the alien is applying for a ***government job***, and the performance of this job is ***closely tied in with politics, justice or public policy***, we use only ***"mere-rationality"*** review. So government may discriminate against aliens with respect to posts like ***state trooper***, ***public school teacher***, or ***probation officer***. See, e.g., *Ambach v. Norwick.*

   a. **Low-level government jobs:** But don't make the mistake of thinking that because what's involved is a government job, strict scrutiny automatically fails to apply. If the job is ***not*** closely tied in with politics, justice or public policy — something that is true of most ***low-level jobs*** — then strict scrutiny applies.

      Example: Strict scrutiny would almost certainly be applied to a city ordinance that said that no resident alien may work for the city government as a sanitation worker.

4. **Education of illegal aliens:** A last quirky rule in the area of alienage is that if a state denies ***free public education*** to ***illegal aliens***, this will be subjected to intermediate-level review, and probably struck down. [*Plyler v. Doe*] (But this comes from a combination of the fact that the plaintiffs were aliens and also that they were children. If a state discriminates against ***adult*** illegal aliens, we don't know whether something higher than middle-level review will be applied.)

E. **Other unpopular groups:** Discrimination against ***other unpopular groups*** might conceivably be subjected to middle-level review. For instance, discrimination against the ***elderly*** or the ***disabled*** might possibly trigger mid-level review, but the Court has not addressed this question. (This would be a good gray area for an exam question — you could argue both the pros and the cons of applying mid-level review to these unpopular, frequently-discriminated-against groups.)

F. Congressional affirmative action plans: Finally, remember that there's one other area where the Court uses mid-level review: affirmative action programs established by *Congress*.

VI. UNEQUAL TREATMENT OF GAYS, AND THE BANNING OF SAME-SEX MARRIAGE — ENHANCED "MERE-RATIONALITY" REVIEW

A. Sexual orientation classifications generally: The Court has decided *three cases* since 1996 in which legislatures seemed to classify based on *sexual orientation*. Two of the three have been basically equal protection cases. In those cases, the Court has been *unwilling* to treat classifications that are based on sexual orientation — and that seemed to have the purpose of disadvantaging gays — as having official *"semi-suspect"* or *"suspect"* status.

   1. Mere-rationality review: Therefore, when the Court hears a challenge to a classification based on sexual orientation, the Court purports to use easy-to-satisfy *"mere-rationality"* review, not mid-level review or strict scrutiny.

      a. Mere-rationality review "with bite": However, the gay *plaintiffs* have *prevailed* in their constitutional challenge in both of these equal protection cases (as well as in the one substantive due process case, *Lawrence v. Texas*, *supra*, p. 84). That has occurred, in major part, because although the Court has purported to apply mere-rationality review, it has in fact given *much less deference* to the legislature's sexual-orientation-based classification system than is typically applied in mere-rationality cases. The level of review used can fairly be described as "mere-rationality review *with bite*."

   2. Animus towards unpopular minority: A persistent theme in these three decisions has been the majority's conclusion that legislative classifications based on sexual orientation have historically been *based solely on animus towards a disfavored minority*, and that such animus *cannot be a "legitimate governmental interest."* Therefore, the Court concludes, the classification system fails mere-rationality review because of the lack of a legitimate interest. (See also *supra*, p. 94, for more about the Court's treatment of legislative actions that seemed to be motivated solely by animus towards disfavored minorities.)

B. Singling out of gays because of animus: In a 1996 case, the Court *struck down* a Colorado state-constitutional amendment that would have *prevented the state or any of its cities from giving certain protections to gays or lesbians*. The Court found that the measure flunked even "mere-rationality" review. [*Romer v. Evans*]

   1. Rationale: The majority concluded that the Colorado amendment was "inexplicable by anything but *animus toward the class that it affects*" (gays and lesbians). And, the majority said, "a *bare ... desire to harm a politically unpopular group cannot constitute a legitimate governmental interest.*" The lack of a legitimate governmental objective meant that the amendment was a violation of equal protection, even though the Court used only mere-rationality review.

C. **Same-sex marriage:** The biggest debate in the area of gay rights currently is whether and when gay and lesbian couples have a constitutional right to *enter into same-sex marriages*.

1. ***Windsor* case:** So far, the Supreme Court has decided only one case relating to same-sex marriage, *U.S. v. Windsor* (2013). There, the Court decided that *when a same-sex couple has been married under the law of a state*, the federal government *may not treat the couple any differently* than it would treat a *heterosexual couple* married under that same state's law.

   a. **DOMA statute:** The *Windsor* decision invalidated, apparently mainly on equal protection grounds, part of a 1996 federal statute called the *Defense of Marriage Act* (DOMA). The part of DOMA at issue said that the federal government *didn't have to recognize a same-sex couple as being married* — even if they were married under state law — for purposes of any *federal* *benefits* or *regulations*. The facts and holdings are set forth in the following example.

   Example: Two women, Windsor and Spyer, are a gay couple who have lived together for decades in New York City. At the time Spyer dies in 2009, New York views the two women as married under New York law (on account of a marriage they entered into in Canada while living in New York). Under the federal estate tax's "marital exemption," when one married spouse dies, any property left to the other passes free of estate tax. But DOMA, by preventing the federal government from recognizing any same-sex couple as being married, deprives Spyer's estate of the deduction, costing the estate (and therefore Windsor as beneficiary) a large amount of tax. Windsor sues the federal government, contending that DOMA violates her equal protection and due process rights.

   Held (5-4), for Windsor. The federal government has a long tradition of "recognizing and accepting state definitions of marriage[.]" DOMA is an "unusual deviation" from this tradition. This unusual deviation is "strong evidence of a law having the purpose and effect of disapproval" of the class of same-sex married couples; the law places "a *stigma*" on every married same-sex couple. The statute's legislative history shows that its purpose was to express "*moral disapproval* of homosexuality[.]" This purpose of injuring and disparaging those whom a state has "sought to protect in personhood and dignity" is *not a legitimate purpose*, and the statute has no other purpose. Therefore, the statute violates equal protection principles, as incorporated into the obligation of due process that the Fifth Amendment imposes on the federal government. [*U.S. v. Windsor, supra.*]

   Note: The majority opinion in *Windsor* is ambiguous on a couple of points. First, it's not clear whether the holding is based mainly on equal protection principles or on substantive due process ones; but it's pretty clear that equal protection is at least one of the principles underlying the

Court's opinion. Second, it's not clear what ***standard of review*** the majority applied in striking down the DOMA provision. My best guess, based on the majority's language and citations, is that the Court is applying only ***mere-rationality*** review, but that it is doing so ***"with bite,"*** by giving virtually no deference to various objectives (beyond simple anti-gay animus) that did motivate or might have motivated some members of the congressional majority who voted for the statute.

b. **State's right to ban same-sex marriage:** *Windsor* does not decide whether a ***state*** violates equal protection (or for that matter substantive due process) if it ***refuses to allow same-sex marriage.*** As we go to press (September 2013), 34 states have some sort of "mini-DOMA," i.e., either a statutory or state-constitutional provision limiting marriage to opposite-sex couples. The constitutionality of such state laws is almost certain to come before the Court within the next few years.

   i. **Prediction:** My prediction is that if the issue comes before the Court as presently constituted, the five-member *Windsor* majority will decide that ***yes***, a state's refusal to permit same-sex marriage is a ***denial of equal protection*** (and perhaps ***substantive due process*** as well).

      (1) **Rationale:** Here's my rationale for this prediction: The majority concludes that Congress in enacting DOMA was motivated solely by animus towards gays, and that DOMA violates the "personhood and dignity" of gay couples that have actually married. Given this perspective, that same majority is likely to find that any randomly-selected state mini-DOMA that comes before the Court was enacted for similar reasons of animus towards gays, and similarly violates gay couples' "personhood and dignity" by refusing them the same right to marry as the state confers on opposite-sex couples.

      (2) **Justice Scalia's view:** Justice Scalia, in dissent in *Windsor*, makes the same prediction, based on a similar analysis of the majority's reasoning.

VII. FUNDAMENTAL RIGHTS

A. **Fundamental rights generally:** Now, let's look at the second way strict scrutiny can be triggered in equal protection cases: there will be strict scrutiny not only when a "suspect classification" is used, but also when a ***"fundamental right"*** is burdened by the classification the government has selected. Whenever a classification burdens a "fundamental right" or "fundamental interest," the classification will be subjected to strict scrutiny ***even though the people who are burdened are not members of a suspect class***.

1. **"Fundamental" defined:** "Fundamental" means something absolutely different in this Equal Protection context than it means in the Substantive Due Process context. Remember that in due process, the fundamental rights are ones related to privacy. Here, the fundamental rights are related to a variety

of other interests protected by the Constitution, but generally having nothing to do with privacy.

2. **List:** The short list of rights that are "fundamental" for equal protection strict scrutiny purposes is as follows: (1) the right to *vote*; (2) maybe the right to be a *political candidate*; (3) the right to have access to the *courts* for certain kinds of proceedings; and (4) the right to *migrate interstate.*

B. **Voting rights:** The right to *vote* in state and local elections is "fundamental," so any classification that burdens that substantially burdens right to vote is often strictly scrutinized.

   1. **The "related to voter qualifications" issue:** In deciding whether to use strict scrutiny, the Court seems to place great weight on whether the voting regulation is *reasonably related to determining voter qualifications.*

      a. **If not reasonably related to voter qualifications:** If the Court decides that the regulation is *not* reasonably related to determining voter qualifications, then the Court *uses strict scrutiny*, and will probably strike down the regulation.

      b. **If reasonably related to voter qualifications:** If, on the other hand, the Court decides that the regulation *is* reasonably related to determining voter qualifications, then the Court generally does *not* use strict scrutiny. Instead, it uses some less stringent review method (typically, an intermediate-level *balancing test*), and is likely to *uphold* the measure.

   2. **Not reasonably related to voter qualifications:** Here are various types of regulations that the Court has found to be *not reasonably related to determining voter qualifications*, and as to which it has therefore *applied strict scrutiny.*

      a. **Poll tax:** *Poll taxes* are not reasonably related to determining voter qualifications. Therefore, a poll tax, no matter how minor, creates an inequality in the right to vote that must be strictly scrutinized, and struck down as an Equal Protection violation. [*Harper v. Virginia Bd. of Elections*]

      b. **Ballot restricted to "interested voters":** The requirement that voters *own property* or otherwise have some *"special interest"* is ordinarily not related to voter qualifications, and is thus usually given strict scrutiny.

         Example: A New York statute limits school district elections to persons who either: (1) own or lease property within the district; or (2) are parents of children in the district's public schools. *Held*, the statute must be strictly scrutinized, and will be struck down because it is not necessary to promote a compelling state interest. [*Kramer v. Union Free School District No. 15*]

         i. **Exception for "special purpose" body:** However, if the Court finds that the governmental unit for which elections are being held has a *limited purpose* which *disproportionately affects* only one group, the franchise may be limited to that group. Thus *"special pur-*

pose bodies" may restrict the vote to persons who are directly affected by the body's activities.

> **Example:** Votes for a special-purpose *"water storage district"* can be limited to landowners, and can be on a "one acre, one vote" basis. [*Ball v. James*]

c. **Duration-of-residence requirements:** A requirement that voters have *resided within the state* for *more than a certain time* prior to Election Day are strictly scrutinized, if the requirement goes beyond what's reasonably required to ensure that the voter really is a local resident.

> **Example:** A state limits the right to vote to people who have resided in the state for at least one year before the election. *Held*, the requirement will be strictly scrutinized and struck down. Such a duration-of-residence requirement violates both the voter's fundamental right to vote and his right to travel. [*Dunn v. Blumstein*]

  i. **Fifty-day statutes:** But *shorter* residency requirements (e.g., 50 days) have been *upheld*, on the theory that these are merely methods of ensuring that the person *really is a resident.*

3. **Reasonably related to voter qualifications:** If the Court finds that the regulation *is reasonably related to voter qualifications*, the Court reviews it by a *less-than-strict-scrutiny* standard (some form of *intermediate-level* review).

   a. **Voter identification requirements:** For example, a state requirement that every voter *present a photo ID* has been *upheld* under this non-strict-scrutiny standard, as a means of protecting the "integrity and reliability of the electoral process." [*Crawford v. Marion County Election Board* (2008)]

   b. **Denial of vote to felons:** Many states deny the vote to *felons*, even ones who have served their sentence and finished any parole. Such disenfranchisement has been *upheld.* [*Richardson v. Ramirez*].

   c. **Burden on right to vote by limiting voter's choices:** Where state regulation of voting merely has the effect of *"burdening"* the right to vote, by *limiting the voter's choices*, the Court does *not* use strict scrutiny, and merely balances the degree of burden against the magnitude of the state's interest.

   > **Example:** A state may completely ban all *write-in votes*. So long as the state gives candidates reasonable access to the ballot (thus preserving each voter's interest in having a reasonable choice of candidates), the state is not required to protect each voter's interest in being able to vote for any candidate of his choosing. [*Burdick v. Takushi*]

C. **Ballot access:** The right to be a *political candidate*, and to have your name on the ballot, seems to be "quasi-fundamental."

1. **Two invalid restrictions:** The two kinds of ballot restrictions that the Supreme Court does seem to give strict or almost strict scrutiny to are:

    a. **Unfair to new parties:** Restrictions that are unfair to ***new, not-yet-established political parties***. (*Example:* A rule saying that a minor party can get its candidate on the ballot only if it presents signatures from 15% of the voters, holds a formal primary, and has an elaborate party structure, violates Equal Protection. [*Williams v. Rhodes*].)

    b. **Based on wealth:** Ballot access limits that are based on ***wealth***. (*Example:* A $700 candidate filing fee, which the state refuses to waive for an indigent candidate, violates Equal Protection. [*Lubin v. Panish*])

  2. Candidate eligibility rules: But reasonable rules concerning the eligibility of the individual candidate, that don't fall into either of these two categories — unfair to new parties, or based on wealth — seem to be generally ***upheld*** by the Court. Thus a state may set a ***minimum age***, or may require that the candidate have ***resided for a certain period of time*** in the state or district where he is seeking office.

D. Court access: Access to the ***courts*** is sometimes a "fundamental right," so that if the right is burdened by a state-imposed classification, that classification will sometimes be closely scrutinized. Basically, what it comes down to is that if the state imposes a ***fee*** that the rich can pay but the poor cannot, and the access relates to a ***criminal*** case, strict scrutiny will be used. (*Example:* The state cannot charge an indigent for his trial transcript in a criminal case. [*Griffin v. Illinois*] Similarly, the state must provide him with free counsel on appeal.)

  1. Civil litigation: When ***civil*** litigation is involved, access to the courts is usually ***not*** fundamental. Only for various family-law proceedings (e.g., ***divorce, paternity suits, termination of parental rights)*** is the state barred from charging fees. [*Boddie v. Connecticut*]

E. Right to travel: The so-called ***"right to travel"*** is generally a "fundamental" right. This term "right to travel" is misleading — it's really the right to ***change one's state of residence or employment.*** So any time the state imposes a classification that burdens one's right to change her state of residence or employment, that classification will be strictly scrutinized.

  1. Duration of residence: This mainly means that if the state imposes a substantial ***waiting period*** on newly-arrived residents, before they can receive some ***vital governmental benefit***, this will be strictly scrutinized.

    Example: Pennsylvania denies welfare benefits to any resident who has not resided in the state for at least a year. *Held*, this one-year waiting period impairs the "fundamental right of interstate movement" so it must be strictly scrutinized, and in fact invalidated. [*Shapiro v. Thompson*].

  2. Vital government benefit: But the key phrase here is ***"vital government benefit"*** — if the benefit is ***not*** vital, then the state may impose a substantial waiting period. (*Example:* A one-year waiting period before a student can qualify for low in-state tuition at the public university probably does not burden a fundamental right, and thus does not need to be strictly scrutinized.)

F. Necessities: The right to ***"necessities"*** is ***not*** fundamental. So if the state distributes necessities in a way that treats different people differently (or if it distributes the money to be used to buy these things differentially), there will be no strict scrutiny because there is no fundamental right.

1. **Education:** For instance, one does not have a fundamental right to a ***public school education***. Therefore, the state may allow or even foster inequalities in the distribution of that public school education, without violating any fundamental right, and thus without having to pass strict scrutiny. [*San Antonio School Dist. v. Rodriguez*]

    Example: The Ps claim that Texas' system of financing public education violates equal protection, because districts with a high property tax base per pupil consistently spend more on education than those with a low base are able to do.

    Held, education is not a fundamental right. Therefore, Texas' scheme merely has to undergo "rational relation" review. Because the use of property taxes to finance education is a rational way of achieving the legitimate state goal of giving each local school district a large measure of control over the education its residents get, this "mere-rationality" standard is satisfied. [*San Antonio School Dist. v. Rodriguez, supra.*]

    a. **Complete deprivation:** Actually, it's still possible that a ***complete deprivation*** of public education might be held to be a violation of a "fundamental" right. If a state simply refused to give any public education *at all* to some groups of residents, this might be such a large deprivation that it would amount to a violation of a fundamental right, and thus be subject to strict scrutiny.

2. **Food, shelter:** There is no fundamental right to the material ***"necessities of life."*** Thus *food*, *shelter*, and *medical care* are not "fundamental" for equal protection purposes. Therefore, the state may distribute these things unevenly. Similarly, the state may give some people but not others money for these things without having to survive strict scrutiny. (*Example:* The state can give a smaller per capita welfare payment to big families than small families, without having the scheme subjected to strict scrutiny. This is because the food and shelter for which the payments are used are not "fundamental rights." [*Dandridge v. Williams*])

CHAPTER 11

MISCELLANEOUS CLAUSES

I. FOURTEENTH AMENDMENT PRIVILEGES OR IMMUNITIES

A. **Privileges or Immunities Clause Generally:** The Fourteenth Amendment has its own "Privileges or Immunities" Clause: "No state shall make or enforce any law which shall abridge the privileges or immunities of citizens of the United States."

1. **National rights only:** But this clause is very narrowly interpreted: it only protects the individual from state interference with his rights of *"national"* citizenship. The most important of these rights of "national" citizenship are: (1) the right to *travel from state to state* (which as we saw is also protected by the Equal Protection Clause); and (2) the right to *vote in national elections*.

2. **Right to change state of residence:** The clause is most relevant where a state treats *newly-arrived residents less favorably* than those who have resided in-state for a longer time: this violates the "right to travel," protected by the clause. (*Example:* If a state gives newly-arrived residents lower welfare payments than ones who have been residents longer, this is a violation of the "right to travel" protected by the 14th Amendment P&I clause. [*Saenz v. Roe*])

3. **Strict scrutiny:** The Court gives *strict scrutiny* to state laws that interfere with the rights of national citizenship. [*Saenz v. Roe*]

II. THE "TAKING" CLAUSE

A. **The "Taking" Clause Generally:** The Fifth Amendment contains the "Taking" Clause: *"[N]or shall private property be taken for public use, without just compensation."*

1. **General meaning:** The gist of the Taking Clause is that the government may take private property under its "power of eminent domain," but if it does take private property, it must *pay a fair price*. This is true even if the property is taken to serve a compelling governmental interest.

2. **Taking vs. regulation:** The government (whether it's federal or state) must pay for any property that it "takes." On the other hand, if it merely *"regulates"* property under its police power, then it does not need to pay (even if the owner's use of his property, or its value, is substantially diminished).

    a. **Land use regulations:** Usually the problem of distinguishing between a compensable "taking" and a non-compensable "regulation" occurs in the context of *land-use regulation*.

    b. **Guidelines:** Here are some guidelines about when a land-use regulation will avoid being a taking:

        i. **No denial of economically viable use:** A land-use regulation must not "deny an owner *economically viable use* of his land," or it will be considered a taking. However, few land use regulations are likely to be found to deny the owner all economically viable use of his land. For instance, if a particular 3-story building is made a landmark, the fact that the owner can't tear down the building to build a skyscraper doesn't deprive him of "all economically viable use." But if the state were to deny the owner the right to *build any dwelling* on the land, this would probably constitute a denial of all economically viable use.

            Example: The state of South Carolina, in order to protect against coastal erosion, prohibits landowners from building any permanent habitable structure at all on certain parcels. P owns 2 vacant parcels (for which he paid $1 million), on which the building ban applies. *Held*, by the Supreme Court, if this regulation indeed prevents P from making any "economically viable use" of the parcels (something for the state court to decide on remand), there has been a "taking" for which the state must pay compensation, even if the state was just trying to protect the health and safety of its citizens. [*Lucas v. South Carolina Coastal Council*]

Note 1: Most zoning, environmental laws and landmark-preservation laws will satisfy this don't-deny-all-economically-viable-uses rule, and will thus *not* be takings, merely non-compensable regulations.

Note 2: If a land-use law merely *temporarily* prevents all economically viable use of a parcel, this will not necessarily constitute a taking — *all surrounding circumstances* must be considered to determine whether the interference with use is significant enough to constitute a taking. For instance, a 2- or 3-year *moratorium on development* of a particular parcel, until a permanent land-use scheme can be enacted by government, might not constitute a taking even though for that period an affected owner can't make any economically viable use of her parcel. [*Tahoe-Sierra Preservation Council v. Tahoe Regional Planning Agency*]

c. **Permanent physical occupation:** If the government makes or authorizes a *permanent physical occupation* of the property, this will *automatically* be found to constitute a taking, no matter how minor the interference with the owner's use and no matter how important the countervailing governmental interests. (*Example:* The state requires landlords to permit cable TV companies to install their cable facilities in the landlord's buildings. *Held*, this compulsory cabling was a taking because it was a permanent physical occupation, even though it didn't really restrict the owner's use of his property or reduce its value. [*Loretto v. Teleprompter*])

d. **Diminution in value:** The more drastic the *reduction in value* of the owner's property, the more likely a taking is to be found. But a very drastic diminution in value (almost certainly much more than 50%) is required.

e. **Landmark:** *Landmark preservation schemes*, just like zoning and environmental regulations, will rarely be found to constitute a taking. This is especially true where the designation of a particular building to landmark status occurs as part of a *comprehensive* city-wide preservation scheme. (*Example:* New York City didn't carry out a taking when it designated Grand Central Station as a landmark; this was true even though this designation prevented the owner from constructing a 55-story office building above the Terminal. [*Penn Central v. New York City*])

3. **Special rule for "dedications":** Suppose the government attempts to *condition* approval of a land-use permit in return for a property owner's willingness to *"dedicate"* (i.e., *give away*) to the public some piece of land, cash or other property in return. In this special situation, the Supreme Court requires a *very close fit* between the *means* chosen by the state (i.e., the particular dedication required) and the governmental *objective* being pursued (typically the avoidance of some environmental or land-use harm that would otherwise likely occur if the permit is given).

   a. **Summary of rules:** Here are the two main rules that ensure this close fit in the case of dedications:

      [1] **"Substantially advance":** First, when government makes a permit conditional on a dedication, the *means* chosen by government (the particular dedication required) must *"substantially advance"* the land-use objective that the government is pursuing (i.e., the avoidance of harm that a grant of the permit would be expected to cause).

      Example: The Ps own an ocean-front house; the ocean runs north-south, and the house is to the east of the ocean. A local land-use Commission says that the Ps can rebuild this house only on condition that they first give the public an easement across a sandy strip of the property running north-south immediately adjacent to and parallel to the ocean. (The Commission is mainly concerned that the Ps will replace their small bungalow with a much bigger house, thus blocking the view of the beach by people on the street on the eastern side of the house.)

      Held, the Commission's conditioning the issuance of the building permit upon transfer of the easement amounted to a taking, for which compensation must be paid. Only if the conditions attached to the grant of the permit "substantially advance" — or have an "essential nexus" with — the legitimate state interests being pursued will the conditions be valid. This requirement is not satisfied here, because the harms feared by the government would not be cured or even materially lessened by the means chosen (the easement). For instance, the easement will not reduce any obstacles to viewing the beach created by the new house, since the easement will only help people already on public beaches north or south of the Ps' property, not people on the street to the east of the ocean whose views would be blocked by a bigger house. [*Nollan v. Cal. Coastal Comm.*]

      [2] **"Rough proportionality":** Second, there must be a *"rough proportionality"* between the *burdens* that issuance of the land-use permit would cause to the public, and the *benefits* that would accrue to the public from the dedication. In other words, the burdens can't be much bigger than the anticipated benefits.

      Example: P is a property owner who wants to enlarge the store she runs on the property. D, a city, issues her a permit to do this, but conditions the permit on P's willingness to (among other things) convey a 15-foot strip of land on her property to D, to be used as an unpaved bicycle pathway. (P would be required to convey approximately 10% of the property.) D justifies this condition in part on the theory that P's bigger store will increase automobile traffic to her site (which the bike path, by increasing the attractiveness of biking, might reverse).

Held, this trade-off requirement is an unconstitutional taking of P's property. For any permit condition to be valid, there must be a "rough proportionality" between the size of the give-back demanded by the city and the burden to the public caused by P's proposed development (for which the give-back is supposed to compensate). Here, D has not satisfied this "rough proportionality" requirement. For example, although D has calculated somewhat precisely the number of additional car trips per day that would be caused by P's expansion, D has not tried to show how much of this extra traffic will be reduced by the proposed bikeway, something D was required to do to satisfy its "rough proportionality" burden. [*Dolan v. City of Tigard*]

4. **Requirement of "public" use:** The Taking Clause says that private property shall not be taken *"for public use"* unless just compensation is paid. This language has been interpreted by the Supreme Court as prohibiting the taking of private property for *private use, even if just compensation is made*. Thus the government cannot simply take private property from one person, and give it to another, without any public purpose.

   a. **"Public use" construed broadly:** However, the Supreme Court has construed the requirement of a "public use" quite *broadly*. Here are two principles illustrating just how broadly the Court stretches the phrase:

      ❏ So long as the state's use of its eminent domain power is "*rationally related* to a *conceivable public purpose*," the public use requirement is satisfied. [*Hawaii Housing Authority v. Midkiff*]

      ❏ The property *need not be open to the general public after the taking.* Therefore, the fact that the property is *turned over to some private user* does not prevent the use from being a public one as long as the public can be expected to derive some benefit (e.g., economic development) from the use.

      Example: The City of New London, as part of an economic-development plan for the City's waterfront area, condemns 15 houses owned by the Ps. The properties are not blighted. The plan contemplates turning the properties over to private developers. The Ps claim that this is not a "public use," and thus violates their rights under the Fifth Amendment even if "just compensation" is paid.

      Held, for the City. Even though the properties are being turned over to private developers (not made available to the public), and even though the properties were not blighted, this is still a "public use" as the term is used in the Fifth Amendment. [*Kelo v. New London*]

III. THE "CONTRACT" CLAUSE

A. The "Contract" Clause: The so-called "Contract" Clause (Art. I, §10) provides that "no state shall ... pass any ... law impairing the obligation of contracts." The clause effectively applies to both federal and state governments. The Clause has a different meaning depending on whether the government is impairing its own contracts or contracts between private parties.

   1. Public contracts: If the state is trying to escape from its *own financial obligations*, then the Court will *closely scrutinize* this attempt. Here, the state attempt to "weasel" will be struck down unless the modification is "*reasonable* and *necessary* to support an *important* public purpose" (basically *middle-level review*).

   2. Private contracts: But when the state is re-writing contracts made by *private parties*, the judicial review is not so stringent. Here, even a *substantial* modification to contracts between private parties will be allowed so long as the state is acting "*reasonably*" in pursuit of a "legitimate public purpose." So we apply what is basically "mere-rationality" review in this situation. (*Example:* If a state's economy is in shambles with widespread home mortgage foreclosures, the state probably may temporarily order a lower interest rate on home mortgages, or impose a moratorium on mortgage repayments, without violating the Contract Clause.)

      a. Incidental effect on contracts: Even this "mere-rationality" standard applies only where the state takes an action that is *specifically directed* at contractual obligations. If the state applies a *"generally applicable rule of conduct"* that has the *incidental by-product* of impairing contractual obligations, the Contract Clause *does not apply at all*.

      Example: Suppose Manco, a manufacturing company located outside the state of Texahoma, contracts with Disposal Corp., which operates a toxic waste disposal facility within Texahoma. The contract runs through the year 2000, and allows Manco to deliver up to 1,000 tons of toxic waste per year to the dump. The Texahoma legislature then enacts a statute that, effective immediately, prohibits anyone from disposing of any additional toxic wastes within the state. Even though this enactment has an effect on the Manco-Disposal contract, it does not trigger Contract Clause review at all, because the statute affects contracts as an incidental by-product, rather than being specifically directed at contractual obligations.

IV. THE SECOND AMENDMENT "RIGHT TO BEAR ARMS"

A. **Text of the Amendment:** The Second Amendment provides: "A well regulated Militia, being necessary to the security of a free State, the right of the people to *keep and bear Arms*, shall *not be infringed*."

B. **Applicable to private individuals:** The *Amendment* confers on *private individuals* a right to keep basic firearms, including handguns, *at home for self-defense*. [*District of Columbia v. Heller* (2008)]

> **Example:** Washington D.C. makes it a crime to keep any type of handgun at home. It also makes it a crime to keep a non-gun (e.g., a rifle) at home unless the weapon is kept unloaded and inoperable (e.g., by a trigger lock). *Held*, both provisions violate the Second Amendment right of private individuals to keep at home operable firearms of the type that were kept by private citizens for self-defense in 1791. [*Heller, supra.*]

1. **Applies to states and cities:** The Second Amendment *applies the same way to state and local governments* as to the federal government. [*McDonald v. City of Chicago* (2010)]

   a. **Selectively incorporated:** This result is due to the Supreme Court's conclusion in *McDonald* that the Second Amendment should be deemed to be *selectively incorporated* into the 14th Amendment's *Due Process Clause*, and thereby made applicable to the states. (The Court believed that the right to bear arms in self-defense is *"fundamental to our scheme of ordered liberty,"* the test for whether any Bill of Rights guarantee should be deemed incorporated into the 14th Amendment guarantee of due process and thus made applicable to the states.)

2. **Review standard to be used:** It's unclear what *standard* the court will use for reviewing governmental restrictions that impair Second Amendment rights (*Heller* and *McDonald* didn't decide this.) The most likely outcome is that *mid-level review*, under which the question is whether the means chosen by government is *"substantially related"* to the achievement of an *"important"* governmental interest, will ultimately be used.

3. **Some regulation allowed:** It seems likely that despite the broad reading of the Second Amendment in *Heller* and *McDonald*, all governments will be allowed to exercise *substantial regulation of gun possession.* So, for example:

   a. **Licensing requirements:** *Licensing requirements* will probably *not* be found to violate the Second Amendment as long as the procedures for obtaining a license are not unreasonably burdensome, and are directed towards keeping guns out of the hands of people who do not have a Second Amendment right to possess them.

   > **Example:** Licensing requirements that deny gun permits to felons and the mentally ill — and that give government a reasonable amount of time to check whether the applicant falls into these categories — are probably valid even after *Heller* and *McDonald*.

    b. Concealed-carry permits: Similarly, the Amendment will probably be found not to prohibit governments from banning the ***carrying of concealed weapons in public places.***

    c. Modern weapons: Probably the Amendment won't be found to block governments from banning the possession of ***modern weapons*** that are much more ***advanced and dangerous*** than those existing in 1791. So ***machine guns, assault rifles*** and ***sawed-off shotguns*** probably may still be banned.

V. *EX POST FACTO* LAWS

A. Constitutional prohibition: Article I prohibits both state and federal governments from passing any "ex post facto" law. An *ex post facto* law is a law which has a ***retroactive punitive effect***. So government may not ***impose a punishment*** for conduct which, at the time it occurred, was ***not punishable***. Also, government may not ***increase*** the punishment for an offense over what was on the books at the time of the act.

    Example: On June 1, Joe smokes a cigarette in a public building. On June 10, the state legislature makes it a crime, for the first time, to smoke in a public building. Because of the ban on *ex post facto* laws, Joe cannot be convicted of the June 1 smoking, since it was not a crime at the time he did it. The same would be true if the legislature on June 15 increased the penalty for such smoking over what it was on June 1.

1. Criminal only: The ban on *ex post facto* laws applies only to measures that are *"criminal"* or *"penal,"* not to those that are civil. Basically, this means that only measures calling for ***imprisonment*** will come within the *ex post facto* ban (so a measure that imposes, say, ***disbarment***, or one that imposes ***deportation***, can be made retroactive, since these sanctions are civil). See, e.g., *Galvan v. Press*.

VI. BILLS OF ATTAINDER

A. Generally: Art. I prohibits both the federal government and the states from passing any *"bill of attainder."* A bill of attainder is a legislative act which "applies either to named individuals or to easily ascertainable members of a group in such a way as to ***punish*** them without a ***judicial trial***." (*Example:* Congress prohibits the payment of salaries to three named federal agency employees, on the grounds that they are engaged in subversive activities. This is an invalid bill of attainder, since it applies to named or easily-identified individuals, and punishes them without a judicial trial. [*U.S. v. Lovett*])

THE "STATE ACTION" REQUIREMENT; CONGRESSIONAL ENFORCEMENT OF CIVIL RIGHTS

I. STATE ACTION

A. **State action generally:** Virtually all of the rights and liberties guaranteed by the Constitution to individuals are protected only against interference by the government. We summarize this rule by referring to the requirement of *"state action."* But sometimes, even a *private individual's act* will be found to be "state action" that must comply with the Constitution. There are two main doctrines that may lead a private act to be classified as state action; if *either* of these doctrines applies, then the private action is "state action" even if the other doctrine would not apply. The two doctrines are the *"public function"* doctrine and the *"state involvement"* doctrine.

B. **"Public function" doctrine:** Under the *"public function"* approach to state action, if a private individual (or group) is entrusted by the state to perform functions that are *governmental in nature*, the private individual becomes an *agent of the state*, and his acts constitute state action.

1. **Political system:** The *electoral process* is a "public function," and is thus state action. Therefore, the carrying out of *primary elections* is state action, even if the acts are directly carried out by "private" political parties. (*Example:* A state convention of Democrats (in essence, a "private" political party) rules that only whites may vote in the Texas Democratic Primary. *Held*, this racial restriction is "state action," and therefore violates the 15th Amendment. The primary is an integral part of the election scheme, and the running of elections is traditionally a "public function," so the running of the primary is state action even though it is directly carried out by private groups. [*Smith v. Allwright*])

   a. **Company town:** Similarly, operation of a *"company town"* is a "public function," and thus is state action, because towns are usually operated by the government.

      i. **Shopping centers not a public function:** But operation of a *shopping center* is *not* the equivalent of operating a company town, so a person does not have any First Amendment rights in the shopping center. [*Hudgens v. NLRB*]

   b. **Parks:** Operation of a *park* is usually deemed a governmental function, so generally the operation of a park will constitute "state action" under the "public function" doctrine. Therefore, even if the park is being operated by private persons, it must still obey constitutional constraints (e.g., it can't be operated for whites only). [*Evans v. Newton*]

2. **The "exclusively public" requirement:** Apparently, the function must be one that traditionally has been *"exclusively"* a public function, in order for the "public function" doctrine to apply.

Example: A warehouseman has a warehouseman's lien on goods stored with him, to cover unpaid storage charges. He sells the goods pursuant to the warehouseman's lien, and the owner claims that due process was required because the resolution of disputes is a "public function." *Held*, the warehouseman's lien and sale was not a "public function" because the resolution of disputes between private individuals is not traditionally an "exclusively" governmental activity — for instance, the parties might have agreed to private arbitration. [*Flagg Bros. v. Brooks*]

C. "State involvement" doctrine: Even if the private individual is not doing something that's traditionally a "public function," his conduct may constitute state action if the state is *heavily involved* in his activities. This is the *"state involvement"* branch of state-action doctrine. Here are some of the ways in which the state and private actor can be so closely involved that the private person's acts become state action:

1. **Commandment:** The state may become responsible for the private party's actions because it *commanded*, i.e., required, the private party to act in that way. (*Example:* The state enforces a private agreement among neighbors that none will sell his house to a black. Because the state has lent its state judicial enforcement mechanism to this otherwise private contract, the combination of enforcement and private discrimination violates equal protection. [*Shelley v. Kraemer*]

2. **Encouragement:** If the state *"encourages"* the private party's actions, then the private action will be converted into state action. (*Example:* The voters of California amend their constitution to prohibit the state government from interfering with any private individual's right to discriminate when he sells or leases residential real estate. This amendment immediately results in the repeal of two state Fair Housing statutes. *Held*, this state-constitutional amendment amounts to governmental "encouragement" of private discrimination. Therefore, the resulting private discrimination will be imputed to the state, and the state constitutional provision violates the 14th Amendment. [*Reitman v. Mulkey*])

3. **Symbiosis:** There is state action if there exists between the state and private actor a *"symbiotic"* relationship, i.e., a relation between the two that is *mutually beneficial*. (*Example:* A Wilmington, Delaware city agency owns and runs a parking garage complex. The agency gives a 20 year lease to a privately-operated restaurant located in the complex. The restaurant refuses to serve African Americans. *Held*, African Americans who are refused service have had their equal protection rights violated. The relation between the restaurant and the publicly-run garage was so close and symbiotic — the garage wouldn't have been able to operate viably without rents from the restaurant — that the restaurant's actions must be imputed to the state, and therefore constitute state action. [*Burton v. Wilmington Parking Authority*])

4. **Entanglement or entwinement:** State action may arise from the fact that the state is so *"entangled"* or *"entwined"* with a private actor that even though the state might not directly benefit from the private actor's conduct,

the conduct will still be treated as state action. This is true where the state and the private party *act together* to carry out the action being challenged.

Example 1: A state allows a private litigant — either a civil litigant or a defendant in a criminal case — to use peremptory challenges to exclude jurors on racial grounds. This conduct constitutes state action, and therefore violates the Equal Protection Clause. [*Edmondson v. Leesville Concrete Co.*; *Georgia v. McCollum*]

Example 2: A state recognizes a private association of high schools as being the regulator of high school interscholastic sports. Most members of the association are public high schools within the state, and these schools are active in the association's affairs as part of the schools' official business of running athletic programs. Because the association's activities are deeply entwined with state affairs, the association's conduct is state action. [*Brentwood Academy v. Tenn. Secondary School Athl. Assoc.*]

  a. **Mere acquiescence not enough:** But if the state merely *acquiesces* in the private party's discrimination, this won't be enough of a state involvement to convert the private actor's conduct into state action.

  Example: The state regulates all utilities. A private utility cuts off plaintiff's service without notice or a hearing, and this fact is known to the state, which does not object. *Held*, the utility's conduct was not state action, because the state merely acquiesced in that conduct, rather than actively participating in it. [*Jackson v. Metropolitan Edison Co.*]

  b. **Licensing:** Similarly, the fact that the state has *licensed* a private person is generally not enough to convert the private person's conduct into state action.

  Example: A private club refuses to serve African Americans. Even though the state has given the club one of a limited number of liquor licenses, this act of licensing is not enough to turn the club's action into state action. [*Moose Lodge v. Irvis*]

II. CONGRESSIONAL ENFORCEMENT OF CIVIL RIGHTS

A. **Congressional enforcement of civil rights:** Congress has special powers to enforce the post-Civil War amendments, i.e., the Thirteenth, Fourteenth, and Fifteenth Amendments.

  1. **13th Amendment:** The Thirteenth Amendment *abolishes "slavery"* and *"involuntary servitude."*

  2. **14th Amendment:** The Fourteenth Amendment requires the states to give *"due process," "equal protection,"* and *"privileges and immunities."*

  3. **15th Amendment:** The Fifteenth Amendment bars the states from denying *voting rights* on the basis of race, color or previous condition of servitude.

B. Congress' power to reach private conduct: The special enforcement powers let Congress reach a lot of ***private conduct*** that it could not reach by means of any other congressional power.

1. **14th and 15th Amendments:**   When Congress enforces the Fourteenth and Fifteenth Amendments, it has some, but not unlimited, power to reach private conduct. So Congress could, for instance, make it a crime for somebody to ***interfere with a state official*** who is trying to guarantee another person's equal protection rights or voting rights. (*Example:* Congress can make it a crime for D to prevent a school principal from allowing African Americans to enroll in an all white school.)

    a. **Can't reach purely private discrimination:**   But Congress under the Fourteenth Amendment ***cannot*** simply make it a crime for one private person to practice ordinary racial discrimination against another. (Congress would instead have to use its power to regulate interstate commerce; this is the basis on which the 1964 Civil Rights Act, forbidding racial discrimination in places of public accommodation, was upheld. [*Katzenbach v. McClung*])

2. **13th Amendment:**   But the ***13th*** Amendment is different. §1 of the 13th Amendment provides that "neither slavery nor involuntary servitude, except as a punishment for crime … shall exist within the United States." §2 gives Congress the power to "enforce this [amendment] by appropriate legislation." The 13th Amendment, unlike the 14th and 15th, is ***not explicitly limited to governmental action.*** Indeed, that's the most important thing to remember about the 13th Amendment, and its principal use today — it's practically the only clause in the entire Constitution that prevents one private citizen from doing something to another. So the 13th Amendment gives Congress important authority to reach certain private conduct that it couldn't reach through the 14th and 15th Amendments.

    a. **"Badges of slavery":**   If the 13th Amendment only meant that Congress could take special action to ensure that slavery itself, in its most literal sense, shall be wiped out, the Amendment wouldn't be of much practical use today. But instead, the Supreme Court has held that the Amendment allows Congress also to stamp out the ***"badges and incidents"*** of slavery. In fact, Congress has the power to determine what the "badges and incidents of slavery" are, so long as it acts rationally — once Congress defines these "badges and incidents," it can then forbid them.

       Example: In 1866, Congress passes a statute, 42 U.S.C. §1982, which provides that "all citizens of the United States shall have the same right, in every state and Territory, as is enjoyed by white citizens thereof to inherit, purchase, lease, sell, hold and convey real and personal property." In a modern case, the Ps argue that the statute prevents D (a private developer) from refusing to sell them a house solely because they are African American.

       Held, this statute applies to block discrimination by D, a private citizen. Furthermore, the statute is constitutional under the 13th Amendment. §2 of the 13th Amendment, which gives Congress enforcement powers under that amendment, gives Congress the power to make a rational determination of *what the badges and incidents of slavery are.* Here, Congress could have rationally concluded that barriers to enjoyment of real estate, and discrimination in housing, are relics of slavery. [*Jones v. Alfred H. Mayer Co.*]

b. **Ancestry, ethnic discrimination:** As we've just seen, the 13th Amendment clearly lets Congress prevent private discrimination against African Americans, on the grounds that it's a "badge or incident" of slavery. *All other racial minorities are also protected* — Congress could probably even bar private racial discrimination against *whites* based on the 13th Amendment (though the Court has never explicitly decided this). But it's not clear whether private discrimination based on *non-racial grounds* (e.g., *ancestry, ethnic background*, religion, sex, etc.) can be barred by Congress acting pursuant to the 13th Amendment.

c. **Must have statute:** The application of the 13th Amendment to a broad range of "badges and incidents of slavery" applies only where Congress has used its *enforcement* powers by passing a *statute* that relies on the Amendment. If private citizen A discriminates against B on the basis of race, but the type of discrimination is not one that Congress has outlawed, then the 13th Amendment's "naked" or "self-executing" scope *won't* be enough to reach that discrimination. Probably actual *peonage* — the keeping of a person as a slave — is the only type of private racial discrimination that is directly barred by the 13th Amendment in the absence of a congressional statute.

C. **Congress' remedial powers:** The Thirteenth, Fourteenth and Fifteenth Amendments all have specific provisions giving Congress the power to *"enforce"* that amendment. See, e.g., §5 of the Fourteenth Amendment, giving Congress the power to enforce the amendment *"by appropriate legislation."*

1. **Remedial powers:** Under this enforcement power, Congress may *prohibit* certain actions that *don't directly violate* these amendments, if it reasonably believes that these actions would or might *lead* to violations of the amendments. That is, Congress has broad *"remedial" or "prophylactic" powers.*

   Example: Congress may use its 15th Amendment remedial powers to forbid, in the Voting Rights Act (further discussed below), any voter literacy test or character test in states with a history of voting rights violations. That's true even though such tests aren't themselves necessarily unconstitutional — Congress' 15th Amendment remedial powers are triggered by Congress' reasonable fears that such tests *may lead* to violations of the 15th Amendment. [*South Carolina v. Katzenbach*]

2. **Reference to "Necessary and Proper" clause:** Congress' power to enforce the Civil War amendments is to be judged generally by reference to the *"Necessary and Proper"* clause (*supra*, p. 51). That is, as long as the *means* chosen by Congress are *"rationally related"* to achieving an objective that one of these amendments is designed to fulfill, Congress has not exceeded its enforcement authority. (But as we'll see below, there is one important limitation on this principle, the special "congruent and propor-

tional" standard for judging Congress' exercise of its Fourteenth Amendment enforcement powers; see *Boerne v. Flores, infra*, p. 129.)

  a. **Easy "rationally related" review standard:** This easy-to-satisfy "rationally related" standard means that if Congress reasonably fears that the *effect* of a state law will include interferences with a right guaranteed by one of these three amendments, Congress can prohibit the state law from being enforced. That's true even if it's clear that the members of the state legislature did not, when they enacted the law, have a *purpose* of promoting violations of any of the amendments.

3. **Obligation to rely on current data (*Shelby County v. Holder*):** Cases like *South Carolina v. Katzenbach, supra*, giving a broad reading to Congress' remedial powers under the Fifteenth Amendment, were decided when massive official racial discrimination against minority voters in many southern states — and Congress' response — were both relatively *recent* phenomena. But recent decades have seen large reductions in such overt racial discrimination in voting. So the question arises, may Congress continue to single out for more-burdensome federal regulation of voting practices certain states based solely on these states' 1960s and 1970s histories of official racial discrimination in voting?

  The answer according to a recent (2013) case is ***"no."*** If in the present era Congress wants to use its Fifteenth Amendment enforcement powers to prevent future violations of the Amendment — rather than punish past violations — Congress must *adjust the measures it uses* to reflect *current rather than historical voting circumstances*.

  > **Example:** In the most recent version of the Voting Rights Act (enacted in 2006), Congress continues to use its Fifteenth Amendment remedial powers to set certain criteria that the Justice Department is to use to compile a list of states and local governments that will be deemed to have had a history of intentional discrimination in voting (this is the "coverage formula"). Congress then says that any jurisdiction on the list must get federal pre-approval ("preclearance") before making any major or minor change to the jurisdiction's voting regulations (e.g., imposition of new Voter ID methods, different voting hours, or redrawing of electoral districts). The coverage formula — and thus the list of covered jurisdiction — is based solely on voter-registration and turnout data from the 1972 elections or earlier. Shelby County, which is covered because it's in a state that's on the list (Alabama), challenges the constitutionality of Congress' assertion of this power.
  >
  > *Held* (5-4), for the county: the formula for compiling the list of jurisdictions exceeds Congress' Fifteenth Amendment powers. There is a *"fundamental principle of equal sovereignty"* among the states. If Congress is going to "divide the States" (as it has done here by means of the coverage formula), this equal-sovereignty principle requires Congress to design the coverage formula on a *"basis that makes sense in light of current conditions."* Given the large amount of progress the covered states have made since 1972 (including the fact that black and Hispanic

registration and turnout percentages are actually higher than for whites in five of the six states covered on account of 1972 data), Congress' failure to use any data from later than 1972 fails this "make sense" standard. Therefore, the coverage formula may not be enforced (though the decision does not prevent Congress from applying preclearance to jurisdictions if Congress enacts a *new* coverage formula based on current conditions). [*Shelby County v. Holder* (2013)]

III. CONGRESS' POWER TO REDEFINE THE MEANING AND SCOPE OF CONSTITUTIONAL GUARANTEES

A. **Congressional power to redefine the scope of constitutional rights:** Congress does *not* have the power to *redefine the scope* of the rights protected by the Civil War amendments in a way that is different from the way the Supreme Court would define their scope.

1. **No power to redefine scope:** This is true whether Congress is trying to *expand* or *contract* the right.

   Example: The Supreme Court issues a decision defining the First Amendment Establishment Clause more narrowly than the Court had previously defined that clause. Congress doesn't like this decision. It therefore passes the "Religious Freedom Restoration Act," which in effect says that all state and local governments must refrain from any action that would have violated the Establishment Clause under the earlier, now-overruled, cases. *Held*, Congress has no power to either expand or contract the scope of constitutional rights, so the Act is an unconstitutional exercise of congressional power. [*Boerne v. Flores*]

IV. CONGRESS' POWER TO ABROGATE THE ELEVENTH AMENDMENT AND THUS AUTHORIZE DAMAGE SUITS AGAINST THE STATES FOR DISCRIMINATION

A. **Private money-damage discrimination suits against states:** Congress often prohibits a certain type of discrimination, and then attempts to make *state and local governments*, not just private individuals, obey the prohibition. Sometimes, Congress goes even further, and attempts to *give private individuals the right to bring private actions* for *money damages* against a *state or local government* that commits the prohibited discrimination.

1. **Significance of Eleventh Amendment:** But because of the existence of the *Eleventh Amendment*, it will often turn out that Congress *has overstepped its boundaries* by such an attempt to let private individuals sue state and local governments for discrimination.

2. **The Eleventh Amendment:** The Eleventh Amendment says, in brief, that the *states are immune* from being sued for *money damages by private citizens in federal court*. We discuss the Amendment in much greater detail

below (see p. 180).

a. **Abrogation of amendment:** It's always been clear, however, that Congress has in some circumstances the power to *abrogate* the states' Eleventh Amendment immunity from private suits. But the Court's view of how and when Congress can do so has changed over the years.

b. **Use of Commerce powers:** Originally, nearly everyone thought that Congress could use its extremely broad *Commerce Clause* powers to abrogate the states' Eleventh Amendment immunity. That is, it was thought that Congress could *ban a particular type of discrimination* by use of its Commerce powers, and then under those same powers (i) require the states to comply with the ban, and (ii) *strip their Eleventh Amendment immunity* so that private citizens could sue the state for violation of the federal ban.

   i. **Use of Commerce powers disallowed:** But in *Seminole Tribe of Florida v. Florida* (discussed in more detail *infra*, p. 181), the Court held that the Commerce powers *cannot* serve as the basis for a congressional abrogation of the Eleventh Amendment, and thus as the basis for letting private individuals sue a state for damages for violating a federal ban on some sort of discrimination.

   ii. **Use of Civil-War-Amendment powers:** On the other hand, it's always been clear that Congress *may* rely on its *Civil-War-Amendment remedial powers* as the source of authority for a general anti-discrimination statute. And under those powers (unlike the Commerce power), Congress can not only ban discrimination that would violate the Civil War amendments, but can subject state governments to the ban, and *abrogate the states' Eleventh Amendment immunity*, so as to let private victims sue a discriminating state for damages.

      (1) **Restrictions:** But as we'll discuss immediately below (in Par. (B)), the Court has placed a special "congruent and proportional" restriction on Congress' powers to enforce the Civil War amendments. This restriction, when coupled with the above-described ban on Congress' use of its Commerce powers to abrogate states' Eleventh Amendment immunity, significantly limits Congress' ability to let private citizens sue state governments for discrimination.

B. **"Congruent and proportional":** When Congress purports to use its enforcement powers to prohibit acts that it fears might lead to constitutional violations, Congress' action must be *"congruent and proportional"* to the threatened violation. If not, the congressional action is *invalid* under the enforcement powers. [*Boerne v. Flores*]

1. **Significance:** The most important consequence of this principle is that if Congress wants to let private individuals *sue the states* in federal district court for money *damages* for state violations of a federal anti-discrimination statute, two conditions must be satisfied:

   [1] Congress must ordinarily have before it evidence of *widespread past con-*

stitutional violations by the states of the sort that Congress is trying to prevent; and

[2] the remedy picked by Congress must be *"congruent and proportional"* to the state violations that Congress is trying to prevent.

Otherwise, Congress' action cannot be justified by its Civil-War-Amendments enforcement powers. And only those powers (not, say, the Commerce power) are sufficient to let Congress overcome states' *Eleventh Amendment immunity from private federal-court damage suits.*

> **Example:** In the Age Discrimination in Employment Act (ADEA) Congress makes the states, when they act as employers, obey the same age-discrimination rules as private employers. And Congress authorizes state employees to sue the states in federal court for money damages for ADEA violations committed by the state. Congress says it has acted under authority of its 14th Amendment §5 remedial powers, to prevent violations by the states of older state employees' equal protection rights.
>
> *Held*, Congress went beyond the scope of its §5 remedial powers, because there was no evidence that the states routinely violated older workers' equal protection rights. Therefore, Congress' regulation was not a "congruent and proportional" response to any threatened constitutional violations, making the regulation not authorized under Congress' § 5 remedial powers. Consequently, the states are free to assert their Eleventh Amendment immunity from private damage suits (which immunity can properly be overcome only by Congress' use of its § 5 remedial powers, not by its use of other powers like the Commerce power). [*Kimel v. Fla. Bd. of Regents*]

a. **Area receiving heightened scrutiny:** But if the federal statute that creates the right of the plaintiff to sue a state for damages deals with an area that involves *either a suspect or semi-suspect class or a fundamental right, Congress has more freedom.* Since the Court applies some form of *heightened scrutiny* to these areas, the Court will be much more likely to find that Congress' decision to allow a damages suit *meets the "congruent and proportional" requirement* and is thus constitutional.

> **Example:** Title II of the Americans with Disabilities Act (ADA) requires states (as well as private citizens) to accommodate disabled persons' access to certain public facilities, including courthouses. The Ps are paraplegics who seek damages from the state of Tennessee because they do not have adequate access to court services. (One P, for instance, has been required to crawl up stairs to answer criminal charges, because the county courthouse has no elevator.)
>
> *Held*, for the Ps. Congress has power to allow damages for violations of ADA Title II, at least in the court-access area. The right of access to courts is subject to *"more searching judicial review"* than the rational-relation review used in ADA Title I disability-discrimination-in-*employment* cases (as to which the Court has held that Congress does *not* have power to subject the states to money-damage awards, because of lack of

evidence that the states as employers have systematically discriminated against disabled employees). [*Tennessee v. Lane*]

b. Right to prohibit direct constitutional violations: Also, if the state conduct that the plaintiff is complaining of was an *actual violation* by the state of the plaintiff's *constitutional rights,* Congress can grant the plaintiff the right to recover damages against the state in federal court without worrying about whether the federal statute is congruent-and-proportional to the overall pattern of constitutional violations that Congress was trying to prevent.

Example: Congress may allow P, a wheel-chair-bound prisoner, to sue a state for actual damages caused to him when his disability was not accommodated. (His cell was too small for him to turn his wheelchair around in it.) Because P's suit is premised on an *actual violation* of his 14th Amendment liberty interest (not merely based on a federal statute that was enacted out of a general fear that states or private citizens would discriminate in the future), the Court will not consider whether the ADA statute is "congruent and proportional" to the constitutional violations feared by Congress. [*U.S. v. Georgia*]

CHAPTER 14

FREEDOM OF EXPRESSION

I. GENERAL THEMES

A. Text of First Amendment: The First Amendment provides, in part, that "Congress shall make no law ... abridging the *freedom of speech*, or of the press; or the right of the people peaceably to assemble, and to petition the Government for a redress of grievances."

1. Related rights: There are thus several distinct rights which may be grouped under the category "freedom of expression": freedom of *speech*, of the *press*, of *assembly*, and of *petition*. Additionally, there is a well-recognized "freedom of *association*" which, although it is not specifically mentioned in the First Amendment, is derived from individuals' rights of speech and assembly.

B. Two broad classes: Whenever you consider governmental action that seems to infringe upon the freedom of expression, there's one key question that you must always ask before you ask anything else. That question is, "Is this governmental action '*content-based*' or '*content-neutral*'?" If the action is "content-based," the government's action will generally be subjected to strict scrutiny, and the action will rarely be sustained. On the other hand, if the action is "content-neutral," the government's action is subjected to a much less demanding standard, and is thus much more likely to be upheld.

1. Classifying: A governmental action that burdens a person's expression is "content-based" if the government is aiming at the *"communicative impact"* of the expression. By contrast, if the government is aiming at something other than the communicative impact of the expression, the government action is "content-neutral," even though it may have the *effect* of burdening the expression.

Example 1 (content-based): Under Maryland tort law, if a speaker (D) intentionally makes outrageous statements attacking another person (P), P may be able to recover against D for intentional infliction of emotional distress (IIED). In a federal-court diversity case based on Maryland tort law, a jury grants P (the father of a Marine killed in Iraq) a civil judgment for IIED against the Ds, who are members of a church that thinks God punishes the U.S. military for tolerating homosexuality. The IIED consists of the Ds' having carried, during and nearby the Marine's funeral, picket signs attributing the Marine's death to God's desire to punish the military for not rooting out homosexuality.

Maryland's common law of IIED is "content based." That's because the "outrageousness" of the Ds' messages on the picket signs results solely from the content of those messages. [*Snyder v. Phelps*]

Example 2 (content-neutral): A city forbids the distribution of all leaflets, because it wishes to prevent littering. This ban is "content neutral" — the government is banning all leaflets, regardless of their content, and the harm sought to be avoided (littering) would exist to the same extent regardless of the message in the leaflets. Therefore, the government action is subject to less rigid review — more or less "intermediate level review" (though it was still struck down on these facts). [*Schneider v. State*]

   a. **Tip:** Here's a tip to help you decide whether a given governmental action is content-based or not: would the harm the government is trying to prevent exist to the same degree if the listeners/readers ***didn't understand English***? If the answer is "no," the action is probably content-based.

      Example: Suppose a funeral attendee in *Snyder v. Phelps* (Example 1 *supra*) didn't speak English. He wouldn't suffer the harm the state was trying to prevent — being emotionally harmed by the statements on the picketers' signs — even if he saw or read the signs, so it's clearly the content of the communication that the state is objecting to. But in the case of the ban on littering (Example 2), even a whole city of non-English-speakers would suffer the same harm — lack of a "right" to litter — so the ban is content-neutral.

   b. **Motive counts:** When a court decides whether a regulation is content-based or content-neutral, ***motives*** count for everything — the question is what the state really ***intends*** to do. If the court believes that the state intends to inhibit certain speech because of its message, the court will treat the statute as content-based (and strictly scrutinize it) even though it is neutral on its face.

C. Analysis of content-based government action: Once we've determined that a particular government action impairing expression is "content-based," we then have to determine whether the expression falls within a category that is **protected** by the First Amendment.

1. **Unprotected category:** If the speech falls into certain pre-defined **unprotected** categories, then the government can basically ban that expression completely based on its content, without any interference at all from the First Amendment.

   a. **List of categories:** Here is a list of these unprotected categories, as the Supreme Court has recognized them:

      [1] ***"Incitement."*** This category includes advocacy of **imminent lawless behavior**, as well as the utterance of **"fighting words,"** i.e., words that are likely to precipitate an immediate physical conflict;

      [2] ***Obscenity***;

      [3] ***Misleading or deceptive speech (i.e., fraud)***;

      [4] Speech **integral to criminal conduct**, such as speech that is part of a **conspiracy** to commit a crime or speech **proposing an illegal transaction**; and

      [5] ***Defamation***.

   b. **Not totally unprotected:** But even speech falling within an "unprotected category" receives one small First Amendment protection: government must regulate in a basically **viewpoint-neutral** way. That is, it can exclude certain subjects entirely, but it can't single out certain viewpoints for less favorable treatment.

      Example: The state may ban all "fighting words." But it may not choose to ban just those fighting words directed at the listener's race, religion, or other enumerated traits. [*R.A.V. v. City of St. Paul*]

2. **Protected category:** All expression not falling into one of these five pre-defined categories is "protected." If expression is protected, then any government ban or restriction on it based on its content will be **presumed to be unconstitutional**. The Court will subject any content-based regulation of protected speech to **strict scrutiny** — the regulation will be sustained only if it (1) serves a **compelling governmental objective**; and (2) is **"necessary,"** i.e., drawn as **narrowly as possible** to achieve that objective (since a broader-than-needed restriction wouldn't be a "necessary" means).

   Example: A District of Columbia statute bans the display of any sign within 500 feet of a foreign embassy, if the sign would bring the foreign government into "public disrepute." *Held*, this regulation is content-based, since a sign is prohibited or not prohibited based on what the sign says. Therefore, the regulation must be strictly scrutinized, and cannot be upheld. Even if the government's interest in protecting the dignity of foreign diplomats is compelling — which it may or may not be — the statute is not "necessary" to achieve that interest, since a narrower statute that only banned the intimidation, coercion or threatening of diplomats would do the trick. [*Boos v. Barry*]

    a. Religious speech gets equal protection: The requirement of content-neutrality is now so strong that it seems to take precedence over the ***Establishment Clause*** (which protects separation of church and state). Thus if the government allows private speech in a particular forum, it may not treat ***religiously-oriented*** speech ***less favorably*** than non-religiously-oriented speech.

    Example: If a public university gives funding for student publications on various topics, the requirement of content-neutrality means that the university must give the same funding to a student publication whose mission is to proselytize for Christianity. [*Rosenberger v. Univ. of Virginia*]

D. Analyzing content-neutral regulations: Now, let's go back to the beginning, and assume that the government restriction is ***content-neutral***.

  1. Three-part test: Here, we have a ***three-part test*** that the government must satisfy before its regulation will be sustained if that regulation substantially impairs expression:

    a. Significant governmental interest: First, the regulation must serve a ***significant governmental interest.***

    b. Narrowly tailored: Second, the regulation must be ***narrowly tailored*** to serve that governmental interest. So if there's a somewhat ***less restrictive*** way to accomplish the same result, the government must use that less-intrusive way. (*Example:* Preventing littering is a significant governmental interest. But the government can't completely ban the distribution of handbills to avoid littering, because the littering problem could be solved by the less restrictive method of simply punishing those who drop a handbill on the street. [*Schneider v. State*])

    c. Alternative channels: Finally, the state must ***"leave open alternative channels"*** for communicating the information. (*Example:* Suppose a city wants to ban all billboards. If a political advertiser can show that there's no other low-cost way to get his message across to local motorists, this billboard ban might run afoul of the "alternative channels" requirement.)

  2. Mid-level review: This three-part test basically boils down to ***mid-level*** review for content-neutral restrictions that significantly impair expression (as opposed to strict scrutiny for content-based restrictions).

E. Overbreadth: The doctrine of ***overbreadth*** is very important in determining whether a governmental regulation of speech violates the First Amendment. A statute is "overbroad" if it bans speech which could constitutionally be forbidden but *also* bans speech which is protected by the First Amendment.

  1. Standing: To see why the overbreadth doctrine is important, let's first consider how a litigant attacks the constitutionality of a statute *outside* the First Amendment area. Here, the litigant can only get a statute declared unconstitutional if he can show that it's unconstitutional in its ***application to him***.

    a. Lets P assert third-party rights: But the overbreadth doctrine lets a litigant prevail if he can show that the statute, applied according to its terms, would violate the First Amendment rights of ***persons not now***

before the court. So overbreadth is really an exception to the usual rule of "standing" — under the usual standing rules, a person is not normally allowed to assert the constitutional rights of others, only his own.

2. **"Substantial" overbreadth:** In cases where the statute is aimed at ***conduct*** that has expressive content (rather than aimed against pure speech), the over-breadth doctrine will only be applied if the overbreadth would be ***"substantial."*** In other words, for the statute to be deemed overly broad, the potential unconstitutional applications of the statute must be fairly ***numerous*** compared with the constitutional applications.

F. **Vagueness:** There is a second important First Amendment doctrine: ***vagueness.*** A statute is unconstitutionally vague if the conduct forbidden by it is so ***unclearly defined*** that a reasonable person would have to ***guess at its meaning.***

1. **Distinguish from overbreadth:** Be careful to ***distinguish vagueness from overbreadth:*** they both leave the citizen uncertain about which applications of a statute may constitutionally be imposed. But in overbreadth, the uncertainty is hidden or "latent," and in vagueness the uncertainty is easily apparent.

   Example: Statute I prohibits anyone from "burning a U.S. flag as a symbol of opposition to organized government." Statute II prohibits anyone from "burning a U.S. flag for any purpose whatsoever." Statute I is probably unconstitutionally vague, because there's no way to tell what the statute means by "symbols of opposition to organized government." Statutue II is unconstitutionally overbroad — it's obviously not vague, since it's perfectly clear that it bans *all* flag burning. But since by its terms it appears to apply to constitutionally-protected conduct (e.g., burning that's intended as a political expression), and since there's no easy way to separate out the constitutional from unconstitutional applications, it's overbroad.

II. ADVOCACY OF ILLEGAL CONDUCT

A. **Advocacy of illegal conduct:** Remember that one of our "unprotected categories" is the ***advocacy of imminent illegal conduct.*** The government can ban speech that advocates crime or the use of force if (but only if) it shows that two requirements are met:

   [1] The advocacy must be ***intended*** to incite or produce "imminent lawless action"; and

   [2] The advocacy must in fact be ***likely*** to incite or produce that imminent lawless action.

   [*Brandenburg v. Ohio*]

1. **Mere membership not enough:** ***Mere knowing membership*** in a group — even a very dangerous and subversive group — cannot be forbidden. Membership in a group can be punished only if the member is an ***active*** (not passive) member who ***specifically intends to further the organization's illegal ends.*** [*Scales v. U.S.*]

a. **Active support by intangible means:** On the other hand, the government *can* constitutionally prohibit virtually any kind of *active support* of an illegal organization, even support that is intended to further the organization's *legal* aims.

Example: After 9/11, Congress makes it a crime to provide "material support" to a designated foreign terrorist organization, and defines "material support" broadly to include such things as training the group's members to use legal methods of accomplishing their objectives. *Held*, Congress did not violate the First Amendment — even support of a terrorist organization's *legitimate* aims can be harmful (e.g., by "free[ing] up other resources within the organization that may be put to violent ends, and "lend[ing] legitimacy" to the group). Therefore, government may forbid such support. [*Holder v. Humanitarian Law Project*]

III. TIME, PLACE AND MANNER REGULATIONS

A. **Time, place and manner generally:** Let's now focus on regulations covering the *"time, place and manner"* of expression. This is probably the area of Freedom of Expression on which you are most likely to be tested, since these kinds of regulations are quite often found in real life. When we give you the rules for analyzing "time, place and manner" restrictions below, assume that the speech that is being restricted is taking place in a *public forum*. (If it's not, then the government has a somewhat easier time of getting its regulation sustained; we'll be talking about these non-public forum situations later.)

1. **Three-part test:** A "time, place and manner" regulation of public-forum speech has to pass a *three-part test* to avoid being a violation of the First Amendment:

    a. **Content-neutral:** First, it has to be *content-neutral*. In other words, the government can't really be trying to regulate content under the guise of regulating "time, place and manner."

    Example: City enacts an ordinance allowing parades or demonstrations "to protest governmental policies" to be conducted only between 10 a.m. and 4 p.m. No such restrictions are placed on other kinds of parades or demonstrations. Even though this restriction is ostensibly merely a "time, place and manner" restriction, it violates the requirement of content-neutrality, because the restriction applies to some expressive conduct but not others, based on the content of the speech.

    b. **Narrowly tailored for significant governmental interest:** Second, it's got to be *narrowly tailored* to serve a *significant governmental interest*. (We saw this above when we were talking more generally about the analysis of all content-neutral restrictions on speech.) This basically means that not only must the government be pursuing an important interest, but there must not be some significantly *less intrusive* way that government could achieve its objective.

Example: Suppose the government wants to prevent littering on the streets. Even though prevention of littering is an important governmental objective, the government may not simply ban all distribution of handbills, because there is a significantly less restrictive means of achieving this objective — a direct ban on littering — so the ban on handbills is not "narrowly tailored" to achieving the anti-littering objective.

c. **Alternative channels:**   Finally, the state must "leave open *alternative channels*" for communicating the information.

Example: City is a medium-sized city, with six public parks and many streets. City enacts an ordinance stating that any parade or demonstration, no matter what the content of the message, shall take place only in Central Park or on Main Street. City argues that its limited budget for police security, and the greater ease of handling crowds in these two places than in other places, justify the ordinance. Even though this time, place and manner restriction is apparently content-neutral and is arguably narrowly tailored for a significant governmental interest, it probably violates the "leave open alternative channels" requirement because it puts off limits for parades and demonstrations the vast majority of locations within City.

2. **Application to conduct:**   These rules on when the state may regulate the "time, place and manner" of expression apply where what is being regulated is pure speech. But much more importantly, these rules apply where the state is regulating *"conduct"* that has an expressive component. *So the state can never defend on the grounds that "We're not regulating speech, we're just regulating conduct."*

Example: It's "conduct" to hand out handbills, or to form a crowd that marches down the street as part of a political demonstration. But since both of these activities have a major expressive component, the state cannot restrict the conduct unless its satisfies the three-part test described above, i.e., the restriction is content neutral, it's narrowly tailored to achieve a significant governmental interest, and it leaves open alternative channels.

3. **"Facial" vs. "as applied":**   A "time, place and manner" regulation, like any other regulation impinging upon First Amendment rights, may be attacked as being either "facially" invalid or invalid "as applied." Thus even a time, place and manner restriction that has been very carefully worded to as to satisfy all three requirements listed above may become unconstitutional *as applied to a particular plaintiff*.

Example: A City ordinance provides that any parade or demonstration participated in by more than five people shall be held only after the purchase of a permit, which shall be issued by the City Manager for free to any applicant upon two days notice. The City Manager normally issues such permits without inquiring into the nature of the demonstration planned by the applicant. P, who is known locally as an agitator who opposes the current city government, applies for a permit. The City Manager denies the permit, saying, "I don't like the rabble rousing you've been doing."

Even though the ordinance on its face is probably a valid time, place and manner restriction, the application of the ordinance to P's own permit request violates P's First Amendment rights, because that application is not being carried out in a content-neutral manner.

B. Licensing: Be especially skeptical of governmental attempts to require a *license* or *permit* before expressive conduct takes place.

1. **Content-neutral:** Obviously, any permit requirement must be applied in a ***content-neutral*** way. (*Example:* Local officials give permits for speeches made for purposes of raising money for non-controversial charities, but decline to give permits for demonstrations to protest the racism of local officials. The requirement of content neutrality in the licensing scheme is not being satisfied, and the scheme will be automatically struck down.)

2. **No excess discretion:** Also, the licensing scheme must set forth the grounds for denying a permit ***narrowly*** and ***specifically***, so that the discretion of local officials will be curtailed. (*Example*: A municipal ordinance cannot require a permit for every newspaper vending machine where the permit is to be granted on "terms and conditions deemed necessary by the mayor" — the grounds for denying a permit must be set forth much more specifically, to curb the official's discretion. [*Lakewood v. Plain Dealer Publ. Co.*])

3. **Narrow means-end tailoring:** Finally, the permit ***mechanism*** must be ***closely tailored*** to the ***objective*** that the government is trying to achieve.

4. **Reasonable means of maintaining order:** But if these three requirements — content-neutral application, limited administrative discretion and close means-end fit — are satisfied, the permit requirement will be ***upheld*** if it is a ***reasonable means of ensuring that public order is maintained.***

   Example: A requirement that a permit be obtained before a large group of people may march would probably be upheld as a reasonable way of maintaining order, if the requirement is applied in a content-neutral way and is drafted so as to apply without exception to *all* large marches.

5. **Right to ignore requirement:** Assuming that a permit requirement is unconstitutional, must the speaker apply, be rejected, and then sue? Or may he simply speak without the permit, and then raise the unconstitutionality as a defense to a criminal charge for violating the permit requirement? The answer depends on whether the permit is unconstitutional on its face or merely as applied.

   a. **Facially invalid:** If the permit requirement is unconstitutional ***on its face***, the speaker is ***not*** required to apply for a permit. He may decline to apply, speak, and then defend (and avoid conviction) on the grounds of the permit requirement's unconstitutionality.

   b. **As applied:** But where the permit requirement is not facially invalid, but only unconstitutional ***as applied to the speaker***, the speaker generally does ***not*** have the right to ignore the requirement — he must apply for the permit and then seek prompt judicial review, rather than speaking and raising the unconstitutionality-as-applied as a defense. (However, an exception to this rule exists where the applicant shows that *sufficiently prompt judicial review* of the denial was *not available*.)

C. **Right to be left alone:** People have no strong *right to be left alone*, and the government therefore can't regulate broadly to protect that right. As a general rule, it's *up to the unwilling listener* (or viewer) *to avoid the undesired expression.*

> **Example:** A city can't make it a misdemeanor to walk up and down the street handing advertising brochures to people without the recipient's express consent. (It's up to the recipient to decline the handbill.)

1. **Captive audience:** But if the audience is *"captive"* (unable to avert their eyes and ears), this makes it *more likely* that a fair degree of content-neutral regulation *will be allowed*. (However, the fact that the audience is captive is just one factor in measuring the strength of the state interest in regulating.)

> **Example:** A state may make it a crime to approach close to a woman who is entering an abortion clinic, if the approacher's purpose is to orally "counsel or educate" the woman and the woman does not consent to the approach. [*Hill v. Colorado*]

D. **Canvassing:** A speaker's right to *canvass*, that is, to go around ringing doorbells or giving out handbills, receives substantial protection.

1. **Homeowner can say "no":** The individual listener (e.g., the homeowner), is always free to say, "No, I don't want to speak to you about becoming (say), a Jehovah's Witness." The city can then make it a crime for the speaker to persist.

2. **City can't give blanket prohibition:** But the *government* cannot say "No" *in advance* on behalf of its homeowners or other listeners.

> **Example:** A city passes an ordinance providing that "All doorbell ringing for the purpose of handing out handbills is hereby forbidden." *Held*, such an ordinance violates the First Amendment, even if (as the city claims) it is a content-neutral ordinance designed to protect unwilling listeners, such as those who work nights and sleep days. The most the city can do is to provide that once the individual homeowner makes it clear he doesn't want to be spoken to, the speaker must honor that request. [*Martin v. Struthers*]

3. **Time, place and manner:** But the authorities may impose "time, place & manner" limits on canvassing, if these limits: (1) are content-neutral; (2) serve a significant governmental interest; and (3) leave open adequate other channels for communication. (*Example:* A town might prohibit canvassing after 6:00 PM, if its policy is truly content-neutral (e.g., it wasn't enacted for the purpose of silencing Jehovah's Witnesses), is enacted to protect homeowners' night-time tranquility, and allows solicitation to take place at other times.)

E. **Fighting words:** One of our other "unprotected categories" consists of *"fighting words."* "Fighting words" are words which are likely to make the person to whom they are addressed commit an *act of violence*, probably against the speaker. Expression that falls within the "fighting words" category can be flatly banned or punished by the state. [*Chaplinsky v. New Hampshire*]

Example: D picks out one member of his audience and calls him a liar, racist and crook. D can be arrested for this speech, because these are words which might well provoke a reasonable person to whom they are addressed into physically attacking D.

1. **Limits:** But the "fighting words" doctrine is tightly limited:

   a. **Anger not enough:** It's not enough that the speaker has made the crowd angry; they must be so angry that they are *likely to fight*.

   b. **Crowd control:** The police must *control* the angry crowd instead of arresting the speaker if they've got the physical ability to do so. (In other words, the police can't grant the hostile crowd a "heckler's veto.")

   c. **Dislike of speaker's identity:** The doctrine doesn't apply where it's the mere *identity* or *lawful acts* of the speaker, rather than his threatening words, that moves the crowd to anger. (*Example*: If D is a black civil rights worker speaking in a small southern town with a history of racial violence, the fact that members of the audience are ready to attack D because they hate all black civil rights activists will not suffice to make D's speech "fighting words" — here the anger is not really coming from the speaker's particular threatening words, but from his identity and his lawful advocacy of change.)

F. **Offensive language:** Language that is *"offensive"* is nonetheless protected by the First Amendment.

   1. **Profanity:** This means that even language that is *profane* may not be banned from public places. (*Example*: D wears a jacket saying "Fuck the Draft" in the L.A. County Courthouse. D cannot be convicted for breaching the peace. The state may not ban language merely because it is "offensive," even if profane. [*Cohen v. Calif.*])

      a. **Sexually-oriented non-obscene language:** This protection of "offensive" material also means that messages or images that are *sexually-oriented* but not obscene are, similarly, protected.

      Example: Congress bans the use of the Internet to display any "indecent" language or images which may be accessed by minors. *Held*, this statute is unconstitutional, because it restricts the First Amendment rights of adults to receive indecent-but-not-obscene material. [*Reno v. ACLU*]

   2. **Racial or religious hatred:** Similarly, this means that messages preaching *racial or religious hatred* are protected (at least if they don't incite imminent violence or come within the "fighting words" doctrine). (*Example*: A member of the American Nazi Party tells a predominantly-Jewish audience, "Jews are the scum of the earth and should be eliminated." D cannot be punished for, or even restricted from, saying these words.)

   3. **Limits:** But offensive language *can* be prohibited or punished if: (1) the audience is a *"captive"* one (e.g., the speech occurs on a city bus or subway); or (2) the language is *"obscene,"* under the formal legal definition of this term (lewd and without socially redeeming value).

G. Regulation of "hate speech": Government efforts to regulate *"hate speech"* — for instance, speech attacking racial minorities, women, homosexuals, or other traditionally disfavored groups — may run afoul of the First Amendment for being content-based.

1. **Four rules:** Here are the general rules about how a state may go about banning hate speech:

   ❑ **General ban:** A ban on speech or conduct intended or likely to incite anger or violence based solely on *particular listed topics or motives* — such as race, color, religion or gender hatred — is *impermissibly content-based.* That's true even if all the speech/conduct banned falls within an *"unprotected"* category such as, here, *"fighting words."* [*R.A.V. v. St. Paul*]

     Example: City bans only those "fighting words" that evoke hatred or conflict based on race, ethnicity or gender (not fighting words based on, say, the listeners' political affiliation). This enactment is content-based, in that it selects speech for proscription based on its content. Therefore, the statute will be strictly scrutinized, and struck down for not being sufficiently narrowly-tailored to achieve the compelling state interest in avoiding dangerous physical conflict. (However, a state could ban *all* fighting words — it just can't select fighting words based only on certain types of hatred.) [*R.A.V.*]

   ❑ **Worst examples:** However, a state *may* impose a content-based ban on *particular instances* of unprotected speech if the ban forbids *only the very worst examples* illustrating *the very reason the particular class of speech is unprotected.*

     Example: The state may choose to criminalize just the very most dangerous "fighting words," just the very most obscene obscene images, etc. [*R.A.V.*]

   ❑ **Penalty-enhancement statutes:** Also, a state may identify particular generally-applicable criminal proscriptions, and may then choose to punish *more severely* those criminal acts that happen to be motivated by hate than those not motivated by hate. This is called the *"penalty enhancement"* approach. [*Wisconsin v. Mitchell*]

     Example: For instance, from within the overall class of acts that constitute arson (all of which are defined as crimes), the state may punish arson more seriously if it's motivated by bias against particular groups.

   ❑ **All intimidating acts:** Finally, a state may select a particular type of expressive act (e.g., cross-burning), and punish *all instances* where that act is done with a purpose of *intimidating or threatening* someone, even though the state doesn't punish other types of intimidating or threatening acts. [*Virginia v. Black*]

     Example: A state may choose to ban all cross-burnings that are done with intent to intimidate another. That's true even if the state chooses not to criminalize other types of expressive activity that are done with intent to intimidate another (e.g., burning that other in effigy).

H. Injunctions against expressive conduct: Where the restriction on expression is in the form of an *injunction* issued by a judge, there is a special standard of review. When a court issues an injunction that serves as a kind of "time, place and manner" restriction, the injunction will be subjected to slightly *more stringent* review than would a generally-applicable statute or regulation with the same substance: the injunction must "*burden no more speech than necessary* to serve a significant governmental interest." [*Madsen v. Women's Health Center, Inc.*]

I. The public forum: Let's turn now to the concept of the *"public forum."*

   1. Rules: Here are the rules concerning when the fact that speech occurs in a public forum makes a difference, and how:

      a. Content-based: If a regulation is *content-based*, it makes no difference whether the expression is or is not in a public forum: strict scrutiny will be given to the regulation, and it will almost never be upheld.

      b. Neutral "time, place and manner": It's where a regulation is *content-neutral* that the existence of a public forum makes a difference; especially regulations on "time, place and manner" are less likely to be upheld where the expression takes place in a public forum.

         i. Non-public forum: When expression takes place in a *non-public forum*, the regulation merely has to be *rationally related* to some *legitimate governmental objective*, as long as equally effective alternative channels for the expression are available.

         ii. Public forum: When the expression takes place in a *public forum*, by contrast, the regulation has to be *narrowly drawn* to achieve a *significant governmental interest* (roughly *intermediate-level* review). It is necessary, but not sufficient, that the government also leaves alternative channels available.

         Example 1 (public forum speech): A city says, "No political campaign messages may be presented in handbills distributed on city streets." Since this rule impairs communications in a public forum (city streets), the city will have to show that its ordinance is necessary to achieve a significant governmental interest, which it probably can't do (anti-littering won't be enough, for instance). The city can't say, "Well, TV or radio ads will let the same message be given" — the existence of alternative channels for the communication is necessary, but is not enough, when the expression takes place in a public forum.

         Example 2 (non-public forum speech): A city says, "No political campaign messages may be displayed on privately-owned billboards, even with the consent of the owner." Here, no public forum is involved. Therefore, as long as adequate alternative channels are available (which they probably are, e.g., radio & TV ads), the city only has to show that its regulation is rationally related to some legit-

imate governmental objective. The city can probably meet this burden (e.g., by pointing to the objective of beautifying the city).

2. **What are public forums:** What places, then, are public forums?

   a. **"True" or "traditional" public forums:** First, there are *"true"* or *"traditional"* public forums. These are areas that are public forums by custom and tradition, not by virtue of any particular government policy. The classic examples are: (1) *streets;* (2) *sidewalks*; and (3) *parks*.

   b. **"Designated" public forums:** There's a second type of public forum: places that the government has *decided to open up* to a broad range of expressive conduct.

   Some examples:

   ❑ places where *government meetings* take place that the government has decided to open to the public at large (e.g., a school board meeting held in a school auditorium);

   ❑ places that government has decided may be *used by a broad range of people* or groups (e.g., *school classrooms after hours*, under a policy that lets pretty much any group use them, or a municipal theater that any group may rent).

   These are called *"designated"* public forums.

      i. **Same rules:** The *same rules* apply to designated public forums as apply to true public forums, except that government can *change its mind* and remove the designation (in which case the place becomes a non-public forum that can be subjected to much broader viewpoint-neutral regulation, as described below).

   c. **Non-public forums:** Still other public places are not at all associated with expression traditionally, so they can be treated as *non-public forums* (also sometimes called "*limited public forums*").

      i. **Illustrations of non-public-forums:** Here are some illustrations of facilities that, even though they are owned by the government, are not public forums: *airport terminals*, *jails*, *military bases*, the insides of *courthouses*, and *governmental workplaces*.

      ii. **Rules for non-public forums:** In a non-public forum, the government regulation just has to be:

      [1] *reasonable* in light of the *purpose served* by the forum; and

      [2] *viewpoint neutral*.

      [*Int'l Soc. for Krishna Consciousness, Inc. v. Lee*]

      iii. **Reasonableness:** The above requirement of *"reasonableness"* has relatively little bite here, as in the due process and equal protection areas. Government may limit speech in the non-public forum even if *less restrictive alternatives are readily available*, and even if the restriction chosen is not the *"most reasonable."*

(1) **All expression banned:**   Often, even a regulation that completely **bans** expression in a particular non-public forum will be found to satisfy this "mere-rationality" test. Or, the government can choose entirely to forbid discussion of **certain subjects** (but **can't** forbid just certain **viewpoints**).

iv. **Viewpoint neutrality:** But the requirement of **viewpoint neutrality** has a real impact in these non-public-forum cases. The government can restrict speech across the board in these forums, but it can't restrict speech by **preferring some messages or perspectives over others.**

(1) **Can't bar religious viewpoint:** For instance, the requirement of viewpoint-neutrality for non-public forums means that when a school district allows after-hours use of **school facilities** by various (even though not all) community groups, **religious groups** must be given **equal access**.

Example: A school district allows an elementary school to be used after hours by any community group that wishes to put on a program about current affairs. However, the district says that "programs of primarily religious content" are excluded. The Good Christians Club wants to hold a discussion of how practicing Christians should view recent events in the Middle East, to be followed by a prayer for peace in that region.

Held, for the Club. The district's program is a non-public forum (or as the Court calls it, a "limited public forum"). Since the program proposed by the Club concerns the appropriate topic (current affairs), the school district cannot exclude it on the grounds of its religious orientation, because that would be illegal viewpoint-discrimination. [Cf. *Good News Club v. Milford Central School*]

J. **Access to private property:**   In general, a speaker does not have any First Amendment right of **access** to another person's **private property** to deliver his message.

1. **Shopping centers:** Most significantly, a person does not have a First Amendment right to speak in **shopping centers**. [*Hudgens v. NLRB*]

Example: State trespass laws may be used to prevent a person from conducting an anti-war demonstration or a religious proselytizing campaign at her local privately-owned shopping center.

IV. REGULATION OF SYMBOLIC EXPRESSION

A. **Symbolic expression:**   Let's consider *"symbolic expression,"* i.e., expression that consists solely of *non-verbal* actions.

1. **Standard:** We use essentially the same rules to analyze restrictions on symbolic expression as we do for restrictions that apply to verbal speech, or to verbal speech coupled with conduct. Thus: (1) any attempt by government to

restrict symbolic expression because of the ***content*** of the message will be strictly scrutinized and almost certainly struck down; (2) any restriction on the ***time, place or manner*** of symbolic expression will have to be narrowly tailored to a significant governmental objective and will have to leave open alternative channels.

Example: The Ds (high school students) wear armbands to school, in the face of a school policy forbidding students from wearing such armbands. Because school officials were motivated by a desire to suppress particular messages — anti-war messages — the ban must be strictly scrutinized, and is struck down. [*Tinker v. Des Moines Schl. Dist.*]

2. **Flag desecration:**   The most interesting example of government regulation of symbolic expression is ***flag desecration*** statutes. The main thing to remember is that if a statute bans flag desecration or mutilation, and either on the statute's face or as it is applied, the statute is directed only at particular ***messages***, it will be invalid. (*Examples:* Both the Texas and federal flag burning statutes have been struck down by the Supreme Court. In the case of the federal statute, the Court concluded that Congress was trying to preserve the flag as a "symbol of national unity." The statute was therefore content-based, so the Court struck it down. [*U.S. v. Eichman*])

V. DEFAMATION, INTENTIONAL INFLICTION OF EMOTIONAL DISTRESS, AND THE BANNING OF "FALSE SPEECH"

A. **Defamation:**   The First Amendment places limits on the extent to which a plaintiff may recover tort damages for ***defamation.***

1. ***New York Times v. Sullivan test:***   Most importantly, under the rule of ***New York Times v. Sullivan***, 376 U.S. 254 (1964), where P is a ***public official***, he may only win a defamation suit against D for a statement relating to P's official conduct if P can prove that D's statement was made either "with ***knowledge*** that it was false" or with ***"reckless disregard"*** of whether it was true or false. These two mental states are usually collectively referred to as the ***"actual malice"*** requirement.

    Example: The *New York Times* runs an ad saying that P — the Montgomery, Alabama police commissioner — has terrorized Dr. Martin Luther King by repeatedly arresting him. Even if these statements are false, P cannot recover for libel unless he can show that the *Times* knew its statements were false or acted with reckless disregard of whether the statements were true or false. [*N.Y. Times v. Sullivan, supra*]

2. **Public figures:**   This rule of *Times v. Sullivan* — that P can only recover for defamation if he shows intentional falsity or recklessness about truth — applies not only to public "officials" but also to public ***"figures."*** Thus a well known college football coach, and a prominent retired Army general, were public figures who had to show that the defendant acted with actual malice. [*Assoc. Press v. Walker*]

    a. **Partial public figure:** Someone who voluntarily *injects himself* into a public controversy will be a public figure for *just that controversy* — thus an anti-abortion activist might be a public figure for any news story concerning abortion, but not for stories about, say, his private life unrelated to abortion.

    b. **Involuntary public figure:** Also, some people may be *"involuntary"* public figures. (*Example:* A *criminal defendant* is an involuntary public figure, so he cannot sue or recover for a news report about his crime or trial unless he shows actual malice.)

3. **Private figure:** If the plaintiff is a *"private"* (rather than "public") figure, he does *not* have to meet the *New York Times v. Sullivan* "actual malice" rule. [*Gertz v. Robert Welch, Inc.*] On the other hand, the First Amendment requires that he show at least *negligence* by the defendant — the states may not impose strict liability for defamation, even for a private-figure plaintiff. *Id.*

    a. **No punitive damages:** Also, a private-figure plaintiff who shows only negligence cannot recover *punitive* damages — he must show actual malice to get punitive damages. *Id.*

4. **Falsity:** The First Amendment also probably requires that the defamation plaintiff (whether or not she is a public figure) show that the statement was *false*.

B. **Intentional infliction of emotional distress:** The *Times v. Sullivan* rule applies to actions for intentional infliction of *emotional distress* as well as ones for defamation. Thus a public-figure plaintiff cannot recover for any intentional infliction of emotional distress unless he shows that the defendant acted with actual malice.

    Example: *Hustler* Magazine satirizes religious leader Jerry Falwell as a drunken hypocrite who has sex with his mother. *Held*, Falwell cannot recover for intentional infliction of emotional distress unless he shows that *Hustler* made a false statement with knowledge of falsity or with reckless disregard of falsity. [*Hustler Magazine v. Falwell*]

C. **Forbidding other types of false speech:** Defamation necessarily involves speech that is false. And as we've seen, in most instances government may ban (or allow damages for) defamatory speech, in part because the falsity of the speech makes it less valuable. This raises the question, can government *categorically forbid factually-false statements*, even ones that are *not* defamatory? Could a state, for instance, *make it a crime to "tell a lie"?*

1. **Can't forbid all false speech:** The brief answer is *"no."* Except for a few narrow *pre-defined sub-categories* (defamation, fraud, and perjury, for instance), as to which there is a long-standing consensus that the type of false speech in question is especially likely to cause severe harm, government *may not forbid statements merely on the grounds that they are factually false.*

    a. **Lying about military honors:** For instance, the Court has held that Congress' decision to make it a crime for a person to falsely state he has won certain *military medals* violates the First Amendment.

Example: In the federal Stolen Valor Act of 2005, Congress makes it a crime for any person to falsely state, even orally, that he has been awarded any Armed Forces decoration or medal. Alvarez falsely claims, in a public meeting, that he was awarded the Congressional Medal of Honor 20 years before. Alvarez does not appear to be seeking any tangible benefit from the lie; he just wants respect.

Held (by a 6-3 vote), the Act violates the First Amendment. A four-Justice plurality applies *strict scrutiny* to the statute, and concludes that the statute cannot survive that scrutiny. That's because criminalizing such lies is not a "necessary" method of achieving the compelling objective of preventing the debasement of military honors — for instance, an online database could list all medal winners, unmasking those who lie. Two more Justices apply *"intermediate scrutiny"*; but they too agree that the statute cannot survive, because the government has not shown that a "more finely tailored statute" could not adequately address the harms. (For instance, the statute might be rewritten to require that the false statement "caused specific harm" or was "material.") [*U.S. v. Alvarez* (2012)]

VI. OBSCENITY

A. **Obscenity:** Another of our "unprotected categories" is **obscenity**. Expression that is obscene is simply **unprotected** by the First Amendment, so the states can ban it, punish it, or do whatever else they want without worrying about the First Amendment.

B. **Three-part test:** For a work to be "obscene," all three parts of the following test must be met:

1. **Prurient interest:** First, the average person, applying today's community standards, must find that the work as a whole appeals to the ***"prurient"*** interest;

2. **Sexual conduct:** Second, the work must depict or describe in a "patently offensive way" particular types of ***sexual conduct*** defined by state law; and

3. **Lacks value:** Finally, the work taken as a whole, must lack "serious literary, artistic, political or scientific value."

[*Miller v. Calif.*]

C. **Significance:** So something will not be "obscene" unless it depicts or describes ***"hard core sex."*** (For instance, mere ***nudity***, by itself, is not obscene.)

D. **Materials addressed to minors:** It will be much easier for the state to keep erotic materials out of the hands of ***minors***. Probably even minors have some First Amendment interest in receiving sexually explicit materials, but this is typically ***outweighed*** by the state's compelling interest in protecting minors against such material. So the distribution of non-obscene but sexually explicit materials may basically be forbidden to minors (provided that the regulations do not substantially impair the access of adults to these materials).

1. **Adult's rights impaired:** But if a measure aimed at minors *does* substantially impair the access of adults to material that's "indecent" but not obscene, the measure will be struck down. (*Example:* If Congress bans all "indecent" material on the Internet (as it has done), out of a fear that the material will be seen by minors, there's a good chance the measure will be found to violate the First Amendment rights of adults.)

E. **"Pandering":** The issue of whether the material appeals primarily to prurient interests may be influenced by the manner in which the material is *advertised* — if the publisher or distributor plays up the prurient nature of the materials in the advertising, this will make it more likely that the materials will be found to appeal mostly to prurient interests and thus to be obscene. The advertisement itself, and expert testimony about the likely effect of the advertising, may be admitted into evidence to aid the determination on obscenity. (The marketing of materials by emphasizing their sexually provocative nature is often called *"pandering."*)

F. **Private possession by adults:** The mere *private possession* of obscene material by an adult may *not* be made criminal. [*Stanley v. Georgia*]

> **Example:** While police are lawfully arresting D at his house on a robbery charge, they spot obscene magazines on his shelf. D may not be criminally charged with possession of pornography, because one has both a First Amendment right and a privacy right to see or read what one wants in the privacy of one's own home.

1. **Child pornography:** However, the states *may* criminalize even private possession of *child pornography.* [*Osborne v. Ohio*]

2. **No right to supply to consenting adults:** Also, the state may punish a person who *supplies* pornography even to consenting adults. In other words, there is a right to *have* pornography for one's own home use, but not a right to supply it to others for their home use.

VII. COMMERCIAL SPEECH

A. **Commercial speech generally:** Speech that is *"commercial"* — that is, speech advertising a product or proposing some commercial transaction — gets First Amendment protection. But this protection is in some ways *more limited* than the protection given to non-commercial (e.g., political) speech.

1. **Truthful speech:** *Truthful* commercial speech gets a pretty fair degree of First Amendment protection. The government may restrict truthful commercial speech only if the regulation meets the three following requirements:

   [1] it *directly advances* ...

   [2] a *substantial governmental interest* ...

   [3] in a way that is *"no more extensive than necessary"* to achieve the gov-

ernment's objective.

[*Central Hudson Gas v. Public Serv. Comm.*]

So basically, the court will apply ***mid-level review*** to government restrictions based on the content of commercial speech (whereas it applies ***strict scrutiny*** to content-based restrictions on non-commercial speech).

Example: Virginia forbids a pharmacist from advertising his prices for prescription drugs. Virginia must show that it is pursuing a "substantial" governmental interest, and that materially-less-restrictive alternatives are not available. Here, the state's desire to prevent price-cutting that will lead to shoddy service is not strong enough to qualify as "substantial," so the measure must be struck down on First Amendment grounds. [*Virginia Pharmacy Board v. Virginia Consumer Council*]

a. "Consume less" objective will fail: The three-part mid-level review described above is often used to strike down advertising regulations that are premised on the government's argument that if advertising of the legal-but-harmful product is limited, people will ***consume less*** of the item. The limitation will usually flunk requirement [3] above (that the limitations be ***"no more extensive than necessary"*** to achieve the government's objectives), because government will almost always be free to ***increase taxes*** on the item, to ***regulate how and where it can be sold***, or to conduct an ***educational campaign*** showing its dangers — and any of these methods would likely be less restrictive than an advertising ban, while still reducing consumption of the harmful product.

   Example: Rhode Island prohibits all advertising of liquor prices, except for price tags displayed with the merchandise and not visible from the street. The state defends the prohibition on the grounds that forbidding price advertising will lower liquor consumption, in accordance with the state's goal of "temperance."

   Held, the prohibition violates the First Amendment, because it fails the 3-part *Central Hudson Gas* test. For instance, that test requires that a regulation of commercial speech be "no more extensive than necessary." The ban here fails this requirement because the state could have limited alcohol consumption by less restrictive means, such as increased taxation, caps on per capita purchases, or educational campaigns. [*44 Liquormart v. Rhode Island*]

b. Protect minors: Similarly, if the government's principal justification for the regulation is to prevent ***minors*** from gaining access to, or being enticed by, the "vice" product, government will have to ***tailor its methods very tightly*** so that there is no undue interference with the rights of ***adults*** to obtain or learn about the product.

   Example: Massachusetts dramatically restricts the advertising of smokeless tobacco and cigars (e.g., by forbidding billboards). The state defends on the grounds that this limit will protect minors from being attracted to the product.

Held, the regulations violate the free-speech rights of the tobacco industry and its adult customers. "No matter how laudable the state's interest in preventing minors' access to tobacco products, the state may not regulate advertising in a way that interferes materially with the legitimate rights of the tobacco industry, and its ***adult customers***, to exchange truthful information." [*Lorillard Tobacco Co. v. Reilly*]

2. **False, deceptive or illegal:** But the principles discussed above assume that the commercial speech — even if it concerns a harmful product — is *truthful. False or deceptive* commercial speech may be *forbidden* by the government.

   a. **Integral to criminal conduct:** This stems from the more general rule that speech that is "***integral to criminal conduct***" is not protected at all (i.e., that such speech constitutes an "unprotected category").

      i. **Proposing an illegal transaction:** Similarly, commercial speech that *proposes an illegal transaction* (e.g., a help-wanted ad that indicates a preference for white males, in violation of anti-discrimination laws) doesn't receive any First Amendment protection.

      ii. **Conspiracy:** And commercially-oriented speech that is part of a ***conspiracy*** to commit a crime ("We hereby agree to rob the First National Bank") may likewise be punished, because such speech is unprotected.

B. **Lawyers:** The qualified First Amendment protection given to commercial speech means that ***lawyers*** have a limited right to advertise. Thus a state may not ban all advertising by lawyers or even ban advertising directed to a particular problem. See, e.g., *Bates v. State Bar of Ariz.* (Thus a lawyer can advertise, "If you've been injured by a Dalkon shield, I may be able to help you.")

   1. **In-person solicitation:** On the other hand, the states may ban certain types of ***in-person solicitation*** by lawyers seeking clients (e.g., solicitation of accident victims in person by tort lawyers who want to obtain a contingent-fee agreement [*Ohralik v. Ohio St. Bar Ass'n.*]).

   2. **Direct mail:** Similarly, the states may ban lawyers from ***direct-mail*** solicitation of accident victims, at least for a 30-day period following the accident. [*Florida Bar v. Went For It*]

VIII. REGULATION IN THE CONTEXT OF POLITICAL CAMPAIGNS

A. **Campaign spending, generally:** The state or federal governments can regulate ***campaign spending*** to some extent, but other campaign regulations would violate the First Amendment.

B. **Contributions:** *Contributions* made by individuals or groups to candidates, political parties, or Political Action Committees may be limited.

Example 1: Congress may constitutionally prevent anyone from contributing more than $1,000 to a candidate for federal office, in order to curb actual or apparent corruption. [*Buckley v. Valeo*]

Example 2: Congress may prevent national political parties from receiving more than $2,000 from any donor, thus outlawing unregulated "soft money" donations. That's because such donations give the appearance that large donors get special access to office-holders, a type of corruption that Congress may constitutionally combat. [*McConnell v. F.E.C.*]

1. **Lower limit:** But contribution limits may not be made *so low* that they substantially interfere with candidates' and parties' ability to *run a competitive election campaign.*

    Example: Vermont prevents any individual or political party from contributing more than $400 to the campaign of any candidate for governor during any two-year period. *Held*, this limit is so low that it violates the free speech and free association rights of individuals and parties (though no majority of the Court can agree on the precise test for "how low is too low"). *Randall v. Sorrell.*

C. **Expenditures:** But a person or entity's *independent* campaign-related *expenditures* (whether he's a candidate or not) may *not* be limited at all.

    Example 1: A candidate may not be prevented from spending as much of his own money on getting elected as he wishes. [*Buckley v. Valeo; Randall v. Sorrell*]

    Example 2: Similarly, private citizen X may spend as much money to try to get Y elected as he wishes, as long as X spends the money in a truly independent manner rather than contributing it to Y or coordinating with Y on how it should be spent. [*Buckley v. Valeo*]

1. **Corporations' expenditures:** *Corporations* (and probably *unions*) can spend *limitless sums* from their general treasuries to advocate or advertise for or against particular candidates, as long as the spending is *"independent,"* i.e., not coordinated with the candidate.

    a. **Rationale:** That's because the First Amendment does not permit corporations to be *treated less favorably than individuals,* and individuals are entitled, under *Buckley, supra,* to make unlimited independent expenditures to get others elected. [*Citizens United v. FEC*]

        Example: Congress forbids any corporation from using its general funds to take out a broadcast advertisement naming a specific candidate for federal office, if the ad runs shortly before a general or primary election. (Individuals are not barred from paying for or running such ads.) The ban applies even if the corporation acts completely independently of the candidate. The consequence of the ban is that if a corporation wants to advertise for or against a named candidate, the corporation has to do so by setting up a highly-regulated Political Action Committee (PAC), which will then be bound by strict contribution and spending limits.

Held, the statute violates the First Amendment rights of corporations. Banning corporations from making independent expenditures to broadcast political messages amounts to censorship. "The Government may not suppress political speech on the basis of the speaker's corporate identity." [*Citizens United v. FEC, supra.*]

IX. SOME SPECIAL CONTEXTS

A. **Public school students:** Students in **public schools** have a limited right of free speech. The student's right to speak freely has to be **balanced** against the administration's right to carry out its educational mission and to maintain discipline.

   1. **Allowable regulation:** Thus a school may ban profanity. It may also ban the school newspaper from running stories that would disturb the school's **educational mission** (e.g., stories about sex and birth control that the principal reasonably believes are inappropriate for younger students at the school). [*Hazelwood Sch. Dist. v. Kuhlmeier*]

      a. **Advocacy of illegal drug use:** Also, schools may ban the **advocacy of illegal drug use,** even where the advocacy does not pose an immediate threat to discipline or the school's educational mission. [*Morse v. Frederick*]

   2. **Non-allowable regulation:** But school officials may **not** suppress students' speech merely because they disagree with that speech on ideological or political grounds. (*Example:* School officials may not ban the wearing of anti-war armbands [*Tinker v. Des Moines Schl Dist.*].)

B. **Group activity:** The rights of a **group** to engage in **joint expressive activity** get special First Amendment protection, generally called the **"freedom of association."** (*Example*: Groups have the right to get together to bring law suits, or to conduct non-violent economic boycotts. Therefore, they cannot be prevented from doing these things by state rules against fomenting litigation or conducting boycotts. [*NAACP v. Button*])

C. **Government as speaker or as funder of speech:** So far, we've looked only at the role of government as the regulator of speech by non-government actors. But sometimes, **government itself wishes to speak**. And sometimes, government wishes to give **financial support** to certain speech by others. In the former situation, government has a broad right to act in a non-viewpoint-neutral way; in the latter situation, the rules are more complex.

   1. **Government as speaker:** When government wishes to **be a speaker itself**, it is pretty clear that government may **say essentially what it wants**, and is not subject to any real rule of viewpoint neutrality.

      Example: Government can pay for ads attacking smoking as a health hazard, without having to pay for opponents' ads saying that the dangers of smoking are overrated.

   2. **Government as funder of third-party speech:** If government **funds speech by third parties**, may government be non-viewpoint-neutral, by fund-

ing only those viewpoints of which it approves? The answer is heavily dependent on the *details* of the government funding.

a.   **Use of agents to deliver government's message:** Government *may* use content-based criteria when government is selecting third parties who will serve as the *government's agents* in *spreading the government's own message*.

   Example: The federal government funds certain family-planning "projects" (essentially, clinics) that are operated by private parties. The program's regulations say that while a person (e.g., a doctor) is working in such a clinic, that person may not discuss the possibility of an abortion with a pregnant clinic patient.

   Held, this limitation of private speech does not violate the First Amendment. When the government appropriates public funds to promote a particular policy of its own, it is *entitled to say what it wishes*. [*Rust v. Sullivan* (as summarized later in *Rosenberger v. Rector & Visitors of the Univ. of Va.*)]

b.   **No forbidding of some topics or messages for disfavor:**   On the other hand, if government decides to *fund* (or *allow* on government property) *some expressions of private citizens' own views*, government must generally *behave not only in a content-neutral but also a subject-neutral way.* That is, government cannot (1) decide that it's going to subsidize (or allow on public property) private messages on various topics, but then (2) decline to fund (or decide to exclude from the discussion) a few *disfavored topics or messages*.

   i.   **Religion:** For example, government cannot decide to fund a broad range of expressive activities and then exclude expressive activities that are *mainly religious.*

      Example: The University of Virginia (a public university) funds certain student publications, by paying for their printing costs. The University disqualifies from this funding any primarily-religious publication.

      Held, this exclusion violates the free speech rights of student religious organizations. If the University were disseminating only its own messages, it would not have to fund opposing viewpoints. But once it chooses to fund some *third-party viewpoints* (i.e., some student-run publications), it may not choose which ones to fund based on the viewpoint of the speaker. [*Rosenberger v. Rector & Visitors of the Univ. of Va.*]

c.   **Unconstitutional conditions:**   Similarly, where government decides to award public funding for a privately-run program, the doctrine of *"unconstitutional conditions"* may prevent government from conditioning the funding on the recipient's agreement to (i) give up its right to speak on certain topics, or (ii) deliver certain messages with which recipient doesn't agree. See our discussion of this doctrine *infra*, p. 158.

3. **Blurry line:** The ***boundary line*** between government speech (where government does not have to be content-netural) and ***government-facilitated private*** speech (where government *does* have to be content neutral) can sometimes be blurry.

   a. **Acceptance of privately-donated monument:** The need to draw the boundary line can arise when government accepts and permanently displays a ***privately-donated monument.*** Here, the Court has held that government is probably ***acting as a speaker***, in which case it is free to ***reject other similar donations*** of property bearing messages with which government does not agree. [*Pleasant Grove City v. Summum*]

   Example: A city has previously permanently placed in a local park a Ten Commandments monument donated by a private group. The Ps (members of the obscure Summum religion) now ask the city to accept and display in the same park a monument showing the "Seven Aphorisms," which the Ps believe were brought down from Mt. Sinai by Moses before he brought down the Ten Commandments. The Ps argue that when the city accepted and displayed the Ten Commandments and other privately-donated monuments, the effect was to turn the park into a public forum, thereby requiring the city to accept other kinds of monuments and displays on a content-neutral basis.

   Held: for the city. The monument display was government speech, which therefore does not have to be content-neutral. Although a park is a traditional public forum for *speeches* and other *transitory expressive acts*, the placement of a *permanent monument* in a public park will be viewed as a form of government speech, which is therefore not subject to strict scrutiny under the Free Speech Clause. [*Pleasant Grove City v. Summum, supra*]

X. FREEDOM OF ASSOCIATION, AND DENIAL OF PUBLIC BENEFITS OR JOBS

A. **Freedom of association generally:** First Amendment case law recognizes the concept of ***"freedom of association."*** In general, the idea is that if an individual has a First Amendment right to engage in a particular expressive activity, then a ***group*** has a "freedom of association" right to engage in that same activity as a group.

   1. **Right not to associate:** Individuals and groups also have a well-protected ***"right not to associate."*** Thus any government attempt to make an individual give ***financial support*** to a cause she dislikes, or to make a group ***take members*** whose presence would interfere with the group's expressive activities, will be ***strictly scrutinized***.

   Example 1: Where public school teachers are required to pay union dues, a teacher has a freedom-of-association right not to have the dues used to support ideological causes the teacher dislikes. [*Abood v. Detroit Bd. of Ed.*]

Example 2: The Boy Scouts can't be forced (by a state anti-discrimination law) to accept an openly-gay male as a scoutmaster, because this would significantly interfere with the Scouts' First Amendment-protected message that homosexuality is immoral. [*Boy Scouts of America v. Dale*]

B. Illegal membership: The freedom of association means that ***mere membership in a group or association may not be made illegal.*** Membership in a group may only be made part of an offense if: (1) the group is ***actively engaged in unlawful activity***, or ***incites others*** to ***imminent lawless action***; and (2) the individual ***knows*** of the group's illegal activity, and specifically intends to further the group's illegal goals. (*Example*: Congress cannot make it a crime simply to be a member of the American Communist Party. On the other hand, Congress can make it a crime to be a member of a party that advocates imminent overthrow of the government, if the member knows that the party so advocates and the member intends to help bring about that overthrow.)

C. Denial of public benefit or job: Freedom of expression also prevents the government from ***denying a public benefit or job*** based on a person's association.

    1. Non-illegal activities: If a person's activities with a group could not be made ***illegal***, then those activities may generally not be made the basis for denying the person the government job or benefit.

    Example 1: A state may not refuse to hire a person as a teacher merely because he is a member of the American Communist Party, since the state could not make it illegal to be a member of the ACP.

    Example 2: At a time when Republicans are in power, a state may not refuse to hire Democrats for non-policy-making jobs like police officer or clerk. [*Rutan v. Republican Party of Illinois*]

    2. No right/privilege distinction: There is no constitutional distinction between a *"right"* and a *"privilege."* Even if, say, a particular public benefit or job is defined by the state to be a "privilege," the state may not deny that job or benefit on the basis of the applicant's constitutionally-protected membership in a group or organization.

    3. Loyalty oath: Government may generally not require an applicant to sign a ***loyalty oath***, unless the things that the applicant is promising in the loyalty oath not to do are things which, if he did them, would be grounds for punishing him or denying him the job. (*Example*: You cannot be required to sign a loyalty oath that you are not a member of the Communist Party in order to get a teaching job. But you can be required to sign an oath that you will not advocate the forcible overthrow of our government.)

    4. Compulsory disclosure: Similarly, the government may not force you to ***disclose*** your membership activities (or require a group to disclose who its members are), unless it could make that membership illegal. (*Example*: The state cannot require the Communist Party to furnish a list of its members.)

    5. Some exceptions: There are some ***exceptions*** to the general rule that associational activities that couldn't be outlawed directly also can't be made the basis for public hiring or benefits decisions. In general, these exceptions are for conduct which, although it includes protected expression, directly (and negatively) relates to ***performance of the job***.

a. **Partisan political activities:** For instance, civil servants can constitutionally be forced to choose between their jobs and engaging in ***partisan political activities***, since there's a very strong government interest in making sure that civil servants can do their jobs without being coerced into campaigning for or contributing to their elected bosses. [*CSC v. Letter Carriers*]

b. **Patronage hirings:** Similarly, some public jobs may be awarded as ***patronage appointments***, ones the performance of which is ***reasonably related to a person's politics***.

   Example: Even though I have a First Amendment right to be a Democrat, the Republican Congressman representing my district doesn't violate my rights when, on the basis of my political beliefs, he declines to hire me as, say, a speech writer, a high advisor, or some other post with a ***heavy political content***.

   On the other hand, if I'm a Democrat, and there's a Republican governor in power, he can't block me from getting a government job as a clerk or secretary or police officer — the old fashioned "patronage" system whereby all public jobs could be restricted to supporters of the party in power has been outlawed as a violation of freedom of association, and only jobs with a heavy political content, like speech writer, say, or Chief of Staff, can be based on party membership.

c. **Speech critical of superiors or inappropriate:** An employee gets limited protection for speech or associational activities that are ***critical of superiors***, or that the employer believes are ***inappropriate for the workplace***. Where such speech involves a matter of ***"public concern,"*** the court will ***balance*** the speech rights of the employee and the government's interest as employer in promoting efficiency on the job. [*Connick v. Myers*]

   Example: P, a government clerical worker, hears that John Hinckley has tried to shoot Pres. Reagan, and says, "If they go for him again, I hope they get him." P is fired for the remark. *Held*, for P. This remark was intended as political commentary and was thus on a matter of "public concern," so P could not be fired unless the remark heavily affected P's job performance, which it did not. [*Rankin v. McPherson*]

   i. **Not a matter of public concern:** But where the speech does ***not*** involve a matter of public concern, *Connick* and *Rankin*, *supra*, do ***not*** apply, and the court gives great ***deference*** to the employer's judgment.

   ii. **Must not be part of employee's job function:** Also, even the limited protection given to employee speech on matters of public concern doesn't apply where the speech occurs as ***part of the employee's job functions*** — here, the employee gets no First Amendment protection at all, no matter how important the issue on which the employee is speaking.

Example: P, a supervising lawyer in a District Attorney's Office (D), is called on to investigate whether an affidavit prepared by a deputy sheriff to obtain a search warrant was properly done. P writes a memo to his supervisor concluding that the affidavit was improperly done. The supervisor retaliates against him for what he says in the memo.

Held, for D. "[W]hen public employees make statements *pursuant to their official duties,* the employees are *not speaking as citizens* for First Amendment purposes, and *the Constitution does not insulate their communications from employer discipline."* Here, because P's investigation and the ensuing memorandum were part of his job responsibilities, D had the right to regulate the content and manner of P's speech. [*Garcetti v. Ceballos*]

D. **Unconstitutional conditions:** Suppose that before government gives a particular *benefit* — such as housing, employment, funding for an activity, or a license — government imposes a *condition*. That is, government says that the recipient must, in exchange for the benefit, agree to *waive her freedom of expression* or other constitutional right. The Court *sometimes* invokes the doctrine of *"unconstitutional conditions"* in order to strike down the condition.

1. **Statement of doctrine:** When the doctrine applies, it holds that government *may not grant a benefit on the condition that the beneficiary surrender a constitutional right*, even if the government may *withhold that benefit altogether*. The idea behind the doctrine is that what the government may not do *directly*, it may not do *indirectly* either.

    Example: Suppose that the Republican-controlled legislature of a state passes a statute saying that no one may get or keep a job working for the state — no matter how low-level the position or what the requirements of the position are — unless the person signs a pledge not to criticize any elected Republican official during the employment.

    The Supreme Court would undoubtedly invoke the doctrine of unconstitutional conditions to strike down this statute as a violation of state employees' and applicants' freedom of expression. Government obviously couldn't directly forbid citizens from criticizing politicians, and letting the state condition a government benefit (state employment) on the waiver of this right would amount to letting the state do indirectly what it could not to directly.

2. **Guiding principles:** The Court seems to apply the unconstitutional conditions doctrine somewhat inconsistently. But here are three principles (some of which we've already discussed) that seem to explain the outcome in most of the Court's unconstitutional-condition cases.

    [1] **Government uses agents to deliver government's own speech:** Since government is *permitted* to say pretty much whatever it wants *when the government is itself the speaker,* government is also free to *pay agents* to

deliver the government's message, and to ***condition that payment*** on the agent's willingness to ***waive his otherwise-protected right*** to engage in speech that would contradict or garble the government message the agent is being paid to deliver.

Example: A state government engages (and pays) P, a celebrity, to make public speeches as part of the government's campaign to have the federal constitution amended so as to limit the scope of abortion rights under *Roe v. Wade*. Government *may*, as a condition to engaging P, insist that P agree that during the course of the campaign, P will not publicly state that P is in favor of a woman's right to choose an abortion as presently construed by the Supreme Court.

[2] **Limits on use of government's payments:** Government is also free to set up ***"subsidy programs,"*** under which government funds private groups to help the groups carry out some function. And when government does this, it is free to ***refuse*** to allow ***the subsidy dollars to be used for particular activities opposed by government***, including otherwise-constitutionally-protected activities like ***speaking*** on certain topics, ***performing abortions***, or lobbying legislators.

Example: Congress provides federal grants to help private groups operate family-planning clinics. When a special-purpose "project" is set up to receive such a grant and operate a clinic, the project's founders are required to prohibit the project's employees (while on the job) from advocating for, or counseling about, abortion.

Held, the condition is not an unconstitutional condition, and does not violate the First Amendment rights of the group that runs the project. "[T]he Government is not denying a benefit to anyone, but is instead simply insisting that ***public funds be spent for the purposes*** for which they were authorized." (The way the statute is written, a group that runs the project/clinic and receives the funds for it can continue to engage in abortion advocacy or counseling; the group simply is required to conduct those activities through a program or project that is separate from the project [the clinic] receiving the government funds.) [*Rust v. Sullivan*]

[3] **No "leveraging" by government:** Although government may (as described in [2] above) put conditions on how the government funds will be used inside a government-subsidized privately-run program, government may not impose conditions that "seek to ***leverage funding*** to ***regulate speech outside the contours*** of the [government] ***program itself.***" [*Agency for Int'l Dev. v. Alliance for Open Soc'y Int'l, Inc.* (2013)]

Example: Congress gives large money grants to various nongovernmental organizations that are fighting HIV and AIDS. Congress says that no funds may be given to any group "that does not have a policy explicitly opposing prostitution" (the "Policy Requirement"). The Ps are various non-profits that say the Policy Requirement violates their free speech rights.

Held, for the Ps; the Policy Requirement is an unconstitutional condition. Past cases on unconstitutional conditions have distinguished between conditions on the actual activities that Congress wants to subsidize (these conditions are constitutional) and conditions that "seek to *leverage* funding to *regulate speech outside the contours of the program itself*" (conditions that are unconstitutional). Here, the Policy Requirement falls on the unconstitutional side of the line. "By demanding that funding recipients adopt — as their own — the Government's view on an issue of public concern, the condition ... affects 'protected conduct outside the scope of the federally funded program.'" [*Agency for Int'l Dev., supra*]

XI. SPECIAL PROBLEMS OF THE MEDIA

A. **The media (and its special problems):** Here is a brief review of some special problems related to the *media*:

   1. **Prior restraint:** In general, the government will not be able to obtain a *prior restraint* against broadcasters or publishers. In other words, only in exceptionally rare circumstances may the government obtain an *injunction* against the printing or airing of a story, and the government will almost never be allowed to require that a publisher or broadcaster obtain a *permit* before it runs a story.

      Example: The *New York Times* may not constitutionally be enjoined from publishing part of the Pentagon Papers, even though these government-prepared materials might contain information that is useful to our enemies or that would embarrass the U.S. [*N.Y. Times v. U.S.*]

      a. **Gag order:** This means that a judge may generally not impose a *gag order* on the media ordering it not to disclose a certain fact about a pending trial.

         i. **Participants:** But the judge may usually order the *participants* not to speak to the press. For instance, a state may prevent a lawyer from making any statement which would have a "substantial likelihood of materially prejudicing" a trial or other court proceeding. [*Gentile v. State Bar of Nevada*]

   2. **Subpoenas by government:** The press does not get any special protection from government demands that the press *furnish information* which other citizens would have to furnish. In particular, if a reporter has information that is of interest to a *grand jury*, the reporter may be required by subpoena to disclose that information to the grand jury even though this would cause him to violate a promise of confidentiality to a source. [*Branzburg v. Hayes*] (But the state is always free to enact a "shield law" making such subpoenas illegal under some or all circumstances.)

   3. **Right of access:** The press does not get any general *right of access* to information held by the government.

a. Right to attend trials: However, the media does have a constitutionally protected right to *attend criminal trials*. This right is not absolute — the government can close the media (and the public) out of a trial if it shows that there is an "overriding" government interest being served by a closed trial, and that that interest cannot be served by less restrictive means. [*Richmond Newspapers v. Virginia*]

    i. Showing rarely made: But this showing will rarely be made, so that as a practical matter the press is usually entitled to attend a criminal trial. (*Example:* A state statute automatically bars the press from hearing any trial testimony by a minor who was allegedly the victim of a sex crime. *Held,* the statute unduly interferes with the public's right of access to criminal trials. [*Globe Newspapers v. Sup. Ct.*])

    ii. Other proceedings: Probably the media also has a qualified constitutional right to attend other proceedings, like *civil trials* and *pre-trial proceedings*. [*Gannett Co. v. DePasquale*]

4. Disclosure of confidential or illegally-obtained information: Government may generally *not* prohibit the media from disclosing information that goverment believes ought to be *secret*. If a media member *lawfully* obtains information about a matter of public significance, government may punish disclosure of the information only if government has "a *need* of the *highest order*," which it will rarely be found to have. [*Smith v. Daily Mail*]

Example: A broadcaster may not be held civilly liable for *publishing the name of a rape victim*, if the broadcaster learns the name from reading a publicly-filed indictment. [*Cox Broadcasting v. Cohn*]

a. Where publisher has acted illegally: If the *publisher itself* has *acted illegally* in obtaining the information, then government *may make it a crime* to publish the information, no matter how newsworthy it is. (*Example:* A newspaper reporter breaks into a private home to steal an audiotape, then publishes a transcript of the tape. The newspaper may constitutionally be punished for the publication.)

b. Where private party has acted illegally but publisher has not: On the other hand, the fact that the secret information was originally *obtained illegally* by a person *acting independently* of the eventual publisher is *not* enough to allow publication to be made criminal, at least where the material has significant newsworthiness.

Example: X, a private individual acting alone, intercepts and tapes a cellphone conversation between the Ps (two teachers' union officials) who are discussing their upcoming negotiation with a school board. The interception violates federal wiretapping laws. X anonymously mails the tape to a radio station, which broadcasts it. The Ps sue the station. *Held,* the station may not constitutionally be held liable for damages to the officials, because the station did not participate in the illegality, and the strong First Amendment interest in disseminating this newsworthy material outweighs the admittedly strong interest in safeguarding cellphone conversations. [*Bartnicki v. Vopper*]

CHAPTER 15

FREEDOM OF RELIGION

I. INTRODUCTION

A. Two clauses: There are two quite distinct clauses in the First Amendment pertaining to religion.

    1. Establishment Clause: First, we have the *Establishment* Clause. That clause prohibits any law "respecting an establishment of religion." The main purpose of the Establishment Clause is to prevent government from *endorsing* or *supporting* religion.

    2. Free Exercise: The second clause is the *Free Exercise* Clause. That clause bars any law "prohibiting the free exercise of religion." The main purpose of the Free Exercise Clause is to prevent the government from *outlawing* or seriously *burdening* a person's pursuit of whatever religion (and whatever religious practices) he chooses.

B. Applicable to states: Both the Establishment and the Free Exercise Clauses by their terms only restrict legislative action by *Congress*. However, both clauses have been interpreted to apply also to the *states*, by means of the Fourteenth Amendment's due process clause. Therefore, you don't have to worry whether the government action in question is federal or state — the same standards apply to each.

C. Conflict: Occasionally, the Establishment and Free Exercises Clauses seem to *conflict* on particular facts. That is, a religious group may be asking for some government benefit; if the benefit is given, there may be an Establishment Clause problem. Yet if the benefit is not given, this may be a burdening of religion. When the two clauses seem to conflict, the *Free Exercise* Clause dominates. In other words, if a particular benefit or accommodation to religion is arguably required by the Free Exercise Clause, then when government grants that accommodation or benefit it is not violating the Establishment Clause.

    Example: A public university makes meeting rooms available to all sorts of student groups. If the university allows religious groups to use the room, there might be an Establishment Clause problem. But if it doesn't allow religious groups to use the rooms, while allowing non-religious groups to do so, there might be a Free Exercise Clause problem. Consequently, it will not be an Establishment Clause violation for the university to allow the religious groups to use the rooms.

II. THE ESTABLISHMENT CLAUSE

A. General rule: The overall purpose of the Establishment Clause is to put a *wall between church and state*. In other words, the government must stay out of the business of religion, and religious groups must to some extent stay out of the business of government.

1. **Some examples:** Here are some things that would clearly be forbidden by the Establishment clause:

    a. **Official church:** Congress cannot establish an "official religion of the United States." In fact, Congress probably couldn't even declare that "the American people believe in God," because the Establishment Clause means that government may not prefer or endorse religion over non-religion.

    b. **Go to church:** The government cannot force people to worship. In fact, the state can't even intentionally ***encourage*** people to worship — for example, it cannot decide that it wants to promote church attendance, and then give people a special tax deduction that applies to church donations but not to other charitable donations. (But it could, as Congress does, give a *general* tax deduction for charitable contributions, and let contributions to churches be eligible. This would be allowable because the government is treating religion the same as non-religion, not preferring religion over non-religion.)

    c. **Preference of one religion over another:** The government cannot intentionally ***prefer one religion over another religion.*** For instance, a state may not decide that since Christians are in the majority, it will allow tax deductions for contribution to Christian churches but not for contributions made, say, to synagogues.

    d. **Participate:** Government may not actively ***participate*** in religious affairs, or allow religious organizations to have a special participation in government affairs. For instance, Congress probably could not constitutionally use public officials and public polling places to run an election to determine the next head of the American Presbyterian Church — this would be an undue governmental entanglement in religious affairs.

B. **Three-part test:** Government action that has some relationship to religion will violate the Establishment Clause unless it satisfies ***all three parts*** of the following test (known as the "*Lemon*" test, from *Lemon v. Kurtzman*):

    1. **Purpose:** First, the government action must have a ***secular legislative purpose***. In other words, there must be some governmental purpose that has nothing to do with religion. (If there is both a religious and a non-religious purpose, then this prong is probably satisfied.)

        Example: Alabama passes a statute saying, "Every public school student shall have the opportunity to engage in silent prayer or meditation for at least two minutes at the start of every school day." If there is evidence that the legislature was *motivated* solely by a desire to help students pray, then the statute will be struck down (and in fact such an Alabama statute was struck down). [*Wallace v. Jaffree*]. This is true even if many of the students who take advantage of the statute engage in non-religious meditation — if the sole purpose was to aid religion, that's enough to make the government action void.

2. **Effect:** Second, the governmental action's principal or ***primary effect*** must ***not be to advance*** religion. (But ***incidental effects*** that help religion do not violate this prong.)

3. **Entanglement:** Finally, the governmental action must not foster an ***excessive governmental entanglement*** with religion. (*Example:* Massachusetts lets a church veto the issuance of a liquor license to any premises located within 500 feet of the church. *Held*, this statute violates the Establishment Clause, because it entangles churches in the exercise of governmental powers. [*Larkin v. Grendel's Den*])

C. **Religion and the public schools:** If the government tries to introduce religion into the ***public schools***, it is probably violating the Establishment Clause.

1. **Instruction:** Thus the government may, of course, not conduct religious instruction in the public schools. In fact, it can't even allow privately-employed religious teachers to conduct classes on the public schools' premises during school hours.

   a. **Accommodation:** However, it's probably allowable for the government to allow students to ***leave school early*** to attend religious instruction somewhere else. It's also probably acceptable for government to let religious groups have access to school facilities, as long as non-religious groups are given equal access. Remember our example of the university that lets all kinds of student groups, including religious groups, use meeting rooms — that's permissible.

2. **Prayer reading:** The official ***reading of prayers*** in the public schools will virtually always be unconstitutional. See, e.g., *Engel v. Vitale*. That is, it will almost always turn out to be the case that either the sole purpose, or the primary effect, of the prayer reading is to advance religion.

   a. **Moment of silence:** Even the setting aside of a ***"moment of silence"*** at the beginning of the school day will generally violate the Establishment Clause, since a moment-of-silence statute will usually turn out to have been solely motivated by the legislators' intent to advance religion, or will at least have the primary effect of advancing religion. (But this will always turn on the actual purpose and effect of the particular statute — there's no absolute *per se* rule against moments of silence. [*Wallace v. Jaffree*]

   b. **Prayer reading at graduation:** Similarly, the school may not conduct a prayer as part of a ***graduation ceremony***, at least where school officials can fairly be said to be sponsoring the religious message. [*Lee v. Weisman*]

   c. **Student-selected speakers don't solve problem:** The school can't easily get around prayer-reading problems by having the student body ***elect a student speaker,*** and then having that speaker decide whether to give a prayer. As long as the school's process can be reasonably viewed as supporting school prayer, the fact that a student-body election intervenes is irrelevant. [*Santa Fe Indep. Sch. Dist. v. Doe*]

3. **Curriculum:**   The state may not design or modify the ***curriculum*** of its schools in order to further religion at the expense of non-religion, or to further one set of religious beliefs over others. (*Example*: A state may not forbid the teaching of evolution. [*Epperson v. Ark.*] Similarly, it probably may not demand that "creationism" be taught in addition to evolution, since "creationism" is mainly a religious doctrine the teaching of which would have the primary effect of advancing religion. [*Edwards v. Aguillard*])

4. **Equal treatment of religion and non-religion:** But it's not a violation of the Establishment Clause for government to treat religion and non-religion ***equally*** in the schools (and government may in fact be *required* to do this because of free-speech principles). (*Example*: If a public university funds non-religiously-oriented student publications, it must fund an evangelical Christian publication on the same terms. [*Rosenberger v. Univ. of Virginia.*])

D. **Sunday closing laws:**   Laws requiring ***merchants*** to be ***closed on Sundays*** generally do ***not*** violate the Establishment Clause. The reason is that these "blue laws" have a primarily secular effect and purpose — they permit everyone (Christian, non-Christian and atheist alike) to have a uniform day of rest. [*McGowan v. Md.*]

E. **Ceremonies and displays:**   Any time your exam question involves a governmentally-sponsored ***ceremony*** or ***display***, beware of Establishment Clause problems.

1. **Ceremonies:**   Thus a ***ceremony*** put on by the government may not have the sole purpose or primary effect of advancing religion. (For instance, as noted above, the government may not normally conduct a prayer as part of a high school graduation ceremony.)

   a. **Long-standing tradition:**   However, if a particular ceremony has a ***long historical tradition*** going back to the time when the Constitution was enacted, then it will probably be allowable, especially outside of the public-school context. (*Example*: The practice of opening a session of the legislature with a prayer by the legislative chaplain dates back to colonial days, so presumably the authors of the Bill of Rights thought that it did not violate the Establishment Clause. Therefore, the practice will be upheld. [*Marsh v. Chambers*])

   b. **Incidental references:**   Similarly, the Establishment Clause probably is not violated when the ceremony has an ***incidental reference*** to God or to a religious theme. (*Example*: The Pledge of Allegiance, with the phrase "One nation, under God," is probably allowable.)

2. **Religious displays:**   Where a ***display*** with religious themes is either put on by the government, or put on by private groups using government property, there is a potential Establishment Clause problem. The problem usually arises where there is a "Christmas" display, "Easter" display, etc. Ask yourself this question: Would a reasonable observer seeing the display conclude that the government was ***endorsing*** religion? If so, there is a violation of the Establishment Clause.

a. **Context:** *Context* is very important. If there is one religious symbol, but it is surrounded by primarily-secular symbols, then the display would be taken as a whole and probably does not violate the Establishment Clause.

Example: For instance, if a nativity scene is surrounded by reindeer, Santa Claus, "Season's Greetings" banners, etc., then as a whole the display would seem to be primarily secular, and the nativity scene won't be a violation of the Establishment Clause. [*Lynch v. Donnelly*] But if the nativity scene or other primarily-religious symbol stands by itself, then that display probably will have a primarily religious effect, and thus violate the Establishment Clause.

b. **History:** The *history* behind the display is also very important. The longer the display has been around without objection or controversy, the less likely it is to be an Establishment Clause violation.

Example: In Case 1, a display of text of the Ten Commandments has existed for 40 years without objection, before the present suit, and was originally donated as part of an anti-juvenile-delinquincy campaign. *Held*, no Establishment Clause violation. [*Van Orden v. Perry*] In Case 2, a display of the text of the Ten Commandments is recent, and replaced two other recent displays that were from the beginning criticized on Establishment Clause grounds. *Held*, an Establishment Clause violation. [*McCreary County v. ACLU of Kentucky*]

F. **Intentional preferences between denominations:** The government may not intentionally *prefer one religion over another*, or one sect over another. That's true even if government thinks that it's merely trying to "accommodate" a particular religion.

Example: The New York legislature creates a special school district whose residents consist solely of members of a particular orthodox Jewish sect, the Satmar Hassidim. The purpose and effect of the special district is to let the Satmars get public funding for a public school in their village to educate their handicapped children. *Held*, the district violates the Establishment Clause, because it was created in a way that singled out the Satmars for a special preference not made available to other groups (and also because it amounted to a delegation of state authority to a group chosen according to a religious criterion). [*Bd. of Educ. of Kiryas Joel Village v. Grumet*]

1. **Unintended effect:** But a regulation that has the incidental unintended *effect* of helping one religion or sect more than another, or hurting one more than another, does not generally violate the Establishment Clause.

2. **Preference for religion over non-religion:** In theory, government can't even "accommodate" *religion generally*, by giving religion in general a preference over non-religion. But in practice, the Court is *less likely to object* to a special accommodation of religion generally than to an accommodation of a particular sect.

Example: In a federal statute, the Religious Land Use and Institutionalized Persons Act (RLUIPA), the federal government orders prison officials to go out of their way to accommodate the religious needs of all prisoners (e.g., by giving them opportunities for group worship and the right to adhere to the dress mandates of their religion). *Held*, even though comparable accommodations are not given to similar needs/desires that are not mandated by religious belief, RLUIPA (at least on its face) does not violate the Establishment Clause. [*Cutter v. Wilkinson*]

G. **Aid to religious schools:** Whenever your fact patterns shows that the government is giving some sort of ***financial aid*** to religious schools, you must immediately think "Establishment Clause." And, of course, you must apply the three-part test.

   1. **General principles:** In general, here are some things to look for when you analyze aid to religious schools:

      a. **Benefit to all students:** A government program that benefits ***all students***, at public, private non-parochial and parochial schools alike, is much more likely to pass muster than aid which goes overwhelmingly to parochial-school students;

      b. **Colleges:** Aid to religious ***colleges*** is easier to justify than aid to high schools or, especially, elementary schools; and

      c. **Aid to parents:** Aid given to ***parents*** in a way that permits them to choose what school to use the aid at is more likely to be sustained than aid given directly to the ***school.***

   2. **Transportation:** Programs by which parents may have their children ***transported*** free to religious schools are probably constitutional, as long as the transport program also covers public and private non-parochial students. [*Everson v. Bd. of Ed.*]

   3. **Textbooks and equipment:** Similarly, ***textbooks*** and *equipment* (e.g., computers) may be loaned to parochial school students as long as loans on the same basis are made to public school and private non-parochial students. But only books and materials that are ***strictly secular*** may be used (e.g., Bibles can't be lent out). [*Bd. of Ed. v. Allen; Mitchell v. Helms*]

   4. **Teachers:** The state ***may*** send ***public school teachers*** into parochial schools, even to teach basic academic subjects, as long as what's taught is free of: (1) religious content and (2) influence from the parochial school's administration. [*Agostini v. Felton*]

   5. **Tuition vouchers:** The state may give ***tuition vouchers*** to parents to enable them to pay religious-school tuition, if the vouchers may also be used in non-religious private schools. That's true even if the tuition is used to cover the costs of educating the children in ***core religious doctrine***, and even if the benefits overwhelmingly go to the parents of ***religious school students***. [*Zelman v. Simmons-Harris*]

H. **The "excessive entanglement prong":** Don't forget the third prong of the test for Establishment Clause violations: governmental action must not give rise to ***excessive entanglement*** on the part of government in the affairs of religion, or vice versa.

1. **The "ministerial exception" from regulation:** For instance, governmental regulation that has the effect of interfering with a religious group's determination of *who is qualified to convey the group's message* and/or *carry out its mission* is likely to violate the Establishment Clause. Thus religious groups are entitled to a *"ministerial exception,"* under which the group's choice of *who may be a minister or leader* will be essentially *immune from regulation*, such as *anti-discrimination* laws. [*Hosanna-Tabor Evangelical Lutheran Church and School v. EEOC*]

III. THE FREE EXERCISE CLAUSE

A. **Free Exercise generally:** Let's now turn to the second clause relating to religion, the Free Exercise Clause. Under this clause, the government is barred from making any law "prohibiting the free exercise" of religion. The Free Exercise Clause prevents the government from getting in the way of people's ability to practice their religions.

   1. **Conduct vs. belief:** The Free Exercise Clause of course prevents the government from unduly burdening a person's abstract "beliefs." (*Example:* Congress cannot ban the religion of voodooism merely because it disapproves of voodooism or thinks that voodooism is irrational.) But the Clause also relates to *conduct*.

      a. **Non-religious objectives:** Free Exercise problems most typically arise when government, acting in pursuit of *non-religious objectives*, either: (1) forbids or burdens conduct which happens to be *required* by someone's religious belief; or conversely, (2) compels or encourages conduct which happens to be *forbidden* by someone's religious beliefs.

B. **Intentional vs. unintentional burdens:** The Free Exercise Clause is much more likely to prevent the government from unduly interfering with religion when the government does so *intentionally* (i.e., with knowledge or intent that a religious practice is being burdened) than when it does so *unintentionally*.

   1. **Intentional burden:** If the interference with religion is *intentional* on government's part, then the interference is subjected to the *most strict scrutiny*, and will virtually never survive.

   2. **Unintentional burden:** If government *unintentionally burdens* religion, it's much harder for a religious person or group to demonstrate a Free Exercise violation. The Free Exercise Clause does not relieve a person of the obligation to comply with a *valid and neutral law* of *general applicability* even though the law forbids (or requires) conduct that his religion requires (or forbids).

   We consider the "intentional" and "unintentional" cases in turn.

C. **Intentional interference:** If the government acts with a *purpose* of interfering with a religious practice — in other words, government *singles out* the religious practice, and burdens it *due to anti-religious motives* — then the interference is subjected to the *most strict scrutiny*, and will virtually never survive. (Cases involving such intentional interference with religion are rare — only one has reached the Supreme Court in recent decades, the one in the following Example.)

> **Example:** The Ps practice Santeria, a religion involving animal sacrifice. D (the local city council), motivated by the citizenry's dislike of this religion and of the sacrifices, outlaws all animal sacrifice (but exempts Kosher slaughter).
>
> *Held*, the Ps' Free Exercise rights have been violated. D has acted with the purpose of outlawing a practice precisely because the practice is motivated by religion, so D's act must be most strictly scrutinized. Because there is no compelling governmental objective here, and because any governmental objective that the city is pursuing (e.g., maintenance of public health) could be achieved by less discriminatory means, the law fails this strictest scrutiny. [*Church of the Lukumi Babalu Aye v. Hialeah*]

1. **Perhaps limited to "punishments":** However, this rule of strict scrutiny probably applies only to criminal or civil *"sanctions"* — in essence *punishments* — that are imposed for the purpose of disfavoring religious practices, not to government conduct that merely *withholds some generally-applicable benefit* so the benefit cannot be used in connection with a religiously-motivated activity.

   > **Example:** A state gives merit scholarships to college-bound student with a certain G.P.A., but excludes anyone who wants to use the scholarship to study for the ministry. *Held*, this exclusion doesn't violate the Free Exercise clause, because it doesn't involve a criminal or civil sanction, merely a refusal by government to grant an affirmative benefit to subsidize an "essentially religious endeavor." [*Locke v. Davey*]

D. **Unintentional burdening of religious practices:** Where government *unintentionally burdens* a religious practice by enacting a *generally-applicable* rule, it is very difficult for the affected individual whose religious practice has been burdened to obtain an exemption from the rule on free exercise grounds. In this situation, the Court has held since 1990 that the right of free exercise does not relieve a person of the obligation to comply with a *valid and neutral law* of *general applicability*, even though the law forbids (or requires) conduct that his religion requires (or forbids). [*Employment Division v. Smith*].

   > **Example:** Oregon makes it a crime to possess the drug peyote, and refuses to give an exemption to Native Americans whose use of the drug is a central part of their religious rites. The Native Americans assert that their rights under the Free Exercise Clause require the state to give them an exemption from the rule, unless the state can show that denial of an exemption is necessary for the achievement of a compelling state objective.
   >
   > *Held*, for the state. Oregon may refuse an exemption. And it may do so without the court's application of strict scrutiny, indeed, without the court's conducting any balancing of the strength of the state's interest in its prohibition against the burden on the individual's religious beliefs.

"[T]he right of free exercise does not relieve an individual of the obligation to comply with a ***valid and neutral law*** of ***general applicability*** on the ground that the law proscribes (or prescribes) conduct that his religion prescribes (or proscribes)." [*Employment Division v. Smith, supra.*]

1. **Other constitutional interests present:** But where the individual's interest in free exercise of religion is ***combined*** with a ***free speech, freedom of association, substantive due process,*** or some other ***separate constitutional interest,*** the individual has a ***better chance of prevailing.***

   > **Example:** In *Wisconsin v. Yoder* (1972), the Court held that Wisconsin must exempt 14- and 15-year-old Amish students from the state requirement that students attend school until the age of 16. The decision came before the 1990 decision in *Employment Div. v. Smith, supra,* that free-exercise rights don't require the government to give an exemption from valid and neutral laws of general applicability. But given the special *substantive-due-process interest* of the students and their parents in the subject of education (parents have a fundamental due process interest in deciding how their children are to be educated; see *Pierce v. Society of Sisters* [p. 83]), even the present post-*Smith* Court might give stricter-than-usual review to the state's refusal to give an exemption.

2. **Anti-discrimination laws vs. group's right to pick its "ministers":** *Smith* does ***not*** apply when the government regulation, even though neutral and generally-applicable on its face, would have the effect of ***interfering with the internal decision-making of a religious group*** regarding the group's ***core faith and mission***. So, for instance, a church will be exempt on free-exercise grounds from a generally-applicable and neutral rule forbidding certain types of ***employment discrimination***, if the rule would interfere with the church's right to ***select the "ministers"*** who will carry out the church's core religious mission.

   > **Example:** Hosanna-Tabor, a combined church and religious school, fires Perich, a minister/teacher. The EEOC claims that this action violated the ADA, a federal anti-discrimination law. The EEOC argues that the case falls within the *Smith* principle that the Free Exercise Clause does not require government to give an exemption from a valid and neutral generally-applicable law.
   >
   > *Held*, for the church-and-school: *Smith* applies only to government regulation of ***"outward physical acts"*** (such as ingesting peyote, in *Smith*). Smith does not apply where government is interfering with "an ***internal church decision that affects the faith and mission*** of the church itself." So the Free Exercise Clause (as well as the Establishment Clause) entitle the church-and-school to a "ministerial exemption," enabling it to fire Perich even if this would otherwise violate the ADA. [*Hosanna-Tabor Evangelical Lutheran Church and School v. EEOC*]

E. **Conscientious objection:** It's not clear whether Congress *must* (as it does) give an exemption for military service for *conscientious objectors* (i.e., those who believe that all war is evil).

    1. **Selective c.o.'s:** But it's clear that Congress need not give an exemption to "selective" c.o.'s (i.e., those who do not believe that all war is evil, but who believe that the particular war in which they are being asked to fight is evil). [*Gillette v. U.S.*]

F. **Public health:** Government may have to sacrifice its interest in the *health* of its citizenry, if individuals' religious dictates so require.

    1. **Competent adult:** Where the case involves a *competent adult*, and only that adult's own health is at stake, government may probably not force treatment on the individual over his religious objection. (*Example:* A state probably can't force a Jehovah's Witness to accept a blood transfusion or other life-saving medical care over that person's religious objections.)

    2. **Child:** However, where the patient is a *child* whose parents object on religious grounds, the state may probably compel the treatment.

    3. **Danger to others:** Also, if the case involves not only a health danger to the person asserting a religious belief, but also a health danger to *others*, then government probably does not have to give an exemption. (*Example:* P may be forced to undergo a vaccination over his religious objections. [*Jacobsen v. Mass.*])

G. **What constitutes a religious belief:** Only *bona fide* "religious beliefs" are protected by the Free Exercise Clause. But "religious beliefs" are defined very *broadly*.

    1. **Non-theistic:** For instance, *non-theistic* beliefs are protected. That is, the belief need not recognize the existence of a supreme being. (*Example:* Public officials cannot be forced to take an oath in which they say that they believe that God exists. [*Torcaso v. Watkins*])

    2. **Unorganized religions:** Similarly, *unorganized* or obscure religions get the same protection as the major religions. In fact, even if a person's religious beliefs are followed *only by him*, he's still entitled to free exercise protection.

    3. **Sincerity:** A court will not sustain a free exercise claim unless it is convinced that the religious belief is *"genuine"* or *"sincere."* (The fact that the belief or practice has been observed by a religious group for a long period of time may be considered in measuring sincerity. But the converse — absence of a long-standing practice — does not mean that the belief is insincere.)

        a. **Unreasonableness:** The court will *not* consider whether the belief is "true" or *"reasonable."* Even a very "unreasonable" belief (that is, a belief that most people might consider unreasonable) is not deprived of protection, so long as it is *genuine*. [*U.S. v. Ballard*] (*Example:* The practice of voodoo, including sticking pins into dolls representing one's enemies, might be considered by most of us to be "unreasonable." But as long as such a practice is part of a person's genuine set of beliefs and religious practices, it will not be deprived of protection merely because most find it unreasonable.)

CHAPTER 16

JUSTICIABILITY

I. JUSTICIABILITY GENERALLY

A. List: In order for a case to be heard by the federal courts, the plaintiff must get past a series of procedural obstacles which we collectively call requirements for *"justiciability"*: (1) the case must not require the giving of an ***advisory opinion***; (2) the plaintiff must have ***standing***; (3) the case must not be ***moot***; (4) the case must be ***ripe*** for decision; and (5) the case must not involve a non-justiciable ***political question***.

II. ADVISORY OPINIONS

A. Constitutional "case or controversy" requirement: Article III, Section 2 of the Constitution gives the federal courts jurisdiction only over "cases" and "controversies." The federal courts are therefore prevented from issuing opinions on ***abstract*** or ***hypothetical*** questions. This means that the federal courts may not give *"advisory opinions."* In other words, the federal courts may not render opinions which answer a legal question when no party is before the court who has suffered or faces specific injury.

> **Example:** Suppose that both houses of Congress approve a bill, but the President has doubts about the bill's constitutionality. The President may *not* go to a federal court and ask the federal court whether the bill is constitutional, so that he may decide whether to veto it. If the federal court were to give its opinion about whether the bill was constitutional, at a time when no party who had been or might soon be injured by the unconstitutionality was before the court, this would be an "advisory opinion" that would violate the constitutional "case or controversy" requirement.

1. Declaratory judgments sometimes allowed: But ***declaratory judgments*** are sometimes allowed, and are not forbidden by the rule against advisory opinions. A declaratory judgment is a judicial decision in which the court is not requested to award damages or an injunction, but is instead requested to state what the legal effect would be of proposed conduct by one or both of the parties.

    a. Requirements: But the plaintiff is not entitled to get a declaratory judgment on just any question about what the legal consequence of the particular conduct would be. If the declaratory judgment action raises only questions that are very ***hypothetical*** or ***abstract***, the federal court is likely to conclude that what's sought here is an illegal advisory opinion, because no specific, concrete controversy exists.

III. STANDING

A. **Function of a standing requirement:**   Probably the most important rule about when the federal courts may hear a case is that they may do so only when the plaintiff has *"standing"* to assert his claim. By this, we mean that the plaintiff must have a significant *stake* in the controversy.

> **Example:** Suppose that during the Vietnam War, P, a federal taxpayer, becomes convinced that, since Congress has never formally declared war, P's tax dollars are being used to support an unconstitutional war. If P were to sue the federal government in federal court to have the war effort enjoined on this ground, the court would not hear his claim — he would be found to lack "standing," since (as we'll see in detail later) a person whose only connection with the controversy is that he is a taxpayer will almost never be deemed to have standing to claim that tax dollars are being used illegally.

B. **Requirement of "injury in fact":**   The key concept behind the law of standing is simple: the litigant must show that he has suffered an *"injury in fact."* At its broadest level, the standing requirement means that the plaintiff must show that *he has himself been injured* in some way by the conduct that he complains of.

C. **Who is kept out:**   The standing rules tend to keep three main types of cases *out* of the federal courts:

1. **Non-individuated harm:**   First, we have cases in which the harm suffered by the plaintiff is *no different* from that suffered by very large numbers of people not before the court. (*Example:* Suppose P's only connection with the suit is that he is a federal "citizen" or a "taxpayer" who is injured the same as any other citizen or taxpayer by the fact that the government is spending tax dollars illegally or otherwise violating some law. P does not have standing.)

2. **"Speculative" future harm:** Second, we have cases in which the plaintiff is trying to avoid *future* harm. Plaintiffs can have standing to try to prevent future harm, but the plaintiff must show that the threatened harm is *reasonably likely to occur* in the near future, not merely *"speculative."*

3. **Third parties' rights:**   Third, we have cases where the rights claimed to be violated are not the rights of the plaintiff, but instead the rights of *third parties* who are not before the court. (But there are some important exceptions to the general rule that the plaintiff can't complain of government actions that violate someone else's rights.)

D. **Taxpayer and citizen suits:**   Here is the single most important context in which standing problems arise: suits that are brought by federal *"citizens"* or *"taxpayers"* arguing that their general rights as citizens or taxpayers are violated by governmental action.

1. **Taxpayer suits:**   Suppose that the plaintiff contends that: (1) he is a federal *taxpayer*; and (2) his tax dollars are being spent by the government in some illegal way. May the plaintiff pursue this suit in federal court? In general, the answer will be, *"no."* The fact that a person's federal taxes are used to fund an unconstitutional or illegal government program is simply not a sufficient

connection with the governmental action to confer standing on the plaintiff. [*Frothingham v. Mellon*]

    a. One exception: There is one very narrow exception: a taxpayer has standing to sue to overturn a congressional *tax or spending program* that violates the *Establishment Clause*. [*Flast v. Cohen*]

        i. Tightly limited: But this "*Flast* exception" is extremely *tightly limited:* it applies only to *congressional* spending that violates the Establishment Clause, not even to *Executive-Branch* spending that might violate the Clause. [*Hein v. Freedom from Religion Foundation*]

    b. State taxpayers: A *state* taxpayer, like a federal taxpayer, does *not* have federal-court standing to litigate the legality of the state's expenditures. [*DaimlerChrysler Corp. v. Cuno*]

    c. Municipal taxpayer: But a *municipal* taxpayer definitely *does* have standing to litigate the legality of his city's expenditures.

  2. Citizen suits: Suppose now that plaintiff argues that he is a federal *"citizen,"* and that as such he has the right to have his government act in accordance with the Constitution. Assume that P has no direct connection with the governmental act he's complaining about (he's merely claiming that, like every other citizen, he has the right to have the federal government obey the Constitution). In this "citizen suit" situation, P will *not have standing*. The Court has always held that one federal citizen's interest in lawful government is no different from the interest of any other citizen, and that an individual litigant relying on citizenship has not shown the *"individualized"* injury-in-fact that is required for standing.

  E. Cases not based on taxpayer or citizen status: Now suppose that the plaintiff is not arguing that his standing derives from his status as citizen or taxpayer. In other words, we're now talking about the vast bulk of ordinary law suits.

    1. Three requirements: Here, there are three standing requirements that the plaintiff must meet: (1) he must show that he has suffered (or is likely to suffer) an *"injury in fact"*; (2) the injury he is suffering must be *concrete* and *"individuated"*; and (3) the action being challenged must be the *"cause in fact"* of the injury.

    2. "Injury in fact": The plaintiff must show that he either *has suffered*, or *will probably suffer*, some concrete *"injury in fact."*

        a. Non-economic harm: This "injury in fact" requirement is pretty loosely applied. For instance, the harm does not have to be *economic* in nature.

        Example: A group of people who use a national forest claim that the construction of a recreation area in the forest will violate federal laws. To get standing, the plaintiffs point to the injury to their "esthetic and environmental well-being" which would result from the construction.

        Held, this esthetic and environmental injury satisfies the "injury in fact" requirement, even though the harm is non-economic and in fact very intangible. [*Sierra Club v. Morton*]

b. Imminent harm: If P has not *already* suffered the injury in fact, he must show that the future injury is not only probable but *"concrete"* and *"imminent."* In other words, a speculation that harm may come about in the indefinite future will not suffice.

Example: The Ps challenge a federal regulatory action that they say will endanger certain species abroad. The Ps say that they have in the past, and will in the future, travel abroad to visit the habitats of these species.

Held, the Ps lack standing, because the lack of specific information about their future plans means the harm to them is not sufficiently concrete or imminent. [*Lujan v. Defenders of Wildlife*]

i. "Certainly impending": In at least one recent case, the Court has said that the threatened harm has to be *"certainly impending."* See *Clapper*, immediately *infra*. This phrase seems to mean that if the harm hasn't already occurred, not only does it have to be the case that if the harm occurs, it will occur soon (the requirement of "imminence"), but it must also be the case that the occurrence of the harm in the near future is *highly probable.*

(1) Government surveillance in the war on terror: The principle that the future harm must be "certainly impending" and not unduly speculative is likely to make it hard for anyone to challenge certain *federal surveillance programs,* such as those enacted as part of the war on terror.

Example: A federal statute, §1881a, permits federal intelligence authorities to conduct secret e-mail and telephone surveillance of non-citizens who are believed to be outside of the country and whom the government suspects of having links to terrorist organizations, where the government's purpose is to obtain "foreign intelligence information" (typically for counter-terrorism purposes). The Ps are various U.S. citizens — including attorneys, reporters, and human-rights workers — who allege that their work requires them to communicate with such non-citizens suspected of having links to terrorist organizations. The Ps say they reasonably fear that §1881a will be used in the near future to eavesdrop on conversations between themselves and these targeted foreigners.

Held (5-4), the Ps don't have standing. Prior standing cases have required that the threatened injury be "certainly impending." The plaintiffs fail to meet this "certainly impending" requirement. Because the Ps have "no actual knowledge" of what foreign targets the government would choose for surveillance, their fear that their own communications will be captured through surveillance targeting others is "necessarily conjectural" and "highly speculative." [*Clapper v. Amnesty Int'l USA* (2013)]

3. Remedy: In addition to showing an "injury in fact," P must show that the injury would be *remedied* by a favorable court decision.

Example: The various plaintiffs claim to have been injured by the zoning rules of Penfield, New York. They claim that these rules were imposed for the purpose of excluding the building of low- and moderate-income housing in the town. Certain Ps (the only ones we'll discuss here) are low- and moderate-income individuals who have never lived in Penfield, but who allege that they sought housing there and would have moved there had affordable housing been available.

Held, these Ps lack standing for several reasons. One reason is that these Ps fail the *"redressability"* requirement: they can't show that if the court awarded the relief being sought — a striking down of the zoning rules — the desired moderate-income projects will in fact likely be built. Therefore, they can't show that a favorable decision would redress (make better) the harm the Ps complain about. [*Warth v. Seldin*]

4. **Individuated harm:** The harm that has been or will be suffered by the plaintiff has to be *"individuated."* That is, it can't be the same harm as suffered by every citizen, or every taxpayer.

   a. **Large number:** But the harm may still be found to be "individuated" even though there are a *large number* of people suffering the harm.

      i. **Same harm:** But remember that if the harm complained of by the plaintiff is truly the same harm as suffered by every citizen or every taxpayer in the country, the harm will not be sufficiently "individuated," and the plaintiffs won't have standing.

   b. **Organizations and associations:** What about organizations and associations — does the organization itself have to suffer the harm, or can it merely assert that its *members* will suffer or have suffered the required harm? In general, the answer is that organizations and associations will be able to sue on behalf of their members. However: (1) the members have to be people who would have *standing in their own right* (so that an organization of citizens or taxpayers could not complain of harm that is suffered by all citizens or taxpayers); (2) the interests being asserted by the organization in the lawsuit must be *related to the organization's purpose* (so that an environmental group could probably not try to pursue its members' interests in, say, an effective criminal justice system); and (3) the case cannot be one which requires the *participation of individual members.* [*Hunt v. Wash. Apple Advt'g. Comm.*] These three requirements are pretty liberally applied.

5. **Causation:** Finally, the action that the plaintiff is complaining about must be the *"cause in fact"* of his injury. Actually, this causation requirement breaks down into two sub-requirements:

   (1) P has to show that the challenged action was a *"but for"* cause of his injury, that is, that the injury would not have occurred unless the challenged action had taken place; and

   (2) P must show that a favorable decision in the suit will probably *redress* the injury to him.

6. **Perhaps easier test for states:** When the suit is brought by a *state*, the injury-in-fact and causation requirements are probably interpreted a bit *less stringently.*

   Example: Massachusetts sues to force the EPA to regulate auto emissions. The state's reasoning is that (1) such regulation will or may slow the speed of global warming "over the next century" (even though non-U.S. sources will concededly grow their own emissions dramatically during this period); and (2) without the slowing, the state's coastal lands will or may be eroded by rising sea levels. *Held*, Mass. has met the injury-in-fact and causation requirements, in part because Mass. is acting as a sovereign state protecting the interests of its citizens. [*Mass. v. EPA*]

F. **Third-party standing:** One of the key functions of the standing doctrine is that this is how courts apply the general rule that a litigant normally may ***not assert the constitutional rights of persons not before the court***. (This principle is sometimes called the rule against use of "constitutional *jus tertii*," — *jus tertii* means "rights of third persons" in Latin.)

   Example: Zoning laws enacted by the city of Penfield, N.Y., intentionally exclude the building of low-income housing. The Ps are residents of nearby Rochester, who claim that because Penfield has refused to allow low- and middle-income housing, the taxes of these Rochester residents have risen, since Rochester has to subsidize or build more low-income housing than it would have to build than had Penfield not practiced exclusionary zoning.

   Held, these Rochester residents lack standing. It is true that their higher taxes are an "injury in fact" to them. But Penfield's zoning laws do not apply to these Rochester residents, and therefore do not violate *their* rights. And the Rochester residents may not claim that the rights of ***other people not before the court*** have been violated (e.g., people who would have moved to Penfield had exclusionary zoning not been practiced). [*Warth v. Seldin*]

   1. **Not constitutionally required:** This rule against the assertion of third-party rights is ***not*** mandated by the Article III "case or controversy" requirement. In other words, it is not a rule imposed by the Constitution on the federal courts; instead, it is a rule of "prudence," a policy decision adopted by the Supreme Court.

   2. **Exceptions:** Since the rule against asserting third-party rights is not required by the Constitution, the Supreme Court is free to make whatever *exceptions* it wishes to the doctrine.

      a. **Associations:** One exception is that an *association* will normally be allowed to raise the rights of its *members*. For instance, if a group of people would be injured by damage to the air they breathe and the water they drink, an organization of which they are members (e.g., the Sierra Club) would typically be allowed to sue on their behalf.

      b. **Overbreadth:** Another sort of exception to the rule against third-party standing is the First Amendment *overbreadth* doctrine, which we covered earlier in our discussion of freedom of expression. Remember that the basic idea behind overbreadth is that even where a statute could constitutionally be applied to the plaintiff's conduct, if he can show that the statute would unconstitutionally restrict the expression of *some other person not before the court,* the court may hear the lawsuit and strike down the statute. We allow overbreadth in the *First Amendment area* but not elsewhere because statutes that purport to restrict expression in an overbroad manner will have a *"chilling effect"* on citizens' general willingness to exercise their freedom of speech.

G. **"Prudential" standing:**   We just saw that the rule against third-party standing is not dictated by the Article III "case or controversy" requirement, and is instead the result of *"prudential"* considerations. More generally, the federal courts retain the right to refuse to hear *any* case on such prudential-standing grounds, even cases falling outside the pure third-party-standing area.

> **Example:** P is the father of a daughter, X, who attends public-school. P claims that the school's policy of reciting the Pledge of Allegiance violates his First Amendment right to have his daughter be instructed in P's atheistic beliefs without government interference. (X's mother, who is divorced from P, opposes the suit.) *Held*, because the suit involves domestic relations questions — typically avoided by the federal courts — and also involves X's rights in a highly controversial matter, the Court's prudential-standing policies dictate that the federal courts not hear the case. [*Elk Grove v. Newdow*]

IV. MOOTNESS

A. **General rule:**   A case may not be heard by the federal courts if it is *"moot."* A case is moot if it raised a live controversy at the time the complaint was filed, but *events occurring after the filing* have deprived the litigant of an ongoing stake in the controversy.

> **Example:** P sues D, a state university, claiming that the university's law school admissions program is racially discriminatory. P is permitted to attend the law school while the case is being litigated. By the time the case arrives at the Supreme Court for review, P is in his final year of law school, and the university says that he will be allowed to graduate regardless of how the case is decided. *Held*, the case is moot. Therefore, the appeal will not be decided. [*DeFunis v. Odegaard*]

  1. **Constitutional basis for:**   Apparently the rule that the federal courts may not decide "moot" cases is *required* by the Constitution. That is, deciding a case when the parties no longer have a live controversy would amount to issuing an advisory opinion, in violation of Article III's "case or controversy" requirement.

B. **Exceptions:**   Nonetheless, the courts recognize a few situations where a case that would appear to be "moot" will nonetheless be heard.

  1. **"Capable of repetition, yet evading review":**   For instance, a case will not be treated as moot if the issue it raises is *"capable of repetition, yet evading review."* This "capable of repetition, yet evading review" doctrine takes care of situations in which, if the case were to be declared moot, a *different per-*

son might be injured in the *same way* by the same defendant, and his claim, too, would be mooted before review could be had.

Example: P, a pregnant woman, attacks the constitutionality of Texas' anti-abortion law. She brings the suit as a class action, in which she is the named plaintiff and other pregnant women who want abortions are unnamed members. By the time the case reaches the Supreme Court, P is no longer pregnant.

Held, the case should not be dismissed as moot. A pregnancy will almost always be over before the usual appellate process is complete. Therefore, if the Court insisted that the named plaintiff who starts the suit must still be pregnant by the time the suit gets to the Supreme Court, no plaintiff could ever get to that Court. So the constitutionality of the Texas anti-abortion law is "capable of repetition, yet evading review." [*Roe v. Wade*]

2. **Voluntary cessation by defendant:** The case will generally not be treated as moot if the defendant *voluntarily ceases* the conduct that the plaintiff is complaining about. So if the plaintiff is seeking an injunction, the defendant can't usually get the case dismissed on mootness grounds merely by saying that he has voluntarily stopped the conduct that the plaintiff is trying to get an injunction against — unless the defendant shows that there is no reasonable likelihood that he will return to his old ways, the court will let the action go forward.

3. **Collateral consequences:** Finally, a case will not be moot even if it is mostly decided, if there are still *collateral consequences* that might be adverse to the defendant. For instance, suppose that a criminal defendant has already served his sentence by the time his attack on the constitutionality of his conviction comes before the federal court. The case will not be moot, because there will probably be future collateral consequences to the defendant from his conviction (e.g., he will lose the right to vote, his reputation or employability will be damaged, etc.).

V. RIPENESS

A. **Ripeness problem generally:** You can think of the problem of ripeness as being the opposite of mootness. A case is moot, as we've just seen, because it *no longer* involves an actual controversy. By contrast, a case is not yet ripe (and therefore not yet decidable by a federal court) if it has *not yet become sufficiently concrete* to be easily adjudicated.

Example: The Hatch Act prohibits federal executive-branch employees from getting involved in "political management or … political campaigns." The plaintiffs are federal civil servants who want to attack the constitutionality of the Hatch Act. The plaintiffs claim that they want to engage in prohibited political activities. But they concede that they have not yet engaged in such activities.

Held, the plaintiffs' claims are not yet ripe. The problem is not that the Ps have not yet violated the statute. Rather, the problem is that the plaintiffs have not been adequately specific about the ***precise acts*** that they wish to carry out. (If the Ps would specify in detail what they want to do, their suit might not be unripe even though they haven't yet violated the act.) [*United Public Workers v. Mitchell*]

B. Uncertain enforcement of criminal statute: One common ripeness problem arises where the plaintiff attacks the constitutionality of a statute and says that he has violated the statute, but it is clear that the statute is ***rarely enforced*** and probably will not be enforced in this particular situation. Here, the rules are pretty blurry — suffice it to say that if the court believes that it is ***very unlikely*** that the statute will be enforced against the plaintiff either for the activity he has already done or similar activity he is likely to do in the future, the court will probably treat the case as being not ripe.

> **Example:** Connecticut forbids the distribution of contraceptives. Two married couples and a physician challenge the law's constitutionality, and allege that they have violated the law. *Held*, the case is not ripe, because the statute has been on the books for 80 years with only one reported prosecution, so there does not exist the required "clear" threat that the plaintiffs will be prosecuted. [*Poe v. Ullman*]

1. Specific threatened harm required: But for a case to be ripe, it is not necessary that the litigant have ***already suffered*** harm. It will be enough that there is a ***reasonable probability*** of harm. However, the anticipated harm has to be fairly ***specific***.

VI. THE ELEVENTH AMENDMENT AND SUITS AGAINST THE STATES

A. The Eleventh Amendment generally: The ***Eleventh Amendment*** specifically bars any federal suit "against any one of the ***states*** by citizens of another state, or by citizens or subjects of any foreign state."

1. Damage suits against states: The Eleventh Amendment has been held to bar most types of ***damage suits*** against a state.

a. Plaintiff not a citizen of defendant state: By its own terms, the Amendment clearly applies to suits against a state brought by citizens of a ***different state*** or by foreigners. (*Examples:* A citizen of Missouri may not bring a damage suit against the state of Illinois. Nor may a British subject bring a damage suit against the state of Illinois.)

b. Suit by citizen of defendant state: The Eleventh Amendment has been ***interpreted*** to apply also to bar a damage suit where the plaintiff is a ***citizen of the defendant state***. [*Hans v. Louisiana*] (*Example:* Suppose P is an employee of the Delmarva state legislature. He is then fired, in apparent violation of his employment contract. P brings a suit for contract damages against Delmarva, in federal court. This suit would be a violation of the Eleventh Amendment, as broadly interpreted by the Supreme Court.)

2. **Suits by states or federal government:** The Eleventh Amendment does *not* bar federal suits brought by *one state* against another state, or by the *federal government* against a state.

3. **No counties or cities protected:** Only the *state itself*, not its *subdivisions*, such as *counties* or *cities*, is protected by the Eleventh Amendment. (*Example:* P, a county worker, is fired. He brings a federal suit for contract damages against the county. Since the suit is not against the state *per se*, the Eleventh Amendment does not apply, even though the county is in essence a subdivision of the state.)

4. **No bar against injunctions:** The Eleventh Amendment essentially bars only suits for *damages*. That is, it does not bar most suits for *injunctions*. For instance, if a private litigant sues a state official to enjoin him from taking acts which would violate the plaintiff's *constitutional* or *federal-law* rights, the Eleventh Amendment does not apply and the suit may proceed. [*Ex parte Young*]

5. **Congress can't override:** *Congress* generally *can't change* the "no federal-court suits against the states" principle behind the Eleventh Amendment, even if it wants to and expressly says it's doing so. [*Seminole Tribe v. Florida*]

   Example: Congress passes a statute saying any state *can* be sued in federal court by private citizens for violating, say, federal patent or environmental laws. This statute won't have any effect — a federal court still can't hear a private suit against a state for damages for violating the federal law. [*Florida Prepaid v. Coll. Sav. Bank*]

   a. **Exception for remedial powers:** But there's an *exception* — if Congress is acting properly pursuant to its *remedial powers* under the Thirteenth, Fourteenth or Fifteenth Amendment, it may *abrogate* the states' Eleventh Amendment immunity.

B. **States' sovereign immunity:** The states have a constitutionally-guaranteed *sovereign immunity* from certain proceedings brought by private parties.

   1. **Suit in states' own courts:** Thus the states have constitutional sovereign immunity from private damage suits brought against the state in the *state's own courts.* This is true even if the suit is based on a *congressionally-granted federal right*.

      Example: Congress passes a valid statute saying that state employees must receive premium pay for overtime just as private-sector employees do. Employees of Maine sue the state in Maine courts on this right. *Held*, the Constitution's structure incorporates the doctrine of sovereign immunity, and that doctrine allows Maine to avoid hearing the employees' suit, even if Congress has expressly said that the states must hear such suits. [*Alden v. Maine*]

   2. **Proceeding before federal administrative agency:** Similarly, the states have sovereign immunity from being required to respond to a private complaint before a *federal administrative agency*. [*Federal Maritime Comm. v. So. Car. St. Ports Auth.*]

VII. POLITICAL QUESTIONS

A. **The doctrine generally:**   The final aspect of justiciability is the requirement is that the case not involve the decision of a *"political question."* This rule is even more vague than the other justiciability rules we've talked about already. The doctrine does *not* mean that federal courts will not decide a case that involves politics. It doesn't even mean that courts will refuse to decide cases where political issues are right at the heart of the controversy. Instead, the court will decline to hear a case on political question grounds only if it thinks that the doctrine of *separation of powers* requires this, or if it thinks that deciding the case would be unwise as a policy matter.

  1. **Two of the factors used:**   Two of the factors that seem to be very important in whether a case will be found to involve a non-justiciable political question are:

    a. **Commitment to another branch:**   First, the fact that the case presents an issue which has been committed by the Constitution to *another branch of the federal government*, i.e., to Congress or to the President instead of the courts.

    b. **Lack of standards:**   Second, the fact that there are no manageable *standards* by which a court could resolve the issue.

B. **"Commitment to other branches" strand:**   The courts will refuse to decide a case on political-question grounds if the case raises an issue the determination of which is clearly committed by the Constitution to *another branch of the federal government*.

   Example: D, a federal judge, claims that the Senate has used improper procedures in convicting him following his impeachment, because the case was heard before a committee of Senators rather than the full Senate (though the full Senate voted, after receiving a transcript of the committee proceedings). D claims that this violates the Impeachment Clause, which says that "the Senate shall have sole Power to try all Impeachments." *Held*, the case presents a nonjusticiable political question, because the Constitution has given the Senate, not the courts, the power to decide what constitutes a "trial." [*Nixon v. U.S.*]

  1. **Other impeachment issues:** The same principle probably applies to *all* aspects of the impeachment process. Thus if the House voted to impeach the President and the Senate voted to convict, the Supreme Court would probably refuse to review either of these decisions on "commitment to other branches" political-question grounds (so that if the President tried to get the Supreme Court to hear his argument that the crime for which he was impeached and convicted was not within the constitutionally-defined category of "high crimes and misdemeanors," the Court would probably refuse to consider the merits of this argument).

  2. **Rare:** It is quite rare for a case to be declined on the grounds that it involves a question committed to some other branch of government.

C. "Lack of judicially manageable standards": The second major factor that may lead the court to decide that there is a non-justiciable political question, is that there are no *manageable standards* by which the courts can resolve the issue.

> **Example:** Article IV, Section 4 provides that "the United States shall guarantee to every state in this union a republican form of government." Some unhappy Rhode Island citizens stage a rebellion. Ultimately, various Rhode Islanders ask the federal courts to decide which of two competing factions is the lawful government of the state.
>
> *Held*, the Court cannot decide this question, because it presents a political question. There are no criteria by which a court could determine whether a particular "government" was "Republican." [*Luther v. Borden*]

D. Reapportionment: Let's now look in some detail at the federal cases on *legislative reapportionment*.

1. One person, one vote rule: The landmark case of *Baker v. Carr,* and cases following it, establish the so-called *"one person, one vote"* principle: any governmental body, whether it's a federal one (like congressional districts) or a state one (like a state legislature) must be apportioned on a *population* basis, so that *all voters have essentially the same voting power.* If a governmental electoral scheme does not comply with this "one person, one vote" principle, it violates the *equal protection* rights of the under-represented voters. [*Reynolds v. Sims*]

a. Justiciable: Such cases raising the "one person, one vote" argument are *justiciable*. The Court has rejected the argument that these cases raise non-justiciable political questions. [*Baker v. Carr*]

b. Both houses of state legislature: One of the consequences of the "one person, one vote" principle is that if a state has a bicameral (two-house) legislature, *both* houses must be elected based on population. Thus, paradoxically, the U.S. Constitution prohibits a state from having one body that awards seats without reference to population (e.g., a house that gives the same number of votes to each county), even though the U.S. Senate is built upon exactly this kind of non-population-based scheme!

2. How much equality is required: The rules for *how much equality is required* vary depending on whether we're talking about a congressional districting scheme or, instead, a state or local districting scheme.

a. Congressional: For *congressional districts*, the districts have to be *almost precisely equal.* Even a scheme where one congressional district within a state was only 1% more populous than another has been struck down. States must make a "good-faith effort to achieve *precise mathematical equality*" in the drawing of congressional districts. [*Kirkpatrick v. Preisler*]

b. State and local: *Much greater deviation* from mathematical equality is allowed where what is being apportioned is *state legislatures* or *local governmental bodies*. So for example, a *10%* or smaller deviation between the voting power of a voter in one district versus a voter in another will generally be ***upheld***. [*White v. Regester*] Even greater disparities will be allowed if there are good reasons for them. (For instance, suppose a state wants not to have to redraw its county boundaries, and wants to have each county elect its own representative to the state Assembly. This desire to "respect pre-existing political boundaries" will probably justify, say, a 15% or even 20% disparity in per-person voting power.)

3. **Gerrymandering:** Consider ***gerrymandering***, that is, the process by which the strength of a particular voting bloc is curtailed by restricting its members to carefully and artificially-constructed districts.

    a. **"Partisan gerrymandering" cases hard to win:** First, consider ***"partisan gerrymandering"*** cases, i.e., cases arguing that a group is being disadvantaged based on its ***political*** rather than racial status. These cases are almost impossible for the plaintiffs to win. See p. 105 *supra*. (In fact, a near-majority of the Court believes that such cases aren't even ***justiciable***. [*Vieth v. Jubelirer*])

    b. **Racial minority:** But if a ***racial or ethnic minority*** can show that the gerrymandering scheme was intentionally designed to hurt, and did hurt, that minority, the plaintiffs' case *will* be justiciable, and probably winnable. For instance, if the state legislature draws districts for the state senate in a way that intentionally gives African Americans control of 5% of the districts when African Americans constitute 10% of the state population, African American voters have a good chance of winning an equal protection suit.

EXAM TIPS

TABLE OF CONTENTS
of EXAM TIPS

EXAM TIPS

Exam Tips on
THE SUPREME COURT'S AUTHORITY

If the facts describe a lawsuit that takes place in federal court (or a state-court lawsuit that is eventually heard by the U.S. Supreme Court) be alert to *limits* on the *federal judicial power:*

☛ **State-court decisions:** If the facts involve a state-court suit that is heard by the **Supreme Court** on **certiorari**, be sure that the state-court decision was **based on federal law.**

 ☞ **Independent & adequate state ground:** Be alert to the possible existence of an **independent and adequate state ground**. That is, if the state court decided some issue of state law in a way that would have been enough to dispose of the case, there is no federal issue that is vital to the case, and the Supreme Court may not decide the federal issue. In particular, be alert for fact patterns where a **state** and **federal constitutional provision** cover the **same territory** — the state court might have decided the state issue as solely a matter of state law, in which case there would be no federal issue necessary to the case.

☛ **Limitations by Congress:** If a fact pattern involves an attempt by **Congress** to **limit the power** of either the Supreme Court or the lower federal courts, the main things to remember are:

 ☞ **No expansion beyond constitutional limits:** Congress can within limits *cut back* on the kinds of cases the Supreme Court may hear, but cannot *expand* the case load beyond the categories set forth as the federal judicial power in the Constitution; and

 ☞ **Lower-federal-court jurisdiction:** Congress may cut back, perhaps even completely eliminate, the **lower federal courts**; as with the Supreme Court, Congress may not *expand* the lower courts' dockets beyond the bounds of the constitutional federal judicial power.

Exam Tips *on*
FEDERALISM AND FEDERAL POWER GENERALLY

Issues covered by this Chapter are often hidden in a fact pattern. Here are some things to watch out for:

☛ **Enumerated powers:** Most importantly, any time your fact pattern tells you that Congress (or, for that matter, the Executive or Judicial Branch) is doing something, be sure that the action taken falls within one of the *enumerated* powers.

☛ **No general federal police power:** Remember that there is *no general federal police power*.

    ☞ **Only power to tax and spend:** It's true that Congress has the power to *tax* and *spend* for the "general welfare." But Congress doesn't have a general power to *legislate* for the "general welfare." Therefore, if your fact pattern indicates that Congress is *regulating* rather than taxing or spending, it is not enough that Congress is acting for the "general welfare"; it must be regulating pursuant to some other enumerated power, typically the Commerce power or the post-Civil War amendments.

☛ **"Necessary & Proper" Clause:** Once you identify an enumerated power that might be relied upon by Congress, invoke the "Necessary and Proper" Clause. Under this clause, Congress may use *any means* that is: (1) *rationally related* to the exercise of the enumerated power; and (2) not specifically *forbidden* by the Constitution.

    ☞ **Broadly construed:** Remember that the Clause is *very broadly construed*, to give Congress *lots of authority* to choose the means with which to carry out an enumerated power. So, if in your fact pattern Congress seems to be trying to exercise some valid source of power, resolve in favor of Congress any doubts about the validity of the particular method Congress has chosen. Perhaps cite to *U.S. v. Comstock* (holding that Congress can civilly commit dangerous prisoners at the end of their prison terms, as a "necessary and proper" means of enforcing Congress' power to pass and enforce federal criminal statutes).

Exam Tips *on*
THE FEDERAL COMMERCE POWER

Any time your fact pattern involves an action by Congress, you've got to keep the *Commerce Clause* in mind. In particular:

☛ **Check Commerce first:** Whenever you've got to decide whether a congressional statute falls within an enumerated power, **check the Commerce Clause first**. It encompasses a broader variety of congressional action than any other congressional power.

☛ **Deference by Court:** Remember that the Court takes a fairly **deferential** view on the issue of whether a particular action falls within the Commerce power. So long as a regulated activity **"substantially affects"** interstate commerce, the regulation will be found to fall within the Commerce power.

  ☞ **Aggregation of intrastate transactions:** For instance, even if a particular commercial activity being regulated seems to take place solely **intrastate**, the Court will usually find that when all similar activities are considered as a **class**, they have a **cumulative effect** on interstate commerce.

  Example: Remember *Gonzales v. Raich*, where the Court upheld Congress' right to ban intrastate cultivation of marijuana for one's own medicinal use because exemption of such cultivation might damage Congress' scheme banning interstate marijuana distribution.

  ☞ **Interstate transport:** Also, remember that Congress may ban or regulate interstate transport as a way of dealing with local problems.

  ☞ **Non-commercial activities:** However, look out for congressional regulation of activities that are **not really commercial**. Here, there's a much better chance that the Court will find that the activity does **not** substantially affect interstate commerce. Cite to *U.S. v. Lopez* in this situation.

  Examples of attempts to regulate activities that probably **don't substantially affect interstate commerce,** so that the regulation is probably **invalid**:

    ❏ Congress prescribes the **curriculum public schools must use**.

    ❏ Congress makes it a federal crime to commit a **gender-based violent crime** against a woman (see *U.S. v. Morrison*).

    ❏ Congress **bans marriage** under the age of 18.

    ☛ **Jurisdictional hook:** But if there's a "jurisdictional book" — like a ban only on those machine guns that passed in interstate commerce — the regulation is probably O.K.

  ☞ **Must purchase product:** Be alert for fact patterns where Congress purports to tell a person who is not presently in the market for a particular product that they **must purchase that product.** This type of command probably goes beyond Congress' Commerce powers. The result in *N.F.I.B. v. Sebelius* — where Congress was found not to have the Commerce power to require most individuals to **buy health insurance even if they don't want to** — is an example of the kind of fact pattern you may get on an exam. Point out that under *N.F.I.B.*, even the fact that millions of individuals' decision not to buy a product substantially (and negatively) affects the interstate market for that product isn't enough to make Congress' decision to require the purchase a proper exercise of the Commerce power.

☛ **Tenth Amendment:** Be alert for fact patterns where Congress is regulating *the states*. Such regulation raises a *Tenth Amendment* issue:

  ☞ **Generally-applicable laws:** So long as Congress has merely passed a *generally applicable* law, this law can apply to the states just as it does to private individuals, and there is no Tenth Amendment violation. (*Example:* Minimum wage laws may be applied to state workers just as to private workers.)

  ☞ **States forced to enforce federal regulatory scheme:** But Congress may not directly compel the states to enact or enforce a federal regulatory program. [*New York v. United States; Printz*] When Congress does this, it violates the Tenth Amendment (But Congress may single out the states for regulation when the states are acting as market participants. [*Reno v. Condon*]

Exam Tips *on*
OTHER NATIONAL POWERS

Here are some of the ways issues discussed in this chapter can appear on exams:

☛ **Taxes vs. regulation:** Professors sometimes test on the blurry line between taxing and regulation. Your fact pattern might give you a *tax* that is principally for *regulatory purposes*. If so, you can probably rely on the taxation power as an independent source of congressional power (distinct from the Commerce Clause, for instance).

  ☞ **"Penalty" label not fatal:** To determine whether a revenue-raising device is a "tax," the Court now performs a *"functional"* analysis: if the measure *behaves like a tax* (most importantly, it raises some *material revenue*), it doesn't matter than Congress has labelled it a *"penalty."* Cite *N.F.I.B. v. Sebelius* on this point.

    ☛ **Can't make the activity a crime:** But to be a valid "tax," it's probably the case that the measure must not make the activity being regulated a *"crime"* or *"offense,"* and the money collected must be small enough that a rational person might choose to pay the "tax" rather than commit the act that Congress is trying to encourage (e.g., buying health insurance).

Example: In the Affordable Care Act (ACA), Congress said that anyone who didn't buy health insurance (at a typical cost of $400 per month for a high-income person) had to pay the IRS a "penalty" (which for a high-income person would be about $200 per month). Since the ACA didn't make non-purchase a serious offense (i.e., there were no criminal penalties for not buying and not paying the penalty), and since the "penalty" was much smaller than the cost of the actual insurance, the penalty was found valid as an exercise of the Taxing power. *N.F.I.B. v. Sebelius.* (But if failure to buy a $400/month policy had caused a $2,000/month "penalty," and non-penalty-payers could be criminally prosecuted, the scheme probably would *not* have qualified as an exercise of the Taxing power.)

☞ **Treaties:** Occasionally, you will be tested on the procedural requirements for a *treaty*. Remember that the President may propose a treaty, but it does not become effective until *ratified* by two-thirds of the Senate.

  ☞ **Executive Agreements:** Also, keep in mind that even where the President cannot get a treaty ratified, the President may create an international agreement as an ***"Executive Agreement."*** (An Executive Agreement is essentially an agreement entered into between the President and some other country but not ratified by the Senate.) An Executive Agreement can't override a prior act of Congress, but is superior to state law.

  ☞ **Foreign affairs:** Your fact pattern may involve *foreign affairs* without any war and without any treaty. In this situation, you should pose the question whether the action falls within the enumerated powers. The answer, typically, is that there is no power over foreign affairs expressly given to either the President or the Congress, but the Court has recognized an implicit power of both branches over this domain.

  Examples: For instance, your fact pattern might involve an attempt by Congress to prevent Americans from travelling abroad, to prevent aliens from visiting this country, or some other aspect of foreign affairs not falling within a specifically-enumerated power. Generally, you should find such an attempt as falling within Congress' implied powers of the foreign-affairs domain.

☞ **District of Columbia:** Be on the lookout for questions involving congressional regulation of the ***District of Columbia***. Congress has a special enumerated power to govern the District of Columbia, so it may regulate there in purely local matters (which would not fall, say, within the Commerce power).

☞ **Federal property:** Similarly, remember that Congress can govern all *federal property*. Fact patterns frequently involve *national parks*, national monuments, *military bases*, and other types of federal property. In all of these areas, Congress has complete regulatory power, so you do not need to worry about whether the activity being regulated falls within the Commerce power or any other general congressional power.

> **Example:** Congress makes it a federal crime to kill a wild boar in any national park. This statute can be most easily justified under Congress' power to supervise federally-owned land.

Exam Tips on
TWO LIMITS ON STATE POWER

Issues involving the dormant Commerce Clause and congressional pre-emption can often be well-hidden in a fact pattern; you must be especially vigilant to spot these issues. Here are some particular things to look for:

Dormant Commerce Clause

☛ **Undue burden on Commerce:** Remember that one main branch of dormant Commerce Clause analysis is the *"burden"* branch: if a state's regulations would burden interstate commerce, the regulation will be struck down unless the burdens are *outweighed* by the state's interest in enforcing its regulation. Thus you must use a *balancing test* to evaluate "burden" problems. Also:

☞ **Conflicts:** Look for *conflicts* between the laws of two or more states. The existence of conflicting regulations is likely to be an undue burden on commerce, since a business operating in multiple states would find it difficult or impossible to comply with all of the conflicting regulations.

☞ **Transportation:** Be on the lookout for regulations affecting *transportation*, especially *trucking*. These are classic scenarios where the states have differing regulations and commerce is directly affected because goods have to pass from state to state.

Example: State A says that any truck driving a load in the state must have mud-guards of at least a certain size. No other nearby state (or the federal government) imposes such a limitation. You should say that a court might conclude that the requirement unduly burdens interstate commerce, in which case it would be invalid even though enacted for legitimate safety reasons.

☞ **Applies even without protectionist motive:** Remember that you must do a "burden" analysis even where the state seems totally *even-handed*, and is not showing any protectionism.

☛ **Health and safety regs:** Common examples of state regulations that are even-handed but nonetheless unduly burdensome are *health* and *safety* regulations.

Example: Suppose a state (or local) government insists on performing its own inspection of goods that are imported from elsewhere. This is likely to be an undue burden on commerce even if the state is truly pursuing health and safety rather than protectionism.

☛ **Protectionism:** Remember that the other main branch of dormant Commerce Clause analysis is the *"protectionist"* branch — if the state is intentionally *discriminating* against out-of-staters, in order to promote its residents' *own economic interests*, this is not a legitimate state objective, so the regulation will almost *automatically* violate the Commerce Clause.

   ☞ **Examples:** Here are some common varieties of protectionism:

      ❑ **Exporting of good stuff:** Look for rules *restricting* the *export* of *"good stuff"* produced inside the state. This is especially likely where *natural resources* are the "good stuff" (e.g., a rule saying, "No more than x% of coal mined from the state may be exported").

      ❑ **Importing of bad stuff:** Look for rules barring the *import* of *"bad stuff"* (e.g., "No out-of-state garbage or toxic waste may be buried in our state").

      ❑ **Importing of good stuff:** Look for rules whose effect is to *limit imports* of *"good stuff"* because the state is trying to *boost demand* for *in-state-produced* good stuff (e.g., "Coal-fired utilities located in this state must buy at least 10% of their coal from in-state mines").

☛ **State as market participant:** Remember that the dormant Commerce Clause does not apply at all where the state is a *market participant*. Therefore, be on the look-out for instances where the state is *operating a factory*, *purchasing goods*, or otherwise *directly engaging in commercial transactions* for its own account (as opposed to regulating the commercial transactions done by private parties).

☛ **Local ordinances:** Don't forget that *local ordinances*, not just state rules, can violate the dormant Commerce Clause. This is true even where the ordinance discriminates against out-of-town in-staters as well as out-of-staters.

☛ **Taxes:** Remember that *taxes* can be a violation of the dormant Commerce Clause (DCC) just as readily as regulations can be. We have the same two branches of analysis for taxes:

   ☞ **Discrimination:** Thus if the state is *discriminating* against interstate commerce by taxing it less favorably than in-staters, this will be a DCC violation.

   ☞ **Unfair burden:** Alternatively, a tax scheme will violate the DCC if the scheme unfairly *burdens* commerce even though it doesn't discriminate against out-of-staters on its face. One common type of illustration: the state puts a *flat tax* on some activity, regardless of its degree of connection with the state.

> **Example:** The state puts a flat annual tax on all trucks entering the state even occasionally, which has the effect of taxing out-of-state trucks much more heavily per mile than in-state trucks. In considering the burden, consider whatever the fact pattern tells you about the tax policies of *other states* — inconsistencies can make the whole scheme burdensome even though each state's scheme is not burdensome when viewed in isolation.

Congressional pre-emption

☞ **Pre-emption by Congress:** Separately, be on the lookout for *federal preemption* problems. Remember that this is an aspect of the Supremacy Clause; if Congress (or a federal agency acting under Congress' direction) has acted in a particular respect or occupied a particular domain, the states are often precluded from regulating.

  ☞ **Same subject:** Be on the lookout for a fact pattern telling you that there are federal and state statutes dealing with the *same subject area*. This is a clue to preemption problems.

  ☞ **Express preemption:** First, check for *"express"* preemption: if Congress has explicitly said that the states may not regulate in a particular area, then any state regulation in that area is invalid under the Supremacy Clause, even if the state regulation seems to be consistent with the federal regulation.

  ☞ **Implied preemption:** Next, check for *"implied"* preemption. This can come in either of two flavors: *"conflicts preemption"* and *"field preemption."*

    ☞ **Direct conflict:** *Conflicts preemption* has two flavors, too, *"direct"* and *"indirect."* First, check for a *direct conflict*. If a person or business *could not simultaneously obey both* the state and federal regulation, then obviously the state regulation must fall. Most fact patterns are *not* of this "direct conflict" type, however.

    ☞ **Indirect conflict:** Next, check for an *indirect conflict*, mainly a conflict due to inconsistencies in the *purposes* of the two regulations. For instance, you may see a fact pattern where there are federal and state statutes dealing with the same activity, and the state statute is *more stringent* than the federal statute. Obviously, a person can obey both (simply by obeying the more stringent state statute). Here, ask yourself whether Congress meant to say, "We're setting a minimum standard, and we'll let the states be more stringent," or meant to say instead, "We're regulating this way, and we don't want states interfering with our scheme by being more stringent." In the latter situation, the state regulation conflicts with the purposes of the federal regulation, so the state regulation is invalid. Remember that it is always a question of *what Congress intended*.

☞ **Field preemption:** Finally, be on the lookout for *"field preemption."* That is, look for a federal statutory scheme that seems to deal with an *entire broad area*. Where Congress has acted in this way, this may represent Congress' intent to *"occupy the whole field,"* in which case even a state regulation dealing with an aspect of the problem that is not addressed in the federal regulatory scheme may be pre-empted. Commonly, this happens in fact patterns involving *nuclear power* and *immigration* — the existence of a broad federal regulatory scheme in these areas may well prevent the states from enacting even non-conflicting regulations dealing with these subjects.

Exam Tips on
INTERGOVERNMENTAL IMMUNITIES AND INTERSTATE RELATIONS

Here are things to watch for in connection with the two main topics from this Chapter, intergovernmental immunities and Art. IV's Privileges and Immunities Clause:

Taxation

☛ **Federal taxation of state activity:** If your fact pattern shows that a *federal tax* is being applied directly to an activity conducted by a *state government*, consider whether the limited state immunity from federal taxation is being violated.

  ☞ **Illustrations:** Typical fact patterns raising this issue are:

  ❏ The federal government requires every user, including states, to pay a fee for *federally-sponsored services* (e.g., a tax on airplanes to support the air traffic controller system), or

  ❏ The federal government applies a *general tax* on certain *wages* (e.g., a payroll tax applicable to state as well as private-sector employees).

  (As you'll see from the "substantial interference" test described below, in both of the above fact patterns the tax would be valid.)

  ☞ **Substantial interference:** Remember the general rule: the only real state immunity from federal taxation is that the federal government may not tax in a way which *substantially interferes* with a state's performance of its *basic governmental functions*.

    ☛ **Basic governmental functions:** Thus if the federal government is taxing a state's public parks or schools, you might have a violation of the state immunity.

☞ **Generally-applicable tax:** But in the vast majority of situations, including virtually all situations where the federal tax is a *generally applicable* tax, there will be *no* interference with basic governmental functions and thus no violation of state immunity. (*Example*: The federal government can tax all airplanes, including state-operated ones.)

☞ **State tax on federal function:** Conversely, any time you spot a *state tax* that is applied to an activity somehow connected with the *federal government*, consider whether this violates the *federal immunity from state taxation:*

  ☞ **Direct taxation:** The federal government is certainly immune from *direct* taxation by any state. For instance, if your fact pattern involves a state or local property tax on, say, a post office, that's a clear violation.

  ☞ **Taxation of federally-linked private party:** But most exam fact patterns do *not* involve a "direct" tax on a federal instrumentality. Instead, the state taxes a *private party*, in a way that (arguably) increases the federal government's costs.

    Example: The classic illustration is a tax on the operations of a *contractor* who is performing tasks for the federal government on a cost-plus basis.

    ☞ **Legal-incidence test:** Here, the rule is that it doesn't matter whether the economic burden is passed onto the federal government; as long as the *"legal incidence"* of the tax is *not* on the federal government, there is *no violation* of the federal immunity.

    Example: A state may impose a sales tax on materials used by a real estate contractor who is building a post office for the U.S. on a cost-plus basis, since the legal incidence of the tax is not on the federal government.

Regulation

☞ **State regulations:** Be on the lookout for state *regulations* that affect the federal government. Such a fact pattern raises the issue of whether the federal immunity from state regulation is being violated.

  ☞ **Federal immunity:** Typically, federal immunity from state regulation arises where the states are attempting to regulate a *federal enclave*, such as a post office or military post. Even if the state is regulating in a generally-applicable way, federal enclaves are *immune* from this regulation unless Congress has expressly consented to it.

    Example: A state may not impose its criminal code on a military base, unless Congress consents.

☞ **Federal regulation of state:** Conversely, if your facts show that the *federal government* is *regulating a state*, consider whether the state immunity from federal regulation is being violated.

    ☞ **Presumption of non-violation:** Here, you should almost always conclude that the state immunity is *not* being violated. State immunity from federal regulation is exceptionally narrow. Only if a federal regulation prevents a state from exercising its *core functions* will there be a violation. (If you do find a violation, it is essentially a violation of the Tenth Amendment.) It is unlikely you will see a fact pattern where the federal regulatory interference with state functioning is so great that this test is satisfied.

Art. IV Privileges and Immunities

☞ **P&I generally:** Issues involving Article IV's *Privileges and Immunities Clause* are easily hidden.

    ☞ **Discrimination against out-of-staters:** You should be looking for fact patterns where there is *discrimination* against *out-of-staters*. When you see such discrimination, your first instinct will be to see if there is a violation of the dormant Commerce Clause, and you will also want to examine the possibility of an equal protection violation. But don't forget to check for an Article IV P&I violation, since where that clause applies, the standard of review is very tough.

    ☞ **"Rights fundamental to national unity" test:** When you do see a state discriminating against out-of-staters, the most important thing to remember about Article IV P&I is that it applies only to rights that are *"fundamental to national unity."* Essentially, the only rights covered are rights related to *commerce*.

        ☞ **Illustrations:** In general, for the "fundamental to national unity" standard to be satisfied, your fact pattern will usually involve an individual who is a *U.S. citizen*, *resides out of state*, and is either *totally blocked* from following his *chosen profession or job* in the state, or is subjected to a *higher license fee* than is charged to in-staters.

        Example: A state law preventing citizens of other states from practicing law or medicine in the state would involve a right "fundamental to national unity," and would in fact violate the Article IV P&I Clause.

    ☞ **Two-part test:** If you conclude that the right in question *is* fundamental to national unity, then be sure to articulate the correct standard for review. Something akin to strict scrutiny is used: the state *loses* unless it can prove *both* that:

        [1] non-residents are a *"peculiar source of the evil"* which the discrimination against out-of-staters is attempting to remedy; and

[2] the discrimination bears a ***"substantial relationship"*** to the problem the discriminatory statute is attempting to solve.

☛ **Test is usually flunked:** Usually, you should conclude that the state has ***failed*** to satisfy one or both of these tests. (The "peculiar source of evil" test is especially hard for the state to satisfy.)

☞ **Recreation:** There is one context in which you should always conclude that a right "fundamental to national unity" is ***not*** involved: where what is involved is the pursuit of ***recreation***. Thus your fact pattern will frequently involve an out-of-stater's right to ***hunt***, ***fish***, use tennis courts, etc.; typically the out-of-stater will either be entirely blocked from doing these things, or charged a much higher fee than in-staters. Even if the ban on out-of-staters is total, you should still conclude that Article IV's P&I is ***not*** violated, because commerce is not involved and thus there is no right fundamental to national unity.

☛ **Professional:** But if the out-of-stater wants to hunt, fish, etc. as a ***professional*** who will earn most of his living that way, then this analysis probably will not apply, and the P&I Clause *will* apply.

☞ **Compared with Equal Protection Clause:** When you spot discrimination against out-of-staters that seems to trigger the Article IV P&I Clause, you typically will want to compare the application of the P&I Clause with the Equal Protection Clause. Keep in mind the important differences between how these two clauses apply to discrimination against out-of-staters:

☛ **Exclusions:** ***Aliens*** and ***corporations*** do ***not*** get to use the Article IV P&I Clause (since it applies only to "national citizenship," and neither aliens nor corporations are "United States citizens.") By contrast, aliens and corporations can benefit from the Equal Protection Clause.

☛ **Stiffer test:** On the other hand, once the P&I Clause does apply, something like ***strict scrutiny*** is applied, and the out-of-stater will almost always win. By contrast, under Equal Protection Clause analysis, non-residency is ***not*** a suspect classification, so a state can usually discriminate against out-of-staters without violating the Equal Protection Clause as long as the state regulation is rationally related to a legitimate state objective. Often, the state will be able to satisfy this easy standard.

☞ **Distinguish from 14th Amendment P&I:** Be sure to specify that it is the ***Article IV*** P&I Clause, ***not*** the Fourteenth Amendment P&I Clause that you're talking about. The Fourteenth Amendment P&I Clause is extremely limited, and is rarely used. Especially on multiple choice questions, be careful not to pick a response stating that the challenged action is a violation of "the Fourteenth Amendment's Privileges and Immunities Clause" — professors love to slip this in as a trick answer.

Exam Tips on
SEPARATION OF POWERS

Separation-of-powers problems are usually pretty easy to spot. The harder part, usually, is to say something intelligent about how the issue should be resolved, since the law in this area is very hazy. Here are some particular things to watch for:

Miscellaneous presidential powers

☛ **Executive orders:** Whenever your fact pattern indicates that the President is issuing an *"executive order,"* consider whether this may amount to the *making of law* rather than the mere carrying out of law. If so, the President is probably treading on Congress' domain. (But remember that if Congress acquiesces, even implicitly, to the President's exercise of power, then the problem disappears. See, e.g., *Dames & Moore v. Regan.*)

☛ **Veto power:** Always remember that "legislation" cannot go into effect unless the President has been given the opportunity to *veto* the bill. Therefore, if your fact pattern has Congress do something by a one-house or concurrent *resolution*, determine whether what Congress is doing amounts to lawmaking; if so, the action is unlawful. (See, e.g., *INS v. Chadha*, the "legislative veto" case.)

☛ **Armed Forces abroad:** One of the most common separation-of-powers issues involves the President's power as Commander in Chief to *commit the use of American armed forces abroad*. The general rule, of course, is that only Congress, not the President, may declare war.

  ☞ **Emergency powers:** However, the President may commit our armed forces even without a declaration of war in order to *repel a sudden attack*, and probably to defend an ally with whom we have a treaty. But if you conclude that one of these exceptions applies, note in your answer that the President probably has the obligation to consult with Congress after the fact, and to bring our troops back if Congress has not passed a declaration of war within, say, a couple of months.

Appointments and firings

☛ **Appointments and firings, generally:** Any time your fact pattern involves the *appointment* or the *firing* of a *federal official*, be alert to possible separation-of-powers problems.

☛ **Appointment:** The President, not Congress, has the power to appoint federal officers. Federal officers include ambassadors, federal judges, Cabinet members, agency heads, etc.

☞ **Advice and consent by Senate:** When the President appoints a *"principal"* officer of the United States (i.e., a top-level officer), the appointment does not take effect until the Senate "advises and consents," i.e., approves. This applies to members of the Cabinet, ambassadors and federal judges.

☞ **Delegation as to inferior officers:** Congress cannot appoint *"inferior"* (non-top-level) federal officers either. But it can decide **which of three players** (the President, the federal judiciary, and the *"heads of departments,"* i.e., Cabinet members) may appoint any given inferior officer.

☞ **Removal:** The most frequently-tested area involving appointment of federal officers involves *removal* of officers once they have been appointed.

☞ **Removal by Congress acting alone:** Congress may *not* itself ever remove a federal officer, *except by impeachment*.

  Example: If Congress decided that it did not like the Secretary of State, it could not pass a law stripping him of his office, even if Congress were able to override the President's veto. Impeachment is the only method by which Congress could remove this officer.

☞ **Limits on President's power of removal:** But Congress **may limit the President's right to remove** a federal official, at least officials working for or heading *"independent"* agencies, and officials who are pure-executive-branch but are *"inferior"* officers.

  Example: Congress can say that no SEC Commissioner may be removed during her fixed term except for cause. (That's so because the SEC is an *independent* agency, i.e., one that's not just in charge of carrying out the President's executive-branch policies.)

☞ **Cabinet members:** Congress may *not* limit the President's right to fire **high-level purely-executive-branch officers** (e.g., **Cabinet members**).

  Example: Congress may not pass a law stating, "The Secretary of State shall have a fixed term of at least four years, and may not be sooner removed by the President without cause." That would violate the separation-of-powers, since it would seriously impair the President's power to carry out his own responsibilities as head of the executive branch.

Impeachment

☞ **Impeachment generally:** *Impeachment* is occasionally tested.

☞ **Procedural rules:** Keep in mind the procedural rules: by majority vote, the House decides whether to "impeach" (which is like an indictment). Then, the

Senate conducts a trial, at which a two-thirds vote is necessary for conviction.

☞ **Abuses of power:** Your fact pattern may involve the issue of whether the President or another federal official may only be removed for crimes, or may also be removed for non-criminal "abuses of power." The constitutional phrase is "high crimes and misdemeanors," but it is not clear what this means.

Immunity

☛ **Immunity generally:** Issues relating to *immunity* of the various branches are sometimes tested:

☞ **"Speech or Debate" Clause:** If a *member of Congress* is sued (either civilly or criminally), or called before a grand jury, be alert to the possibility that the member may be protected by the *"Speech or Debate"* Clause, which is basically a form of immunity.

☞ **Executive-Branch immunity:** There is a common-law immunity for the *President* and other members of the *Executive Branch*.

☛ **Qualified immunity for lower officials:** Members of the Executive Branch other than the President get only *qualified* immunity from civil suits. (Focus on whether the right violated by the official was "clearly established" at the time he acted; if it was, he can be liable, if not, he'll be immune.)

☛ **Criminal prosecutions:** Remember that there is *no* Executive-Branch immunity from *criminal* prosecutions.

Executive privilege

☛ **Qualified privilege:** If your fact pattern involves a President or other Executive-Branch member who wants to *decline to disclose* material, consider the possibility that the doctrine of *"executive privilege"* may apply. If you discuss the doctrine, remember that the privilege is merely a *qualified* one, which can be outweighed by other interests (e.g., the need to develop all facts at a criminal trial). Also, mention that claims of executive privilege are justiciable — that is, the Court will typically decide these claims, rather than avoiding them as non-justiciable political questions.

Exam Tips *on*
DUE PROCESS OF LAW

In virtually any fact pattern where an individual or company is not permitted to do something, you must be alert to the possibility that there is a *due process* violation. A large portion of all complex-fact-pattern essay questions will raise at least one due process ("DP") issue. Here are the most important things to keep in mind:

Substantive/procedural distinction

☛ **Making the distinction:** Determine whether it is an issue of *substantive* DP or *procedural* DP that you're faced with.

   ☞ **Nature of substantive DP problem:** In a *substantive* DP problem, the government is completely taking away a whole group's ability to do something, and there is no issue of whether the particular plaintiff falls into the governmentally-defined group or not.

      Example: The state says, "No woman may have an abortion after the third month of pregnancy." If the facts make it clear that P is a woman who is four months pregnant, we have a substantive DP problem, not a procedural DP problem.

   ☞ **Nature of procedural DP problem:** In a *procedural* DP problem, the overall issue is whether P as an individual does or does not fit into the legislatively-defined group, and the sub-issue is what if any *individualized, case-specific, procedures must be followed* before the government can determine which group P falls into.

      Example: A city says, "Public school teachers may only be fired for acts of moral turpitude." If there is an issue about whether P did or did not commit such an act, then we're dealing with procedural due process, i.e., the procedures used to determine whether P did or did not commit such an act.

Substantive DP, generally

☛ **Fundamental vs. non-fundamental:** If you're dealing with a *substantive* DP problem, decide immediately whether the right at issue is *fundamental* or non-fundamental.

   ☞ **Catalogue of fundamental rights:** Remember that the only rights that are fundamental for substantive DP purposes are those that involve the *"right of privacy"* or *"right of autonomy."* The key examples are:

❏ The right to *marry*. (But there's no evidence so far that the right of a *same-sex* couple to marry is fundamental — only *opposite-sex* couples have thus far been recognized as having a fundamental right of marriage.)

❏ The right to *bear* (or decide *not* to bear) *children*.

❏ The right to decide how to *rear* one's children.

❏ Perhaps the right to decline *unwanted medical treatment* (and possibly the right to *commit suicide* if competent and terminally ill).

❏ Possibly, the right to control one's *dress* and *personal appearance*.

☞ **Strict scrutiny:** If you conclude that the right is "fundamental," state that the court must *strictly scrutinize* the regulation. The state *bears the burden* of defending its regulation. The state loses unless *both* the following are true:

[1] The state is pursing a *"compelling"* (not just "legitimate") objective; and

[2] The means chosen by the state are *"necessary"* to achieve that compelling end. (If there are *less restrictive means* that would do the job just as well, or almost as well, then the means chosen aren't "necessary.")

☞ **Mere-rationality review:** By contrast, if you conclude that the right involved is *non-fundamental*, then state that *"mere-rationality"* review is used. That is, it just has to be the case that the state is:

[1] Pursuing a *legitimate governmental objective*; and

[2] Doing so with a means that is *rationally related* to that objective.

☛ **Economic regulation:** If the government regulation is essentially *economic*, you should almost certainly conclude that the rights involved are non-fundamental, and apply the mere-rationality test.

☛ **Social-welfare regulation:** The same is true of most health, safety or other "social welfare" legislation — unless it treads on one of those narrow areas (marriage, child-bearing, child-rearing, "right-to-die"), it's non-fundamental, and you should be using "mere-rationality" review.

Fifth vs. Fourteenth Amendment

☛ **Importance of distinction:** Be sure to distinguish between the *Fifth* Amendment's DP Clause and the *Fourteenth* Amendment's DP Clause. If the regulation is imposed by the *federal* government, the relevant clause is the Fifth Amendment. If the regulating is being done by a state or local government, the Fourteenth Amendment is the relevant one.

☛ **Trap:** Especially on multiple-choice tests, profs love to try to trip you up on this distinction.

Example: The question asks you which of four actions is least likely to be a violation of the Fourteenth Amendment. The correct answer is an action taken by the federal government — this could be a violation of the 5th Amendment's DP clause, but not a violation of the 14th Amendment's DP clause.

Particular substantive DP areas

☛ **Testable areas:** Here's an overview of some of the most testable issues relating to the substantive due process protection given to *fundamental* rights:

☞ **Contraception:** Most regulations restricting access to *contraception* will be strictly scrutinized and will fail. However, it is not clear that *minors* have a substantive DP right to birth control without parental consent — this makes a good testable issue.

☞ **Abortion rights:** A pregnant woman's interest in *abortion*, of course, gets some substantive DP protection. Your professor will expect you to know that this is so, as a general proposition. The particular sub-issues she is likely to test you on are:

❏ Whether the state may require that the woman's *spouse* be given notice prior to the abortion. (The answer is *"no."*)

❏ Whether a *minor* may be required to have *parental consent.* (The answer is generally *"yes,"* but there must be a "judicial bypass" offered as an alternative.)

❏ Whether *late-term* abortions may be tightly regulated. (The answer generally seems to be *"yes"*, but only if the health of the mother is taken into account. Cf. *Stenberg v. Carhart*, striking down a ban on "partial-birth" abortions because it did not contain an exception to protect the health of the mother.)

☛ **"Undue burden" test:** In general, when you're analyzing an abortion problem, remember to say that under *Planned Parenthood v. Casey*, the standard is whether the regulation *"unduly burdens"* the woman's interest in deciding whether to have the baby or not.

Also, in any case involving *regulations* on the abortion process (rather than outright bans), mention that under the recent *Gonzales v. Carhart* partial-birth-method decision, the Court has grown more likely to uphold regulations that are justifiable by a desire to spare the woman from *later regret* about her decision to use a particular method.

☞ **Sexual activities:** If the regulation interferes with *sexual* activities, distinguish between interferences with the rights of *married* opposite-sex couples, and virtually all other types of sex.

☛ **Marital privacy:** Thus if your facts involve a government attempt to make certain practices unlawful when practiced between members of an opposite-sex *married* couple in *private*, you should usually be applying strict scrutiny, and you should conclude that the interference violates substantive DP.

Example: A state makes it a crime to engage in "sodomy," and the statute is applied to the activities of a heterosexual married couple. Probably the statute is to be strictly scrutinized, and violates the couple's substantive DP rights.

☛ **Gay sex:** Where the activity consists of *homosexual sex*, you should conclude that (1) the activity is *not* "fundamental," and the regulation is therefore not to be strictly scrutinized; but that (2) the *"mere rationality"* review that's used should have real *"bite,"* and should be used to *strike down* as "irrational" any regulation that seems motivated solely by the majority's *"moral disapproval."*

Example: If government bans "sodomy" in a way that restricts gay sexual activity, say that even under mere-rationality review the measure must be struck down as an irrational substantive due process violation of the right to sexual expression. Cite to *Lawrence v. Texas*.

☞ **Same-sex marriage:** If a state chooses to allow *same-sex marriage*, and a couple is validly-married according to the state, you should note that the *federal government may not treat the couple differently* than it treats opposite-sex married couples. (*Example:* Same-sex couples married under state law must receive the same federal income and estate tax treatment as opposite-sex married couples.) Cite to *U.S. v. Windsor* (but note that it's not clear whether *Windsor* is based on equal protection, substantive due process, or both).

☛ **Unmarried minors:** If the activity is by unmarried *minors*, it is especially clear that it is not "fundamental," and may be extensively regulated (or probably even forbidden) by the state.

☞ **Unwanted medical attention:** If the state has placed restrictions on a person's right to decline *unwanted medical attention*, say that a fundamental interest is probably at stake.

☛ **Living wills and health-care proxies:** If the state is declining to honor a properly-prepared *living will* or *health-care proxy* (delegating the health-care decision to another person if the patient is incompetent), conclude that the state is violating substantive DP.

☛ **No documents present:** But where there is no living will or health-care proxy, and the patient is incompetent, the state does **not** violate substantive DP by setting very high *evidentiary standards* before concluding that the medical care is really unwanted. Cite to the *Cruzan* case in this kind of situation (where the Court held that the state may require "clear and convincing evidence" that the incompetent really would not have wanted the medical attention).

☛ **Assisted suicide:** If the patient is terminally ill (and competent) and the issue is whether a relative or doctor may *assist in the patient's suicide*, indicate that whatever due process interest the patient may have in committing suicide is certainly *not fundamental*, and that the state's countervailing interest in preventing the suicide is stronger. Therefore, the state *may make it a crime* to attempt suicide, or to assist another in committing suicide.

Other possibly-fundamental interests

☛ **Some contexts:** Here are some other contexts where you might find that fundamental interests are being impaired in violation of substantive DP:

❑ The state has impaired opposite-sex couples' right to *get married* to each other (e.g., by disallowing marriage until one party pays some fine or satisfies a back obligation like child support — see *Zablocki v. Redhail*).

❑ Be alert for a question on the constitutionality of a *state's ban on same-sex marriage.* Note that *U.S. v. Windsor* doesn't explicitly address this issue. Note also that even if such a ban is given *minimal rational-relation* review, the ban might flunk, on the theory that the ban is motivated simply by moral disapproval of gay people, and that that's not a legitimate state interest.

❑ Relatives are being prevented from *living together* (e.g., by restrictive *zoning* rules such as the no-cousins rule in *Moore v. East Cleveland*).

❑ Parents are being deprived of freedom to choose how their child is to be *educated* (e.g., a state statute banning home-study or private-school education, or unduly restricting these alternatives) or how the child is to be *raised at home* (e.g., a state court order compelling a mother to give lengthy visitation rights to the child's paternal grandparents).

❑ Adults are unfairly restricted in their attempts to *adopt* a child (e.g., by a requirement that the *race* of the parent and child, or the *religion* of the parent and child, *match*).

Procedural due process

☛ **Procedural DP generally:** Whenever you have government denying a person a job, license, benefit, etc., consider whether the individual was entitled to ***procedural due process***, and if so, whether the requirements of procedural DP were complied with.

☞ **Governmental action:** First, make sure that there is ***government action*** in the denial.

> **Example:** Suppose the facts tell you that a private employer is firing someone. In your answer, you'll never even need to get to the issue of procedural due process because there is no state action.

☞ **Deprivation of life, liberty or property:** Next, check to make sure that what is being denied is *"life," "liberty"* or *"property."*

☛ **Life:** You'll never have to worry about "life" being taken unless your fact pattern deals with the death penalty in criminal cases.

☛ **Liberty:** Here are some typical situations where "liberty" is at stake:

❏ P is deprived of the right to ***drive***;

❏ P is denied a ***license*** that she needs in order to practice her profession (e.g., law, medicine, accounting, teaching, or even truck-driving or tour-guiding);

❏ P is deprived of the right to ***raise his family***, because of charges of child abuse or neglect.

☛ **Property:** Most commonly, though, you'll see fact patterns suggesting that *"property"* may have been taken.

> ☞ **Government benefits:** Many situations involve government ***benefits***. If you are ***already*** getting the benefit, the government is probably depriving you of a "property" interest if it tries to ***terminate*** the benefit. On the other hand, if you are first ***applying*** for the benefit, then you probably do not yet have a property interest, so the government probably does not have to use procedural DP — it can arbitrarily or irrationally reject your application.
>
> Here are some typical kinds of government benefits that pop up on exam questions:
>
> ❏ receipt of ***welfare*** payments;
>
> ❏ right to occupy ***public housing***;
>
> ❏ right to take certain ***courses*** in public school, or to participate in ***extracurricular activities*** sponsored by the public school.
>
> ☞ **Legitimate claim of entitlement:** Remember that a key part of the analysis is whether state law, or perhaps even government custom,

gives P a *"legitimate claim of entitlement"* to have the benefit continue.

Example: If state law says that welfare benefits must be paid to every applicant in certain circumstances, that's probably enough to make receipt of the benefits a property interest. In that event, a person's benefits can't be terminated without due process.

☞ **Government job:** When you're dealing with a state or local government *job*, the same analysis applies: if you've already got the job, you may or may not have a "legitimate claim of entitlement" to it (depending on what state law says about how and when you can be fired).

Example: Suppose a government employee is given a booklet describing the circumstances under which he can be fired. The employee is likely to have a "property" interest in being able to avoid being fired except on the terms described in the booklet. If so, he can't be fired (at least on terms different from those in the booklet) without procedural due process.

☞ **Applicant:** On the other hand, a mere *applicant* for a government job probably has no legitimate claim of entitlement to the job, and therefore she can be denied the job without due process.

☞ **Protection from third-party misdeeds:** If P's claim is that government owed P a duty to *protect P from some private third-party's bad deeds*, probably P did *not* have a property or liberty interest in receiving that help from government, even if some statute required government to give that help.

Example: A statute says that police "shall arrest" anyone who violates a protective order. P asks the police to protect her by arresting her husband, H, who has just violated such an order. The police refuse, giving H the chance to murder P's children. P has not been deprived of a property or liberty interest. [*Castle Rock v. Gonzales*]

☞ **Significance:** So to re-summarize: If you do have a legitimate claim of entitlement, then you have a "property" interest that can only be taken away by complying with procedural DP. If you don't have a legitimate claim, then you have no procedural DP rights either.

☞ **What procedures are due:** If you've decided that P has a "property" or "liberty" interest that is being taken away, you know that P is entitled to some sort of procedural DP. Now, you must decide exactly *what procedures* are due to P.

☛ **Balancing test:** Here, remember to do a *balancing* test: for each procedural safeguard that may or may not be due, weigh the state's interest in making a prompt disposition against the damage to P in being denied the safeguard.

Example 1: Suppose P is a school teacher who is suspended based on suspicions that he has sexually abused a student. P's interest in being given a formal hearing with counsel *before* the suspension is clearly outweighed by the system's need to get him out of the classroom quickly. (P's interests can be adequately protected by, for instance, suspending him with pay pending the hearing.)

Example 2: By contrast, suppose the state wants to cut off P's welfare benefits. Here, P's probably entitled to a hearing before any suspension, because the cost to the state of a delay is not very great, and the damage to P from an erroneous determination would be great.

☞ **Punitive damages:** If P has been awarded *punitive damages* against D, consider the possibility that the award is so excessive (or so inappropriately takes account of harm done by D to persons not present in the litigation) that the award violates D's due process rights.

☞ **Judicial bias of elected judge:** If there is evidence that an *elected judge* may be *biased* because one litigant has made unusually large *campaign contributions* to her, consider the possibility that the opposing litigant may have a due process right to have the judge recuse herself. (Cite to *Caperton v. Massey* on this point.)

☞ **Sample safeguards:** Some of the procedural safeguards that you should consider are (in ascending order of the burden that they typically put on the state):

❑ the right to receive a *statement of reasons* why the benefit is being cut off;

❑ the right to a *hearing* at which P can plead her case;

❑ the right to have *counsel present* at the hearing;

❑ the right to *appeal* the adverse decision to a higher body.

☞ **What safeguards are due:** In general, you should conclude that P has the right to counsel and appeal only where the proceedings are criminal or quasi-criminal, but you should be relatively quick to conclude that P has a right to a statement of reasons or a hearing, even in a non-criminal situation such as loss of a job or loss of a financial benefit.

Exam Tips on
EQUAL PROTECTION

Equal protection issues, like due process ones, are often hidden, and are likely to be part of almost any complex fact pattern. It is not uncommon for 20-25% of a total Constitutional Law exam to consist of equal protection issues, scattered throughout multiple fact patterns. Here's what to look for:

Nature of classifications

☞ **Classes generally:** Above all else, anytime you see a legislative *classification* — a placement of people or businesses into *two or more groups* — think about the possibility that the classification might violate equal protection.

  ☞ **Distinction:** For there to be an equal protection problem, the issue must be whether the government has behaved reasonably in *setting up* the classes in the first place. If the issue is whether the government has correctly placed an *individual* into the "right" group or class, you have a problem of procedural due process, not equal protection.

    Example: If the government says, "All firefighters must retire at age 55," there is an EP problem because the issue is whether the government can set up the classes in this way. But if the government says, "Any firefighter too weak to do the work will be discharged," and the government then says, "Norman, you are too weak," the issue of whether Norman has been treated fairly is a procedural DP issue, not an EP issue, because the issue is whether the government has given Norman procedural regularity in deciding which class he falls into.

  ☞ **Invidious discrimination:** For there to be an EP problem, there must be *"discrimination"* against members of one of the classes, i.e., one class must be treated intentionally less favorably than the other. Use the adjective *"invidious"* to describe the required discrimination.

☞ **Facial vs. as-applied attacks:** If you state that P can make an EP attack on the classification at issue, state whether the attack would be "on the statute's *face*" or *"as applied."* Remember that a "facial" attack is used where the statute itself in its text discriminates against a class; an "as applied" attack is used where discrimination against one class stems from how the statute or regulation is *carried out*.

    Examples: If government imposes a literacy test, or allows public prosecutors to use peremptory challenges, you're likely to be dealing with an "as applied" test.

☞ **State vs. Federal:** Examine whether the discrimination is being practiced by a *state/local* government, or by the *federal* government. If it's the state or local government, then you're using the Fourteenth Amendment's EP Clause. If it's the federal government, you're using the Fifth Amendment's Due Process Clause, which by the process of "reverse incorporation" includes the principle of equal protection.

☞ **Trap:** Especially in multiple choice tests, profs like to give you an instance of federal discrimination and then try to tempt you to make a choice that involves "the Fourteenth Amendment's Due Process Clause." That's the wrong answer, for the reason just stated.

Choosing the correct level of review

☞ **Selecting the correct level:** Once you have identified an EP problem, devote extreme efforts to choosing the correct *level of review*. Remember that there are three levels used in evaluating EP situations:

❑ *Strict scrutiny* is used where either a classification is based upon a *suspect class* (race, national origin or alienage) or where the classification impairs the exercise of a *fundamental right* (e.g., the right to vote or the right to change your state of residence).

❑ *Mid-level* review is used for two "semi-suspect" classifications, those based on *gender* and *illegitimacy*.

❑ The *"mere-rationality"* standard is used for all other types of classifications.

☞ **Suggestion:** After you identify the issue, immediately state what the likely standard of review is, including details of that test.

Sample language to use: Here's a sample of how you might phrase the beginning of your answer: "Since the classification here is on the basis of gender, the Court will use a mid-level standard of review. That is, the Court will strike down the statute unless it is shown to be important to the achievement of a substantial governmental objective."

Mere-rationality standard

☞ **"Mere-rationality" standard generally:** Here are the main things to remember about the *"mere-rationality"* standard, and the places where it is used:

☞ **Economic regulation:** If the classification relates to *economic* regulation, you will almost certainly be using the "mere-rationality" standard.

Example 1: The state says no one can put a sign on a rooftop, but gives an exception for a sign advertising goods produced by the owner of the building. Use mere-rationality review (and say that the statute will almost certainly be upheld).

Example 2: The state taxes one group more heavily than another (e.g., there's a sales tax on "refined petroleum," but not on "unrefined petroleum"). Again, use mere-rationality review, and say that the tax scheme will almost certainly be upheld.

☞ **Social-welfare legislation:** Most types of *"social welfare"* classifications will also be judged by the "mere-rationality" standard.

Examples:

❑ Discrimination based on *age*;

❑ Discrimination against *aliens* where the function relates to the heart of representative government (see further discussion of aliens below);

❑ Discrimination in the issuance of *licenses* or *permits*;

❑ Discrimination against *out-of-staters*;

❑ Discrimination against the *poor* (in the sense that government fails to pay for things the poor need that the rich can pay for themselves).

☞ **"One step at a time":** If there's no suspect or semi-suspect class or fundamental right, and the government is trying to *combat an evil*, you'll probably note that the government has only attacked *part* of that evil. The question becomes whether the government has violated EP by not attacking the other evil. Here, you should say something like: "The regulation is valid, because the government is entitled to combat evils *one step at a time*." You might then want to cite to *Williamson v. Lee Optical Co.*

Example: The government requires lawyers, but not doctors, to take mandatory continuing education — this is OK, because the government may combat the evil of non-up-to-date professionals one step at a time.

☞ **Unpopular group:** If the government is trying to *single out an unpopular group* (but one that doesn't get suspect or semi-suspect status) for unfavorable treatment, indicate that although only "mere-rationality" review is used, that review will likely be applied *"with bite,"* and the scheme may well be struck down.

☛ **Gay marriage; rights of mentally retarded:** Unequal treatment of *gays* and the *mentally retarded* seems to fall into this category. So, for instance, Congress' decision in the Defense of Marriage Act not to recognize state-sanctioned *same-sex marriages* apparently flunked even mere-rationality review. (Cite to *U.S. v. Windsor*, where the Court doesn't expressly say it's applying the mere-rationality standard, but seems to be applying that standard "with bite.")

Racial classifications

☛ **Race generally:** If the classification has to do with *race*, here are the key things to remember:

☞ **Suspect class:** Race is a *"suspect class."* Therefore, any intentional discrimination based on race — either in the face of the statute/regulation, or in the way it is applied — must be *strictly scrutinized*. That is, the classification must be struck down unless it is *necessary* to achieve a *compelling governmental interest*. You should almost always conclude that this standard is *not* satisfied. Typically, your reason will be because there is some alternative non-race-conscious method of handling the problem, so the race-conscious means are not "necessary."

☞ **Purpose, not just effect:** Remember that race as a suspect classification will not be deemed to be involved unless government is acting with the *purpose*, *not just the effect*, of classifying based on race. *This is the single most commonly tested aspect of strict scrutiny*.

Example: If government takes an action which happens to disadvantage more blacks than whites, there's no suspect class, and thus no strict scrutiny, unless there's evidence that government acted with the purpose of disadvantaging blacks.

☛ **Tip off:** Your fact pattern will usually *not* contain a racial classification "on its face." Yet, the facts will indicate to you that some racial group is affected more than other groups. This should be your tip-off that you have an " 'effect' vs. 'purpose' " problem.

☛ **Circumstantial evidence:** Keep in mind, however, that *circumstantial evidence* can always be used to show that government has the *intent* to discriminate against the unfavored group, and that the effect is not merely an unintended by-product.

Example: If government chooses grand jurors from the rolls of registered voters, the fact that this produces far fewer black grand jurors than other methods would is admissible as circumstantial evidence that the government really intended to discriminate against black grand jurors.

☞ **Invidious:** Remember that the discrimination must be *"invidious."* That is, there must be an attempt to treat some racial group in a *less favorable*, stigmatizing, way. You will want to examine whether this element of "invidiousness" is present whenever the governmental scheme tends to merely *record* racial differences, or to impose some kind of racial *"matching."*

Examples: If the government publishes the race of each political candidate, or the government requires that the race of an adoptive parent match the child's race, or the government imposes a sickle-cell test applicable only to African Americans, you'll want to examine whether there is a "stigmatizing" or "invidious" discrimination. Often, but not always, you will conclude that the answer is "yes."

☞ **Segregation:** Be on the lookout for *segregation* — any government program that intentionally *separates* the races, or intentionally encourages the races to separate themselves, is likely to be invidious and thus needs to be strictly scrutinized.

Example: If a state university allows dormitories to classify themselves, by vote of the existing residents, as "primarily black" or "primarily white," this probably represents intentional governmental support of segregation, and probably requires strict scrutiny.

☛ **Affirmative action:** Special rules apply to race-conscious *affirmative action*:

☞ **Strict scrutiny:** *Strict scrutiny* is applied to the affirmative action situation just as much as to the "invidious" situation. Cite to *Richmond v. Croson* when you have a race-conscious affirmative action program.

☛ **Eradication of past discrimination:** Typically, the only governmental objectives that are strong enough to overcome strict scrutiny in the affirmative action context are: (1) the eradication of *past discrimination* by government (and only if the discrimination is shown by *clear evidence*); and (2) the pursuit of *diversity* in a *student body*.

☞ **Congress vs. state/local government:** The fact that it's *Congress*, rather than state or local government, that's doing the affirmative action now makes *no* formal difference — strict scrutiny is still applied. (Cite to *Adarand* if a congressional act is at issue.) However, you may want to allude to the possibility that even though the Court applies strict scrutiny, it may end up giving *slightly greater deference* to Congress' conclusion that race-conscious measures are needed, than it would to a similar conclusion by a state or local body.

☞ **University admissions:** Be on the lookout for race-conscious affirmative action in *university admissions*. Here, say that this is OK (because student-body diversity can be a compelling objective) *if* the school (1) evaluates each applicant as an *individual*; (2) treats minority-race as merely *one "plus factor" among others*; (3) *doesn't use mechanical means* (like *quotas* or a fixed number of "points") to obtain the desired number of minority-group admittees; and (4) proves that there were no *"workable race-neutral alternatives"* available to achieve the desired "educational diversity."

☛ **Key cases:** On these four rules, cite to the three cases of *Grutter v. Bollinger* (race as an individualized "plus factor" is OK), *Gratz v.*

Bollinger (mechanical point systems are not OK) and *Fisher v. Univ. of Texas* (workable race-neutral methods for achieving student-body diversity must be shown to be unavailable).

☞ **Pupil-assignment plans:** Also, be on the lookout for race-conscious *pupil-assignment plans* for *public elementary or high schools.* Here, any plan that classifies each student's race, and then makes any pupil assignment based on whether the student's presence would improve or worsen the target school's racial imbalance, will almost certainly flunk the requisite strict scrutiny. Cite to *Parents Involved v. Seattle School District* on this point.

☞ **Some contexts:** Here are some contexts in which race-conscious affirmative action programs may pop up on exams:

❏ preferential *admissions* to universities and public schools (see above);

❏ minority set-asides in the award of public *construction* and other *contracts*;

❏ allocation of public-sector *jobs* (including layoffs and promotions as well as original hiring);

❏ the drawing of *election districts*.

National origin

☞ **National origins:** The drawing of classifications based on *national origin* is also to be *strictly scrutinized*. However, exams rarely pose a national-origin problem.

Gender-based classifications

☞ **Gender generally:** Here's what to look for when there is a classification based on *gender*:

☞ **Mid-level review:** Remember that *mid-level* review is used for gender-based classifications. That is, the governmental objective must be *"important,"* and the means must be *"substantially related"* to that objective. (But note that this mid-level review is now a pretty tough standard, with the court requiring an "exceedingly persuasive justification," and giving "skeptical scrutiny." Cite to *U.S. v. Virginia*, the VMI case, as the source for these new descriptions of how the mid-level review is to be conducted.)

☞ **Invidious vs. benign:** Remember that the same review standard is in theory used whether the sex-based classification is *"invidious"* (intended to harm women) or *"benign"* (intended to help women). Any classification that derives in part from "stereotypical" views about women (e.g., that women's place is in the home, or that women are physically weak) is especially likely to be struck down.

☞ **Disadvantaged men:** Where the classification disadvantages *men*, the same rules apply: mid-level review is used.

☞ **Purpose, not just effect:** As with race-conscious discrimination, only governmental action whose *purpose*, not mere effect, is to discriminate against one gender, will be considered.

   Example: A strength requirement for paramedics would not be subjected to mid-level review, if the requirement's purpose was not to discriminate against women, and it was merely an unintended effect that fewer women than men could qualify.

☞ **Sample areas:** Here are some areas where gender-based classifications have popped up on exams:

   ❏ The government provides that *pregnant women in the work force* are to be treated differently than all others, e.g., with respect to exposure to toxic substances. (This is not necessarily true gender discrimination, since women who are not pregnant are not impacted, so probably you don't apply mid-level review, just "mere-rationality" review.)

   ❏ Women are given different *school activities* than men.

   Example: Women are not allowed to play football. Probably it's appropriate to use mid-level review, but the classification system will probably survive that review in light of the different average size and strength of women.

Illegitimacy

☛ **Illegitimacy is semi-suspect:** Classifications based on *illegitimacy* are also "semi-suspect" and thus get mid-level review. Most commonly, you would be tested on a state statute that discriminates against illegitimates with respect to the right to *inherit*.

Alienage

☛ **Alienage generally:** Discrimination against *aliens* is very frequently tested.

   ☞ **Strict scrutiny:** As a *general* rule, remember that discrimination against aliens is subjected to *strict scrutiny*.

   Examples:

   ❏ A state's refusal of welfare benefits to aliens will be strictly scrunitized.

   ❏ A state's refusal to let an alien practice a profession will be strictly scrutinized.

☞ Note that discrimination against "aliens" typically refers to discrimination against *legal* aliens. Probably strict scrutiny is *not* used for discrimination against *illegal* or "undocumented" aliens.

☞ **Heart-of-representative-government exception:** Remember that there is a key *exception* to the general rule of strict scrutiny: where the alien has applied for a *job* that goes to the *"heart of representative government,"* only mere-rationality review is used. Most government jobs that have a *policy*, *law enforcement* or *education* component fall within this "representative government" exception.

Examples: Jobs as a *public school teacher*, *police officer*, or *probation officer* are all within the exception, so the state merely has to be rational in its decision to close these positions off from foreigners.

☞ **Not covered:** But there are some jobs that are sufficiently ministerial that they do not fall within the "representative government" exception. (*Examples:* Secretary in a governmental agency; meter reader for a publicly owned electric utility.)

Fundamental rights

☞ **Fundamental-rights restrictions:** Classifications impairing a *"fundamental right"* are tested less frequently than those involving a suspect or semi-suspect class. Nonetheless, these classifications sometimes pop up on exams.

☞ **Voting:** Any impairment of the right to *vote* is an impairment of a fundamental right, and thus strictly scrutinized, if it is *not reasonably related to determining the voter's qualifications.*

Examples: (1) Poll taxes; (2) a requirement that the voter have resided in the jurisdiction for one year before the election; and (3) a requirement that the voter be a landowner or tenant, are all generally not reasonably related to determining the voter's qualifications. Therefore, such measures will be strictly scrutinized and struck down.

☞ **Reasonably related to voter qualifications:** But if the measure *is* reasonably related to determining the voter's qualifications, then it will be subjected only to *mid-level review*, and probably upheld.

Examples: (1) A requirement that a voter present a government-issued photo ID; and (2) A requirement that a voter prove that he's a bona fide resident (e.g., by having lived in the jurisdiction for 50 days) won't be strictly scrutinized, and will probably be upheld.

☞ **Candidacy:** A person's right to be a *candidate* seems to be "semi-fundamental," and thus gets more-than-mere-rationality review.

Example: A high candidate filing fee that is imposed even on indigent candidates violates EP.

☞ **New-party restrictions:** Similarly, restrictions that unfairly keep *new, not-yet-established, political parties* off the ballot get this semi-fundamental review.

☞ **Court-access:** Access to the *courts* is sometimes a "fundamental interest." Look for situations where the state imposes a *fee* that it refuses to waive for indigents. The two contexts that count are *criminal* cases (so that the state may not charge an indigent for a trial transcript or for counsel) and *family law* cases (so that the state may not charge a filing fee to indigents who want a *divorce*). But other types of civil access (e.g., small claims court or bankruptcy court) are not deemed "fundamental," so the state's refusal to subsidize indigents gets only mere-rationality review.

☞ **Right to travel:** The *"right to travel"* (really the right to *change* one's state of *residence* or *employment*) is "fundamental."

☞ **Illustrations:** Therefore, look for patterns where the state imposes a substantial *waiting period* on newly-arrived residents: if they have to do this wait before they get some *vital governmental benefit* (e.g., *welfare*), a fundamental right has been impaired. But non-vital benefits are not "fundamental" (so that there's only mere-rationality review where the state makes newcomers wait for, say, low in-state university tuition rates).

☞ **"Necessities":** The right to *"necessities"* is *not* fundamental. So if your fact pattern involves the state's refusal to equalize the right of indigents to such items as *public school education, food, shelter or medical care*, you probably need to apply only "mere-rationality" review, not strict scrutiny fundamental interest review.

Exam Tips on
MISCELLANEOUS CLAUSES

The Clauses covered in this chapter are easy to miss on an exam, because each applies to fairly specialized facts and is likely to be buried within a much larger fact pattern.

Most of your work will therefore consist of spotting the issue; once you do so, analyzing it correctly shouldn't be too hard. Here are some things to look for:

14th Amendment Privileges or Immunities

☞ **P-or-I Clause generally:** If your fact pattern happens to involve a person who is prevented from *travelling* from state to state, or blocked from *voting* in a national election, consider whether the *14th Amendment's Privileges or Immunities Clause* has been violated. A 1999 decision (*Saenz v. Roe*) makes questions on this Clause more likely — if the state is discriminating against people who recently moved into the state, the clause is probably violated.

☞ **Distinguish from Art. IV Clause:** But if your fact pattern involves a target state that discriminates against out-of-staters who have *not moved into* the target state, probably it's the *Article IV* P&I Clause, *not* the 14th Amendment P-or-I Clause, that's been violated.

Takings Clause

☞ **Takings Clause generally:** If you have a fact pattern that involves *land-use regulation* by the state or federal government, be alert to a *Takings* Clause issue.

☞ **Illustrations:** The main kinds of regulations that should put you on notice to look for a Takings problem are:

[1] *zoning* regs;

[2] *environmental-protection* regs; and

[3] *landmark-protection* regs.

☞ **Tip-off:** In general, if government is telling the owner, "You can't do such-and-such with your property" or "If you want to do such-and-such with your property, you'll have to submit to the following conditions … ," there is likely to be a Takings issue.

☞ **Economically-viable-use standard:** Remember that for a land-use regulation to avoid being a taking, it must *not deprive an owner of all economically viable use* of his land.

☞ **Typical zoning regulation:** The typical zoning regulation, which is generally-applicable and leaves the owner with at least some reasonable alternative uses of the property, will *not* normally be a "taking."

☞ **Permanent ban on building:** But a *permanent ban* on constructing any building on a lot *would* be a "taking," if there was no economically attractive use of the property (e.g., recreational) that did not involve construction.

☞ **"Public use" requirement:** Also, if you have a fact pattern in which the government has clearly exercised its *eminent domain powers*, don't forget to say that the taking must be for a *"public use."* But "public use" is a very watered-down standard — there must merely be some "public benefit," and almost anything qualifies (e.g., economic development such as more jobs or tax revenues). It can still be a public benefit even though the condemned property is turned over to private developers. Cite to *Kelo v. New London* on this point.

Contract Clause

☞ **Gov't rewrites the rules:** If your fact pattern has the government *"rewriting the rules"* in a way that seems to *change previously-executed contracts*, consider whether the *"Contract"* Clause has been violated. It's important for you to distinguish between government's attempt to re-write contracts to which it's a party, and government's attempt to re-write contracts between private parties:

☞ **Government's own deal is changed:** Where government is trying to escape from *its own "bad deals,"* you should be quick to find a Contract Clause violation. Remember that the Court scrutinizes this type of government action closely, and will allow it only if a *"significant public need"* exists that cannot be reasonably handled in any other way.

> **Example:** Suppose a state government faces bankruptcy unless it re-writes the payment schedule on some bonds, and the problem can't be handled by borrowing fresh funds. This might be a sufficient "significant public need" justifying the changing of the payment schedule.

☞ **Private deals:** Where government is re-writing contracts made by *private parties*, remember that the judicial review is *not so tough*. So long as the government is dealing with an emergency, and protecting broad social interests (rather than a narrow, favored group), the Court will tend to uphold any contract-rewriting that is *"reasonable"* in the circumstances.

☞ **Generally-applicable rules:** If the state applies a *"generally applicable* rule of conduct" that merely has the *incidental by-product* of impairing contractual obligations, the Contract Clause *doesn't come into effect at all*. This element is perhaps the most frequently tested aspect of the Contract Clause — fact patterns typically involve some general environmental or other regulatory change that happens to make one party's promised performance under a private contract no longer legal. Here, you should conclude that the Contracts Clause never comes into play, because the government action wasn't "directed at" (enacted for the purpose of affecting) the contractual obligation.

Ex Post Facto laws

☞ **How to spot:** *Ex post facto* laws are fairly easy to spot — whenever you see government *making something a crime* that wasn't a crime when it was done, or *increasing the penalty* for something beyond what was on the books when it was done, you may have an *ex post facto* violation.

☞ **Criminal penalty required:** Remember that only *"criminal"* penalties, not "civil" or "regulatory" ones, are covered. Often this distinction is what's being tested.

Bills of Attainder

☛ **How to spot:** *Bill of attainder* issues are rare. Only when you see the legislature trying to punish a group that is so *narrowly-defined* that it's possible to name all the affected people in advance, should you even think about bill of attainder. Typical example: The legislature holds that members of a particular named *organization* may not hold a certain post or receive a certain benefit.

Exam Tips on
STATE ACTION

You need to be on the lookout for State Action problems in any question that involves the rights of individuals (i.e., due process, equal protection, freedom of expression, freedom of religion, etc.). Remember that these constitutional guarantees only come into play when government is acting. Here are some specific things to watch for:

☛ **General tip:** Before you start to write about how the due process, equal protection, or other guarantee has been violated, make sure that there is "state action," i.e., that the challenged action is really *action by the government*, or at least that the challenged action can somehow be *ascribed* to the government.

☛ **Acts by private parties:** If a private individual is doing something that would clearly pose constitutional problems were it done by government, that's a tip off to a state action problem.

Examples:

❏ A private apartment owner refuses to rent to a black;

❏ A private employer refuses to hire a person because of her gender;

❏ A private shopping center refuses to allow P to distribute political campaign literature.

☞ **No state action:** In all of these situations, there will be *no state action* (and thus no constitutional violation), unless additional facts are presented that somehow tie the state in to the private actor's conduct.

☞ **Public function:** Be alert to situations where the only action is by a private individual, but the activity in question is one that is a ***"public function,"*** i.e., a function ***"traditionally" done by the states.*** Thus you may have at least an issue of whether a "public function" is being performed if your facts involve any of the following:

❑ a private (but partly state-funded) ***school***;

❑ a privately-operated ***park***;

❑ a ***political party*** conducting a primary or other party business;

❑ a ***"company town;"***

❑ a person taking some action typically done by the ***judicial system*** (e.g., a seller or lender foreclosing on collateral).

☞ **Public function must be exclusively by state:** Remember that today, the "public function" doctrine applies only where the function has traditionally been done ***"exclusively"*** by the states. This requirement knocks out a large percentage of the cases (including at least the private-school situation above).

☞ **State involvement in private conduct:** Also, be on the lookout for situations where the state is somehow heavily ***"involved"*** in the private actor's actions. The common scenarios for this are:

❑ **Commanded or required:** The state has ***"commanded"*** or ***"required"*** the private action.

Example: Recall the facts of *Shelley v. Kraemer*: the state, by enforcing restrictive covenants in real estate deeds, in effect commanded private individuals not to sell their homes to blacks. Because the state effectively commanded or required the private action, the private action became the equivalent of state action.

☞ **Testable issue:** A good testable issue is, May the state enforce some ***neutral state law*** where this has the effect of facilitating private discrimination?

Example: A private store owner refuses to serve blacks and wants them evicted. Does the state's use of its trespass laws turn the property owner's action into "state action?" The answer is probably "no," as long as the state is evenhanded in how it uses the trespass law.

❑ **Encouragement:** The state has ***"encouraged"*** the private action.

❑ **Symbiosis:** The state has a ***"symbiotic relationship"*** with the private action, i.e., the state and the private actor ***benefit from each other's conduct.***

Classic illustration: Remember *Burton v. Wilmington Parking Authority* — the state builds a state-operated building, and rents space in it to a restaurateur who discriminates. Because the state is getting major benefits from the restaurateur's operations (symbiosis), his conduct is transformed into "state action."

❏ **Involvement or entanglement:** The state is heavily *"involved," "entangled"* or *"entwined"* in the activity.

☛ **Mere license:** But where the state merely *licenses* the private activity, that's not enough involvement or entanglement to produce state action.

Example: Where government gives a liquor license to a private club, that's not enough to turn the club's discriminatory actions into state action. [*Moose Lodge v. Irvis*]

☛ **Heavy participation:** On the other hand, if state entities *participate* heavily in the private activity, and the state *recognizes* that activity as being closely related to important state concerns, this *will* probably be enough entanglement to make the activity state action.

Example: A state statute provides that a private association of high schools, all of which are located within a single state, has the role of regulating interscholastic sports in the state. Most association members are public high schools, and nearly all public high schools are members. The association's activities will probably found to be so entwined with state concerns as to make the association a state actor. [*Brentwood Academy*]

Exam Tips on
CONGRESSIONAL ENFORCEMENT OF CIVIL RIGHTS

Exam questions on the subjects covered in this Chapter are relatively rare. Here are the few things to keep in mind:

☛ **Can't reach purely private conduct:** Probably most important, the 14th and 15th Amendments cannot be used to reach *purely private conduct*, i.e., conduct not involving the state in any way. (This is another way of stating that "state action" is required.)

☞ **Combination:** But where government action and private action *combine*, then Congress can reach this activity. (*Example:* Congress can make it a crime for a private citizen to interfere with government desegregation efforts.)

☛ **13th Amendment:** The *13th* Amendment is the only Amendment that can reach *purely private conduct*. That is, Congress gets to say what is a "badge or incident of slavery," and to then forbid it. Profs love to test this special quirk.

> **Example:** Congress can ban purely private discrimination in housing, under authority of the 13th Amendment. [*Jones v. Alfred H. Mayer Co.*]

☞ **Basis for federal statute:** This means that the 13th Amendment can be the basis for federal anti-discrimination legislation that would otherwise have to be based on the Commerce Clause.

☞ **Non-whites:** The 13th Amendment can be used to ban racial discrimination against *non-blacks* (e.g., whites, Asians, etc.).

☞ **Testable issue:** A good testable issue is, Can Congress ban, under the 13th Amendment, discrimination on *other than racial grounds*? Probably Congress can attack discrimination based on *national origin* and *ethnicity*, but not on other characteristics (e.g., gender or sexual orientation). Also, probably only *purposeful* discrimination can be reached.

☛ **Remedial powers:** Where Congress is trying to combat a clear problem of *discrimination by a state*, its *remedial* powers are *relatively broad*. So as long as Congress is behaving rationally in combatting discrimination, you should conclude that it is acting constitutionally under its power to enforce the 13th, 14th and 15th Amendments.

☞ **"Up-to-date information" must be used:** But where Congress wants to use its remedial power to *prevent* state discrimination that has *not yet occurred*, Congress must act on *reasonably up-to-date information* about where discrimination is likely to be occurring.

> **Example:** Congress uses its 15th Amendment remedial powers to single out certain states, and to require only those states to get federal preapproval of any changes to state voting laws. Congress can't rely solely on 40-year-old voter data as the basis for picking which states must get the federal preapproval. (*Shelby County v. Holder*)

☞ **"Congruent and proportional" requirement:** Also, even where Congress is using its 14th Amendment powers to combat state discrimination, Congress' response must be *"congruent and proportional"* to the discrimination — Congress can't choose methods that are much *broader* than the discrimination being cured. [*Boerne v. Flores*] So Congress can't ban certain state discriminatory conduct, and then make the states liable in damages to private plaintiffs for that conduct, unless Congress had evidence that the states frequently violated people's constitutional rights in that area. Otherwise, the Eleventh Amendment blocks even Congress from imposing private-suit damage-liability onto the states.

Example: Suppose Congress rationally concludes that states, acting as employers, occasionally (but not frequently) violate the Fourteenth Amendment equal protection rights of disabled employees. Congress still can't give state employees the right to sue the state for damages for violating the statute — the states have Eleventh Amendment immunity from private damage suits, and that immunity can be overcome only by proof that Congress' response was congruent and proportional to widespread state discrimination of the type being addressed, something not present here. [*Bd. of Trustees of Ala. v. Garrett*]

☛ **Heightened scrutiny:** But where the area of discrimination that Congress is trying to prevent is one that gets *heightened scrutiny* (i.e., involves a *suspect or semi-suspect class*, or a *fundamental right*), then Congress can allow private damages based on a *lesser showing* that the states have discriminated.

> **Example:** Congress orders state and private employers to give employees various rights to take unpaid leave to care for sick family members. In doing so, Congress is acting to combat gender discrimination. Even if the states have practiced only occasional leave-related gender discrimination against their employees, Congress can still let state employees sue for violations of the state, because gender-discrimination gets heightened (mid-level) review. [*Nevada Dept. of Hum. Res. v. Hibbs*]

☛ **Expansion or contracting of constitutional guarantee:** Occasionally, you'll notice buried in a fact pattern that Congress is arguably *expanding* or *contracting* the *scope* of a right guaranteed under one of the Civil War Amendments. Say that under *Boerne v. Flores*, Congress may *neither* expand nor contract the boundaries of any constitutional right, even under Congress' power to "enforce" the Civil War Amendments.

Exam Tips on **FREEDOM OF EXPRESSION**

Freedom of expression typically makes up a larger portion of a full-year Constitutional Law exam than does any other single topic. Almost any regulation of an individual's conduct may pose a free expression issue, so think very broadly. Here are some particular things to keep in mind:

General concepts

☞ **Speech vs. conduct:** Remember that free expression issues are posed not just where government is regulating "speech" but also where government is regulating *"conduct"* that includes an *expressive component*. So for each activity that's being restricted, first deal with the issue: "Is there an expressive component to the activity?" If you answer "yes," you've got a free expression issue. (*Example:* Panhandling on the subway has been held to be expressive — and thus protected — conduct.)

☞ **Unprotected categories:** Always keep in mind the five *"unprotected categories,"* the categories thought to be of *so little value* that they get *no First Amendment protection at all* (as long as government is not singling out particular disfavored *viewpoints,* something that will trigger strict scrutiny even for an unprotected category). If your facts fall into an unprotected category, you don't have to worry about whether the government is unreasonably restraining expression, as long as government is being content-neutral.

   ☞ **List of 5:** Here is a list of the five unprotected categories:

      [1] *"Incitement."* This category includes advocacy of *imminent lawless behavior*, as well as the utterance of *"fighting words,"* i.e., words that are likely to precipitate an immediate physical conflict.

      [2] *Obscenity.*

      [3] *Misleading or deceptive speech (i.e., fraud).*

      [4] Speech *integral to criminal conduct*, such as speech that is part of a *conspiracy* to commit a crime or speech *proposing an illegal transaction*.

      [5] *Defamation.*

      Example: A state can flatly *forbid all obscenity,* without even trying to make its ban narrowly tailored to achieve a significant governmental interest (something government would have to do for a content-neutral regulation outside an unprotected category).

☞ **Content-neutral vs. content-based:** Once you've identified a situation where government is "substantially impairing" protected speech or expressive conduct, decide whether the regulation is *"content-neutral"* or not.

   ☞ **"English" tip:** A tip to help you decide: Ask whether the harm the government is trying to prevent would exist to the same degree if the listener/reader didn't understand English. If the answer is "no," the government's action is probably content-based.

   ☞ **Government motive:** Always consider the government's *motive* in regulating the speech — the issue is what the government wished to do: did it want to suppress/control ideas, or did it really want to regulate "secondary" concerns not related to the expressive content?

☛ **Strict scrutiny:** If you decide that the regulation is "content-based," apply *strict scrutiny.* That is, write that the regulation must be struck down unless the government shows that the restriction is *necessary* to achieve a *compelling* governmental purpose. You should almost always then conclude that the government restriction can't survive. (Usually, the key reason will be that there is some less restrictive way to deal with the problem, even if that less restrictive way is not an absolutely perfect way of handling the problem.)

☞ **Use of public school:** One commonly-tested scenario: A public school district allows community groups to use the school for their own purposes after hours. A particular group is denied access because of the type of activity, or because of the group's controversial views. (Typically, you should conclude that the restriction here is content-based, and therefore apply strict scrutiny.)

☞ **IIED liability:** Keep in mind that strict scrutiny for content-based regulations limits a state's right to *impose civil liability for hurtful speech.* So, for instance, be ready to say that there is a First Amendment violation if the state lets a person against whom *intentionally-offensive speech is directed* recover under state law for *intentional infliction of emotional distress (IIED).* (Cite to *Snyder v. Phelps*, where funeral picketers who were carrying offensive signs were shielded from IIED liability.)

☞ **Subject-neutrality:** For a regulation to be "content-neutral," the regulation must be more than just *"viewpoint"* neutral. "Content neutral" means "without reference to the content." For instance, restrictions that put *whole topics* off limits usually are not content-neutral.

Example: Suppose a city requires a permit for political demonstrations, but does not require one for sports victory celebrations. The city's scheme is not content-neutral, because the general type of speech or emotion being expressed serves as the basis for imposing or not imposing the permit requirement.

☛ **Test for validity of content-neutral regulation:** If you conclude that the regulation is truly "content-neutral," use a three-part test. For instance, any regulation of the "time, place and manner" of demonstrations or other expressive conduct will be analyzed by this test if you find that it is content-neutral. Here are the three parts (*all* of which must be satisfied):

❑ The regulation must serve a *"significant* governmental interest";

❑ The regulation must be *narrowly tailored* to achieve that objective; and

❑ The regulation must leave open adequate *alternative channels* for communication.

☞ **Narrowly-tailored is most important:** Of these three, the *"narrowly tai-lored"* requirement is the one most commonly violated — if there is some *less restrictive means* available for dealing with the problem, that means must usually be selected. (However, the less restrictive means probably counts only if it is truly *"as effective,"* not just "almost as effective," as the means chosen by government. This makes it hard for the plaintiff challenging the restriction to establish that the "narrowly tailored" requirement has been violated. Cf. *Rumsfeld v. FAIR*.)

☞ **Significance of public forum:** In assessing a "time, place and manner" restriction, consider whether a *public forum* is involved. The "narrowly tai-lored" and "alternative channels left open" requirements are more strictly construed when a public forum is involved. (The public forum is discussed further below.)

Overbreadth and Vagueness

☛ Always consider whether either of two key First Amendment doctrines applies:

☞ **Overbreadth:** First, consider *overbreadth*. Remember that most litigants in Constitutional Law are not permitted to assert the rights of others. But under First Amendment overbreadth, P is allowed to assert that the government regulation violates the rights of a person who is not now before the court.

Example: A city bans the sale of "sexually explicit" materials. P is charged with violating the statute. The materials sold by him are clearly obscene. Yet, he can defeat the prosecution by showing that the ban also applies to non-obscene sexually explicit materials, which cannot be constitutionally prohibited.

☞ **Vagueness:** Second, consider *vagueness*. Remember, a statute or regulation is unconstitutionally vague if a person of normal intelligence wouldn't know whether the action in question was forbidden or not.

Examples: Statutes forbidding conduct that is "demeaning," "offensive," or "disruptive to public order" might all be found to be unconstitutionally vague, because it is not clear where the line is between what they do and do not proscribe.

Subversion / Advocacy of Illegality

☛ **Advocacy generally:** Many exam questions involve a speaker who tries to rouse the crowd to take *subversive* or *illegal action*. Be on the lookout for persons charged with "inciting to riot," "urging the overthrow of the government," "advocating illegal conduct," or the like. When you have such a fact pattern, check for three things:

- ❏ **Imminence of illegality:** Was the riot or illegality *imminent*, as opposed to something that would take place at a later date? Only speech urging imminent illegality may be punished.

  Example: If the speaker says, "Start thinking about forming guerrilla units …," the required imminence is not present.

- ❏ **Intent:** Was the advocacy *intended* to produce illegality? (If illegality was the *unintended by-product* of the speaker's speech, he can't be punished for it.)

- ❏ **Likelihood:** Was the advocacy *likely* to produce the illegality? Ineffectual efforts don't count.

  Example: If people are in a park for other purposes, happen to listen to the speaker, and then go about their business, the "likely to produce illegality" requirement probably is not met.

License and permit requirements

- ☛ **License or permits generally:** When government attempts to require a *license* or *permit* before expressive activity (typically a speech or demonstration) may occur, here are the things to check for:

  - ☞ **Content-neutral:** Make sure that the license/permit requirement is truly *content-neutral*, both as written (i.e., "on the face" of the statute) and as applied (i.e., as the permits are actually handed out by officials). A permit/license requirement cannot be used as a smokescreen for suppressing unpopular views or unpopular topics.

  - ☞ **No excess discretion:** Make sure that the scheme does not give *excessive discretion* to the official charged with issuing the permit. (*Example:* If the fact pattern tells you that the permit is to be issued "based on the Police Commissioner's overall assessment of the good of the community," that's excessive discretion.) This is a commonly tested aspect.

  - ☞ **Right to ignore requirement:** Profs frequently test on whether a speaker has a right to *ignore* a permit requirement.

    - ☛ **Facial unconstitutionality:** If the permit requirement is unconstitutional *on its face* (e.g., it's content-based, in that it requires a permit for certain topics but not others), the speaker is *not* required to apply for a permit. He may decline to apply, speak, and then defend on the grounds of the permit requirement's unconstitutionality.

    - ☛ **As-applied unconstitutionality:** But if the permit is not facially invalid, only unconstitutional *as applied* to the speaker, then the speaker generally does *not* have the right to ignore the requirement. He must apply for the permit, then seek prompt judicial review rather than just going ahead and speaking. (But an exception exists where the applicant shows that *sufficiently prompt judicial review* of the denial was not available.)

☛ **Injunction:** When the speaker is judicially *enjoined* from speaking, marching, etc., he generally may *not* ignore the injunction and then raise the constitution as a defense in a subsequent contempt proceeding. Instead, he must seek prior judicial review.

☞ **Summary:** If the above requirements are satisfied, then the permit requirement is valid.

Example: A permit will not be invalid merely because it is issued upon conditions that the marchers or demonstrators not block the public's access to a particular place, e.g., an abortion clinic or government building.

Fighting Words

☛ **Fighting words generally:** Be on the lookout for expression that may constitute *"fighting words."* These are words that are likely to induce the addressee to *commit an act of violence*, typically against the speaker. Government may forbid fighting words, or punish them after they are spoken.

☞ **Crowd control:** But be skeptical of claims by the government that the speech in question really constituted "fighting words." Most importantly, remember that the police must *control the crowd* if they have the ability to do so — they can't stand back, then punish the speaker for rousing the crowd to violence.

☞ **Distinguish from offensive speech:** Also, distinguish fighting words from mere "offensive speech." Speech may not be forbidden merely because the listeners are likely to find it offensive.

Examples: Nazis demonstrating in front of Holocaust survivors, or black students calling white students "honkey" at a public university, are probably not using "fighting words," merely "offensive speech" — unless the circumstances made violence very likely, the speech cannot be forbidden.

☛ **"Hate speech" restrictions:** Look out for attempts to restrict *"hate speech."* A *broad ban* on *all fighting words* is OK. So is a broad ban on all words or acts intended to *harass* or *intimidate* others. Government can even single outs certain intimidating acts and forbid them (e.g., *cross burnings*, when done as a threat or intimidation), while declining to forbid other intimidating acts (e.g., burnings in effigy). But government *can't forbid just those fighting words or threats that are motivated by particular kinds of hatred* (e.g., racial or gender hatred). (Cite to *R.A.V. v. St. Paul* on this point.)

Example: University, a public university, passes a speech code that says

"All students are forbidden to harass or threaten other students on the basis of race, gender, or sexual orientation. Violations are punishable by suspension." Since the code bans just certain types of harassment or threats (those based on race, gender and sexual orientation) and not others (e.g., those based on political affiliation), the code is a content-based regulation, and must be strictly scrutinized. It will probably fail that scrutiny, since there are content-neutral alternatives that are less restrictive of speech and will do the job almost as well (e.g., a code banning *all* harassments and threats, regardless of the speaker's motive).

☛ **Profanity not enough:** Speech cannot be banned on the mere grounds that it is *profane*. This merely makes it "offensive," not "obscene" or "fighting words."

     Example: D can wear a jacket saying, "Fuck the Draft." [*Cohen v. California*]

☛ **Vagueness:** Whenever you're dealing with a ban on "offensive" conduct or "harassment," consider the possibility that there may be a *vagueness* problem with the regulation.

Public Forum vs. Private Property

☛ **Public forum generally:** Whenever your fact pattern involves a restriction on speech that takes place in a *public forum*, note this fact, and try to explain what difference it makes.

     ☞ **Content-neutrality:** The fact that the expressive conduct is taking place in a public forum only makes a difference if the regulation is *content-neutral.*

         ☛ **Mid-level review:** Assuming that the regulation *is* content-neutral, the principal difference is that we use *mid-level review* (the restriction must be *narrowly drawn* to serve a *significant governmental interest*, while leaving open *adequate alternative channels* for the communication) as opposed to "mere-rationality" review for non-public-forum speech.

     ☞ **"Traditional" and "designated" public forums:** There are two types of public forums: "traditional" and "designated":

         ❏ **Traditional:** The classic *"traditional"* public forums are: *streets, sidewalks and parks*.

         ❏ **Designated:** There are also *"designated"* public forums, where government has decided to open the place to a broad range of expressive activity.

         Examples of designated forum: (1) An open City Council meeting; (2) a school whose classrooms are made available after hours to a broad variety of community groups.

☞ **Same rules apply to both:** The same rules apply to designated forums as to true forums, except that in the case of a designated forum government can *change its mind* and make the place a non-public forum.

> **Example:** A school district that allows most community groups to use its classrooms after hours can change its mind and adopt a no-use, or limited-use, policy.

☞ **Non-public forums:** The mere fact that something is public property does not mean it is a traditional public or designated-public forum. There are public spaces that are *"non-public forums,"* as to which "mere-rationality" review is all that is used.

> **Examples of public properties that are non-public forums:** Airport terminals, jails, military bases, courthouses, government office buildings.

> ☞ **Rationality and viewpoint-neutrality required:** But even in a non-public forum, regulation must still be *rational* and *viewpoint-neutral*. Be especially alert for a violation of viewpoint-neutrality when government *excludes religious groups* from benefits that it gives to a wide range of non-religious groups.
>
> > **Example:** A school district allows a variety of local community groups to use elementary school classrooms after hours to run programs promoting the "general welfare." However, the district excludes from this program any activity or group that is "primarily of a religious nature." This will be unconstitutional viewpoint-based discrimination, even though school classrooms used this way are probably a non-public forum.

☞ **Speech by government itself:** Even if a private group is somehow involved in speech, check to see whether *government* is the *real speaker.* If the real speaker is government, *don't use public-forum analysis.* Instead, say that government-as-speaker can behave in a content-based way, delivering just the message it wants.

> **Example:** A private group donates a message-bearing monument that a city goverment decides to take and display in a park. Government will be deemed to be the speaker by virtue of its decision to accept and display the monument. Therefore, the city can discriminate based on the message: the city doesn't have to accept other donated monuments with messages that the city doesn't approve of. [Cite to *Pleasant Grove v. Summum*.]

☞ **Private property:** Fact patterns often involve speech that takes place on *private property*. Here are the two aspects that are most frequently tested:

☞ **No right of access:** The *public* has no First Amendment right of access to private property.

Example: A person does not have a First Amendment right to distribute literature in a privately-owned shopping center.

☞ **Limitations by government:** Government may limit an owner's right to use, or to rent his property to others, for expressive purposes. Here, use standard "time, place and manner" analysis, except that no public forum is involved. Therefore, the regulation will usually be upheld if it is content-neutral and other avenues are left for the message.

Example: Government may prevent owners from putting signage on their property advertising their wares, as long as the ban applies to all types of signage, and there are other advertising channels available.

Symbolic Expression

☛ **Symbolic expression generally:** The same rules apply to regulation of *"symbolic* expression" as apply to speech and speech-mixed-with-conduct. "Symbolic expression" refers to *non-verbal acts*.

☞ **Flag-destruction:** For instance, if government wants to ban destruction of the flag, it must do so in a content-neutral way. Thus it cannot ban flag burning that is intended as a means of political dissent while allowing flag burning that is intended as a means of destroying worn-out flags.

Defamation and Making it a Crime to Lie

☛ **Defamation generally:** Remember that when the government regulates *defamation*, there are First Amendment limitations:

☞ **Suits by public officials and public figures:** Most important, under *New York Times v. Sullivan*, if P is a *public official* or *public figure*, he may only win a defamation suit against D for a statement relating to P's official conduct if P can prove that D's statement was made either "with *knowledge* that it was false" or "with *reckless disregard*" of whether it was true or false. Use the phrase *"actual malice"* to describe this requirement.

☞ **Distinguish from private figure:** Be sure to examine whether the plaintiff is truly a public or, rather, private figure. If P is a private figure, he merely has to prove negligence rather than "actual malice."

☞ **Intentional infliction of emotional distress:** Remember that in an action for "intentional infliction of emotional distress," P must, similarly, follow *New York Times v. Sullivan* and prove "actual malice," if P is a public figure.

☛ **Can't make lying a crime:** Remember that government *can't generally make it a* *crime to "tell a lie."* Government can forbid making factually-false statements within certain long-established **pre-defined categories** (e.g., defamation, perjury, fraud). But outside those categories, government can't pass a law making it a crime to lie, even if the lie would be likely to cause harm.

> **Example:** Congress can't make it a crime to falsely state that the speaker has received the Congressional Medal of Honor. Cite to *U.S. v. Alvarez* on this point.

Obscenity

☛ **Obscenity generally:** *Obscenity* is frequently tested. Here are some of the most commonly-tested sub-issues:

☞ **Community standard:** The relevant standard is the *"community"* standard — if the relevant sale and trial take place in a small town in Kansas, what counts is whether the average member of that town would find that the work as a whole appeals to the "prurient" interest.

☞ **Nakedness not enough:** The fact that the work shows **nakedness** is not enough — there must be real or simulated sex that is described or portrayed.

> ☛ **Pandering:** The fact that D, the seller of the obscene material, has engaged in *"pandering"* is relevant on the issue of whether the material appeals primarily to "prurient interests." D has "pandered" if he has marketed the goods by emphasizing their sexually provocative nature (e.g., by using sexually explicit advertising, packaging materials, etc.).

☞ **Private possession:** Remember that no matter how obscene the work is, its **private possession** by an adult in the privacy of his own home cannot be punished. (But the **seller** can still be punished.)

☞ **Indecency vs. obscenity:** Be sure to distinguish between material that is truly "obscene," and material that's merely *"indecent."* Mere nakedness, for instance, doesn't make something obscene (e.g., because of the possibility that the material may have artistic or social value, or because the material may not be "patently offensive").

> ☛ **Strict scrutiny:** So if government tries to regulate "indecency," indicate that the material gets First Amendment protection and that government has to satisfy strict scrutiny.

> **Example:** Congress prohibits the furnishing of "indecent" material on the Internet, hoping to keep this stuff away from minors. You should apply strict scrutiny, and strike down the restriction, because the total ban is overbroad — the ban covers material that could be proscribed because it's obscene, but also material that's not obscene and thus protected as to adults. Cite to *Reno v. ACLU*.

Same analysis if Congress, trying to avoid having minors access indecent material, says that a Web site can show such material only if the user is required to provide proof that he is an adult; this will flunk strict scrutiny if a less-restrictive and equally-effective alternative — say, user-installed filtering — is available. Cite to *Ashcroft v. ACLU*.

☛ **Secondary effects:** But government has a relatively free hand to regulate the *"secondary effects"* of indecent speech.

Example: A town can ban live nude dancing if it reasonably believes that nude dancing establishments contribute to increased drug use, prostitution, etc.

Commercial Speech

☛ **Commercial vs. political speech:** Ascertain whether the regulated speech is *"commercial"* (as opposed to core political) speech. Commercial speech is speech proposing a sale or other commercial transaction. Here are the things to remember about regulation of commercial speech:

☞ **Mid-level review:** If the commercial speech is truthful and proposes a *legal* transaction, the Court uses mid-level review. The restriction survives if and only if it:

[1] *directly advances*

[2] a *substantial* governmental interest

[3] in a way that is *"not more extensive than is necessary"* to achieve the government's objective.

☞ **Content-based:** This is true even if the regulation is *content-based*. (So it's somewhat easier for government to do content-based regulation of commercial speech than of non-commercial speech, as to which strict scrutiny has to be used.)

☞ **False or deceptive speech:** If the speech is *false*, *deceptive* or proposes an *illegal transaction*, government can *flatly ban* it.

☞ **Truthful advertising about harmful products:** Profs frequently test on whether the government may prohibit or regulate truthful advertising about products that are *harmful* but *lawful*. Generally, this regulation gets mid-level review, which it will often *flunk* because *substantially less-restrictive means are available*.

Examples: If government tries to prohibit or tightly regulate truthful advertising for *cigarettes*, *liquor* or *gambling*, the Court is likely to say that less-restrictive means like educational campaigns, or higher taxes, must first be tried. Cite to *Lorillard*, the Mass. case that banned outdoor tobacco advertising, on this point.

☞ **Lawyer advertising:** Restrictions on *lawyer advertising* are often tested. Except for some *in-person solicitation* by profit-motivated lawyers seeking clients, states generally can't block truthful advertising.

> **Example:** States can't block a public-interest lawyer or advocacy group from soliciting clients, even through direct mail or in-person contacts.

Public School Students

☛ **Balancing test:** If the regulation is of *public school students*, state that the courts apply a "balancing" test: the student has a limited right of free speech, to be balanced against the administration's right to carry out its educational mission and to maintain discipline.

> **Examples:** So officials may not suppress students' speech merely because they disagree with it on ideological or political grounds. But they may ban profanity, or ban school-newspaper stories that would disturb the school's educational mission, such as stories about sex.

Freedom of Association; Public Jobs and Benefits; Unconstitutional Conditions

☛ **Group activity:** If you have a fact pattern that involves *group activity* of an expressive nature, refer to the protected *"freedom of association."*

> **Example:** If a group gets together and pursues class action litigation, their right to do so is protected by the associational freedom.

☞ **Right not to associate:** Remember that there's also a "right *not* to associate": for instance, a group can't be required to take unwanted members whose presence will detract from the group's expressive activities.

> **Example:** The Boy Scouts can't be forced to accept homosexuals as troop leaders.

☛ **Denial of public jobs or benefits:** Many fact patterns involve the denial of *public jobs or benefits* to persons based upon their expressive conduct. This is a very commonly tested area. Here are some key aspects to keep in mind:

☞ **Standard:** In general, the standard for whether government may refuse to hire, or may fire, based on expressive conduct is the same as for when government may *prosecute*.

> **Example:** Since a person may not be prosecuted for belonging to an organization unless there is a showing that he had the specific intent to further the organization's illegal aims, so a person may not be fired for belonging to the organization without such a showing of specific intent.

☞ **Loyalty oath:** A person may be required to sign a ***loyalty oath*** as a condition for getting or keeping a public job, but he may not be forced to promise to refrain from doing anything that he would be constitutionally permitted to do.

Example: You may be forced to sign a loyalty oath that you have not belonged to the Communist Party while specifically intending to further the overthrow of the government, but you may not be required to sign a loyalty oath stating simply that you do not belong to the Communist Party — since you can't be prosecuted for mere membership without specific intent to further illegal aims, you can't be forced to sign a loyalty oath that you won't be a mere member.

☞ **Interference with job performance:** There is an ***exception*** to these limits: you can be deprived of expressive freedom where the expression would truly interfere with your ***job performance***.

Example: Civil servants can be forced to choose between their jobs and engaging in partisan political activities, since there's a strong governmental interest in making sure that civil servants don't get coerced into campaigning for their elected bosses.

   ☛ **Public benefits:** Where a public ***benefit*** as opposed to a job is at stake, there is no "performance" exception, and it's hard for government to restrict free speech.

   Example: A person's right to continue as a tenant in public housing, or to receive welfare payments, generally can't be made contingent upon their forfeiting their freedom of expression, because they generally don't have a "performance" obligation that would be impaired by pursuit of expressive conduct or speech.

☛ **Unconstitutional conditions:** Look out for ***"unconstitutional conditions,"*** where government ***unfairly conditions*** the award of funding or other benefits on the recipient's ***waiver of constitutional rights.***

   ☞ **No limits on how non-subsidy funds are spent:** Government *can* sometimes require as a condition to giving you a financial benefit (e.g., a subsidy) that you waive your right to free expression. But that condition can generally apply only to ***how you use the particular government-supplied funds***, not how you spend privately-raised ***non-subsidy dollars***.

   Example: Congress gives subsidies to private groups fighting AIDS. Congress can require that each grantee promise not to spend subsidy dollars on activities that will likely promote prostitution (e.g., use of subsidy money to buy condoms that are then distributed to prostitutes). But Congress may ***not*** require that recipients promise that they won't even use ***private (non-subsidy) funds*** on speech or activities that will promote prostitution — that's an "unconstitutional condition," because it tries to "leverage" the government dollars to restrict speech *outside of the activities receiving the government funding.* Cite to *Agency for Int'l Dev. v. Alliance for Open Soc'y Int'l, Inc.*

Regulation of Media

☞ **Media restrictions:** If your question involves restrictions placed on the *media* (publishers or broadcasters), there are some special considerations:

   ☞ **Prior restraint:** If the governmental action consists of a *prior restraint*, you should almost certainly conclude that the restraint is *not valid*. For instance, if the government is trying to get an injunction against a newspaper that will publish a story, it's almost impossible for the government to succeed.

   ☞ **Subpoena:** The media must obey a *subpoena* (e.g., to give information to a grand jury) pretty much the same as a private citizen must.

   ☞ **No special right of access:** The press does not get any special *right of access* to government-held information, beyond what the public as a whole has.

   ☞ **Different types of media:** Some issues turn on the *type of media*:

     ☞ **Over-the-air broadcasts:** *Over-the-air broadcast radio and TV* may be subjected to somewhat greater *"time, place and manner" regulation* than print media, because these are scarce resources, and they are potentially intrusive (someone may stumble upon unwanted content while dial-turning).

     ☞ **Print and Internet:** *Print publications*, and the *Internet*, by contrast, are neither scarce nor intrusive. So these media get *very great freedom* from "time, place and manner" regulation. Cable TV seems to be somewhere in between, but closer to print/Internet.

Exam Tips on
FREEDOM OF RELIGION

Issues involving freedom of religion are usually easy to spot: the fact pattern has to refer to religion, religious beliefs, church, parochial school, God, prayer, or some symbol commonly associated with religion (e.g., a creche, a Star of David, etc.). So the trick with freedom of religion issues is to analyze them correctly, not to spot them. Here's what to concentrate on:

Establishment Clause vs. Free Exercise Clause

☛ **Choosing the Clause that's in question:** Of utmost importance: decide whether the issue poses an *Establishment* Clause or a *Free Exercise* Clause problem. A given governmental action will rarely pose the danger of both (though the government will often have a ***choice*** of two actions, each posing the risk of violating a different clause).

　☞ **Tip for choosing:** Here's a tip for deciding which Clause is involved: if government seems to be *favoring* religion generally, or favoring a particular religion over the "rest of society," you probably have an Establishment Clause problem. If government seems to be *disfavoring* a particular person relative to the rest of society, in a way that is related to that person's religious beliefs, then you probably have a Free Exercise Clause problem.

　　❏ **Classic illustration of Establishment Clause problem:** school prayer.

　　❏ **Classic illustration of Free Exercise Clause problem:** P can't get unemployment benefits if she doesn't make herself available for Saturday work forbidden by her religion.

Establishment Clause

☛ **Three-part test:** In analyzing an ***Establishment Clause*** problem, the first thing to do is to recite the three-part test (which you should cite as the *"Lemon v. Kurtzman"* test):

　[1] The government action must have a ***secular legislative purpose*** (but it's OK if there is ***also*** a religious purpose);

　[2] The act must have a ***primary secular effect***; and

　[3] The government action must not involve ***undue entanglement*** of government in religious affairs, or religion in government affairs.

　　☛ **Primary-secular prong:** Of these three prongs, the one that is most likely to be violated in your fact pattern is probably the "primary secular effect" prong, since a large variety of government programs seem to assist religious groups more than they benefit other groups.

☛ **Public schools:** The most common type of Establishment Clause problem that you will see on an exam involves ***religion in the public schools***. Typically, the state gives some sort of financial aid to religious schools or to students who attend religious schools. Here are some rules of thumb in analyzing these:

　☞ **Benefit to all students:** If the program benefits ***all students***, or even all ***pri-***

vate-school students (including non-parochial students), the fact that the biggest beneficiaries are religious students is not fatal.

Example: Tuition vouchers which can be used to send a student to any private school, religious or non-religious, are allowable. That's true even if 95% of the users are religious-school students. [*Zelman v. Simmons-Harris*]

☞ **Post-secondary:** If the assistance is being rendered to a ***college or university***, it's more likely to pass muster than where it is rendered to a secondary or elementary school.

☞ **Tangible objects:** Loans of ***tangible objects*** (e.g., text books or school buses) are easier to justify than loans of ***personnel***, since the loans of tangible objects involve fewer supervisory/entanglement problems for government. But even a loan of personnel to teach inside the religious school is OK, so long as the religious school authorities don't have any influence over the curriculum or the style of teaching.

☛ **After-hours school use:** A common type of fact pattern involves a school district that makes school premises available ***after hours*** to various groups. The issue becomes, "Must religious groups be excluded?" The correct answer: religious groups typically need ***not*** be excluded, as long as the government does not get entangled with what the group is doing, as by having public officials co-sponsor the activity. In fact, exclusion of religious groups from a program open to other sorts of groups generally violates the religious groups' free exercise rights.

Example: A school district opens elementary school classrooms after hours to various community groups. If religious groups are allowed to participate (even if their programs are worship services), this is not an Establishment Clause program, because the religious groups are just getting equal treatment. (And if the religious groups were excluded, this would violate their free expression rights. [*Good News Club*])

☛ **Government funding:** Another common fact pattern occurs where government gives funds to some religious organization for use in some theoretically non-religious "socially beneficial" charitable purpose. (*Example:* Government gives grants to religious and non-religious groups for use in running family planning clinics, legal services clinics, etc.) In this type of fact pattern, use the three-part *Lemon* test. Pay special attention to the risk of entanglement: how does government know that the particular religious organization isn't using the funds to advocate religious doctrine, or to favor its co-religionists? But say that the present Court seems inclined to find that there is no Establishment Clause violation in this type of fact pattern.

☛ **Favoring one sect:** A special type of establishment problem is posed where government ***favors one sect*** or religion over another. (*Example:* Government gives tax breaks to certain religions, or gives certain sects free time on government-owned broadcast stations.) This kind of preference is virtually per se *violative* of the Establishment Clause.

Free Exercise Clause

☛ **Free Exercise generally:** In analyzing *free exercise* problems, be on the lookout for two different kinds of scenarios:

    ❏ In one scenario, P wants to do something that is required by P's religion, and the government blocks him from doing so.

    ❏ In the other scenario, P doesn't want to do something that is forbidden by her religion, and the government requires her to do so (typically, as a condition to the receipt of some kind of government benefit).

    ☞ **Either can apply:** *Either* of these scenarios can lead to a Free Exercise violation.

☛ **Intentional interference:** If government's interference with a religious practice or belief is *intentional* (i.e., motivated by government's desire to interfere with the religion), the interference is virtually per se illegal. This kind of fact pattern is rare on exams.

    Example: Government bans animal sacrifices, in circumstances showing that government is acting out of dislike of an unpopular minority religion (*Lukumi*, the Santeria case). This is a violation of the Free Exercise Clause.

    ☞ **Applies to "serious sanctions" only:** But this principle probably applies only to *serious "sanctions" — punishments* — intentionally directed against religion, not to minor withdrawals of generally-applicable government *benefits*.

    Example: If government funds college scholarships, but doesn't let the scholarship be used for training for the ministry, this is not a Free Exercise violation, because there is no "sanction" or punishment intended here, just avoidance of church-state conflicts. [*Locke v. Davey*]

☛ **Incidental interference:** In the more usual free exercise case, the government's interference with religious practices or beliefs is *unintended* and *incidental*. Here's what to look for in this usual situation:

    ☞ **Valid and neutral general law:** The key rule is that where government enacts a *"valid and neutral law* of *general applicability,"* a person has *no* free exercise right to disobey the law, even if the law forbids (or requires) an action that the person's religion requires (or forbids). In other words, *government does not have to give an exemption from the general rule.*

    Example: Recall *Employment Div. v. Smith*: Oregon can make it a crime to possess or smoke peyote. Native Americans must obey the ban, even though smoking peyote is a core part of their religious rites.

Some additional examples:

❏ Government bans all cruelty to animals, defined to include any death not administered in a painless manner. Assuming that there is no motive to disfavor particular religions, this ban may be applied to groups sacrificing animals as part of a religious ritual, since the ban is a rule of general applicability.

❏ Government bans polygamy. Again, since this is a generally-applicable law that is neutral to religion, government need not give an exemption to groups for whom polygamy is a religious requirement.

❏ Government requires an autopsy in the event of any death that appears to be "non-natural." Government need not give an exemption in the case of a decedent for whom an autopsy would violate the decedent's religious beliefs.

☛ **Choice of ministers:** On the other hand, religious groups *do* have a free exercise right not to have government interfere with the group's *choice of "ministers"* to carry out the group's religious mission. This may require government to grant an exemption from a generally-applicable and neutral rule, such as an anti-discrimination law.

Example: A church fires a minister, after the minister claims that the church has discriminated against her because she is disabled, in violation of the Americans with Disabilities Act (ADA). The church is entitled to a "ministerial exception" from the ADA, since the Free Exercise Clause prevents the government from interfering with "an *internal church decision that affects the faith and mission* of the church itself." Cf. *Hosanna-Tabor Evangelical Lutheran Church and School v. EEOC.*

☛ **Court scrutiny of the religious belief:** In any free exercise case, be on the lookout for an issue concerning, *"What is a religious belief?"* Here are the key aspects of this issue:

☞ **Bona fides of the belief:** The courts may insist that the belief be *"bona fide."* So the court is permitted to gauge the *"genuineness"* or *"sincerity"* of the individual's belief.

☞ **Truthfulness of the belief:** But the court is *not* permitted to gauge the *"truthfulness"* or *"reasonableness"* of the belief. No matter how bizarre or out-of-the-ordinary the belief, only sincerity counts.

☛ **Unusual beliefs:** Even *unorganized* beliefs, and beliefs practiced by just a *single person*, are protected. Thus the court may not consider that a particular practice is "not traditional" — if it's part of P's own practice of the religion, it doesn't matter that it's a deviation from the general practices of the sect to which P belongs.

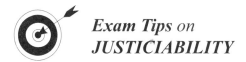

Exam Tips *on* JUSTICIABILITY

Justiciability questions are pervasive and often hidden. Typically, your fact pattern will *not* contain the key words "standing," "ripe," "moot," "abstain," "political question," etc. — it will be up to you to spot these issues. Worse, these issues can be hidden in absolutely *any type* of fact pattern, so you can't let your guard down for a moment. Here are some specifics to watch for:

☞ Here's a brief checklist of justiciability issues:

[1] *advisory opinions;*

[2] *standing;*

[3] *mootness;*

[4] *ripeness;*

[5] *11th Amendment's* ban on certain *suits against the states;*

[6] *abstention;* and

[7] *political questions*.

Advisory Opinions

☞ **How issue arises:** "Advisory opinion" problems usually arise on exams where a *state court* issues an advisory opinion (as allowed by the procedures of most states), and the loser seeks review in the U.S. Supreme Court. Typically, you'll say that even if the state court advisory opinion is based on federal law, the Supreme Court cannot hear the issue because there is no true "case or controversy" as required by Article III.

Standing

☞ **Concrete, individualized harm:** The overwhelmingly most important aspect of justicability on exams is *"standing."* For *every claim* asserted anywhere on your exam, ask yourself, "Has P suffered, or is she about to suffer, a *concrete, individualized harm*, that would be *redressed* by a favorable result in the lawsuit?" Unless the answer is "yes," there's probably no standing.

☞ Here's a checklist for standing, with the five individual elements broken out:

[1] P must have suffered an *"injury-in-fact,"* or be *likely* to suffer one reason-

ably *soon*;

[2] P's harm must be *concrete*, not abstract;

[3] P's harm must be *"individuated,"* i.e., not the same as that suffered by every other citizen or taxpayer;

[4] The action that P is complaining about must have been the *"but for" cause* of P's harm; and

[5] A favorable decision in the suit must be likely to *redress* the injury to P.

☞ **Common fact pattern:** One common fact pattern: P has a contract with the government, and some statute or rule would prevent (or dissuade) the government from honoring the contract. Here, there's usually standing because P is likely to suffer an "injury in fact" from losing the benefit of the contract.

Example: P has a contract to build a school for state X. A federal statute would withdraw funds that X was expecting to receive and pay over to P. In this situation, P has standing.

☞ **Imminent or past harm:** Remember that P need not have already suffered the harm. But if not, the threatened harm needs to be pretty *imminent* and pretty likely — some small chance of harm at some indefinite future time won't suffice.

Example: A first-year law student doesn't have standing to challenge a state's Continuing Legal Education requirement, because that requirement won't apply to her for several years.

☛ **Challenge to secret government procedures:** Be on the lookout for a fact pattern where the plaintiff is contending that the *government* is likely to take some adverse action against him in the future. If the government's procedures are shrouded in *secrecy*, it will be difficult for the plaintiff to prove the *requisite likelihood* that the government will really take the feared action soon.

Example: P has email contacts with two foreign terror suspects, X and Y, and is afraid that the National Security Agency will intercept these emails under a statute letting the agency do secret surveillance on terror-related emails. If P can't show how the NSA chooses its surveillance targets and thus whether X and Y have been targeted, P won't have standing to challenge the constitutionality of the surveillance. (Cite to *Clapper v. Amnesty Int'l.*)

☞ **Organizational standing:** An *organization* will generally be allowed to sue *on behalf of its members*, if the members would individually have standing, and if the suit is *related* to the organization's *purposes*. Most organization-based suits you'll see on an exam will *satisfy* these conditions.

☞ **Taxpayer & citizen standing:** If P is asserting rights as a *federal "taxpayer"* or as a *"citizen,"* and P is not part of the transaction in question, probably P does *not* have standing. Three special cases (exceptions to the general rule of no standing for taxpayer or citizen suits):

❏ If P is a *state* taxpayer challenging a state *expenditure*, then probably all that's required for standing is that there be a "direct expenditure of funds" by the state. Normally, this will be satisfied in your fact pattern.

❏ If P is a *federal* taxpayer who is challenging the *tax itself*, which P would have to pay unless the suit succeeds, P has standing.

❏ If P is a federal taxpayer or citizen challenging a federal expenditure that *directly violates some constitutional guarantee*, P may have standing. Probably, this exception only applies to federal expenditures that violate the First Amendment's *Establishment Clause* (e.g., the federal government pays money to private schools to be used in furthering their religious message).

☞ **Asserting third persons' rights:** Regardless of whether P has standing on her own, P will *not* usually be allowed to assert the rights of *third persons* not then before the court. You can refer to this as the rule against *"jus tertii"* to sound erudite. There are three important exceptions:

☛ **First Amendment exception:** In free-expression cases, litigants get to use the First Amendment *overbreadth* doctrine. This lets P say, in effect, "This statute blocks expressive conduct of mine that may constitutionally be proscribed, but it also could be interpreted to block expressive conduct or speech on the part of others not present, for whom it would violate their free speech rights."

☛ **Exception where third party has difficulty appearing:** The litigant can assert the third party's rights if these rights would be impaired, and it's legally or practically *difficult* for the third party to be present in the suit.

Example: Vendors are often permitted to assert the rights of their customers, who would each individually have too little at stake to sue.

☛ **Associations:** Associations get to assert their members' rights, as noted above.

Mootness

☛ **How to spot:** You can spot a *mootness* problem by the fact that P "doesn't really seem to have a problem anymore."

Example: P has been kept out of a public university by an allegedly discriminatory policy; if the university then allows P to enroll, the case has become moot.

☞ **Collateral consequences:** Before you conclude that P doesn't really have a problem anymore, look for *"collateral consequences."* Most common: the litigant (he can either be P or D) has been *convicted*, then paroled or discharged — there will still be collateral consequences to him from having a conviction on the books (e.g., job or voting problems), so the case is not moot.

☞ **Capable of repetition, evading review:** Look for issues that are "capable of *repetition*, yet evading review." This happens where P is one of a series of similarly-situated people, each of whom would face the same problem that would always turn out to be moot.

Classic illustration: P is a pregnant woman seeking to overturn restrictions on abortion; she's no longer pregnant by the time the suit gets heard, but all other pregnant women similarly situated would have the same problem, so a court will hear the case now. Another illustration: a political group is prevented from doing something until "after the election"; the election is now over, but other political groups, or this very group, would be likely to face the same mootness problem in a future context.

Ripeness

☛ **How to spot:** You can spot a *ripeness* problem by looking for a situation that's *"too early"* or *"not concrete enough."*

☞ **Classic illustration of ripeness:** there's a criminal statute on the books that P wants to violate or has violated, but there's very little risk that the statute will in fact be enforced against P. (In this scenario, P is generally seeking a declaratory judgment that the statute is unconstitutional.) This type of problem is especially acute where P *hasn't committed* the violation yet, and we're not sure that he will.

Example: A statute prevents people from distributing literature on private property, including shopping centers. P says he wants to do this kind of distribution, but hasn't done it yet, and it's not even clear that the owner will object or that the police will arrest. P's case is probably unripe.

☞ **Too abstract:** Another type of scenario that will lead to a finding of unripeness: the risk is too *abstract*.

Example: A state keeps a secret file on citizens; P, one of the monitored citizens, claims that his First Amendment rights are being "chilled." The Court will probably hold that any chilling problem is too speculative and abstract, and the case unripe, unless P can show what activity he is being dissuaded from engaging in.

11th Amendment

☛ **Private suits against states:** Whenever a suit for damages is brought in federal court by a *private citizen* against a *state*, there's a good chance that the suit is blocked by the *11th Amendment*. This is true whether P is a citizen of the defendant state or of some other state.

> **Example:** P, a citizen of state D, is injured when a state D employee runs him over while the employee is on the job. P sues state D in federal court for damages. The suit will be blocked by the 11th Amendment.

☞ **Exceptions:** Some *exceptions* to the 11th Amendment:

❏ Suits against a state by *another state* or by the *federal government*;

❏ Suits against *counties*, *cities*, or anything but the state itself;

❏ Suits for an *injunction* against state *officials* directing them to *cease violating federal law*. (But a suit to force a state official to obey *state* law *is* covered by the 11th Amendment and thus not allowed in federal court.)

☞ **Congress can't change:** Keep in mind that *Congress generally can't change* this "no federal-court suits against the states" law, even if it wants to. Cite to the *Seminole Tribe* case on this point.

> **Example:** Congress passes a statute saying any state can be sued by private citizens for violating federal environmental-protection laws. This statute won't have any effect, and the federal court won't be allowed to hear a private suit against a state for damages for environmental violations.

> ☛ **Post-Civil-War Amendments:** But also remember that Congress *can* provide for federal-court suits by private citizens when the right being sued on stems from Congress' power to enforce the *post-Civil War Amendments*.

> > **Example:** Congress passes a broad statute banning racial and gender discrimination in employment, and says that workers can sue states in federal court for violations. The 11th Amendment won't block such suits, because Congress has the power to say that the Amendment won't apply to suits brought under federal statutes passed under Congress' authority to enforce the 14th Amendment.

> ☛ **Suit in state's own courts:** If the question involves a private damages suit brought on a congressionally-guaranteed right, but brought *against a state in its own courts*, remember that the newly-recognized constitutional doctrine of *sovereign immunity* (the *Alden v. Maine* case) means that the state *doesn't have to hear the case.*

Political Questions

☛ **Two ways to be "political":** Be alert to possible non-justiciable *"political questions."* Remember that there are two different ways a question can become a non-justiciable political one:

   ☞ **Given to another branch:** First, this can happen where, at least arguably, the Constitution gives the problem to the *executive* or *legislative* branch to resolve, rather than to the judiciary.

      Classic illustration: anything to do with the procedures or grounds for *impeachment*.

      Another illustration: A federal court is asked to overrule Congress' decision that P doesn't satisfy the age, citizenship or residency requirement to be a member of Congress.

   ☞ **Lack of manageable standards:** Second, a question can be a non-justiciable political one because there are *no "manageable standards"* to guide the judiciary in deciding. This type of fact pattern is relatively rare.

      Example: P claims that a particular tax is so burdensome that it amounts to an uncompensated "taking" in violation of the Fifth Amendment. This issue is a non-justiciable political one, because no standards exist to tell the Court how to decide.

   ☛ **Reapportionment:** One area that you might think would fall into this "no manageable standards" category — *reapportionment* — doesn't. The Court has decided that the "one person, one vote" principle applies to virtually all federal and state elections, and that this principle can be successfully applied by the judiciary.

SHORT-ANSWER QUESTIONS

Note: These questions are selected from among the "Quiz Yourself" questions in the full-length *Constitutional Law Emanuel Law Outline*. We've kept the same question numbering here as in the *Outline*. Since some questions have been omitted here, there are gaps in the numbering.

CHAPTER 2

THE SUPREME COURT'S AUTHORITY

1. The Constitution of the state of Ames contains a due process clause whose language is identical to the Due Process Clause of the U.S. Constitution's Fourteenth Amendment. Tom was a teacher in the Town of Aaron, in Ames. Because Tom's status was that of "probationary teacher," the custom in Aaron was that Tom could be fired at the end of any school year without cause. Tom was fired without cause. He sued Aaron in Ames state court. His suit was premised on the argument that his firing violated the Ames due process clause, in that he was not given a hearing before being fired. The Ames state court agreed, and the highest appeals court in Ames affirmed. Now, the Town of Aaron has appealed the case to the U.S. Supreme Court. May the U.S. Supreme Court hear the case? Give your reasons. _____

2. Same basic fact pattern as prior question. Now, however, assume that Tom in his Ames state court litigation asserted that his firing violated both the Ames constitution's due process clause and the federal Due Process Clause. The state trial court agreed with Tom that both constitutional provisions were violated, and the Ames Supreme Court affirmed the trial court decision in all respects. The trial court's decision on the state-constitution issue was based solely upon the court's reading of prior Ames state court decisions that in turn relied upon the intent of Ames voters in adopting the Ames due process clause. The portion of the decision relating to the federal constitution relied on U.S. Supreme Court cases construing the federal Due Process Clause. May the U.S. Supreme Court review the decision of the Ames Supreme Court? _____

3. Congress, in an effort to streamline the federal judiciary, passes a statute eliminating diversity jurisdiction (i.e., jurisdiction over cases brought by a citizen of one state against a citizen of another state). The legislation would prevent diversity suits from being brought in federal district court, so that they would have to be brought in state court. (The legislation does not directly change the Supreme Court's appellate jurisdiction, so that the Supreme Court can continue to review the judgments of state courts, including state court suits that turn on a federal

question.) Is the congressional legislation constitutional? _____

CHAPTER 3

FEDERALISM AND FEDERAL POWER

4. Congress, pursuant to its power to establish and regulate copyrights, has decided that there is far too much counterfeiting of copyrighted musical recordings. Therefore, Congress has passed a statute making it a felony, punishable by up to five years in prison, to give a "bootlegged" (i.e., not authorized by the copyright owner) CD or MP3 recording to any other person, even if it is the donor's neighbor or relative, and even though no compensation is charged. Dennis, charged with a violation of this statute, asserts that it is unconstitutional because it is beyond the scope of Congress' authority. Should the Court agree with Dennis' assertion, and why? _____

CHAPTER 4

THE FEDERAL COMMERCE POWER

5. Congress makes it a federal felony for any individual to place a bet with another individual on a sporting event, or to propose such a bet. The statute is written broadly, so as to cover two friends who bet with each other primarily for purposes of friendship rather than profit. The House and Senate Committee Reports on the bill show that Congress believed that ostensibly "friendly" betting creates a climate that is tolerant of gambling, which in turn increases the interstate gambling profits of organized crime, a multi-million dollar nationwide problem. Devon is charged with violating the statute by placing a bet on the Super Bowl with her best friend, Elaine. They made the bet face to face within a single state.

(A) If Devon challenges the constitutionality of the statute on the grounds that it goes beyond Congress' enumerated powers, what enumerated power should the prosecutors point to in defending the statute's constitutionality? _____

(B) Is the statute in fact constitutional? State your reasons. _____

6. By 2020, the federal government is paying approximately 50% of total health-care costs for the nation out of general revenues. Congress, concerned that Americans are living increasingly sedentary, unhealthy, and medically-costly lifestyles, enacts the Walk to Fitness Act of 2020 ("WFA"). The WFA provides that each American over the age of 16 must purchase a specified government-manufactured pedometer, which when attached to the hip measures how many miles the wearer walks each day. The pedometer is sold to the public at a price of $20 (which provides a small profit to the government, made possible by the huge volumes expected to be sold). The device is custom-fitted so that it can work only on the body of the particular purchaser to whom it is registered. Another provision of the WFA says that after the end of each year, the device-wearer shall print out the total miles registered on the device during the prior year, and enclose the printout with his tax return. Anyone whose age-adjusted total annual mileage walked does not reach a pre-specified threshold (150 miles for a young adult) must pay a "penalty" of $200, payable to the IRS together with the person's taxes. Exemptions are given for those whose doctor certifies that the person is not medically capable of walking the threshold amount. Anyone who does reach the threshold, and sends in the printout, gets a one-time government refund of the $20 cost of the pedometer. Congress defends the constitutionality of the WFA on the grounds that the pedometer program encourages fitness, and that fitter people will cause the nation's ever-increasing health-care bill to decline, leading to a substantial lowering of costs billed in the interstate market for health-care services. Therefore, Congress asserts, the WFA is valid as a regulation of commerce.

Is the WFA a proper exercise of the Congress' Commerce power? _____

7. After several years of rising unemployment nationally, and falling wage levels, Congress passes a statute prohibiting the employment of any person under the age of 19. Congress' intent is to keep teenagers in high school or college, where they may or may not learn something but will at least not be competing with adults for jobs, thus allowing wage rates to rise. The state of Alahoma employs many 17- and 18-year-olds, for such posts as cleaners in state parks and apprentice state troopers. Alahoma estimates that its total payroll costs will rise by 8% if it is required to obey the new federal statute (which by its terms applies to government as well as private-sector employees).

(A) Assuming that the federal statute falls within Congress' power to regulate commerce, what is the strongest argument that Alahoma can make as to why the Constitution requires that the state's own hiring be exempted from the statute? _____

(B) Will this argument succeed? _____

8. Congress has concluded that cigarette smoking raises the nation's annual health-care budget 15% above what it would otherwise be. Congress has therefore enacted a statute that requires each state to: (1) place a tax of at least 10% on the sale of cigarettes (in addition to existing federal cigarette taxes); (2) compile a registry of every premises in the state where cigarettes are sold, and audit those premises quarterly to make sure they're collecting the tax; (3) modify its health-care financing scheme so that the state does not pay any hospital or doctor for the costs of treating any condition found to be caused by cigarette smoking; and (4) modify its tort law so as to treat cigarettes as a "defective product" for which strict liability is allowed under state tort law. Congress does not allocate any funds for the carrying out of these objectives. It provides that if a state is found not to be in compliance one year after enactment of the act, the federal district courts for that state shall have authority to direct the legislature and agencies of the state to comply, and to hold state officials in contempt if they do not comply.

(A) If you are given the job of arguing on behalf of a state that this provision is an unconstitutional infringement of your state's sovereignty, what constitutional provision should you point to? _____

(B) Will your argument succeed? _____

(C) If you are charged with improving the likelihood that the federal scheme will pass muster, what fundamental change will you urge to be made in that scheme? _____

CHAPTER 5

OTHER NATIONAL POWERS

10. Congress, after concluding that the states have lagged behind in educating school children to be tolerant towards homosexuals, enacts a program providing a small subsidy to any public elementary school that conducts a program teaching a better understanding of, and tolerance of, gay people.

(A) Putting aside the Commerce power, what constitutional provision best supplies constitutional authority for this statute? _____

(B) A parent whose child is about to receive such instruction sues to have the provision found unconstitutional, on the grounds that it encourages homosexuality and thus detracts from the general welfare of the nation. Assuming that the federal court hearing the case concludes that the measure will probably make the nation worse off than it was before, will this constitutional attack on the statute succeed? _____

11. Congress, alarmed about the dramatic rise in teenage pregnancies, passes the Underage Procreation Act of 2012. That Act requires any person under the age of 17 to obtain a federal permit before becoming pregnant. The permit is granted to any woman who shows that she has received one hour of counselling about the dangers of teen pregnancy from a state-licensed social worker. Violators are to be fined. A 16-year-old woman who wishes to become pregnant files suit to attack the statute's constitutionality on the grounds that it is beyond Congress' enumerated powers. The federal government defends the statute on the grounds that it is a proper exercise of Congress' power to regulate for the "general welfare." Will the plaintiff's attack on the statute succeed? (Ignore any issues relating to a woman's constitutional right to privacy or right to become pregnant. Assume that the Court decides that nothing in the activity being regulated affects interstate commerce.)

CHAPTER 6

TWO LIMITS ON STATE POWER

12. The City of Fairhaven is located in the state of North Texarkansas. The border with the neighboring state of South Texarkansas is three miles south of the Fairhaven city limits. After a serious outbreak of food poisoning, traced to improperly butchered meat, the Fairhaven City Council passed an ordinance forbidding the sale within Fairhaven of any meat not killed at a slaughterhouse inspected by the Fairhaven Department of Sanitation. All evidence suggests that the Fairhaven ordinance was in fact motivated solely by health and safety objectives, not by any desire to favor local producers. Fairhaven Sanitation inspectors survey all slaughterhouses within a 70-mile radius of the city, but do not attempt to cross the boundary to inspect South Texarkansas slaughterhouses. South Texarkansas, at the state level, conducts its own inspections of slaughterhouses for sanitation, using standards that are closely similar to those used by the Fairhaven inspectors.

Chopem, the owner of a butcher shop in Fairhaven, sells meat purchased from a slaughterhouse in South Texarkansas. Chopem was charged with selling meat that had not been slaughtered in a Fairhaven-inspected slaughterhouse. Chopem would like to get the charges dismissed on the grounds that the statute, as applied here, violates the U.S. Constitution.

(A) What is the strongest argument that Chopem can make for the unconstitutionality of the Fairhaven ordinance? _____

(B) Will this constitutional attack succeed? State your reasons. _____

13. The state of New Wales has a single nuclear power plant. Because the power plant has been in operation for over 20 years, it is now time for the plutonium used in the plant to be disposed of. The safest and cheapest way to do this is to bury it in a lead-enclosed structure 200 feet below the surface. Because residents of the state are worried that their state will become a "toxic dumping ground" if strict measures are not taken, the New Wales state legislature has enacted the following statute: "No plutonium imported into this state after 1994 may be buried anywhere within the confines of this state." The effect of this statute is to permit the state's existing utility to make a one-time disposal of its pre-1994 plutonium by the burial method described above. The owners of a nuclear reactor located in South Brunswick, the state directly east of New Wales, have attacked the new statute on the grounds that it violates the Commerce Clause because it prevents them from shipping their spent plutonium into New Wales and burying it there. Assume that Congress has not spoken on the issue of nuclear-waste disposal at all. Should the court hearing this action agree with the plaintiff? _____

14. The state of Rouge decided to build a new and large state office building. Quarries in Rouge had for years produced fine granite. However, in recent years, the in-state granite industry had begun to suffer because of high costs. In an effort to give a shot in the arm to the local industry, the Rouge legislature provided that all granite used in the new building should be purchased from in-state granite producers, even though the price would inevitably be higher than if the materials were bought from out-of-staters. A granite producer in a neighboring state has sued Rouge in federal District Court, asserting that Rouge's preference for in-staters violates the Commerce Clause. Should the court agree with the plaintiff's argument? _____

16. Same facts as Question 13 (on plutonium disposal). Now, assume that Congress has passed the following statute: "Any state may define the circumstances, if any, under which nuclear waste products [defined to include plutonium] may be buried or otherwise disposed of within the confines of that state." If the New Wales statute is attacked on the grounds that it violates the dormant Commerce Clause, should the Court find the statute invalid? _____

CHAPTER 7

INTERGOVERNMENTAL IMMUNITIES & INTERSTATE RELATIONS

17. Arms Co. is a government military contractor. Its sole business is to manufacture M-16 rifles, all of which are then sold by it to the U.S. government. Arms Co.'s contract with the U.S. government is of a "cost plus fixed fee" variety. Okra, the state in which Arms Co. is located, has enacted a generally-applicable sales tax on all wholesale sales of tangible property made within the state. Okra applies this tax to Arms Co., with the result that Arms Co. must pay a tax of 8% on all goods bought by it for use in the manufacture of the M-16 rifle. The net effect of this tax is to increase by 4% the price paid by the U.S. government to Arms Co. for each M-16 rifle.

(A) If Arms Co. wishes to attack the constitutionality of the Okra sales tax as applied to its purchase of materials for use in the M-16, what is its best argument? _____

(B) Will this argument succeed? _____

18. The state of River provides that no physician may practice within the state unless that physician resides in the state. The state has enacted this rule because its legislators believed (with at least some rationality) that doctors are frequently called upon to give emergency service after hours, and doctors who live out-of-state will be, on the whole, less able to do this than those who live in-state. Doc, a person who has satisfied all other requirements for a license to practice in River (e.g., passage of the national medical boards), lives in the neighboring state of Lake.

(A) If Doc wishes to challenge River's residency requirement on constitutional grounds, what is his best argument? _____

(B) Will this argument probably succeed? _____

CHAPTER 8

SEPARATION OF POWERS

19. Congress passes the Personal Communications Services Act of 2009. The PCSA authorizes the FCC to award to private applicants, based on competitive bid, various pieces of radio spectrum for use in a new method of providing cellular phone service. The PCSA provides that any spectrum award by the FCC shall become permanently effective 90 days after it is first made, unless Congress has within the 90-day period enacted a Joint Resolution cancelling the particular award. According to the statute, such a Joint Resolution is to take effect immediately, without further action by any government official. The FCC then awards a particular spectrum license to Comm Co. Sixty days after this award, Congress passes a Joint Resolution purporting to cancel the award to Comm Co.

(A) If Comm Co. wishes to attack the constitutionality of the Joint Resolution stripping it of its license, what is the best argument it can make? _____

(B) Will this constitutional attack succeed? _____

20. The Caribbean island of Grenoble is a small but strategically important ally of the United States. Grenoble holds a popular election, but the military refuses to allow the democratically elected president to take office. The military then begins to seize the property of American businesses located in Grenoble. The President of the the U.S., concerned that U.S. strategic interests are endangered, and invoking his powers as Commander in Chief, sends 20,000 U.S. troops onto the island. This action is taken after the President confers with congressional leaders, but with no other congressional action. With Congress still inactive, fighting continues for six months, due to the Grenoble military's well-entrenched

status. A member of Congress, Senator Piper, then brings suit for a declaratory judgment that the President has acted unlawfully in using U.S. forces in this manner.

(A) What is the best argument that Senator Piper can make against the constitutionality of the President's actions? _____

(B) Will Piper's attack succeed? Assume that there is no existing relevant federal legislation. _____

21. Congress has established the Federal Truck Safety Board (FTSB). In the statute setting up the FTSB, Congress has provided that the Director of the FTSB shall be appointed by the President, without the need for House or Senate confirmation. The enabling legislation also provides that at any time, without cause, the House and Senate, acting together in the form of a Joint Resolution, may remove the Director. The Director is given certain powers, including the ability to issue an order suspending certain types of truck traffic if the Director concludes that the suspension is needed to protect the safety of interstate commerce.

In the 30 years since the FTSB was set up, Congress has played no role in the appointment or removal of the FTSB's Director. The incumbent, Derrick, was appointed 10 years ago. Recently, there have been a rash of accidents on the highway involving trucks of more than six feet in width. Derrick has decided that such wide trucks are dangerous, and has, therefore, issued an order suspending any truck of that width or greater from moving on the federal highways across a state border. Truck Co., owner of many extra-wide trucks, wishes to challenge the constitutionality of Derrick's action.

(A) What is the best grounds on which Truck Co. can challenge the constitutionality of Derrick's order? _____

(B) Will this attack succeed? _____

CHAPTER 9

DUE PROCESS

23. The legislature of the state of Utopia was worried about the large number of consumers being abused by the harassing tactics of debt collectors. A committee of the legislature investigated, and discovered that the vast majority of complaints involved debt collection techniques used by non-lawyers. Therefore (and at the urging of the state Bar Association), the Utopia legislature passed a statute providing that no person not admitted to the Bar of the State of Utopia may engage in the business of collecting debts owed by consumers. Kneecap, a non-lawyer debt collector, wishes to challenge the statute's constitutionality.

(A) Putting aside any possible First Amendment issues, what right held by Kneecap is most likely to have been violated by the Utopia statute? _____

(B) With respect to the right you listed in your response to (a), what is the standard for determining whether the right has been violated? _____

(C) Will Kneecap's attack on the statute succeed? _____

24. The state of Aha has enacted a statute that proscribes what the statute refers to as "unnatural sexual acts." The acts described include oral sex. The statute applies to conduct between married persons as well as to conduct between unmarried persons, but contains an exemption for conduct that takes place in a dwelling that is the residence of one or both parties. Joe and Martha Danzig, a married couple, were vacationing at the Happy Times Motel, when a state police officer burst into the room acting on a tip (reasonable-seeming but erroneous) that the couple was using drugs. The officer happened to see Joe and Martha engaging in oral sex at that moment, and arrested them.

(A) If Joe and Martha want to challenge the charges on constitutional grounds, what is their best argument? _____

(B) Will this argument succeed? _____

25. A number of states have enacted regulations bearing on specific aspects of abortion. Consider the following:

(A) The state of Aloha provides that no abortion may be performed within the state if at the moment of the procedure the fetus is more than three months old.

(B) The state of Brie provides that no abortion may be performed on a married woman unless she signs an affidavit that she has notified her spouse. However, the prohibition does not apply if the married woman instead signs an affidavit that she and her husband are not living together, or that her husband is not the father of the child, or that she has not given notice because she fears that he will abuse her if he finds out that she is planning an abortion. The statute is challenged by P, a woman who is two months pregnant, wants an abortion, and does not want to notify her spouse (with whom P lives, whom she believes to be the father of the child, and who is not likely to abuse her if she tells him she wants an abortion).

(C) The state of Caledonia provides that no abortion may be performed on a woman under the age of 18, unless one parent of the woman has received one hour of counselling about alternatives to abortion, and this mandatory counselling has been followed by a 24-hour waiting period. The young woman may avoid the need for parental consent by taking advantage of a procedure under which she is entitled to try to persuade a judge that either: (i) an abortion is in her best interests; (ii) she is living apart from her parents and is effectively emancipated; or (iii) abortion is made necessary by a medical emergency.

State whether each of these provisions is constitutional. (Assume that the suits in (A) and (C) are attacks on the face of the statute, and that the attack in (B) is "as applied.")

---

26. In recent years, in the state of North Rockland, there has been an increase in the number of marginally-funded, educationally-inadequate private schools, as well as a rise in the number of parents who have been teaching their children at home rather than sending them to the public schools. The North Rockland legislature has, therefore, just passed a statute providing that every child between the age of 6 and 16 must be educated in the state's public schools. Parents who do not comply face criminal punishment. The statute does not allow any exceptions for even educationally-sound private schools or educationally-sound home instruction. Paula, the parent of a seven-year-old son, wishes to educate him at home. Paula was until last year a first-grade teacher in a state public school, and all concerned agree that she is well qualified to teach her child at home provided that she does so full time, which she expects to do. Paula has sued to overturn the statute, as applied to her and her son, on substantive due process grounds.

(A) What standard of review should the court use in deciding Paula's suit?

_____

(B) Will the statute be found constitutional as applied to Paula and her son?

_____

27. The state of Centuria has a criminal statute prohibiting "sodomy," defined to include any instance in which one person's mouth or anus touches another person's genitals. Century Village, a town in Centuria, has a school-board regulation providing that any person who the school board finds to have violated any state statute involving moral turpitude shall be dismissed, and further providing that a violation of the sodomy ban shall be deemed to constitute moral turpitude. Darwin, a non-tenured teacher at Century Village High School, was involved in a sexual relationship with Fred. After Darwin broke up the relationship, Fred sent a video to the Century Village school board, showing Darwin and Fred involved in conduct of the sort proscribed by the Centuria criminal statute. The school board viewed the video, concluded that Darwin had violated the statute, and dismissed Darwin. In recent years, the statute has rarely been enforced, and on those rare occasions has been enforced principally against same-sex sodomy. Darwin has now attacked his firing on the grounds that it violates his substantive due process rights. Assume that issues of procedural due process are ignored.

(A) What standard should the court use for deciding Darwin's challenge?

_____

(B) Was Darwin's firing constitutional? _____

28. The town of Tinsel originally did not have any written regulation concerning the beard or hair styles of fire fighters. At the time Jordan was hired onto the fire fighting force, he had a beard and hair that was neatly combed but of shoulder length. After Jordan had been on the force two years, Tinsel enacted a regulation providing that no male firefighter could wear a beard or hair extending below his neck. Jordan has challenged this regulation as violating his substantive due process rights. Tinsel has defended the regulation on the grounds that: (i) uniformity of hairstyle is necessary to generate a feeling of esprit de corps among firefighters; and (ii) facial hair and long hair are more likely to catch fire even if the person dons the usual safety equipment.

(A) What standard should the court use in deciding whether Jordan's substantive due process rights have been violated? _____

(B) Is the regulation constitutional? _____

30. The town of Corinth advertised an opening for a position as secretary to the City Clerk. The ad described the job briefly, and said nothing about the criteria that would be used to fill it. Jane Brown applied for the job. She was given a typing test, and then an interview with George Crako, the City Clerk. Crako chose somebody else for the job. Brown asked for a statement of why she didn't get the job, but the Clerk's office refused to respond.

Brown later heard from the grapevine that Crako had told someone else in the department that he thought Brown was probably the best at performing the technical tasks, but that he had declined to hire her because he had heard she was gay. Brown, who was not gay, realized that Crako was probably thinking of another member of the community, Jane Browne, who was widely known to be gay. Brown asked for a hearing at which she could present what she called "information which would cause the Clerk to reverse his decision," but town officials again refused. Brown has now sued, arguing that the procedures used to fill the opening deprived her of her Fourteenth Amendment due process rights. Should the court find in Brown's favor? _____

31. Tennant, a single mother who was receiving Welfare, resided in a public housing project owned by the city of Pretoria. She had lived in the building for over 10 years, pursuant to a series of two-year leases. The rules of the housing project, posted on a bulletin board in the complex, stated that "customarily, residents who are well behaved and current on all of their obligations will be offered the opportunity to renew their leases upon their expiration." There is no statute or other body of state or local law bearing on whether one in Tennant's position is entitled, as a contractual matter, to a renewal. At the end of Tennant's current two-year term, she was not offered the opportunity to renew her lease. Instead, the apartment was given to a woman who turned out to be the niece of Pretoria's Buildings Commissioner, who would not have been given an apartment had the ordinary informal allocation procedures that had previously been followed in the housing project been followed here. Tennant was at no time given an explanation for why she wasn't permitted to renew, or a hearing regarding the decision.

    (A) If Tennant wishes to challenge the city's handling of her tenancy on constitutional grounds, what is the strongest argument she can make? _____

    (B) Will this argument succeed? _____

32. Netsville High School, a public high school, was known for its strong boys' and girls' tennis teams. The administration caused to be published in the school newspaper an invitation for tryouts. This invitation included the following sentence: "All students in good academic standing have the right to compete for the 7 spots on each team. These spots will be awarded to the best players." Priscilla, a high school freshman, had not been on the team previously. However, she had had some strong results in non-school tournaments the summer before her freshman year. During tryouts, the head coach watched Priscilla play only briefly. He very quickly reached the conclusion that her game was not mature enough to make her a varsity player. After one day of practice, he cut her from the team. He did not give her any statement of reasons, or opportunity to present her view of why she should make the team; he merely stated that she was "not good enough." The coach awarded team spots exclusively to those who had been on the team in prior years, including at least one girl whom Priscilla had soundly beaten in a non-school tournament the summer before. Priscilla has sued the school board, arguing that the procedures by which she was dropped from the team violated her due process rights to be awarded a post if she was one of the "best players."

    Assuming that Priscilla can demonstrate that most tennis coaches would have found her to be one of the seven strongest players trying out for the team, should the judge order the coach to reconsider her status? _____

CHAPTER 10
EQUAL PROTECTION

33. The state of Chartreuse has delegated to the state bar association the job of determining requirements for the practice of law. Until recently, the bar association imposed no continuing legal education requirements. However, there has been a large rise in the number of malpractice actions against lawyers in the state, some of which appear to derive from the fact that lawyers have not kept pace with changing legal principles. Also, there has been a rise in the disdain with which the public in Chartreuse holds lawyers. The bar association, therefore, imposed a mandatory continuing legal education requirement of 12 course-hours per year. The state imposes on doctors a continuing education requirement of only 4 hours per year. There is strong evidence that, in general, changes in medicine happen faster than changes in law. Amos, a lawyer in Chartreuse, has challenged the continuing legal education requirement on the grounds that by imposing a much higher requirement on lawyers than on doctors, the state has violated his equal protection rights. Assume that the state bar association's conduct constitutes state action.

(A) What standard should the court use to test whether the legal education requirement satisfies the demands of equal protection? _____

(B) Will Amos' attack succeed? _____

34. The town of Solon established a regulation that all members of the fire department must retire at the age of 50. The Town Council enacted the regulation after reading a news report that in a neighboring town, a 53 year-old firefighter with a bad back was unable to carry a child out of the fourth floor of a burning building, leading to the child's death. The Town Council members reasoned that on average, those over 50 are less able to perform the highly demanding physical functions of firefighting than those under 50. Prentice is the Chief of the Solon Fire Department. His duties are exclusively desk-bound. He has just turned 50, and has challenged the retirement regulation, as applied to him, on the grounds that it violates his right to equal protection. Will Prentice's attack on the regulation succeed? _____

35. The state of Minnetonka has enacted an adoption statute that specifies the criteria to be used when public agencies make adoption placements. (No private adoptions are permitted in the state.) According to the statute, the "racial compatibility" between the child and the adoptive parents is the most important factor to be considered, though many other factors are also to be considered. Peter and Jill, a white couple in their 40's, wished to adopt a child. They learned that a large number of African American children were being raised in state-sponsored orphanages, because no homes could be found for them. The couple applied to a state adoption agency, requesting to adopt any African American child under the age of four, who was currently living in an orphanage. The adoption agency replied, "Because applicable statutes require us to give racial matching heaviest weight in making adoption placements, and because you are seeking a relatively young child who may well be placeable with a racially-compatible, i.e., African American family in the future, we cannot grant your request." Peter and Jill have sued in federal court for a ruling that the statute providing for race-matching violates their equal protection rights. They have presented evidence that African American children are staying longer in orphanages than white children who are otherwise similar, and that this lengthier stay is due in part to the heavy statutory weight placed on race-matching.

(A) By what standard should the court test the constitutionality of the race-matching statute as it applies to Peter and Jill? _____

(B) Should the court agree with Peter and Jill's contention that their equal protection rights have been violated? _____

36. Carolene High School, a public high school, has for years maintained special remedial reading classes. Students can take these classes in lieu of the regular English class, if they are shown to have learning disabilities or otherwise shown to be behind on their reading skills. Students of African American ancestry make up 12% of the student body of the high school. Forty-five percent of the students in the remedial reading program are African American. Because of reduced federal aid to education and a local recession, the school board has reluctantly concluded that it must reduce expenditures. Therefore, it has cancelled the remedial reading program, which is about 15% more expensive per student than the regular English program. The school board has not cut funding for the honors English program, which similarly costs about 15% more per student than regular English. About 9% of the students in the honors English program are African American. All of the evidence is that the school board made the decision it did on the honest belief that the honors program accomplishes more per dollar and strengthens the school system more, than does the remedial reading program. Carl, an African American student enrolled in the remedial reading program, has now challenged the termination on the grounds that it violates his right to equal protection.

(A) What standard should the court use in deciding Carl's challenge?

_____

(B) Will Carl's challenge succeed? _____

37. Smithville is a small town located near the Canadian border. A significant minority of the children attending Smithville High School are American citizens of French-Canadian descent. The school board has just canceled the honors French program. The decision was made by the school principal, an American of Anglo-Saxon descent, who told school board members, "If we keep running an extensive French program, we'll just attract more Americans of French-Canadian ancestry to the town, and soon they'll be a majority." Since the school board was completely dominated by Anglo-Saxon Americans, they concurred with the decision. Jacques, an American student at the school of French-Canadian descent, has sued the school district, arguing that the cancellation has violated his constitutional rights.

(A) What standard of review should the court use to judge the school district's cancellation decision? _____

(B) Will Jacques' challenge succeed? _____

38. Same facts as prior question. Now, however, assume that the town of Smithville, and its school board, both contain a majority of Americans of French-Canadian descent. The board has now voted to dramatically expand the French program, and to cancel the honors English program. Strong evidence suggests that the board was motivated by a desire to

attract more French-Canadian Americans into town, and to solidify this group's majority over Anglo-Americans. Does either of your answers to question 41 change here, and if so, how? _____

39. The city of Monroe enacted an ordinance providing that 10% of all procurements of office supplies in the city for the coming year must be purchased from office supply companies majority-owned by either African Americans or Hispanics, the two largest ethnic groups in the city. African Americans and Hispanics together make up a substantial minority (approximately 40%) of the city's population. The City Council did not conduct legislative hearings or investigations prior to enacting the bill. However, minutes of the Council's deliberations show that Council members enacted the bill primarily because they felt that minority business people, especially in the office supply industry, had had less general economic opportunity than white-owned firms, and that the 10% set-aside was the best way to increase the opportunities for minority owned companies. At the moment the bill was enacted, firms owned by African Americans or Hispanics amounted to approximately 10% of the total office supply companies in the city, but these companies did only about 4% of the total office supply business in the city, since the average minority-owned firm was much smaller than the average white-owned firm.

Anglo Office Supply, a white-owned office supply firm, has challenged the Monroe set-aside on equal protection grounds.

(A) What standard should the court use in evaluating the constitutional sufficiency of the set-aside? _____

(B) Will Anglo's attack succeed? _____

40. The Oneanta state legislature mandated that any employer with five or more employees grant a paid six-month maternity leave to any woman who gave birth while on the company's payroll. The legislature imposed no requirements regarding paid or unpaid family leave for men who had just had a child. In deciding to enact the measure, the legislators relied principally on evidence that various rising social problems, such as drugs and crime, were caused in part by the rise in working women and a consequent failure of mothers to bond with their infants. Frank, the father of a newborn infant who wished to have a paid paternity leave, has challenged the statute on the grounds that it violates his equal protection rights.

(A) What standard should the court apply in evaluating Frank's challenge to the maternity-leave statute? _____

(B) Will Frank's attack succeed? _____

41. Congress was dismayed by statistics indicating that although African Americans and Hispanics now compose approximately 22% of America's university-age population, these two groups comprise only 9% of enrollees at colleges and universities nationally. Most members of Congress believed that the shortfall was due to the residual effects of past official discrimination by state and local governments, including public university systems. Therefore, Congress enacted a statute providing that any college or university receiving federal funds was required to treat an applicant's African American or Hispanic status into account as a "positive factor," and to "make best efforts" to enroll as high a percentage of African American and Hispanic students as are present in the school-age population for the geographical area being served by that college or university. The statute further provided that statistics regarding actual enrollments would be treated as follows: a university would be rebuttably presumed to have failed to comply with the statute if the number of African American and Hispanic students actually enrolled was less than 80% of what would be predicted from the pool of recent high school graduates in the region from which the university draws the bulk of its enrollees. The statute's preamble recited Congress' belief that enrollment disparities stemmed in major part from past governmental discrimination, but neither the statutory text nor the statute's legislative history either (1) described the particulars of this discrimination (e.g., whether it was national, whether it was by universities or other governmental actors, etc.) or (2) considered whether race-neutral methods might suffice to cure the lingering effects of the discrimination.

Penny, a white female with good grades and test scores, was denied admission to Statesville University, a large and prestigious public university. She sued the University, pointing out that her grades and test scores were above the average for those accepted at the University, and arguing (correctly, as a factual matter) that but for the federally-required racial preference, she would probably have been admitted. She therefore contends that the federal statute violates her equal protection rights.

(A) What standard should the court use in deciding whether the federal statute violates Penny's equal protection rights? _____

(B) Will Penny's attack succeed? _____

42. In the state of Delta, 12% of recent high school graduates are African-American. The state's premier public university, Delta State, has historically made its decisions about whom to admit on a "holistic basis." Under the holistic system, admissions officials look at the student's entire academic and extracurricular profile, without ever explicitly treating (or even knowing) the student's race as a factor. Two years ago, the university's administration observed that its entering freshman class during the prior four years had been, on average, 6% black. A survey done by the university administration then determined that 75% of seminar classes at the university — "seminar" meaning classes having between 5 and 16 students — contained either zero or one African-American student. The administration decided that it would be vital to admit — and hopefully enroll — a substantially greater number of African-American students, so as to increase the critical mass of such students in seminar classes and thereby increase the overall educational diversity of the undergraduate experience. To that end, the admissions department considered two different plans. Under Plan A, half the entering class's seats would no longer be allocated on the holistic method, and would instead be subjected to a "Top Seven Percent" arrangement, under which any applicant who had been in the top 7% of his in-state public high school graduating class would automatically be offered admission. A statistician consulted by the university predicted that because of the highly segregated nature of Delta's public high schools, the adoption of Plan A would result in many more offers to (and acceptances by) black students, so that the percentage of seminar classes without at least two black students would likely drop from 75% to about 45%. Under Plan B, the university would amend its existing holistic plan so that race could be explicitly considered as one factor among many; under this plan, all seats would be allocated under the newly-revised race-

conscious plan. Admissions officials determined, after some modeling, that Plan B would result in an increase in black students (and a decrease in seminars with fewer than two black students) comparable to that anticipated from Plan A.

Admission officials decided to use Plan B instead of A. They made this choice mainly because they reasonably concluded that Plan B would result in the admission of a slightly-more-highly-credentialed group of black students than Plan A, because Plan B would enable the school to attract a significant number of black students graduating in the top 15% (but not top 7%) of their class at relatively affluent and high-achieving majority-white public high schools in the state. Paula, a white non-Hispanic student who graduated 5th in her class of 100 at a high-achieving in-state suburban high school, was denied admission to Delta State. She has sued the university in federal district court, alleging that its use of Plan B violated her federal equal protection rights by discriminating against her because she was white. The university has defended on the grounds that its use of Plan B, although admittedly race-conscious, conforms with applicable Supreme Court precedents. Assume that (1) pursuit of a "critical mass" of two or more black students in a larger percentage of seminar classes constitutes a compelling governmental interest in "educational diversity"; and (2) had Plan A been in force instead of Plan B, Paula would have automatically been offered admission.

(A) Which party, Paula or Delta State, bears the burden of proof on the issue of whether Paula's equal protection rights have been violated by Delta State's use of Plan B?

_____

(B) What standard of review should the trial court use in deciding whether the party who bears the burden of proof (as identified in your answer in (a)) has carried that burden?

_____

(C) When the court applies the review standard you specified in (b), which party is likely to win? _____

43. The state of Pacifica enacted a statute providing that no person who is not a U.S. citizen could hold title to beach-front land located in the state. Pacifica's west coast consists entirely of ocean-front property. The statute was enacted in part because state residents were annoyed that Japanese nationals and citizens of other Pacific rim countries were paying high prices for Pacifica beach-front property, making it harder for U.S. citizens living in Pacifica to compete for ownership of that property. Yukio, a Japanese citizen who resides permanently in the United States, and who wishes to buy ocean-front property in Pacifica, has sued to have the statute overturned on the grounds that it violates her equal protection rights.

(A) What standard of review should the court give to the Pacifica statute?

_____

(B) Will Yukio's attack succeed? _____

44. The city of Xenon was concerned that many applicants for posts as public school teachers in the town, and some hires, were foreigners who spoke with a hard-to-understand accent. Therefore, the Xenon school board enacted a regulation that henceforth, all new hires for the post of school teacher in the local school system must at the time of their application

be United States citizens. Ted, an Englishman married to an American citizen, was a permanent resident of the U.S. but had no desire to become a U.S. citizen (even though his marital status entitled him to become one). Ted sued Xenon to have its citizens-only rule overturned, on the grounds that it violated his equal protection rights.

(A) What standard should the court use in reviewing the Xenon citizens-only provision?

_____

(B) Will Ted's attack on the provision succeed? _____

45. The village of Tesla had a fine school system, generally believed to be better than that of surrounding towns. Tesla is located less than 100 miles from the border with Mexico, and has a large number of both Mexican Americans as well as undocumented aliens from Mexico. In order to discourage enrollment by students who in fact reside in other towns, the village enacted a set of strict regulations providing that only students who satisfied two conditions could attend the village's schools: (1) they had a bona fide residence within the village limits; and (2) they were either U.S. citizens or resident aliens. One effect of this regulation, as intended by the town elders, was to make undocumented aliens unable to attend the village schools even if they resided in the village. The principal motive for the no-illegal-aliens rule was to conserve tax dollars, because undocumented aliens on average pay lower property taxes, and education in the state is financed principally through property taxes. The village allowed an exception to its enrollment restrictions for anyone willing to pay a tuition fee of $4,000 per year.

Pedro, a resident of Tesla who was undocumented, sued the village, arguing that as applied to him the enrollment restrictions violated the Equal Protection Clause.

(A) When the court reviews Pedro's challenge to the enrollment restrictions, what standard of review should it use? _____

(B) Will Pedro's attack succeed? _____

47. Many members of Congress observed that as more and more states allowed same-sex marriages, there was in these states a corresponding increase in same-sex marriages between a U.S. citizen and a non-citizen. The House Committee on Immigration and Naturalization conducted hearings on the issue, and then reported out to the full House a bill called "The Defense of Heterosexual Naturalization Act of 2014" (DHNA). The bill directed the federal Citizenship and Immigration Service (CIS) to deny a green card (conferring permanent-resident status) to the non-citizen member of any same-sex marriage, even though existing federal immigration law automatically granted a green card to the non-citizen spouse in any *opposite*-sex marriage between a citizen and non-citizen. The Committee's report on the DHNA bill said that "A majority of the Committee disapproves of same-sex marriages on moral grounds, and wishes to discourage the creation of additional same-sex marriages in the U.S. by denying a path to naturalization for non-citizens who enter into such marriages when permitted by state law." There was no other legislative history on the bill. The DHNA passed both houses without significant debate, and was signed into law by the president. After the bill became law, two men, Bill and Li, entered into a marriage in California, where both live and where same-sex marriages are legal. Bill is a U.S. citizen; Li is not. After the marriage, Li applied for green-card; the application was denied by the CIS under authority of the DHNA. Li has sued the CIS in federal district court; he contends that the agency's denial of a green card violated his federal constitutional right to equal protection as applied to the federal government under the Fifth Amendment. The CIS has defended the statute's constitutionality on all available grounds. Will Li's claim succeed? _____

48. The state of Booth has enacted a statute governing the issuance of absentee ballots in state elections. Under the statute, any male under the age of 65 will be issued an absentee ballot only upon written proof that the applicant will be unable to be present at the voting place on the scheduled day for the election. If the applicant is a female, however, no written proof is required, and the applicant's statement that she cannot be present at the polling place is accepted at face value. The motivation for the statute was the legislature's belief that many women voters are the mothers of infants, who cannot easily get to the polling place to vote. Marvin, a male resident of Booth, has attacked the requirement of written proof on the grounds that it violates his Fourteenth Amendment equal protection rights.

(A) What standard should the court use in reviewing the requirement of written proof?

_____

(B) Will Marvin's attack succeed?   _____

49. The county of Gardenia has established a Forest Conservation District. The purpose of this district is to levy a special tax on owners of forested property, and to use these funds to buy certain parcels of forested property in the county from willing sellers so that the property can remain forested. The ultimate purpose of the District is to ensure that there is enough forested land that erosion will not get a foothold locally, something that would happen if many forested parcels become denuded by logging. The district is to be administered by a Board of Directors having five members. The five members are to be elected annually. Only owners of forested property in the county are permitted to vote in the election for directors. Bruce, the owner of non-forested real estate, has sued for a declaration that the "one person, one vote" principle has been violated by this arrangement.

(A) What standard of review should the court use in deciding Bruce's challenge?

_____

(B) Will Bruce's attack succeed?   _____

50. The state of Illowa provided that in order for a "minor" party to have its presidential candidate appear on the ballot, the party must file petitions containing the signatures of 15% of all eligible voters in the state. (A party was defined as "minor" if it had not received at least 10% of the votes cast in the state in the previous presidential election.) The petition had to be filed nine months before the general election. Also, a minor party did not qualify for the ballot unless it conducted a primary election. Other Illowa electoral provisions prevented anyone from running for president as an independent, and did not allow for write-in candidacies for president. The Anti Washington Party, a newly-formed party dedicated to "throwing the rascals out of Washington," wished to have its candidate appear on the Illowa presidential-election ballot. The AWP sued on the grounds that these restrictions violated the equal protection rights of minority parties, as well as the freedom-of-association rights of party members.

(A) What standard should the court use in hearing this challenge? _____

(B) Will the AWP's attack on the restrictions succeed? _____

51. The state of Amazonia has a program called MedAmaz, which provides emergency medical assistance for indigent citizens. Under the rules for the program, a person who has moved to Amazonia is not eligible to receive emergency medical care until he or she has resided in the state for at least one year. Penelope, who moved to Amazonia three months ago from Ohio, needed an emergency appendectomy. The hospital refused to perform it because she did not meet the residency requirement, and Penelope almost died. Now, she has sued the state for damages, arguing that the residency requirement violated her right to equal protection of the laws.

    (A) What standard of review should the court use? _____

    (B) Will Penelope's attack succeed? _____

52. The state of New Canada has set its maximum welfare payment at $1,250 per month. For families of one child through three children, extra sums are paid for each additional child (with the $1,250 figure being paid for a family with three children). The net effect of the scheme is that a family does not receive any extra money for children after the first three. A further effect is that for a family of five children, the maximum paid by the state is 25% less than the federal poverty level. Hilda, a single mother of five children, whose only income comes from New Canada welfare payments, has sued the state, arguing that her family's equal protection rights have been violated, in that the state has discriminated against large families such as hers.

    (A) What standard of review should the court use in evaluating the statute? _____

    (B) Will Hilda's attack succeed? _____

CHAPTER 11

THE PRIVILEGES & IMMUNITIES, TAKING, OBLIGATION OF CONTRACTS, EX POST FACTO AND BILL OF ATTAINDER CLAUSES

53. The state of Okansas has a state-paid health plan, whereby the state pays the medical bills of indigent families after a $1,000-per-family annual deductible. Because of the generosity of this plan, the state has become concerned that some impoverished residents of other states offering less-generous (or no) medical coverage have been moving to Okansas to take advantage of the plan. Therefore, the Okansas legislature has provided that a family moving to Okansas from another state shall, for its first year of genuine residence in Okansas, be entitled only to those medical-bill payments that the family would have received in the state in which it previously resided.

    (A) You represent a poor family that has just moved to Okansas from Nebraska, which has no indigent medical coverage at all. What is the best constitutional argument you can make that Okansas' provision violates your client's rights? _____

(B) Will the claim you make in (a) succeed? _____

54. Mill Co. has operated a steel mill in the Township of Fuschia for many years. Mill Co. owns both the factory and the land on which it is located. The mill has always obeyed all state and federal pollution control requirements. However, operation of a steel mill is inevitably a somewhat messy enterprise, with a fair amount of noise, smoke, etc. As the township has become more affluent and residential in character, the inhabitants have become increasingly unhappy with having a steel mill in their midst. Now, the township has amended its zoning ordinance so as to provide that no "heavy industry" (defined in a way that includes Mill Co.'s steel mill and a variety of other manufacturing operations) shall be permitted to operate anywhere in the town after four years from the ordinance's adoption. The effect of the ordinance is that Mill Co. or the next owner of its property may build houses, stores or warehouses on the site, but not operate a heavy manufacturing plant. Although the end of the four-year period is still two years away, Mill Co. wishes to challenge the ordinance.

(A) Assuming that the ordinance was enacted in a procedurally satisfactory manner, what is the strongest argument that Mill Co. can make attacking the constitutionality of the zoning ordinance as applied to it? _____

(B) Will this argument succeed? _____

55. The village of Green Valley wished to incinerate its trash and garbage in an ecologically sound way, rather than using up scarce landfill. It also wished to raise revenue as part of the process. Therefore, it entered into an arrangement with Waste Co., a trash management company. The arrangement provided for Waste Co. to build an incinerator in Green Valley, and for Waste Co. to pay Green Valley a 50¢ per ton "franchise fee" for every ton of trash or garbage processed by the plant over a 15-year period. (Waste Co. would make money by charging the public a fee for each load processed.) In return, Green Valley agreed to require by law, for the 15 years, that all trash and garbage produced in the town be sent to the Waste Co. facility. The arrangement operated as expected for the first five years, during which time Waste Co.'s fees to the town averaged about $2 million per year.

Then, New Co., another waste company that competed with Waste Co., proposed a new deal to Green Valley. New Co. asked Green Valley to require that trash (i.e., dry refuse) but not garbage (wet refuse, like food) be sent to *its* facility. In return, New Co. would pay Green Valley a minimum of $1.5 million per year. Green Valley agreed, and changed its laws so that now, the Waste Co. plant would only get garbage, and the New Co. plant would get the trash. The net effect was that Green Valley's receipts went from $2 million a year to $3 million per year. (Green Valley, like most municipalities, could certainly benefit from the extra $1 million per year, but the town is not faced with extreme financial hardship.) The effect on Waste Co. was to reduce its profits by $500,000 per year.

(A) If Waste Co. wishes to challenge Green Valley's conduct on constitutional grounds, what is its best argument? _____

(B) Will this attack succeed? _____

56. Last year, Byer purchased a small shopping center in the town of Happy Farms. There were several other similar shopping centers in town, as well as various other types of retail

stores. At the time of the purchase, Happy Farms allowed retail stores to operate seven days a week, 24 hours a day, if they wished. At the time of the purchase, the shopping center had so called "percentage leases" with its tenants, whereby the rent paid was a percentage of the retail sales generated by the stores. Each percentage lease required the store owner to maintain hours on Sunday from noon to 6:00 p.m. Byer computed the amount that it was appropriate for him to pay for the center based on this flow of percentage rent. Six months after Byer made the purchase, Happy Farms changed its zoning ordinance to prohibit any retail store from opening on Sunday. This action (taken at the request of certain small store owners who wanted to be able to take Sundays off without losing sales to their competitors), caused Byer's tenants to suffer a 10% drop in revenues, which translated into a substantial loss of rent for Byer.

Byer now asserts that the Sunday closing law constitutes an impairment of his contractual rights, in violation of the Obligation of Contracts Clause. Is Byer's assertion correct? State your reasons. _____

57. In 2008, Dennis had sex with a 14-year-old girl, who purported to give consent. However, the state's criminal statutes regarded sex with a female under the age of 15 as statutory rape, regardless of ostensible consent. The penalty for rape was a prison sentence of up to five years. In 2009, the state legislature changed the penalty for statutory rape from a maximum of five years to a maximum of 10 years. Dennis was tried and convicted in 2010, and was sentenced to a prison term of seven years.

(A) If Dennis wishes to attack his conviction and/or sentence on constitutional grounds, what is his strongest argument? _____

(B) Will this argument succeed? State your reasons. _____

58. The Phrenic Brotherhood is a small, dedicated group of religious fundamentalists, located throughout the United States, whose stated mission is to dissuade the U.S. from opposing the rise of the religion of Phrenology throughout the world. Certain acts of terrorism have been traced to the Brotherhood, though it is not known who in particular committed these acts. The state of New Righteous, in response to a recent act of terrorism in the state thought to be associated with the Brotherhood, passed the following statute: "No member of the group known as the Phrenic Brotherhood shall be hired or retained on the payroll of any branch of the government of this state." Oren, who was employed as a file clerk at the New Righteous Department of Social Security, was known to his superior to be a member of the Brotherhood. The superior, citing the newly enacted statute, fired Oren.

(A) If Oren wishes to attack the statute on constitutional grounds, what argument (putting aside any argument based directly upon the First Amendment) has the best chance of success for him? _____

(B) Will this attack succeed? _____

CHAPTER 12

STATE ACTION

59. Pablo, an American of Hispanic origin, attempted to receive treatment at Green Valley

Hospital. He believes that he was denied admission solely because he was Hispanic. Green Valley Hospital is owned by the Little Sisters of Green Valley, a private religious order. Pablo has brought suit against the Little Sisters, arguing that they have violated his right to equal protection under the Fourteenth Amendment. Assuming that the facts are as asserted by Pablo, will his suit succeed? _____

60. A statute enacted by the state of Albatross makes it a felony for any individual to "interfere with any right guaranteed by the Equal Protection Clause of the Fourteenth Amendment of the U.S. Constitution." Delbert was the manager of a housing project funded and operated by a federal housing agency. Delbert refused to rent to a family solely because they were black. If Delbert is charged with violating the Albatross statute, should he be convicted? _____

61. Ninety percent of the kindergarten-through-twelfth-grade students who attend school in the state of Mongoose attend public schools. The other 10% attend private schools, some of which are parochial and some of which are not. Beaver Academy is a non-sectarian private school, 40% of whose operating funds are supplied by the state as part of an innovative program to encourage excellence in education. The state does not prescribe any aspect of the Beaver curriculum, beyond checking to make sure that students achieve a minimum level of competency in core subjects like reading. Pamela, a sixth-grade student, has brought suit against Beaver Academy, asserting that she was denied admission to Beaver solely on the grounds that she is black. Because Mongoose has extremely limited civil rights statutes, Pamela's suit consists solely of the assertion that the school's failure to admit her violated her Fourteenth Amendment equal protection rights. Assume that Pamela's factual assertions are true.

(A) When Pamela attempts to prove the presence of state action, what doctrine offers her the best chance of success? _____

(B) Will Pamela's suit succeed? _____

62. State U is a large public university located in the fairly small town of Arborville. Students at the university represent a substantial share of the local demand for housing. Much of the housing stock in Arborville consists of two-family homes, in one part of which the owner lives and the other part of which is rented to students. State U's housing department maintains a list of local homeowners who have such housing to offer to students. State U allows a homeowner to indicate his or her racial or ethnic preferences on the listing; thus one who prefers whites may request that a "W" designation be affixed, one who prefers blacks that a "B" be affixed, etc. The university does not charge for these listings. Because State U does not have enough dormitory space to house all students, the availability of private housing like that contained in the list is an important resource for the university. There is evidence that some homeowners who have participated in the list would not do so if they were not able to indicate their racial preferences and thus reduce the possibility of an embarrassing face-to-face refusal to rent to minorities.

Bernard, a black student at State U, has been unable to find what he considers suitable housing. He believes that there are substantially fewer housing units available to black students than to white students, and that on average the ones that are available to blacks are either more costly or less attractive. Assume that no federal or state statute bars discrimination by an owner/occupier of a two-family house in the selection of a tenant. Bernard has sued State U for an injunction against continued use of the racially-coded housing list, on the grounds that the U's maintenance of that list violates his equal protection rights.

(A) What is the best argument Bernard can make as to why maintenance of the list violates his equal protection rights? _____

(B) Assuming that many private landowners on the list are in fact discriminating against black students, and that black students on average have to pay more for less attractive accommodations than whites when they rent from the list, should Bernard's request for an injunction be granted? _____

CHAPTER 13

CONGRESSIONAL ENFORCEMENT OF CIVIL RIGHTS

63. The U.S. Congress has decided that it would now be desirable to extend the reach of federal anti-discrimination laws to the rental of units in 1-4 family homes, which have previously been exempt from such laws. Therefore, Congress proposes to make it a crime for any homeowner, regardless of the size of his dwelling or the number of units in it, and regardless of whether the owner resides in it, to decline to rent to another person on the grounds of the latter's race, ethnic group or national origin. Do Congress' enforcement powers under the Fourteenth Amendment furnish adequate constitutional support for this statute? _____

64. Same facts as prior question. Now, however, assume that you are asked to find a constitutional basis for the proposed statute other than the Fourteenth Amendment and other than the Commerce Clause. What provision would you point to? _____

65. After a sharp rightward shift in the politics of the nation, Republicans and conservative Democrats gained a majority in both houses of Congress. They passed, and the President signed into law, a statute providing as follows: "It shall be a federal felony for any person to perform an abortion on a woman who is more than three months pregnant, unless the pregnancy was caused by rape or incest or the abortion is necessary to save the woman's life." Assume for purposes of this question that if a state passed a comparable statute, Supreme Court precedents already on the books would compel the conclusion that the state statute was an unconstitutional violation of women's right of privacy. A woman and her doctor have challenged the federal statute on the grounds that it is a violation of the right to privacy, as embodied in the Fifth Amendment's Due Process Clause. Will this attack on the statute succeed? _____

CHAPTER 14

FREEDOM OF EXPRESSION

66. Darwin and 10 others were all members of the basketball team of State U, a public university. The Chancellor of State U had recently suspended Xavier, one of the members of the team, from both the team and the school for alleged cheating in an exam. At 10:00 a.m. on a Tuesday morning, Darwin and his 10 teammates stood in front of the University administration building, which contained the Chancellor's office. They carried signs saying, "Reinstate Xavier"; they also chanted and sang. The Chancellor happened to be away from the office that day (unbeknownst to Darwin and his friends), and nobody in the building was considering Xavier's case at the time.

A statute of the state in which State U is located provides as follows:

> "No group of 10 or more persons shall demonstrate on the sidewalk or other public way in front of a state or local government office building during business hours, unless the demonstration is related to matters currently under consideration by government officials working in the building. Violation of this provision shall be punishable as a misdemeanor."

Darwin has been charged with violating this section. He wishes to defend on the grounds that the section violates his First Amendment freedom of expression.

(A) What is the best argument he can make as to why his First Amendment rights would be violated by a conviction? _____

(B) May Darwin constitutionally be convicted of violating the provision?

_____

67. The city of Munford has enacted the following ordinance: "No person shall attempt to give to passersby on any sidewalk or public thoroughfare any handbill during a Restricted Time Period. 'Restricted Time Period' shall mean the hours between 8:00 and 9:30 a.m. and the hours between 4:30 and 6:00 p.m., Monday through Friday. 'Handbill' is defined to include any piece of printed literature, four pages or less, dealing with a single topic." The purpose of the definition is to cover advertising circulars and brochures, but not to cover newspapers and magazines. The ordinance was enacted in response to two fears: (1) that during the busy rush hour, people were handing out so many handbills that the flow of pedestrian traffic was frequently impaired; and (2) that an extraordinary amount of litter was being generated when people who had handbills thrust into their hands dropped them on the sidewalk. Kermit, a political candidate who was giving out brochures in support of his own candidacy, was charged with violating the statute. Kermit now argues that a conviction would violate his First Amendment rights. Should the Court agree?

_____

68. Picketers picketed on the public street adjacent to the house of CEO, the head of a company that makes drones used in an unpopular foreign war. The signs they carried contained intentionally hurtful messages (e.g., "CEO is a cowardly murderer"). The state common law of intentional infliction of emotional distress (IIED) allows recovery for any "outrageous and intentionally offensive" language carried on a picket sign near the plaintiff's house. In a suit brought by CEO against the picketers for IIED, a jury imposed a $100,000 civil judgment in favor of CEO. May the judgment be constitutionally imposed?

_____

69. Leonard, a resident of a state that bordered Mexico, believed that the federal government should vastly increase the physical barriers to illegal immigration from Mexico. One day he went to a park that was frequented by people on both sides of the immigration issue.

Before a moderately interested audience of about 20 people, all of whom had come to the park for other purposes, Leonard began to make a speech. He said, "If the federal government doesn't start doing a whole lot more to keep out illegal immigrants, we'll have to make 'em do it. Let's start by building up an arsenal of automatics and machine guns. Eventually, we'll have guerilla cells throughout the Southwest to make the federal government's life such a hell they'll build the kind of huge border fence we need." A few of the listeners applauded, one asked a question, but no one took any other action in apparent response to Leonard's speech. Immediately after his speech, Leonard was arrested by the police for violating §123 of a state statute. That statute provided that it is a felony to "advocate insurrection against the state or federal government or any local subdivision thereof." Leonard now defends on the grounds that a conviction would violate his First Amendment rights. May Leonard constitutionally be convicted of violating the statute?

_____

70. Robert was a tenured teacher in a public high school, in the state of Cartesia. He was also a member of NAMBLA, the National Association of Man Boy Love Affairs. NAMBLA's charter says that it is dedicated to the furtherance of social and sexual interaction between men and boys. Cartesia makes it a crime for an adult male to have sexual relations with a boy under the age of 17. Robert knows the aims of NAMBLA, and supports those aims; in fact, he himself has in the recent past had sexual relations with a boy. School officials, worried about recent publicity concerning teachers who belong to NAMBLA, asked Robert and all other teachers at the school to sign an affidavit stating that "I am not now nor have I ever been a member of NAMBLA." (The affidavit said nothing else.) School officials announced that if a teacher did not sign the affidavit, they would consider that refusal to sign presumptive evidence of unfitness to be a teacher. Robert has so far refused to sign the affidavit. He wishes to challenge the constitutionality of the school's insistence that he sign.

(A) What is the strongest argument Robert can make as to why the affidavit requirement is unconstitutional? _____

(B) Will Robert's attack on the requirement's constitutionality succeed?

_____

71. Becky, a young woman, walked topless on the boardwalk of Straitsville. She was arrested for violating a town ordinance that banned "lewd or lascivious public conduct." The statute contains no other relevant language, and there is no legislative history. For purposes of this question, assume that it would be possible to draft a statute in such a way that it could constitutionally proscribe appearing topless in public. Instead, concern yourself only with whether Becky may be convicted for violating *this* statute.

(A) What is Becky's strongest argument as to why she cannot constitutionally be convicted of violating the statute? _____

(B) Will Becky's argument succeed? _____

72. Centerville is a small town. Its two biggest streets are Broadway and Main. After several recent parades and demonstrations that badly snarled traffic, Centerville's City Council enacted an ordinance that forbade all parades from taking place on either Broadway or Main. The ordinance did not forbid parades on the other, smaller streets in town. There is no evidence that the ordinance was motivated by hostility to particular types of parades, and the ban has been enforced even-handedly as to all parades. Citizens Against Corruption, a group wishing to protest what it believed was corruption in the mayor's office, paraded in an organized way down Broadway, and its leaders were arrested. The city has asserted that its ban on parades is a valid "time, place and manner" regulation.

(A) What standard should the court use in evaluating the ordinance as applied here?

_____

(B) Should the court uphold the ordinance, and convict the marchers, under the test you specified in (a)? _____

73. An ordinance in the town of Harmony provides that "no demonstration or parade involving more than 20 persons shall take place on the town's streets, parks or other city-owned property without the prior issuance of a permit." The permit is free, and is to be granted by the mayor's office, "if the mayor concludes, acting in a reasonable manner, that the proposed activity would not be detrimental to the overall community, taking into account the time, place and manner of the activity." Firebrand, the head of a local group of anarchists, wished to conduct a demonstration in the park, at which he planned to urge his followers to immediately attempt a "sit in" of the mayor's office. The mayor, without knowing the precise purpose of the demonstration and knowing only that it was to be a demonstration against the local government, refused to issue the permit. In announcing the refusal, the mayor stated that "there has been too much demonstration, and not enough cooperation, around here recently." Firebrand then brought suit for an injunction against continued application of the permit requirement, and for a declaratory judgment that the permit requirement as drafted was unconstitutional. Should the court find the ordinance unconstitutional on its face? _____

74. Same facts as prior Question. Now, however, assume that Firebrand ignored the ordinance, did not ask for a permit, and held a demonstration involving 30 people in a city park. He was arrested and charged with violating the ordinance. He now wishes to defend on the grounds that the ordinance is overbroad and thus facially invalid. Assuming that the ordinance is indeed overbroad, should the court acquit Firebrand? _____

76. The city of Blue Bell has enacted an ordinance providing as follows: no "canvasser or solicitor" may ring the doorbell of a private home, or knock on the door of a private home, where her purpose is to distribute handbills or to solicit an order for goods, services or charitable contributions. The ban does not prevent a person from simply sticking advertising material under the door or into the mail slot, so long as there is no bell-ringing or door-knocking. The purpose of the ordinance is to avoid disturbing residents (including those who work nights and sleep days), and also to prevent crime (e.g., people who want to see into the residence to "case the joint" for a later burglary).

Delrina, a Jehovah's Witness, was charged with violating the statute in that she rang doorbells so that she could personally hand inhabitants the literature requesting donations to the Jehovah's Witness organization. She has defended on the grounds that the ordinance represents an unconstitutional infringement of her right to free expression. May Delrina be convicted? _____

77. The city of Crooklyn had two substantial ethnic populations that were frequently at odds

with each other, Middle-eastern Muslims and Orthodox Jews. After complying with a city requirement calling for a permit before the making of a public address, Mohammed, a self-proclaimed Islamic Fundamentalist, gave a speech in a park in Crooklyn. There were approximately 100 Islamic followers in the audience, as well as a group of about 30 Orthodox Jews. The Jews carried signs opposing Mohammed. Mohammed then made various anti-Semetic inflammatory statements, such as "Jews are corrupt" and "Jews control the U.S. government." He also addressed the Jews in the audience, saying, "You Jews in the audience today, you're not fit to kiss the dung-stained shoes of my poorest follower." At no time did Mohammed urge his audience to attack any of the Jewish onlookers or to otherwise commit immediate illegal acts.

Some of the Jews in the audience began to shake their fists and yell back at Mohammed; five of them then began to move towards the podium with upraised fists. There were 15 police officers at the scene to prevent disturbances, most of them ringed around the podium. They immediately arrested Mohammed and charged him with violating an ordinance prohibiting anyone from inciting a riot or causing a breach of the peace. Mohammed has defended on the grounds that his arrest violated his freedom of expression.

(A) What doctrine can the prosecution point to as justifying the arrest?

_____

(B) Do First Amendment principles prevent Mohammed's conviction?

_____

78. The Women's Health Alliance is a clinic that principally performs abortions. Abortion protesters decided to demonstrate outside the clinic. The protesters waved signs containing messages such as "Abortion Equals Murder." Whenever the protesters saw a woman leaving the clinic, they shouted, "Baby Killer," at her. The protesters remained at least 20 feet away from the front door of the clinic, and they did not block anyone's access to or from the clinic. All protesting took place on public property. A local ordinance forbids "the making of any public statement or the showing of any sign where the speaker knows the statement or sign is likely to be offensive to the person to whom it is addressed." May a protester who has waved the sign and shouted the epithet described above be convicted of violating the statute? _____

79. State U, a public university, recently added the following provision to its Student Code: "No student or faculty member shall address to any other student or faculty member any verbal slur, invective, insult or epithet based on the addressee's race, ethnicity, gender, handicap or sexual orientation." The penalty for a first offense is suspension, and for the second offense is expulsion. Desmond, a white student at the university, addressed the following remark to Vera, a black student, "You nigger, go back to Africa where you belong." State U has commenced disciplinary proceedings against Desmond. You are the university's general counsel. The president has asked you the following question: "May the university constitutionally suspend Desmond for making this remark?" If your answer is "no," please describe the types of changes that might be made in the Code to alleviate the problem. _____

80. The state of Morality makes it a crime to post any "indecent" photo on a computer system located in the state, if the computer is connected by means of a physical wire or a tele-

phone line to any other computer. "Indecent" is defined to include "any photo of a naked man or woman that would be offensive when measured by local community standards." The legislature means for its prohibition to apply even to pictures that would not be "obscene," including photos having significant artistic value. The legislature's purpose is to prevent minors from seeing indecent material. *Playpen* magazine puts a photo of a naked woman (which is not obscene under U.S. Supreme Court rulings) on its dial-in computer, located in Morality. Peter, a 16-year-old, dials in and retrieves the photo. A local prosecutor in Morality prosecutes the owner of *Playpen*, Hugh, and shows that Hugh had ordered that the photo be placed on the system. May Hugh constitutionally be convicted? _____

81. The Grand Union Station is a large train station owned and run by a public agency, the Tri-State Transit Authority. The Authority has enacted a "policy statement," prominently posted on the walls of the Station, which says, in part, that "no person or organization shall solicit for funds within this Station." Hussan, a member of the Hari Krishna religious sect, approached numerous passengers in the Station one day, asking each one, "Would you like to contribute to my religious organization?" Authority police stopped him and politely but forcibly removed him from the station for violating the no-solicitation policy. The police appear to enforce the no-solicitation rule uniformly, i.e., they stop everyone from soliciting, regardless of whether the solicitation is religiously-oriented, regardless of whether it appears to be "begging" or on behalf of an organized charity, etc.

     (A) Is the Station a "public forum" for purposes of First Amendment analysis? _____

     (B) Was the police's treatment of Hussan constitutional? _____

82. For many years, Acadia High School, a public high school, has had a School Dress and Appearance Code. The Code provides that, among other things, no student may go barefoot, hair must be worn in a way that will not interfere with school functions (including getting caught in machinery in shop and home economics classes), and that girls may not wear skirts more than one inch above the knee. One of the purposes behind the Code (including specifically the skirt-length provision) was to avoid dress or appearance that might distract other students or cause discipline problems. Alicia is a member of an informal group of girls who call themselves the "Sexed Up Girls." The members of this group, all of whom attend Acadia High School, wish to dress in a way that expresses their notion of themselves as sexually active women who are aware of that fact and wish other students to know it. Alicia came to school wearing an extremely short and tight mini skirt, four inches above the knee. She was suspended for violating the Code. She has defended on the grounds that the Code, as applied to her, violates her First Amendment rights.

     (A) Does the application of the Code to Alicia's skirt impair any expression on her part (putting aside the issue of whether any interference is justified)? _____

     (B) Assuming, for purposes of this part only, that some expression by Alicia has been interfered with, is the application of the Code to Alicia's skirt constitutionally permissible? _____

83. Joe was the owner of "Joe's Jewelry," a jewelry store that was the only such store in the town of Liberty. Since Liberty was a small town, most people knew who Joe was, but they

didn't know much about his personal life, and he had never been involved in politics. One day, the local newspaper, the *Liberty Post*, reported that Joe had shot Tim, a shopper in the store, based on Joe's mistaken belief that Tim was attempting to rob the store. In fact, Tim was shot in Joe's store, but by Pete, Joe's employee, who Joe then immediately fired. (Tim was not in fact trying to shoplift, and Pete simply made a bad mistake.) Joe has brought a libel action against the *Post*. The state's policy is to allow a libel recovery whenever such a recovery would be allowed at common law and would not be forbidden by the U.S. Constitution. At the end of the case, the judge charged the jury that Joe could recover against the *Post* if the jury found that the *Post* had been negligent, but not if it found that the *Post* had made a non-negligent error as to the underlying facts. Does this charge correctly reflect the relevant constitutional principles? _____

84. After Emilio failed to pay numerous traffic tickets, the police came to his house to arrest him on a bench warrant. While they were standing inside the foyer of his house making the arrest, they saw copies of two unusual publications. One was *Kiddie World*, which contained pictures of nude adolescents; the adolescents were suggestively posed, but were not engaged in real or simulated sexual activities. The second publication was *Barnyard Illustrated*, which consisted exclusively of pictures of men and women having real or simulated sex with a variety of barnyard animals, including sheep and goats. A state ordinance forbids the sale or possession of "any pictorial material containing sexually explicit photographs that are obscene under prevailing constitutional standards." Assume that Emilio can be shown to have known the contents of both of these magazines.

(A) Can Emilio be convicted for violating the ordinance as to *Kiddie World*?

_____

(B) Can Emilio be convicted for violating the ordinance as to *Barnyard Illustrated*?

_____

86. There have been several bombings of government office buildings on the island of Puerto Rico recently. After each bombing, an anonymous caller has told the local newspaper that the bomb was planted by "People for a Free Puerto Rico" (PFPR), an organization dedicated to using any means necessary to end Puerto Rico's status as a United States territory and establishing it as a sovereign nation. There is evidence that the PFPR was able to plant the bombs so successfully inside the buildings because its members or sympathizers have jobs in government agencies located in those buildings, who could furnish information and access for placement of the bombs. To deal with the threat, the territorial government of Puerto Rico has now imposed a requirement that any new applicant for any government position must before being hired sign a loyalty oath stating, among other things, that "I am not a member of the People for a Free Puerto Rico or of any group advocating the use of force to alter the territorial status of Puerto Rico." Ramona, an applicant for a position as a clerical worker in the Puerto Rican government, has declined to sign the oath, without specifying her reasons. Can the government constitutionally decline to hire her on the grounds that she has refused to sign? _____

87. Sheryl was a low-level clerk in her state's Department of Motor Vehicles. News reports were published stating that Horace, the Commissioner of the Department of Motor Vehicles (and thus, ultimately, Sheryl's boss) may have taken payments from Computer Systems Inc. in return for helping Computer Systems get a contract to install a large new

computer system at the Department. Horace protested his innocence, and the District Attorney eventually decided that no charges should be brought. Shortly thereafter, Sheryl said to a co-worker, while on the job, "I still think Horace took the money, and I think he's a crook." Another employee who overheard the remark reported it to Horace, who immediately fired Sheryl for insubordination and fomenting discord in the Department. Under the relevant Civil Service rules, Sheryl was an at-will employee who had no reason to expect continued employment. Sheryl now seeks a court order restoring her position, on the grounds that she was fired in violation of her First Amendment rights. Should the court grant reinstatement to Sheryl? _____

88. The state of Calizona, which shares a border with Mexico, was in the middle of a divisive in-state political battle about whether the nation's immigration rules should be reformed so as to make it easier for immigrants, especially ones from Mexico, to become U.S. citizens. The party with a majority in the state legislature opposed this type of immigration reform, but supported efforts to register more voters. That party caused the legislature to enact the Get Out The Vote Subsidy Act (GOTVSA), under which Calizona would provide a $100,000 subsidy to any private non-profit group whose principal function was to organize voter-registration and voter-turnout drives. As a condition to any group's eligibility for the funds, the Act required the group to promise that the group would not expend any sums — regardless of whether or not the funds came from the subsidy — to advocate or lobby for "national immigration reform." Hispanic Voters Unite (HVU) is a non-profit group devoted principally to increasing the voter registration and turnout percentage of Calizona citizens of Hispanic ethnicity, but secondarily to advocating and lobbying for national immigration reform. HVU would have been eligible for the subsidy except for its refusal to make the immigration-reform promise. HVU brought a federal suit against the state, claiming that the Act's ban on immigration-reform-related activities violated the group's First Amendment freedom of expression. Should the court find in favor of HVU, and why/why not? _____

90. Roger is a reporter for the Hillsdale Star, a local newspaper. In the most celebrated crime to hit Hillsdale in many years, Joshua, an eight-year-old boy, was found strangled in front of his house. The police have not found any suspects. One week after the killing, Roger published an article saying, "A source that I cannot identify saw the crime from a distance, and believes that the perpetrator was a young white male about 22 years old, six feet tall, weighing about 175 pounds." In the ensuing months, the police have never been able to find this or any other witness to the crime. The prosecutor called Roger in front of a grand jury, and demanded that he identify the witness who served as his source. Roger stated under oath that the witness was fearful that the killer would kill her to silence her. Roger further stated that he had signed a written pledge to the witness that he would never reveal her name; only in response to this pledge did the witness agree to speak to him. Roger did say, however, that the witness lived in the neighborhood and that in his opinion, she could be identified by good police work. The judge then ordered Roger to disclose the witness' identity, or be found in contempt of court. Roger refused. There is no state law relevant to the issue. Can Roger constitutionally be found in contempt and imprisoned until he divulges the name of the witness? _____

CHAPTER 15

FREEDOM OF RELIGION

91. The town of Amity has a religiously diverse population. In October, the mayor announced that he and the City Council believed it would be nice to have some sort of public display celebrating the upcoming holiday season. Therefore, he said, a small area would be set aside in Amity's biggest and most centrally-located park, in which a display could be assembled. He established a "Committee for a Happy Holiday," to which he appointed several eminent local citizens. Anyone else who wished to join the committee was permitted to do so. The purpose of the committee was to design and assemble a display. The committee put together a display consisting of: (1) a crèche or nativity scene, portraying the birth of Christ in the manger; (2) a Christmas tree; (3) a Menorah; (4) a Santa Claus riding reindeer; and (5) a banner reading, "Have a Happy Holiday." There was no instance in which a citizen (whether a member of the committee or not) proposed a figure or item that was rejected.

(A) You are volunteer counsel to the local branch of the ACLU. Your members wish you to bring suit attacking the constitutionality of this display. What constitutional provision should you base your suit on? _____

(B) Will your attack succeed? _____

92. The state of Carginia requires every religious organization operating in the state to register with the state Attorney General, and to submit financial statements, if the institution wishes to be exempt from state property taxes and state income taxes. (An institution is always free to forego these tax advantages, in which case it need not register or submit financial statements.) After numerous small community churches, synagogues and mosques claimed that the paperwork involved was terribly burdensome to them, the registration and financial-statement provisions were amended to grant an exemption for any institution "50% or more of whose financial support derives from donations by persons who consider themselves members of the institution."

The state legislature considered eliminating the registration/financial-statement requirement altogether, but did not do so because of a fear that groups that solicit donation from non-members are likely to practice fraud, harassment, and other abuses. There is evidence that the legislature was especially concerned about groups that did their fund-raising by ringing doorbells at private homes, such as "Moonies" and Jehovah's Witnesses. A local group of Jehovah's Witnesses gets most of its financial support by selling Bibles door-to-door to non-members. This group has sued to overturn the statutory scheme as a violation of its Establishment Clause rights. Should the court find in favor of the plaintiff?

---

93. The legislature of the state of Largesse was concerned that students in the state's biggest and most financially-troubled city, Bigtown, were not getting a good public-school education. To increase school competition, and to give parents of Bigtown students a choice of schooling options, the Largesse legislature enacted the "Tuition Voucher Plan of 2002." Under this plan, the parents of any elementary- or middle-school student living in Bigtown could attend any licensed private school (including parochial schools) in or near Bigtown, and receive a state voucher worth $2,000 to be used towards the private school's annual tuition. Mostly because the average non-religious private school's annual tuition in Bigtown is $15,000, and the average religious school's annual tuition is just $2,500, about 95% of the students who took advantage of the voucher program in its first year attended religious schools, where they were given intensive instruction in religious subjects (e.g., Roman Catholic catechism) as well as secular subjects. There are no other special programs in Bigtown designed to solve the educational problems that the Largesse legislature has identified. A parent of a public-school attendee, Paul, has sued the state, arguing that the voucher program violates the Establishment Clause. Should the court find in Paul's favor? _____

94. The religion of Weejun is practiced primarily on a small island in the South Pacific Ocean. A number of adherents have made their homes in the West Coast town of Pacifica. The Weejuns speak their own language, and practice their own rituals in a church located in the town. As part of their rituals, the Weejuns drink a beverage called nectaria, made from fermented nectarines. The beverage is smelly and of quite high alcoholic content. Practitioners sometimes get drunk from using it in their rituals. The Weejuns are, in general, relatively uneducated, of lower income status, and seem quite strange to most non-Weejun residents of Pacifica. For some time, non-Weejun Pacificans had been complaining at Town Council meetings that the Weejuns and their nectaria-based rituals were leading to public drunkenness, and a consequent burdening of the police and lowering of Pacifica's "image." The Town Council then enacted an ordinance whose sole provision was to ban the sale or public use of nectaria. "Public use" was defined to include the use in any gathering of more than three people who were not related to each other and who were not meeting in a private home. Since the Weejun church was a free-standing building, the sole effect of the ordinance was to ban the use of nectaria as part of the Weejun church rituals.

(A) If the members of the Weejun congregation wish to attack the constitutionality of the Pacifica ordinance, what constitutional provision should they rely upon?

_____

(B) What test or standard of review should the court apply in evaluating the challenge you referred to in (a)? _____

(C) Is the ordinance constitutional, when judged by that standard of review?

_____

95. Practitioners of the religion of Parentism believe that it is up to the parents of the child to carry out that child's education, and that the teaching of the child by strangers (i.e., non-parents) is against God's will. Consequently, each child born to parents who practice Parentism is schooled at home, and no private religious schools following the Parentism religion exist. The state of Gomorra has been worried that students who are taught at home by their parents fail to receive necessary socialization, and frequently don't learn needed skills like cooperation, as well as knowledge of more advanced subjects like trigonometry. Therefore, the state has recently enacted a ban on any kind of home education (though parents are free to send their children to any private or religious school they wish, so long as children from more than one family attend). There is no evidence that the Gomorra regulation was motivated by any particular dislike, or even awareness, of Parentism; in fact, the practitioners of Parentism are so few that state education officials are barely aware that

they exist. Priscilla, an adherent of Parentism who has been teaching her child Pamela at home, has applied to the state for an exemption from the no-home-schooling requirement, on the grounds that the ordinance would otherwise violate Priscilla's and Pamela's free exercise rights. Must the state grant an exemption so that Pamela may be schooled at home? _____

96. A central element of the Sharkist religion is to possess and pray to a piece of a fin from a Great White Shark. Because the Great White Shark is a nearly extinct species, and because it has been relentlessly hunted as a source of shark fin soup and other delicacies, the U.S. (acting together with other western nations) has recently enacted a ban on the possession or importing of any fin or other body part from Great White Sharks. When Congress enacted this ban, few if any members of Congress were aware of the existence of the Sharkist religion, which has very few adherents. The federal legislation makes it a felony, punishable by up to five years in prison, to knowingly possess a Great White Shark's fin. Samark, a practitioner of Sharkism, has petitioned the U.S. for an exemption from the ban, contending that the ban violates his free exercise rights. Religious experts estimate that there are fewer than 100 Sharkists in the United States, and that granting them an exemption would have no material effect on the rate at which Great White Sharks are hunted. Must the U.S. grant the exemption? _____

CHAPTER 16

JUSTICIABILITY

98. The President, in an attempt to restore democracy in Haiti, dispatched American troops to that island without a congressional declaration of war. The troops have now remained there for 60 days, still without a congressional declaration. Their expenses have been paid for out of the general Defense Department budget, appropriated by Congress before the troops were sent and without the expectation that they would be sent. Paul, a U.S. citizen and taxpayer, has sued the President seeking an injunction requiring the President to withdraw the troops. The substance of Paul's suit is that only Congress has the power to declare war, and that the President's action amounts to an illegal declaration of war. Paul further asserts that his federal tax dollars are being unconstitutionally spent to support this illegal action.

   (A) If you are the President's lawyer, what is the first defense you should assert?

   _____

   (B) Will this defense prevail? _____

99. Same basic facts as above question. Now, however, assume that Paul asserts that he has standing to pursue his claim in federal court, because he is a citizen of the United States, and his right to have his government not behave in an unconstitutional manner has been abridged. Is Paul correct? _____

100. A federal statute places restrictions on the extent to which private companies may be permitted by the U.S. government to engage in logging in national forests. Penzel, a private individual, sues the U.S. Secretary of the Interior. His suit contends that the Secretary has administered regulations on logging in a way that contravenes the statute. The suit

contends that the effect will be to allow more logging in the forests than permitted by statute. Penzel asserts that he uses a particular national forest for a one-week hike twice per year, and that the unauthorized logging affects a part of the forest that he expects to hike in during the next year. At least four million hikers each year will cross through parts of federal forests that are likely to have been affected by the allegedly excessive logging. The Secretary asserts that Penzel lacks standing to make this claim. Does Penzel have standing? _____

101. Same facts as prior question. Now, however, assume that the plaintiff is Friends of the National Forests, Inc. (FNF), a non-profit corporation whose members are users and lovers of the national forests. No individual plaintiffs are named. Does FNF have standing to pursue the suit? _____

102. George Brensteiner was the owner of the New York Strikers of the National Soccer League. Brensteiner's existing stadium was about to be demolished, and he needed to pick a new site for a stadium that he would build. After some preliminary investigation, Brensteiner announced that there were three "finalist sites," of which one was Yonkers, New York. Brensteiner applied for clearances from the federal Environmental Protection Agency (EPA) for all three sites. He received quick clearances for the other two. As to Yonkers, the local EPA administrator covering Yonkers determined that the proposed stadium would be on a protected wetland, and that the stadium could not be built unless Brensteiner first filed an Environmental Impact Statement (EIS) showing that the wetlands would not be damaged. Brensteiner then announced, "Because of the expense of preparing an EIS for the Yonkers site, I have selected one of the other sites as the winner, namely, Rutherford, New Jersey." Brensteiner acquired land in Rutherford, and quickly completed about 10% of the construction.

At that moment, Steve, a Yonkers resident, brought suit against the EPA. Steve's suit argued that the EPA's requirement of an EIS for the Yonkers site was in violation of federal statutes, and that the effect of this violation was to deprive him, Steve, of easy access to a soccer stadium (in Yonkers) in which to view Strikers games. Steve's suit asked for a declaratory judgment that an EIS was not required for the Yonkers site. The EPA has defended on the grounds that Steve lacks standing. Is the EPA's contention correct?

_____

103. Fred, who is black, is a police officer on the force of the town of Suburbia. Suburbia's population is 30% black, but Fred is the only black out of 15 officers on the force. Fred has sued the department, arguing that the department's failure to hire more black patrol officers is intentional, and constitutes a violation of the Equal Protection Clause. Fred asserts that this failure to hire additional black officers harms him, by making him racially isolated on the force and leading to a department that is generally insensitive to the concerns of the minority community, thus making Fred's own working conditions less attractive. Does Fred have standing to bring this suit? _____

104. A local school district allows non-profit community groups to use classrooms at the district's public high school at night. The Old Christians Association (OCA), a group of senior citizens who want to pray together, applied for a room. The school district turned them down on the grounds that to allow them to use the room would constitute an unconstitutional establishment of religion. The OCA began a suit in federal district court against the school board, asserting that the denial of a room violated their free exercise rights. After the suit was begun, the school board issued a statement reversing its policy against allowing religious groups to use classrooms, and granted the OCA's permit request. The OCA would like to continue with the suit, so that they may obtain a judicial opinion in their favor that can be cited as precedent in other school districts.

(A) What defense should the school board defendant raise? _____

(B) Will this defense succeed? _____

105. Pintard is a 52-year-old trooper in the police department of the State of New Spain, and is a resident of that state. New Spain has fired him because, in the department's judgment, no one over the age of 50 is physically fit enough to carry out the duties of state trooper. A federal statute, the Federal Age Discrimination Act, applies to all employees and forbids firing on account of age. Pintard has sued the state of New Spain for damages. (He does not want to be reinstated, because he has found a new job.)

(A) What defense should the state raise? _____

(B) Will this defense succeed? _____

106. The state of Caledonia was running short of funds, due to a budget crisis. To save money, the Governor ordered that only one copy be purchased of any personal-computer software package needed by the state government, and that staff members make copies. A staffer made 2,000 copies of the "PC-Word" word-processing package (published by PC Word Corp., a Caledonia company), and distributed these to each state office, where they were used. The retail value of each copy of PC Word is $295. PC Word Corp. has sued the state in federal court for the district of Caledonia, alleging that the state has violated the federal copyright act and seeking money damages ($295 x 2000). Assume that the federal copyright act expressly allows a state to be sued in federal court (whether by its own citizen or by a citizen of another state).

(A) What defense should Caledonia raise? _____

(B) Will this defense succeed? _____

107. Jose won a U.S. congressional seat from a district located in New York City, in a close race against Martin. The House routinely determined that Jose met the constitutional requirements to be seated (that he was at least 25 years old, a U.S. citizen, and a resident of the state from which he had been elected). Martin then brought a federal district court suit against the House of Representatives and Jose, seeking to have Jose ruled unqualified to sit in the House. The essence of Martin's suit was that Jose really "inhabits" (as that term is used in Art. I, §2, second sentence) not the state of New York but rather, the State of Pennsylvania. Martin has come forward with evidence from voting records, state income tax filings, and other documents strongly suggesting that Jose spends the vast bulk of his time in, and considers himself a resident of, Pennsylvania.

(A) What defense should Jose raise to these proceedings? _____

(B) Will this defense succeed? _____

ANSWERS TO
SHORT-ANSWER QUESTIONS

1.   No, because the case does not involve a federal question. The federal judicial power extends, by Article III, Section 2, to cases arising under the U.S. Constitution and federal laws. That power does not extend to cases decided solely on state-law grounds. Here, although the Ames due process clause may have mirrored the language of the U.S. Constitution's Due Process Clause, the state decision was solely based on the Ames courts' interpretation of the Ames constitution. Since no federal issue was involved, the Supreme Court has no jurisdiction (whether by appeal or by certiorari).

2.   No. In contrast to the prior question, here at least a decision on an issue of federal law (the meaning of the U.S. Constitution) was part of the state court decision. However, the federal judicial power does not extend to Supreme Court review of any state court case for which there is an ***"independent and adequate state ground."*** Because Tom's firing would be unlawful even without any finding that the federal Constitution had been violated (since the state constitution was found to have been violated as well), an independent and adequate state ground exists here. (If the Ames state court decision on the meaning of the Ames constitution's due process provision had derived in part from the court's belief that the clause should mean the same thing as it means in the federal Constitution, the state ground would not be truly "independent." But the facts make it clear that the finding on the meaning of the state constitution here derived solely from Ames state-law sources.)

3.   Yes. The Constitution gives Congress full control over the jurisdiction of the lower federal courts. In fact, these lower federal courts do not even exist until Congress creates them; Article III, Section 1 grants the federal judicial power to the Supreme Court and to "such inferior courts as Congress may from time to time ordain and establish." This language has been interpreted to mean that Congress may also define the cases that may be heard by the lower federal courts, and that Congress may do this by refusing to let the lower federal courts hear cases that fall within the general federal judicial power (e.g., cases between citizens of different states).

4.   No, because the statute is valid under the "Necessary and Proper" Clause. *McCulloch v. Maryland*, 17 U.S. 316 (1819), establishes that when Congress is acting in pursuit of a constitutionally-specified objective, the means chosen merely has to be ***rationally related*** to the objective, not "necessary" to the objective's attainment. Here, Congress is exercising its enumerated power to regulate copyrights. Congress could rationally have believed that even non-profit-motivated transfers of copyright-violating recordings contribute to the general decline of copyright protection, and that felony punishment for such transfers is a reasonable way of combatting the problem. The Court will show great deference to Congress' choice of the means to attain constitutionally-enumerated objectives, so the statute here will certainly be sustained.

5.   (A) Congress' power to regulate commerce.

(B) Probably, but this is no longer as certain as it once was. Before the 1995 decision in *U.S. v. Lopez*, it was enough that there was a "rational basis" for Congress' belief that a regulated activity "affects" interstate commerce. But *Lopez* establishes that the activity which Congress is regulating must *in fact* have a *"substantial effect"* on interstate commerce.

Where an activity is "commercial," the Court still seems willing to find regulation of it to be within Congress' Commerce power even if the particular act is wholly intrastate, as long as the act is part of a *class* of activities which, collectively, substantially affect interstate commerce. See, e.g., *Wickard v. Filburn* (farmer's growing of wheat for family use only can be regulated, because the cumulative effect of all such intrastate wheat-growing decisions significantly affects the interstate price of wheat). The bet here seems to qualify — the bet is probably itself a "commercial" transaction (i.e., one primarily motivated by the desire to make a profit), and private bets taken as a group probably have a substantial effect on interstate commerce (e.g., they are often made over interstate phone lines, they contribute to the use of interstate "handicapping" services and interstate money transfers, etc.). Once the Court finds that the activity substantially affects commerce, the Court apparently requires only that the means selected by Congress be "rationally related" to the objective being sought. Here, prohibition of the damaging activity — friendly sports betting — would certainly seem to be a reasonable means of combatting that activity. The scenario seems a lot like that in *Gonzales v. Raich*, where the Court held that Congress could regulate a purely intrastate but commercially-oriented activity regarding a commodity (personal cultivation of marijuana for one's own medicinal uses) because such regulation was reasonably tied in to Congress' regulation of the interstate commercial aspects of that same commodity.

6.   No. *N.F.I.B. v. Sebelius* (the health-insurance case) establishes that five members of the Court believe that Congress' Commerce powers do not allow Congress "to *compel individuals not engaged in commerce to purchase an unwanted product.*" The case also says that "the power to regulate presupposes the existence of commercial activity to be regulated." Since the WFA requires people who are not in the market for a pedometer to buy one, it seems to run afoul of these principles: these individuals are "not engaged in commerce" (at least, not the relevant commerce of purchasing walking-measurement devices), and at least some don't want to purchase the pedometer. So it's hard to see how the Commerce power can extend to this compulsory-purchase program. That's true even though Congress is probably correct in reasoning that if everyone either bought and used the device, or paid the penalty, the interstate market for health-care expenditures would be substantially affected.

7.   (A) The Tenth Amendment. That Amendment provides that "the powers not delegated to the United States by the Constitution, nor prohibited by it to the States, are reserved to the States respectively, or to the People." Alahoma could make a plausible argument that Congress, by precisely detailing whom the state may hire, has interfered with the sovereignty reserved to the state by the Tenth Amendment.

(B) No, probably. At one time, Alahoma would probably have succeeded with this argument, because of *National League of Cities v. Usery*, which held that the Tenth Amendment prevented Congress from regulating the states in a way that might impair their "ability to function effectively in the federal system"; state employees were exempted from federal wage/hour regulations on this theory. But *National League of Cities* was overruled in *Garcia v. San Anto-*

nio Metropolitan Transit Authority. Garcia seems to mean that when Congress, acting pursuant to its Commerce power, regulates the states as part of a generally applicable regulatory scheme, the fact that it is a state being regulated has no practical significance — if the regulation would be valid where applied to a private party, it is also valid as to the state. Consequently, since Congress would almost certainly have the power to set a minimum age for employment in the private sector (on the theory that this directly affects commerce, because of its effect on unemployment and wage limits), the state is not entitled to an exemption.

8.   (A) The Tenth Amendment.

(B) Yes. The Tenth Amendment does not have very huge scope in light of *Garcia* (see previous question), but it has some. In particular, Congress may not simply "commandee[r] the legislative processes of the States by directly compelling them to enact and enforce a regulatory program." *New York v. U.S.* Thus in *New York v. U.S.*, *supra*, the Court held that Congress could not force states to regulate nuclear waste. So, here, the Court would almost certainly conclude that Congress may not force a state to enact a specific regulatory framework for dealing with the cigarette/health-care problem. Nor may Congress force state official to carry out administrative tasks (such as the audits of cigarette vendors here); see *Printz* and *Mack*. Congress is always free to regulate health care directly, but it may not thrust onto the states the job of doing this.

(C) Supply federal funds, and make the loss of those funds the only penalty for failure to comply. Congress is always free to use its power to tax and spend for the general welfare in order to carry out a regulatory scheme. Furthermore, it may do this by giving an incentive to the states to get them to do the regulating. See, e.g., *South Dakota v. Dole* (Congress may induce states to prevent underage drinking by withholding 5% of federal highway funds from states that don't prohibit drivers under age 21 from drinking). So long as the only penalty is "mild encouragement" via a loss of funds that are related to the new congressional program, there should not be a constitutional problem. However, Congress cannot cut off major funding for a pre-existing program that has no relation to the regulatory scheme desired by Congress; thus Congress probably couldn't cut off, say, *all educational funding* to states that refuse to enact the cigarette/health-care scheme. That's because when financial inducements are combined with conditions, in a way that is "so coercive as to pass the point at which 'pressure turns into **compulsion**'," and that leaves the states with "no real option but to acquiesce," the scheme goes beyond the spending power. See *N.F.I.B. v. Sebelius*. Assuming that federal educational funding is so great a portion of the average state's budget that most states couldn't afford to refuse to enact the cigarette/health-care regulation, the scheme would be found to go beyond the spending power under *N.F.I.B.*

10.   (A) The spending power. Art. I, Section 8 gives Congress power to "lay and collect Taxes … to pay the Debts and provide for the … general Welfare of the United States. … " This language includes the "spending" power, although the word "spend" is not used.

(B) No. It is true that the spending power of Art. 1, Section 8 is phrased specifically in terms of providing for the "general welfare" of the nation. However, the requirement that a federal spending program be for the "general welfare" has almost no bite at present — certainly, the Court is not entitled to substitute its own judgment of what would be "best" in lieu of Congress'.

11.   Yes. There is *no federal "police power."* That is, Congress does not have the right to *regulate "for the general welfare."* Congress' only powers regarding the general welfare are the right to tax and to spend to achieve that welfare. Since nothing in the statute provides for either a tax or an expenditure, the statute is not supported by the taxing and spending power or any other enumerated power. Normally, a federal regulatory scheme could be supported by the Commerce power (since the Court takes an extremely expansive view of what activity can be found to "affect commerce"), but the facts tell us to ignore the Commerce power here.

12.   (A) That the ordinance unreasonably burdens interstate commerce.

(B) Yes. The dormant Commerce Clause prevents a state or local government from placing *undue burdens* on interstate commerce. Most violations of the dormant Commerce Clause occur when government acts in a "protectionist" manner, i.e., with an intent to favor the economic interests of local residents over out-of-staters. But even a non-protectionist "neutral" regulation will be found to violate the dormant Commerce Clause if it amounts to an *unreasonable burden* on commerce. This can be true, for instance, of regulations that are enacted for the good-faith purpose of protecting the safety or health of local residents. The Court performs a "balancing test," weighing the state or local government's interest in its regulatory scheme against the national interest in unburdened free-flowing interstate commerce. A major part of this balancing is whether there were *less burdensome alternatives* which the government might have adopted.

Here, since South Texarkansas conducts a similar inspection, Fairhaven could simply have accepted the results of South Texarkansas's inspection without materially compromising its own health standards. Therefore, the Fairhaven ordinance will probably be found to have been an "unreasonable" burden on commerce. See *Dean Milk Co. v. Madison.* The fact that Fairhaven is a municipality rather than a state, and its ordinance might have discriminated against out-of-town but in-state slaughterhouses, i.e., those beyond the 70-mile inspection radius, does not save the ordinance from a dormant Commerce Clause attack.

13.   Yes. Any state or local action that is taken for a *protectionist purpose* — that is, for the purpose of preferring in-state economic interests over out-of-state interests — will be *strictly scrutinized*. This is true even where the measure is taken for what are basically environmental or other non-economic motives. Thus in *City of Philadelphia v. New Jersey* (a garbage disposal case), the Court held that one state could not ban the importation of another's garbage, unless there were no less-discriminatory alternatives. Here, New Wales is clearly preferring local nuclear plant operators to out-of-state operators. New Wales clearly has a less-discriminatory alternative (allow importation, and simply limit the total amount of plutonium that may be buried in the state), so the measure would almost certainly be struck down.

14.   No. Ordinarily, if a state prefers the economic interests of in-staters over out-of-staters, we have a classic violation of the Commerce Clause. But there is an important exception: where the state acts as a *market participant*, spending its money to acquire goods or services, dormant Commerce Clause analysis is not applied, and the state may favor local interests over out-of-staters. Here, Rouge is clearly spending its own money, so it is free to limit that money to acquisitions from in-state producers. See, e.g., *Hughes v. Alexandria Scrap Corp.*; *Reeves v. Stake.*

16.   No. Dormant Commerce Clause analysis is only to be performed when Congress has not expressly allowed the type of discrimination against out-of-staters in question. Here, by the federal statute, Congress has in effect allowed a state to prefer its own citizens over out-of-staters.

17. **(A) That the tax violates the federal immunity from state taxation.**

(B) No. It is true that the federal government is itself immune from taxation by any state. See *McCulloch v. Maryland.* But this immunity generally does not extend to federal government employees or to contractors who work for the federal government. It does not matter that the "economic incidence" of the tax falls on the federal government — as long as it is not the federal government itself that is being *directly obliged* to pay the tax, the fact that the economic burden of the tax may fall on the federal government is irrelevant.

18. **(A) That the requirement violates the Privileges and Immunities Clause of Article IV.**

(B) Yes. Art. IV, Section 2, provides that "the Citizens of each State shall be entitled to all Privileges and Immunities of Citizens in the several States." This Clause prevents states from discriminating against out-of-state individuals. It applies only to rights that are "fundamental to national unity." The right to practice one's profession has been found to be such a right. Once such a "fundamental right" is shown to be at stake, then the defenders of the statute will lose unless they show that non-residents are a "peculiar source of the evil" which the law was enacted to remedy, and that there are no less discriminatory alternatives that would satisfactorily solve the problem.

Here, the unavailability of physicians after-hours may be an important problem, but it is unlikely the state can show that non-residents are a "peculiar source of the evil" (since resident physicians will also frequently be unavailable after hours). Furthermore, it is highly unlikely that there are no less discriminatory alternatives; for instance, the state could simply require that each physician be reachable after hours and have a method of furnishing service within a certain period of time. Therefore, the statute will almost certainly be found to violate at least one of the two required tests, and will thus be struck down. See *Supreme Court of New Hampshire v. Piper*, holding that a state requirement that lawyers practicing within the state reside within it violated the P&I Clause.

19. **(A) That the Resolution violates the Presentment Clause, by which the President is given the opportunity to veto any bill.**

(B) Yes. The scheme described here is a classic two-house *"legislative veto,"* under which Congress attempts to keep oversight over administrative action by reserving the power to cancel that administrative action by means of a Resolution. The scheme here, insofar as it calls for the Joint Resolution to take effect immediately, deprives the President of his opportunity to veto any bill. Therefore, the scheme is invalid. See *INS v. Chadha.* (The theory behind the invalidity of the legislative veto is that the Resolution is itself the exercise of legislative power, so it must be carried out by the same procedures as for any other legislative act, i.e., passage by a majority of each house and presentment to the President for his signature.)

20. **(A) That it violates Congress' sole power to declare war.**

(B) Yes, probably. It is true that Article II, Section 2, explicitly grants the President the power of Commander in Chief of the U.S. Armed Forces. However, the President must use this power subject to oversight by Congress. In particular, the power to "declare war" is given solely to Congress, in Art. I, Section 8. While the President may, without a declaration of war, probably commit our troops to repel an immediate emergency, it is very unlikely that the President may wage a prolonged ground war, without a declaration of war, especially where the United States has not been directly attacked.

Also, the 2006 decision in *Hamdan v. Rumsfeld* indicates that in cases where the President asserts broad power to act in wartime, and it is not clear that Congress has acquiesced to what the President is doing, the Court will favor Congress over the President. So here, probably the Court will say that the President's action violates Congress' sole power to declare war.

21.   (A) That by retaining the right to remove Derrick, Congress has improperly vested executive functions in its own agent.

(B) Yes, probably. Congress and its agents can only exercise "legislative power," not "executive power." The FTSB Director's powers are clearly executive — the Director is carrying out the laws (by determining what is required for safety) rather than "formulating" the laws. Congress, by retaining the right to remove the Director without cause, converted the post of Director into an agent of Congress, thus in effect taking executive powers onto itself. Therefore, Derrick is not permitted to exercise his statutory powers, including issuance of the order. See *Bowsher v. Synar*, striking down certain powers of the Comptroller General on the similar analysis that Congress improperly converted him into an agent of Congress by retaining the power to remove him.

23.   (A) Kneecap's substantive due process rights have been violated.

(B) Whether the statute bore a rational relation to a legitimate state objective.

(C) No. Where a state statute regulates a purely economic matter, and does not involve any fundamental right, all that is required is that the means chosen be rationally related to a legitimate governmental objective. Here, the objective of reducing the harassment of consumer debtors falls within the state's police power, and is clearly "legitimate." The relation between the means chosen (ban on all non-lawyer collections) and achievement of the objective of reducing harassment is tenuous. But so long as the legislature could rationally have *believed* that non-lawyers were worse offenders on average than lawyers, the requisite "rational relation" between means and end is satisfied. In fact, for over 50 years, no state economic regulation has been overturned for substantive due process purposes, assuming an absence of a fundamental right. (The right to engage in the business of debt collection will almost certainly be held not to be "fundamental," a status limited in substantive due process cases to the "right to privacy," i.e., the areas of sex, marriage, child-bearing and child-rearing.)

24.   (A) That the charges violate the defendants' substantive due process right to "privacy."

(B) Yes, probably. The Supreme Court has held that every individual has a "zone of privacy," and that government action which invades that zone will be found to violate the individual's substantive due process rights unless the government action is necessary to achieve a compelling governmental objective (strict scrutiny). The Supreme Court has never explicitly held that the sexual acts of a married couple, taken in private, fall within the zone of privacy for all purposes. However, the Court has held (in *Griswold v. Connecticut*) that the right to privacy is violated when the state interferes with a couple's attempts to use birth control. Later cases suggest that state interferences with a married couple's sexual intimacy would similarly violate the right to privacy, assuming that the conduct took place in private (even if it took place in a hotel room or other non-residential but non-public setting). See, e.g., *Lawrence v. Texas*, the homosexual-sodomy case, where the majority opinion refers to "an emerging awareness that liberty gives substantial protection to adult persons in deciding how to conduct their private lives in matters pertaining to sex." In summary, since Joe and Martha are married and were performing the activity in private, their conduct probably fell within the protected zone of privacy. (It is a bit less clear that their "right of privacy" argument would prevail if they had been unmarried, or engaged in an adulterous relationship.)

25. (A) Unconstitutional. *Planned Parenthood v. Casey* and *Gonzales v. Carhart* make it substantially easier than it was formerly for the states to regulate abortion. Nonetheless, even under these cases, the states may not place ***"undue burdens"*** on the right of abortion. A state regulation will constitute an undue burden if the regulation has the purpose or effect of placing a "substantial obstacle" in the path of a woman seeking an abortion of a ***non-viable fetus***. *Casey*. Since a four- or five-month-old fetus is certainly not viable even under present medical advances, the blanket prohibition on abortions during this time frame would likely be found to be a "substantial obstacle" and thus an "undue burden," even given the Roberts Court's more-circumscribed view of abortion rights. (But a state probably could bar all abortions past the moment of viability.)

(B) Unconstitutional, probably. *Casey* struck down a spousal notification provision. The provision here, while it may contain slightly more escape hatches, would likely be found to be a substantial obstacle to the plaintiff (who is not covered by any of the escape hatches). Notice that the attack here is "as applied" rather than "on the face" of the statute. That is, the suit argues that the statute directly violates the rights of the plaintiff, rather than asking the Court to prevent the statute from being enforced against anyone because it violates the rights of persons not before the Court. Even the Roberts Court that decided the *Gonzales* partial-birth-abortion case would likely find that the statute acts as an undue burden *upon P*, even if that Court wouldn't allow a facial attack on the spousal notification provision. (*Gonzales* indicates that the Court will allow facial attacks only if the plaintiffs prove that the statute would be unconstitutional "in a large fraction of relevant cases"; the plaintiffs in a facial attack might not be able to make this "large fraction" showing, given the various escape hatches.)

(C) Constitutional. A provision much like the one here was upheld in *Casey*. In particular, the Court held in *Casey* that states may require the parent to listen to alternatives to abortion, and may establish a 24-hour waiting period following this mandatory counselling. The Court in the post-*Casey* case of *Gonzales v. Carhart* — upholding a federal ban on partial-birth abortions — emphasized the state's strong interest in warning women of the likely emotional regret that they may come to feel after an abortion, so *Gonzales* makes it even more likely that the Court would uphold the provision here than would have been the case before *Gonzales*.

26. (A) Strict scrutiny, probably. That is, the statute will probably be struck down unless shown to be ***necessary*** to achieve a ***compelling*** state interest. The question is really whether the right to make core decisions about how one's children shall be educated is a ***"fundamental"*** right. The Supreme Court has not addressed this issue directly in recent years. However, several cases (discussed further in part (b) below) suggest that the Court would hold that the right to direct the education of one's children is indeed "fundamental," in which case strict scrutiny must be applied to any governmental regulation that substantially impairs that right.

(B) No, probably. In *Pierce v. Society of Sisters* (a 1925 case), the Court struck down a state statute requiring children to attend public schools. The decision seems to have been on substantive-due-process-like grounds, and seems to have applied essentially strict scrutiny. Similarly, in more recent years, the Court has held that parents have something approximating a fundamental right to decide whether their children should be committed to mental institutions; *Parham v. J.R.* (though the child has important countervailing rights).

Assuming that the right to choose how one's children are to be educated is in some sense fundamental, it is very unlikely that the statute here could survive strict scrutiny. Ensuring a good education for children is certainly an important state objective, and probably a "compelling" one. However, it is highly unlikely that foreclosing all options other than public schools is a "necessary" means of attaining that objective. For instance, allowing a program of home instruction by one who is clearly a qualified elementary school teacher certainly seems to be an adequate way to assure a good education. And the state could adopt a monitoring program to make sure that home study programs satisfy a minimum quality standard. So the statute will probably flunk strict scrutiny, if strict scrutiny is applied.

27. (A) The "rational relation," not "strict scrutiny," standard. The Supreme Court has held that a state may not criminalize sodomy defined in this way. *Lawrence v. Texas* (2003). But in reaching this conclusion, the Court applied the easier-to-satisfy rational-relation standard. However, the Court found that such a ban on sodomy — generally enforced only against homosexual sodomy — could not satisfy even the rational-relation test, because it pursued only the illegitimate aim of expressing moral disapproval of homosexuality. The Court would presumably use the same rational-relation standard in evaluating whether a public body may fire a person for engaging in such sodomy.

(B) No, probably. Although the Court would (as noted in part (a) above) probably apply the rational-relation standard to the school-board regulation here, it is likely that the regulation would be found invalid even under that relatively easy-to-satisfy standard. The essence of the regulation is that one who violates a state statute forbidding a particular act of turpitude may be fired. Since the underlying state statute is no longer valid in light of *Lawrence*, it is hard to believe that the Court would find that it was rational for the school board to fire someone for violating this no-longer-valid statute. This is especially likely given that the governmental objective that the school district seems to be pursuing here — punishing gay people for "moral turpitude" — is the very one that *Lawrence* found to be illegitimate. The conclusion that the state was pursuing an illegitimate objective would be buttressed by the Court's several cases holding that "a ***bare [governmental] desire to harm a politically unpopular group***" cannot be a legitimate governmental objective. (See, e.g., *U.S. v. Windsor* (2013), using this rationale while striking down Congress' refusal to recognize state-sanctioned same-sex marriages; the Court found that Congress was motivated solely by anti-gay animus.)

28. (A) The "rational relation" standard, not strict scrutiny. The choice of standard depends on whether the right of a firefighter to wear a beard, etc., is found to be "fundamental." In a case almost completely on point, *Kelley v. Johnson*, the Supreme Court held that a policeman's right to wear his hair as he wished was not "fundamental," and that the hair-length regulation there should be judged on a rational relation standard.

(B) Yes, probably. Assuming that the rational relation standard is used, the regulation here almost certainly passes muster. The town certainly has a legitimate interest in preserving *esprit de corps* and promoting safety. The contribution of short hair to fulfillment of these objectives may be questionable, but it is certainly "rational." (For instance, the town could reasonably have believed that long-haired male firefighters would not fit in as well.) Certainly the comparable hair-length regulation in *Kelley* was found to be rationally related to a legitimate governmental objective, and was thus upheld, so the same result is likely here.

30. No. The Fourteenth Amendment's Due Process Clause only prevents the government from depriving a person of "*life, liberty,* or *property*" without due process of law." Unless Brown can show that she had a "liberty" or "property" interest that was impaired, she will not even get to the point of being allowed to show that fair procedures were not followed. In other words, the Due Process Clause does not bar the government from procedural irregularities per se, only procedural irregularities in connection with the taking of life, liberty or property. It is very clear that a person applying for an initial government position has no liberty or property interest in the position, so the government may turn the applicant down for totally arbitrary or irrational reasons (so long as the reasons are not themselves violations of independently-guaranteed constitutional rights, such as refusing to hire a person because she is, say, black). So the fact that the Clerk's decision was completely "wrong," in the sense that he had the wrong person in mind, is completely irrelevant. We never get to the question of what type of process (e.g., right to a statement of reasons, or right to a hearing) would have been due.

31. (A) That it violated her right not to have her "property" taken without due process, and that this right included the right to a hearing.

(B) Yes, probably. The core issue is whether Tenant had a *"property" interest* in her apartment. The Court has held that even *informal practices or customs* may be sufficient to create a *legitimate claim of entitlement* to a benefit. See, e.g., *Perry v. Sindermann* (in which a college was found to have created a de facto tenure program that created in P, a college professor, the "understanding" that he would be entitled to tenure). Here, the statement regarding the customary right of renewal was probably enough to create in Tenant such a legitimate claim of entitlement to renew, in view of the lack of any other law bearing on whether Tenant did indeed have such a right. (If there were a statute or body of case law holding that as a matter of state law there is no right to renew despite a seeming indication to the contrary in a housing project's rules and regulations, then this body of state law would be dispositive, and Tenant would not have any "property" interest.)

If Tenant indeed had a legitimate entitlement to being allowed to renew provided that she was in good standing, then she was presumably entitled to at least a hearing before this property interest could be taken away. (The precise procedures that would have to followed are not clear, but for a right as important as the right to continue to live in subsidized housing, it is likely that some sort of hearing and statement of reasons, however informal, would be required.)

32. No, probably. The facts are enough to establish that Priscilla indeed probably had a "property" interest (albeit a weak one) in being awarded a spot if she was in fact one of the best seven players. That is, the notice in the newspaper probably was sufficient to constitute a binding offer on the part of the school to award a place to anyone who tried out and proved that she was indeed among the seven best players, and this contract was enough to give rise to a "property" interest. However, the case really turns on exactly what procedures were "due" to Priscilla when it came time to determine whether she was in fact one of the seven best players. The Supreme Court uses a *balancing test* for deciding whether a particular set of procedures should be required once a property interest (or liberty interest) is at stake. On one side is placed the amount at stake for the individual, multiplied by the likelihood that administrative error will be reduced by using the procedure in question; on the other side is the cost to the government of granting that procedure.

Here, the amount at stake for Priscilla is relatively weak, compared with, say, the right to continue receiving welfare benefits or the right to keep one's job. The likelihood that "administrative errors" would be reduced by requiring, say, a statement of reasons before anyone is cut, or a right to present one's case, is relatively small — a coach would still have to be the decision-maker, and that decision would still be based principally on what the coach saw, so that a hearing and statement of reasons are unlikely to reduce error by much. Conversely, there is a substantial cost to the government (here, the school board) in having to set up detailed, judicially-challengeable procedures for awarding every spot on an athletic team. Consequently, the court is very likely to decide that such litigation-like procedures as a statement of reasons and an opportunity to present one's case are not worth their cost.

(On the other hand, probably an applicant who has a property interest in being allowed to compete for a spot on the team at least has the right to marginally "fair" procedures, so that, for instance, an applicant who could show that the coach favored the coach's own child or own private-coaching pupils might be able to show that her procedural rights had been violated.)

33. **(A)** The court should ask whether the classification is rationally related to a legitimate state objective.

(B) No. Unless there is a suspect or semi-suspect class involved, or a fundamental right, the Supreme Court will uphold a state legislative classification against equal protection attack so long as the classification scheme bears a *rational relation* to some *legitimate legislative objective*. The desire to have lawyers be better trained, and to increase public confidence and reduce suits, certainly seem to constitute legitimate governmental objectives. The link between the classification system chosen and the objective being pursued does not have to be a close one. In fact, there does not need to be an actual empirical link between means and end, merely a *rational belief* on the part of the legislature that there is a link between means and end. Here, a bar association (acting as a government body) certainly could rationally have believed that lawyers who take mandatory legal education will be more up to date, and thus less likely to make mistakes through outmoded training. The fact that doctors might need refresher courses even more than lawyers will be ignored by the court, because reform may take place *"one step at a time"* (i.e., the government does not commit an equal protection violation every time it addresses one aspect of a problem without solving all related aspects).

34. No. As in the prior question, the threshold issue is what standard of review the court will give to the challenged classification. Unless a suspect or quasi-suspect class, or a fundament right, is at issue, the court will use the "mere-rationality" standard. The Supreme Court has held repeatedly that age is not a suspect or semi-suspect class. See, e.g., *Mass. Bd. of Retirement v. Murgia* (police officers may be required to retire at age 50). Therefore, the Court applies mere-rationality review to age-based classifications such as the one here. The goal of assuring that each firefighter is fit for the particular duties of the profession is clearly a legitimate one. There is some question about whether the means chosen (outright ban on all over-50 firefighters) is a good way to accomplish that objective, since there are less drastic alternatives (e.g., testing of each applicant, or an exemption for those who perform only desk duties). But all that is required between means and end is a ***rational relation***. Here, the blanket-ban approach was certainly a rational way of assuring physical fitness, even though it was not the best possible approach or even a very well-tailored one. The classification will be upheld unless it is completely irrational, which this one is certainly not.

35. (A) The court should apply strict scrutiny, and ask whether the statute is necessary to achieve a compelling governmental objective.

(B) Yes, probably. The Supreme Court has generally given strict scrutiny to any race-based classification scheme, even if it does not appear to be enacted for the purpose of disadvantaging African Americans. In a somewhat analogous situation involving child custody, the Court held that child custody decisions could not be made by taking into account race-matching or social prejudices; see *Palmore v. Sidoti*. So unless the mandatory consideration of race here is shown to be a necessary method of achieving a compelling state objective, it will be struck down. The state undoubtedly has a compelling interest in guaranteeing that a child be raised by a family that will be compatible. All other factors being equal, a racial match probably will make it easier for the child to develop a strong sense of identity. However, it is hard to see where the mandatory first-preference for a racial match is a "necessary" means of achieving state objectives, especially in light of evidence that it may keep children in institutional care longer. Therefore, the odds are that the court will find that the "necessary means" part of the equation has not been satisfied, and will strike down the mandatory first preference. (But a scheme merely requiring that race be considered as one factor among many, without making it the most important factor, probably would survive even strict scrutiny.)

36. (A) The court should use the mere-rationality standard, not the strict scrutiny standard.

(B) No, probably. Race is a "suspect category," and classifications based on race are therefore ordinarily subject to strict scrutiny. However, strict scrutiny will only be applied where the court finds that there was a governmental ***intent*** to discriminate against the disfavored group. The mere fact that a law has a less favorable ***effect*** on a racial minority than it has on the majority is ***not*** sufficient to trigger strict scrutiny. Disparate effect can be used as circumstantial evidence of an intent to discriminate, but such evidence is not dispositive. Here, the facts tell us that an intent to disfavor African American students was not present on the part of the school board. Therefore, strict scrutiny will not be applied, and instead the "rational relation" standard will be used. Under this standard, the classification will be upheld so long as it is rationally related to the achievement of a legitimate state objective. Here, cutting an expensive program is certainly rationally related to saving money for the school system, and saving money is certainly a legitimate state of objective in a time of economic hardship.

37. (A) Strict scrutiny. Classifications based on ***national origin*** are suspect. Similarly, classifications based on ethnic ancestry are suspect. So whether the French-Canadians are being discriminated against because they or their ancestors came from another country, or because they are part of a different ethnic group that speaks a different language, they are clearly a suspect class. Since all the evidence indicates that the decision was made for the purpose of disadvantaging members of this group (i.e., the disadvantage was not merely an inadvertent effect of action taken for some other reason), the requisites for strict scrutiny have been satisfied.

(B) Yes. Once strict scrutiny is applied, the challenged classification will only be upheld if it is necessary to achieve a compelling governmental objective. Preventing a particular group of citizens from becoming a majority in a town or school system is certainly not a compelling state objective (and probably not even a "legitimate" objective). Therefore, even if the challenged classification is a "necessary" means of achieving that objective, the classification must fall.

38.   No. Discrimination against *any* racial, ethnic or national-origin group will be strictly scrutinized, even if that group has traditionally not been the victim of widespread prejudice or discrimination. Thus even discrimination against whites of Anglo-Saxon Protestant descent will be strictly scrutinized. This is the result of *City of Richmond v. J.A. Croson Co.*, striking down a minority set-aside program that disadvantaged whites. So the analysis, and outcome, should be exactly the same as in the prior question.

39.   (A) Strict scrutiny.

(B) Yes. The facts here are fairly similar to those of *Richmond v. Croson*. That case makes it clear that any race-based affirmative action scheme will be strictly scrutinized, and will thus be struck down unless it is necessary to achieve a compelling governmental objective. Here, the scheme has at least two shortcomings, each of which is probably separately fatal. First, the city is not trying to remedy past official discrimination, or even explicitly trying to remedy past unofficial discrimination — the facts tell us merely that there has been an inequality of "economic opportunity," which is not the same as racial discrimination. In the absence of a legislative finding of discrimination in the office supply industry in the city of Monroe itself, any attempt to give a racial preference would probably be struck down regardless of how that preference was carried out. Secondly, the plan here is essentially a *quota* — it allocates a particular fixed percentage of city contracts for minority-owned firms. Rarely if ever will quotas be found to be a "necessary" means of redressing even clear past discrimination — certainly a city needs to consider, and probably try, less restrictive measures first, such as voluntary goals, an outreach program to solicit more bids from minority-owned firms, or some other means that is less hard-and-fast than an absolute set-aside.

40.   (A) Mid-level scrutiny, i.e., whether the statute is "substantially related" to the achievement of an "important" governmental objective. (*U.S. v. Virginia* says that gender-based classifications will now need an "exceedingly persuasive justification," and will be "skeptically scrutinized," but the case seems not to officially reject mid-level scrutiny, merely to indicate that mid-level scrutiny will now be applied in a rigorous way.)

(B) Yes, probably. Government classifications involving suspect or semi-suspect claims are evaluated by the same standard regardless of whether the purpose is to discriminate against the traditionally disfavored class or to redress past discrimination. In other words, there is no easier standard for "affirmative action." Thus the Supreme Court applies the same mid-level review to all gender-based classes, whether the classification is old-fashioned discrimination against women or affirmative action designed to improve the lot of women. In both cases, the gender-based classification will be upheld only if it is substantially related to the achievement of important governmental objectives.

Here, encouragement of bonding between parent and newborn child is probably an "important" governmental objective. However, a court would probably conclude that there is no "substantial relation" between a mother-only parental-leave program and achievement of this objective. It is highly likely that whatever social problems are caused by not having either parent at home during a child's infancy, those problems can be redressed as well or almost as well by having the father be at home. Therefore, a scheme that entitled either parent, but not both parents, to take a paid maternity leave would accomplish the legislative purposes as well or almost as well as the mother-only scheme. Consequently, the court will probably, thought not certainly, strike down the statute.

In general, courts are likely to strike down any statute that reflects *stereotypes* about the "proper place of women." See, e.g., *U.S. v. Virginia*, finding Virginia's belief that VMI's intense military training program is unsuitable for women to be an unconstitutional generalization about "the way women are." The scheme here — which implies that a mother's place, but not a father's place, is to be home with the newborn infant — reflects similar stereotypical thinking.

41. (A) Strict scrutiny — the statute must be necessary to achieve a compelling governmental objective.

(B) Yes, probably. There are three key issues here: (1) whether the fact that the preference was enacted by ***Congress*** rather than by a state or local government should change the standard for judicial review; (2) whether Congress' attempt to ***wipe out past discrimination*** renders the measure constitutionally acceptable; and (3) whether the Court's decision in *Grutter v. Bollinger*, allowing race-conscious university admissions, affects the answer.

As to the first issue — whether the fact that the preference was enacted by ***Congress*** rather than by a state or local government should change the standard for judicial review — the answer is ***"no."*** Because of the decision in *Adarand Constructors v. Pena*, strict scrutiny will be given to race-conscious congressionally-enacted affirmative action plans. Since the statute clearly classifies on the basis of race, it falls within this rule.

As to the second issue — whether Congress' desire to wipe out past governmental discrimination renders the measure acceptable — the answer is again ***"no."*** The eradication of past governmental discrimination is indeed probably a "compelling" goal. However, the preference probably would ***not*** be found to be ***"necessary"*** for the rooting out of the effects of past governmental discrimination. Congress did not make detailed *findings* about which geographical regions this discrimination exists in, or about which governmental units (e.g., universities versus other governmental actors) caused it. Also, there is no indication that Congress considered ***race-neutral means*** (e.g., use of "socio-economic" criteria rather than racial ones) as a possible way to solve the problem. As the Court said in another race-conscious university-admissions case, *Fisher v. Univ. of Texas* (2013), strict scrutiny "require[s] a court to examine with care, and not defer to, a university's '***serious, good faith consideration of workable race-neutral alternatives***.'" If there was a ***"workable race-neutral alternative available"*** to the university, then the race-conscious means can't be deemed to have been "necessary." *Id*. There's no evidence here that Congress ever gave "serious, good faith consideration" of race-neutral alternatives to see whether they might be workable.

The "rebuttable presumption" used here is better than an outright quota, but *Adarand*, which involved a similar presumption-based scheme, suggests that racially-based presumptions will nonetheless be hard to justify (though the *Adarand* Court didn't actually decide whether the preference there survived strict scrutiny). Also, the Court might give slightly greater deference to Congress than it would to a state or local body. Nonetheless, the best guess is that the statute here would be struck down.

As to the final issue — whether the Court's decision in *Grutter v. Bollinger*, allowing race-conscious university admissions, changes the outcome — the answer once again is *"no."* Race-conscious affirmative action was allowed in *Grutter* because the majority was satisfied that the University there was pursuing the compelling goal of achieving diversity in the student body, and doing so in a narrowly-tailored way by use of individualized evaluations of each applicant. Here, there is no indication that Congress was seeking true diversity in each student body — Congress seems to have been nakedly pursuing *"racial balancing"* (i.e., making the portion of minority students at each university mirror the local student-age population), and the *Grutter* majority opinion makes it clear that this is not a legitimate objective. The numerically-based presumption of illegality just makes things worse, since such a presumption is more like the point system struck down by the Court in *Gratz v. Bollinger* than it is like the individualized evaluations upheld by the Court in *Grutter*. The Court's post-*Gratz* decision in *Parents Involved in Community Schools v. Seattle School District*, where a majority struck down pupil-assignment plans that gave a preference to students whose presence would lessen the racial imbalance in the target public school, further buttresses the conclusion that the racial preference here would be found to be in essence an illegitimate quota or "racial balancing" plan. The same is true of the even-more-recent decision in *Fisher, supra,* repeating *Grutter*'s holding that strict scrutiny will be applied to any race-conscious admissions method, and quoting approvingly *Parents Involved*'s statement that "Racial balancing is not transformed from 'patently unconstitutional' to a compelling state interest simply by relabeling it 'racial diversity.'"

42. (a) Delta State. Plan B, by amending the holistic method to explicitly take account of a student's race, makes use of a suspect classification (race). When government uses a suspect classification and is challenged on equal protection grounds, the burden of proof as to whether the classification is constitutional is imposed on the government. So it will be up to Delta State to show, by a preponderance of the evidence, that its use of a race-conscious admissions method was constitutional.

(b) Strict scrutiny. That is, Delta State will have to show that Plan B was a *"necessary" means* of accomplishing the university's admittedly-compelling interest in educational diversity. To decide whether Plan B was a "necessary" means, the court will have to make "a careful judicial inquiry into whether [the] university could achieve sufficient diversity *without* using racial classifications." *Fisher v. Univ. of Texas* (2013). If there *was* a *"workable race-neutral alternative available"* to the university, then the race-conscious means can't be deemed to have been "necessary." *Id.* And a race-neutral plan will be deemed to be a workable alternative if it would "promote ... the [governmental] interest *about as well* [as the selected race-conscious method] and at *tolerable administrative expense.*" *Id.* Furthermore, the court *may not defer* to the university's conclusion about what workable race-neutral alternatives might have existed — the court must make its *own* determination on that issue. *Id.* These aspects of *Fisher* will all combine to make it difficult for the university to make the required showing that the race-conscious means it chose were "necessary" for achieving diversity.

(c) Paula. It's pretty clear that Plan A was a "workable race-neutral alternative." Why? Since the University has defined its compelling goal of achieving educational diversity largely in terms of getting a critical mass of two or more students into more than the previous 25% of seminar classes, and since you're told that Plan A would likely do this essentially as well as Plan B, it's hard to see how the court can conclude that Plan A *wasn't* a workable race-neutral alternative. And where a workable race-neutral alternative existed, that alternative **must be used** in preference to a race-conscious method. *Fisher.* The university's best hope is to argue that Plan A was not "workable" because it had the drawback of resulting in admission of a *somewhat-less-academically-qualified* group of black students (because that plan will do worse than Plan B in bringing about the admission of academically-talented black students ranking between the 8th and 15th percentile in stronger mostly-white school districts). But the court is likely to conclude that even if this assertion is true, Plan A was still "workable" — nothing says that a plan that fails to enroll the absolutely most-academically-talented class consistent with educational diversity cannot be "workable." (Indeed, in *Fisher* itself, about 75% of the University of Texas' students were admitted under a "Top Ten Percent" plan very similar to Plan A's Top Seven Percent component; both the University and the Court implicitly concluded that this method was workable and race-neutral, and no one seems to have made a serious argument that students admitted under this feature were on average seriously academically-underqualified.)

43. (A) Strict scrutiny.

(B) Yes, probably. Discrimination against aliens (at least aliens who are legally in this country) is to be strictly scrutinized, because aliens as a class are politically powerless and frequently discriminated against. Therefore, any statute that discriminates against aliens on its face, or whose purpose is to disadvantage aliens, will be struck down unless it is necessary to achieve a compelling governmental interest. Here, the state's interest in keeping land prices low for American citizens is almost certainly not "compelling." In any event, discrimination against aliens is not a "necessary" way to achieve that objective, since there are other less-discriminatory options available (e.g., price controls that apply to everybody).

44. (A) The mere-rationality standard.

(B) No. As noted in the answer to the prior question, discrimination against aliens is generally subjected to strict scrutiny. However, under the so-called "*Sugarman* exception," this strict scrutiny does not apply to discrimination against aliens who apply for jobs that *"go to the heart of representative government."* The Court has held that the post of public school teacher falls within this "heart of representative government" exception, because of a teacher's opportunity to "influence the attitudes of students towards government, the political process, and a citizen's social responsibilities." *Ambach v. Norwick.* Therefore, only a mere-rationality review is used, and the regulation will be upheld if it is rationally related to the achievement of a legitimate state objective. Here, the regulation almost certainly satisfies this standard. Hiring teachers who can be easily understood is surely a legitimate state objective, and there is at least a rational relation between citizenship and ease of understanding (since non-citizens on average probably have harder-to-understand accents than citizens).

45. (A) Intermediate-level review, under which the measure will be invalidated unless it is "substantially related" to the achievement of an "important" governmental objective.

(B) Yes, probably. The Court held in *Plyler v. Doe* that intermediate-level review should be given to any state law denying free public-school education to illegal aliens of school age. In *Plyler*, the Court held that the various state interests advanced there (e.g., preventing an influx of illegal immigrants, conserving tax dollars, etc.) were not sufficiently weighty to overcome this mid-level review. The enrollment restriction here is essentially identical to that struck down in *Plyler*. The fact that non-residents of the village are also excluded is irrelevant — the key fact is that among residents of the village, those who are illegal aliens are excluded, whereas those who are citizens or resident aliens are allowed. Even if the village shows that it has to spend tax dollars on educating these additional students, and even if it is able to show that it does not get state aid to compensate it for these incremental burdens, the interest in conservation of resources is likely to be found insufficient to overcome the mid-level review (and similar fiscal interests were found insufficient in *Plyler* itself).

47. Yes. The facts of this question are fairly closely modeled on the facts of *U.S. v. Windsor* (2013), where the Court invalidated a section of the Defense of Marriage Act that forbade the entire federal government from recognizing, for any federal purpose, any state-consecrated same-sex marriage. Although the majority's reasoning in *Windsor* is somewhat opaque, the opinion seems to mean that (1) if Congress acts solely for the purpose of expressing moral disapproval of or ***animus towards gays***, this is ***not a legitimate governmental objective***; and (2) therefore, if Congress, acting with such a purpose, decides to treat same-sex couples validly married under state law significantly differently from similarly-situated married opposite-sex couples, Congress has violated the same-sex couples' right to equal protection (as imposed on the federal government by operation of the Fifth Amendment's due process clause). The Court's opinion in *Windsor* does not make it clear what standard of review is to be used in cases (like *Windsor* itself) attacking a federal classification system based solely on animus towards gays, but the case seems to mean that such a classification system cannot survive ***even mere-rationality review***, given the absence of a legitimate state objective.

Here, the only legislative history indicates that the Committee with jurisdiction over the bill was acting solely out of hostility towards gay people, the same motive as (the Court found) motivated the passage of DOMA. Therefore, a lower federal court interpreting *Windsor* should find that DHNA was, similarly, not supported by any legitimate governmental objective, and therefore fails even mere-rationality equal protection review. (When the plaintiff contends that the federal government has failed to comply with equal protection principles, the claim is properly brought — as Li's was — under the *Fifth* Amendment, whose grant of the right to "due process" has been interpreted by the Court as obligating the federal government to follow equal-protection principles.) Therefore, regardless of what standard of review the trial court believes the Supreme Court to have chosen in *Windsor*, the trial court should conclude that *Windsor* means that the CIS' denial of a green card violated Li's Fifth Amendment rights.

48. (A) Strict scrutiny — the differential treatment must be necessary to achieve a compelling governmental interest.

(B) Yes. Normally, a statutory scheme that distinguishes on the basis of gender must undergo merely mid-level review, i.e., it must be "substantially related" to the achievement of an "important" governmental interest. However, because the right to vote is *"fundamental,"* classifications disadvantaging this right are subjected to strict scrutiny. Therefore, unless the state can show that distinguishing between men and women in issuance of absentee ballots is necessary to achieve a compelling governmental interest, the restriction must fall. Here, even if the state is pursuing some kind of compelling interest (perhaps the need to avoid the fraudulent use of absentee ballots), it is highly unlikely that the gender-based discrimination chosen here is a "necessary" means to achieve that interest. For example, a provision that *each* person who wants to use an absentee ballot must furnish a written excuse would appear to be a satisfactory way to handle the fraud problem.

49. (A) "Mere-rationality" review.

(B) No, probably. Normally, any deviation from the "one person, one vote" principle, will be strictly scrutinized, and will probably be found to violate the Equal Protection Clause. But the Supreme Court has made a limited exception for **"special purpose"** bodies, that is, governmental units having a strictly limited purpose which disproportionately affects only one group. In that situation, the right to vote may be limited to the disproportionately-affected group. Here, since all funds disbursed by the district come from taxes on the owners of forested lands, and only such owners can receive the disbursed funds, this standard is probably satisfied. If so, the court will only give mere-rationality review to the arrangement. Since limiting votes for a body to those who have some interest in the body's actions is a rational way to achieve the body's purposes, the mere-rationality standard is probably satisfied. See *Ball v. James*.

50. (A) Strict scrutiny.

(B) Yes, probably. States are certainly entitled to impose ballot restrictions to ensure that only parties with a certain degree of popular support appear on the ballot. However, where ballot restrictions are so severe that they prevent virtually any but the two established parties from getting candidates on the ballot, these restrictions will be strictly scrutinized and probably struck down. The restrictions here seem to be so severe that they would be almost impossible to meet, so the court will probably invalidate the restrictions. See *Williams v. Rhodes*, one of the few ballot-access cases containing a restriction so severe that the statute was struck down; the restrictions here are virtually identical to those in *Williams*.

51. (A) Strict scrutiny.

(B) Yes, probably. Normally, when the state furnishes free goods or services, and does not discriminate against a suspect class, only a "mere-rationality" level of review is used. But when the state is dispensing a **"vital government benefit or privilege," and** the state treats **newly-arrived resident**s significantly less favorably than those who have lived in the state longer, strict scrutiny is used. The Supreme Court has held that even non-emergency medical care is a "vital government benefit or privilege" (*Memorial Hospital v. Maricopa County*), so emergency care certainly would be. The one-year residency requirement has the effect of treating recently-arrived people less favorably, so the conditions for strict scrutiny are met. It is doubtful that there is any state interest here that is "compelling" (the state's fiscal interest probably is not), and even more doubtful that a flat ban on any assistance to those who have not yet lived in the state for a year is a "necessary" method of achieving the state's objectives.

52. (A) The "mere-rationality" standard.

(B) No. First, large families (or any particular family size) have has never been found to constitute a "suspect" or "semi-suspect" class. Nor are poor people members of such a class. Hilda's only hope would be to establish that one has a "fundamental interest" in the "necessities of life." However, the Supreme Court has explicitly held that welfare benefits and other "economic necessities" are ***not*** fundamental interests. See, e.g., *Dandridge v. Williams* (no fundamental interest in welfare benefits). Therefore, any classification system used by the state in allocating such economic necessities is judged by the easy-to-satisfy "mere-rationality" standard. Here, the state's scheme bears a rational relation to several legitimate state objectives (e.g., encouraging employment by prohibiting payments that might compare favorably with what a job would provide).

53.   (A) That it violates the "right to travel," a right protected by the 14th Amendment's Privileges or Immunities Clause.

(B) Yes, probably. The Court held in *Saenz v. Roe* that a state may not provide that when a family moves into the state, for one year after arrival the family's welfare payments shall be limited to the amount that the family would have received in their prior state of residence. The Court reasoned that this violates the "right to travel" — one of the rights of "national citizenship" guaranteed by the 14th Amendment's P-or-I clause — because the state's action was irrational except as an attempt to carry out the forbidden objective of discouraging poor people from moving into the state. There is no reason why the same principle shouldn't apply here, since we're told the state's action is based upon this same unlawful motive.

54.   (A) That the ordinance constitutes a "taking" in violation of the Fifth Amendment.

(B) No, probably. The Fifth Amendment provides that "nor shall private property be taken for public use, without just compensation." This clause, though by its terms applies only to the federal government, also applies to states and municipalities via the Fourteenth Amendment's Due Process Clause. An enactment that is labelled a "land use regulation" will generally not constitute a "taking," unless it "den[ies] an owner economically viable use of his land." Here Mill Co. is not being deprived of ***all*** economically viable use of its land — it is free to build houses, stores or warehouses on the site. The fact that the ***particular*** use being made of the property at this moment is now being foreclosed is not enough to meet this "no economically viable use" standard. See, e.g., *Goldblatt v. Hempstead* (town does not commit a "taking" where it bans the continued operation of a sand and gravel pit). If the ordinance had ***immediately*** taken effect, without any "amortization" period (here, four years), this might have tipped the balance in favor of a finding that a taking had occurred. But the amortization period, together with the fact that the mill owners had already had many years to derive value from the plant, remove this difficulty.

55.   (A) That it violated the Obligation of Contracts Clause.

(B) Yes, probably. Art. I, Section 10, provides that "no State shall … pass any … Law impairing the Obligation of Contracts. … " This provision applies both to states and to municipalities. The Clause has been interpreted by the Supreme Court to mean that a state's attempt to ***escape from its financial obligations*** will be sustained only where a ***significant public need*** exists that cannot be ***reasonably handled*** in any other way. Here, Green Valley has in effect modified the terms of its agreement with Waste Co., by changing the law so that Waste Co. no longer gets the town's trash. The fact that Green Valley is somewhat better off financially as a result of this decision, and even the fact that the gain to Green Valley is greater than the loss to Waste Co., will not be enough to meet the requirement that there be a significant public need that cannot be reasonably handled in any other way. Court decisions show that an impairment will be "reasonable" only if it was induced by ***unforeseen developments*** occurring after the original contract was made; here, it was certainly foreseeable that some other waste management company might come along with a more financially attractive deal. Also, the Court has refused to merely balance the benefit to the public against the damage to the other party to the contract. See *U.S. Trust Co. v. New Jersey*. If Green Valley had been on the verge of insolvency, with this modification able to make the difference, then the impairment might stand; however, the facts do not indicate this level of hardship. Therefore, the Court would probably find that the Obligations of Contracts Clause was violated.

56. No. The Obligation of Contracts Clause applies only where the state takes an action that is *specifically directed* at contractual obligations. If the state applies a *"generally applicable rule of conduct"* which has the *incidental by-product* of impairing contractual obligations, the Contract Clause does not apply at all. See *Exxon Corp. v. Eagerton*. Here, Happy Farms has enacted a generally applicable rule, one requiring Sunday closings. The fact that certain contractual obligations (the store owners' contractual duty to remain open on Sundays) happen to be impaired is irrelevant. Therefore, we never get to the point of even determining whether the impairment here was justified by pressing needs of public policy (as we would have to do in a situation where the state specifically directed its new law at contractual obligations).

57. (A) That it is an *ex post facto* law.

(B) Yes. The Constitution prevents a state government from enacting an *ex post facto* law; see Art. I, Section 10. An *ex post facto* law is one which has a retroactive punitive effect. Some *ex post facto* laws are ones which outlaw conduct that was not criminal at the time it was committed. But there is a second kind of *ex post facto* law: one which *increases* the *severity* of a criminal punishment, compared with that authorized at the time the act was committed. Here, Dennis could not have been sentenced to more than five years in prison at the moment he committed the offense, so his sentence now constitutes a violation of the *ex post facto* ban.

58. (A) That the statute violates the prohibition on bills of attainder.

(B) Yes, probably. The Constitution prohibits both the federal government and the states from passing any "bill of attainder." (See Art. I, Section 10, for the provision as it applies to states.) The term covers any legislative act which "applies either to *named individuals* or to *easily ascertainable members of a group* in such a way as to *inflict punishment* on them without a judicial trial. ... " Here, since the Phrenic Brotherhood is a relatively small group, and its members are fairly easily ascertained, the requirements seem met. Assuming that dismissal from the state payroll is found to be "punishment," the law seems to be a bill of attainder. Measures taken solely for the purpose of *regulation*, and which have no substantial stigmatizing element, are not prohibited by the Bill of Attainder Clause. Here, however, since the law applies to all state government jobs, and applies without respect to whether the individual has a specific intent to espouse the terrorist beliefs of some Brotherhood leaders, the law seems more like punishment than regulation. Especially since there is a risk that freedom of association values will be infringed, the Court will probably conclude that the law is a bill of attainder. See, e.g., *U.S. v. Brown* (law making it a crime for a Communist Party member to serve as an officer of a labor union is struck down as a bill of attainder).

59. No. The Fourteenth Amendment, like all aspects of the Constitution (except the Thirteenth Amendment) only restricts *government* action. Here, the facts tell us that Green Valley Hospital is operated by a private religious order. Since there is no government involvement, there cannot be an equal protection violation.

60. No. This is essentially a "trick question." The Fourteenth Amendment applies only to conduct by *state* and *local* governments. Therefore, any conduct by or on behalf of the housing agency here could not have violated the Equal Protection Clause, because it was conduct of the federal government, not the state government. Delbert therefore did not cause any interference with equal protection rights. (Equal protection *principles* are binding on the federal government via the Fifth Amendment's Due Process Clause, and these equal protection principles are interpreted the same way as are the Fourteenth Amendment's equal protection principles. But the question here has been carefully worded to refer only to conduct that violates the Fourteenth, not the Fifth, Amendment.)

61. (A) The "public function" doctrine.

(B) No. The "public function" doctrine holds that when a private actor (or group) is entrusted by the state with the performance of functions that are governmental in nature, that actor or group becomes an *agent of the state* and his/their acts constitute state action. However, for the "public function" doctrine to apply, the function must be one which has traditionally been *exclusively* the domain of the government. The Court has held that the providing of education is *not* the exclusive prerogative of the state, even though it is a function normally provided by the state out of public funds. Therefore, the "public function" doctrine will not apply to Beaver. See *Rendell-Baker v. Kohn*, refusing to treat a private school as involving a public function, even where the school's income came primarily from public grants. (It is also conceivable that the state might be found to have been so heavily "involved" or "entangled" in the private school here that state action should be found, but the Court has held that mere government funding of a private actor's operations does not convert those private operations into state action, so this argument, too, would almost certainly fail.)

62. (A) That there is a symbiotic relationship between State U and the private landowners, sufficient to turn the private acts of discrimination into state action.

(B) Yes, probably. If the state is deeply involved with private discrimination, that private discrimination can sometimes be viewed as itself being state action. One of the ways this can happen is if there is a *"symbiotic,"* i.e., mutually beneficial, relation between the state and the private discriminator. Here, a strong argument can be made that the university is benefitting greatly from private acts (the rental of housing to State U students), and that the private discriminators are receiving important benefits from the state (free listings and a free flow of potential tenants).

To the extent that the pool of homeowners willing to list their properties has been increased by the coding option, it can be argued that State U has actually achieved a benefit not just from the overall listing program, but from the very acts of discrimination being complained of; if so, this makes it even more likely that state action would be found. All in all, there is a better than even chance that State U would be found to be so heavily involved with the private acts of discrimination that state action should be found in the maintenance of the list. The symbiosis here is reminiscent of that in *Burton v. Wilmington Parking Authority* (where restaurant paid rent for space in publicly-owned building, discrimination by restaurant was state action).

63. No, probably. The Fourteenth Amendment is generally triggered only where there is "state action." Thus the clause dealing with equal protection provides that "[n]o State shall make or enforce any law which shall … deny to any person within its jurisdiction the equal protection of the laws." On the other hand, §5 of the Fourteenth Amendment grants Congress the power to enforce that amendment "by appropriate legislation." The issue is whether Congress may "appropriately" enforce the Equal Protection Clause by proscribing private, as opposed to governmental, conduct.

Certainly some types of private conduct may be reached under Congress' enforcement power. For instance, Congress may prevent a private person from interfering with a state official's attempts to furnish equal protection (e.g., Congress may punish private individuals to who prevent local school board officials from carrying out desegregation). But where the conduct being proscribed is *purely* private, involving the interaction of one private individual with another, it is doubtful whether Congress' power to enforce the Equal Protection Clause extends that far.

64. The Thirteenth Amendment. The Thirteenth Amendment provides that "[n]either slavery nor involuntary servitude, except as a punishment for crime … shall exist within the United States. … " The Thirteenth Amendment, unlike the Fourteenth and Fifteenth, is thus not explicitly limited to governmental action. Section 2 of the Thirteenth Amendment gives Congress the power to "enforce this [amendment] by appropriate legislation." This §2 enforcement power has been construed to mean that Congress has the right to decide what the ***"badges and incidents of slavery"*** are. If Congress makes a finding that one of the badges and incidents of slavery is the refusal of private homeowners to rent to others on the basis of race, the Court would uphold the proposed statute here as a valid exercise of this enforcement power. All that is required is that Congress act "rationally" in determining that a particular aspect of private conduct is indeed a badge or incident of slavery, and Congress' conclusion here would certainly be found to be "rational." See *Jones v. Alfred H. Mayer Co.* (Thirteenth Amendment is broad enough to let Congress conclude that private racial discrimination in real estate transactions is a badge or incident of slavery.)

65. Yes, probably. The question boils down to, "May Congress reduce the substantive content of individuals' constitutional rights?" The answer to this question is "no." The Court held in *Boerne v. Flores* that Congress' power to enforce the post-Civil War Amendments does not include the power to redefine the substantive boundaries of the rights given by those Amendments. Here, Congress has tried to reduce the substantive contours of a woman's substantive due process right to abortion, and under *Boerne* (and other Court cases), Congress may not do this.

66. (A) That the section is a content-based regulation on speech, and is thus invalid unless necessary to achieve a compelling state interest.

(B) No. Government may impose reasonable regulations on the time, place and manner of speech that takes place on public forums. However, government's right to do this is contingent on its behaving in a ***content-neutral*** way. If government chooses to allow some messages and not allow others based on the content of the speech, then the restriction will be strictly scrutinized, and will be struck down unless it is: (1) necessary to achieve a compelling objective; and (2) narrowly drawn to achieve that objective. See, e.g., *Widmar v. Vincent*.

Here, government allows messages that pertain to matters under discussion inside the office building, but not messages pertaining to other matters. The government might defend on the grounds that it has not objected to the content of the messages, but has merely allowed some whole "categories" of speech while not allowing other whole categories. However, even distinctions between topics or categories is likely to be found to be content-based. See, e.g., *Consolidated Edison v. Public Serv. Comm.* (state may not prevent utilities from discussing the issue of nuclear power's desirability, because "[t]he First Amendment's hostility to content-based regulation extends not only to restrictions on particular viewpoints, but also to prohibition of public discussion of an entire topic.") In any event, the speech here is taking place in a public forum, so the court will be especially reluctant to allow such a broad interference with it.

67. Yes. First, we need to analyze whether the restriction is content-neutral. In contrast to the restriction in the prior question, the one here probably *is* content-neutral; that is, the government truly does not seem to be interested in what topics are described in the materials being given out, so long as the materials are essentially single-topic short pieces, rather than newspapers and magazines. Although it could be argued that distinguishing between newspapers/magazines on one hand and all other communications on the other is not content-neutral, the court would probably conclude that the distinction here is at such a high level of generality that there is no attempt to suppress a particular message or group of messages.

Assuming content-neutrality, the regulation here must be evaluated by the standards for testing "time, place and manner" restrictions. In general, such restrictions must be *"narrowly tailored"* to serve a *"significant governmental interest,"* and must *"leave open alternative channels"* for communicating the information. The restriction here probably *fails* to satisfy the "narrowly tailored" requirement. That is, the city could probably find methods that are less intrusive of freedom of expression than the total ban on handbills for large parts of the day. For instance the city could strictly enforce its ordinary anti-littering laws, or could prohibit anyone from blocking other pedestrians' right of easy passage on the street or sidewalk. It is important to note that the communication here is occurring in a *public forum* (the street or sidewalk), and the availability of different public forums or the present public forum at a different time, usually will not be enough to constitute an "alternative channel." (This is especially true here, where large segments of the population, i.e., commuters, will be on the street *only* during rush hours, and will thus never get to hear Kermit's message if the regulation is enforced.)

68. (a) No. It would be a violation of the picketers' First Amendment rights for them to be held liable under this statute, because such liability would effectively allow for content-based regulation of the picketers' speech, and cannot survive strict scrutiny. The case is comparable to *Snyder v. Phelps*, where picketers located on a public street who carried signs that intentionally offended the family of a soldier killed in Iraq were found to be shielded on First Amendment grounds from state-court liability for IIED.

69. No. The government may forbid a person from advocating illegal conduct, such as insurrection or overthrow of the government. However, under *Brandenburg v. Ohio*, speech advocating such illegality may only be proscribed if two conditions are satisfied: (1) the advocacy is directed to inciting or producing *imminent* lawless action; and (2) the advocacy is *likely* to incite or produce such action. Here, neither of these requirements seems to be met. Leonard is not calling for *imminent* illegality — he says "let's start … ," but he does not indicate that action should take place immediately. Furthermore, although his statement about having guerilla cells could probably be interpreted as a call for illegality, his statement about "building up an arsenal" is not necessarily a call for illegality, since there are many legal ways to buy guns, even automatics and machine guns. Even if the court decides that Leonard was attempting to incite imminent lawless action, it is pretty clear that there was very little risk that his speech was *likely* to produce that effect, since he had only a small crowd in front of him, they were in the park for other reasons, and they did not in fact respond with immediate illegal actions.

70. (A) That it is overbroad. A statute or regulation is overbroad if, in addition to proscribing activities which may constitutionally be forbidden, it also sweeps within its coverage future conduct which is protected by the guarantees of free speech or free association.

(B) Yes, probably. The government is clearly entitled to insist that Robert not commit crimes, and that he not advocate that others imminently commit crimes. However, the government may *not* make mere membership in an organization, without more, a crime, and it may not deprive a person of a government job or benefit for being merely a member or for refusing to say that he is not a member. Here, the affidavit merely requires Robert to say that he has not been a member; since Robert would be entitled to be a mere member of NAMBLA, so long as he did not agree with its aim of advocating imminent commission of the crime of man-boy love, the affidavit requirement would punish some membership that is constitutional. Robert's own membership here is *not* constitutionally protected, since he in fact knows of NAMBLA's stated aims and supports those (illegal) aims. But under the overbreadth doctrine, Robert is permitted to say, in effect, "The affidavit requirement would be unconstitutional if applied to (hypothetical) other people who merely belong to NAMBLA without supporting its criminal aims, so it should be struck down as facially invalid."

Under the requirement of *"substantial* overbreadth," the overbreadth doctrine would not be applied unless the invalid applications of the requirement are substantial compared to the legitimate applications. Here, however, this requirement of substantial overbreadth is probably satisfied, since quite a number of people are likely to belong to NAMBLA just to get information about the law and politics surrounding this question rather than to advocate or practice illegal man-boy sex. Therefore, Robert's overbreadth attack will probably succeed.

71. (A) That the statute is unconstitutionally vague.

(B) Yes, probably. A statute will be held void for vagueness if the conduct forbidden by it is so unclearly defined that a person of ordinary intelligence would not know what is forbidden.

Here, the statute uses the words "lewd or lascivious," but furnishes no further information about what type of conduct is being forbidden. A reasonable observer would probably be in doubt as to whether it is necessarily lewd for a woman to appear topless. Because of the ordinance's lack of specificity, undue discretion is given to local law enforcement officials, who depending on how they felt about Becky or toplessness generally could decide to look the other way rather than making an arrest. Therefore, while the city might be entitled to ban women from appearing topless in public if the ordinance specifically applied to toplessness, the formulation here is probably unconstitutionally vague.

72. (A) The ban must be: (1) content-neutral; (2) narrowly tailored to serve a significant governmental interest; and (3) leave open alternative channels for communication of the information.

(B) No, probably. The facts indicate to us that the ban is content-neutral both in terms of the purposes for which it was enacted and the way in which it is applied. However, it seems not to be "***narrowly tailored*** to serve a ***significant*** governmental interest." Since the proposed speech would take place in the most traditional of all public forums — the streets — mere convenience, such as avoiding traffic obstructions, probably does not qualify as a "significant governmental interest." Also, there are more narrowly-tailored restrictions that could be used, such as an advance permit requirement which would give the police time to detour traffic and thereby reduce disruption. Finally, the requirement that alternative channels be left open is strictly construed in a public-forum context; the fact that there may be other public places (e.g., smaller streets) where the same expression is allowed will not generally be enough to qualify as an adequate alternative channel.

73. Yes. An advance permit requirement will be upheld if it is content-neutral, adequately constrains administrative discretion, and is a reasonable means of insuring that public order is maintained. However, in order to avoid giving the official charged with granting or denying permit applications too much ***discretion***, the grounds upon which a permit may be denied must be set forth ***specifically*** and ***narrowly*** in the ordinance. Here, the standard given for granting or denying a permit — that the proposed activities "not be detrimental to the overall community" — gives the mayor virtually uncontrolled discretion, and acts as an invitation to him to behave in a content-based way. This excessive discretion makes the statute overbroad and vague. Therefore, even though Firebrand's own proposed conduct might be capable of being prohibited by an appropriately-drawn ordinance, the ordinance here must be struck down as invalid on its face.

74. Yes. If a permit that is required prior to the exercise of First Amendment rights is unconstitutional ***on its face***, the speaker is ***not required*** to apply for a permit. He may decline to apply, then speak, and avoid conviction on the grounds of the permit requirement's unconstitutionality. See, e.g., *Lovell v. Griffin*. Because a statute that is overbroad is facially invalid, this rule applies to overbreadth claims. Therefore, Firebrand may assert overbreadth even though he failed to ever apply for a permit.

76. No. As with any "time, place and manner" restriction, the ordinance will be valid only if it is content-neutral, is narrowly tailored to serve a significant governmental interest, and leaves open alternative channels for communicating the information. Here, probably the requirement of content-neutrality is satisfied (unless there is evidence that, say, Jehovah's Witnesses were a special target of the ordinance). The government probably has a significant government interest in preventing homeowners from being disturbed at home when they do not want to be. However, it is doubtful that the ordinance is "narrowly tailored," since there are less restrictive alternatives (e.g., permitting a homeowner to indicate on his door that he does not wish to be disturbed by solicitors) — when the city makes a blanket assumption that ***no*** homeowner wishes to receive a solicitor, this is probably not a sufficiently narrowly tailored approach. Furthermore, it is doubtful whether alternative channels have been left open, since for many types of organizations, door-to-door and face-to-face is the only affordable means, given the large expense associated with, say, newspaper and TV advertising. Upon facts similar to these, the Court struck down a blanket ban. See *Martin v. Struthers*.

77. (A) The "fighting words" doctrine.

(B) Yes, probably. Among the classes of speech which are not protected by the First Amendment are "fighting words," which the Court has defined as "those which by their very utterance ... tend to incite an immediate breach of the peace." *Chaplinsky v. New Hampshire*. However, there are several exceptions and clarifications to the "fighting words" doctrine, which make it seldom applicable. One of those exceptions is that if the police have the physical ability to ***control the angry crowd*** as a means of preventing threatened violence, they ***must do so*** in preference to arresting the speaker for using "fighting words." *Cox v. Louisiana*. Here, it seems probable that the 15 police officers could have either arrested or at least restrained those Jews who were moving forward towards the podium, and probably any other hostile Jew in the audience. At the very least, the police needed to make some effort to do this, rather than immediately arrest the speaker.

78. No. In general, government may not forbid speech merely because it would be ***"offensive"*** to the listener. For example, language cannot be forbidden merely because it is profane. *Cohen v. California* (D cannot be punished for wearing a jacket bearing the legend "Fuck the Draft"). Here, the statute is phrased specifically to reach only "offensive" conduct, so it runs afoul of this principle. Furthermore, the statute is probably unconstitutionally vague, since a reasonable reader of it would not know exactly what types of language would be forbidden.

79. No. The problem is that the ban here is ***content-based***. That is, it proscribes only certain types of speech, based on the content or message of that speech. Thus insults based on race, ethnicity and three other attributes are banned, but insults based on other attributes are not (e.g., the addressee's politics, intelligence, short or tall stature, etc.). Even if the university interprets the ban so as to bar only "fighting words," this will not be enough to save the statute, because *R.A.V. v. City of St. Paul* (striking down an anti-cross-burning statute) establishes that government may not ban some fighting words but not others, based on the words' precise message. The best way for State U to solve the problem is to amend its code so as to ban "all slurs, invectives, insults or epithets that would have the likely effect of either inducing the listener to respond with violence, or which would be likely to create in the listener an apprehension of imminent physical harm." Such a formulation would essentially ban all fighting words, plus all words that would constitute an assault; these two categories may clearly be constitutionally proscribed, as long as the proscription occurs in a content-neutral way. (Of course, this re-write would fail to prohibit a lot of hate speech, so it would not be a perfect solution, but at least it would be content-neutral.)

80. No. The Supreme Court has held that computer networks are more like newspapers than like broadcast TV, and that content-based restrictions on what is placed on such networks must therefore be strictly scrutinized. See *Reno v. ACLU*. Applying strict scrutiny, the measure is clearly unconstitutional, since it's content-based (only materials with an "indecent" message are proscribed), and it's not narrowly tailored towards the (admittedly "compelling") objective of keeping indecent materials away from minors — for instance, the state could give parents free filtering software that would block access to these materials by minors. See *Ashcroft v. ACLU*. Furthermore, the statute is overbroad: it applies to viewing by adults (who have a right to see the photo), as well as to viewing by minors (who probably don't have a First Amendment right to see such a photo, though this is not completely clear). Since the rights of adults are being curtailed in a content-based way, the statute will surely fail strict scrutiny. *Reno v. ACLU*.

81. (A) No. The Supreme Court has held that airport terminals are not "public forums," even though they are public places. *Int'l Soc. for Krishna Consciousness, Inc. v. Lee*. Assuming that train stations are analyzed the same way as are airport terminals — which seems virtually certain — the terminal here falls into the category of "non-public forum." Non-public forums are public facilities that are used for purposes that are not especially linked to expression; thus the terminal here is primarily linked to transportation, and has never historically been viewed as a center for expression.

(B) Yes. A non-public forum offers the *least* constitutionally-protected access for First Amendment expression. Government regulation of expression in a non-public forum must merely be: (1) *reasonable* in light of the *purpose* served by the forum; and (2) *viewpoint neutral*. See *Krishna v. Lee, supra*. The Court in *Krishna* held that these tests were met by a ban on funds solicitation in airport terminals; presumably the same analysis would apply to the fund solicitation in the train station here. The ban on face-to-face solicitation of money was found to be reasonable in *Krishna* because such solicitation might slow pedestrian traffic within the terminal, interfering with its transportation-related function. (But a *total ban* on *literature distribution* was found not to be even "reasonable" in *Krishna*.)

82. (A) Yes, probably. The Supreme Court has never spoken on whether a public school student's choice of clothing or other aspects of appearance is sufficiently "communicative" that the choice receives First Amendment protection. (The only relevant case is *Tinker v. Des Moines School District*, holding that the wearing of a black armband as a protest was expressive conduct.) However, a majority of the Court believes that "nude dancing" contains enough expressive content to be protected by the First Amendment. See *Barnes v. Glen Theatre*. Regardless of whether a typical student's selection of clothing would be found to be sufficiently communicative to be covered by the First Amendment, Alicia's selection here has a clear expressive component, in that she is trying to make a statement about her sexuality. Therefore, Alicia probably would receive some First Amendment protection for her choice of skirt (though, as described in the answer to the next part, the fact that she receives some protection does not mean that the Code is invalid as applied to her).

(B) Yes, probably. The first question is whether the restriction is "content neutral." If there were evidence that the skirt-length provision was enacted principally for the purpose of suppressing statements about the wearer's sexuality or sexual availability, then we would have a content-based regulation, which would have to survive strict scrutiny (which it probably could not). However, on the facts here, all aspects of the Code seem to be directed at the maintenance of discipline and order, and not at the suppression of any particular type of message. Therefore, the Code is probably content-neutral. If so, we apply the standard "track 2" analysis: the regulation must be *narrowly tailored* to serve a *significant governmental interest*, and must leave open *"alternative channels"* for communicating the information. Probably all parts of this test are satisfied. The school district certainly has a significant interest in maintaining discipline and avoiding distraction. Assuming that there is at least some evidence that short mini skirts would lead other students to gawk, make sexual propositions to the wearer, or otherwise be distracted, the requisite "narrow tailoring" is probably present. And there probably are adequate alternative channels for women such as Alicia to communicate their sexual availability (e.g., by making verbal statements of availability, by wearing tight-fitting sweaters, etc.).

83. Yes, probably. The first question is whether Joe is a *"public figure."* If he is a public figure, he may not be permitted to recover unless he shows "actual malice" on the part of the *Post*, i.e., that either the *Post* had knowledge that its statement about who did the shooting was false, or that the *Post* acted with "reckless disregard" of whether the statement was false or not. So if Joe is a public figure, then the judge's instruction is wrong. Joe might be held to be an "involuntary public figure" because of his involvement in this matter of obvious public interest; however, since he is not a criminal defendant, and since the Court has construed the "involuntary public figure" category narrowly, probably Joe does not fall into this category. Joe is certainly not a generally famous person (even locally), nor one who has voluntarily injected himself into a public controversy, so he probably doesn't fit into either of the other public figure categories recognized by the Court.

If Joe is in fact a "private figure," then the judge's charge is correct. Under *Gertz v. Robert Welch,* where P is neither a public official nor a public figure, there is no constitutional requirement that he prove that the defendant knew his statement to be false or recklessly disregarded the truth. (On the other hand, the state would not be permitted to grant Joe a recovery based on strict liability; the First Amendment requires that the *Post* be proven to be at least negligent, even in a suit brought by a private figure.)

84.   (A) Yes. On these facts, Kiddie World is probably not, strictly speaking, "obscene" under Supreme Court definitions. The reason is that mere nudity, without any attempt to portray sexual activity, is not considered "obscene." However, the state's interest in preventing the sexual exploitation and abuse of children is so strong that states may prohibit the sale, and even the private possession, of sexually explicit nude pictures of children, even though these are not strictly speaking "obscene." *Osborne v. Ohio.*

(B) No. The material here is almost certainly "obscene." Under *Miller v. California*, material is obscene if it depicts "patently offensive representations or descriptions of ultimate sex acts, normal or perverted. … " It must be the case that the average person, applying contemporary community standards, would find that the work taken as a whole appeals to the prurient interest, and that the work taken as a whole lacks serious literary, artistic, political or scientific value. These tests all seem to be satisfied by the material here. However, the mere ***private possession*** of obscene material by an adult may not be made criminal. *Stanley v. Georgia.* Therefore, even though the state might be able to punish the person who sold the magazine to Emilio, it may not punish Emilio for knowingly possessing the material in his house. (As noted in part (a), possession of material showing sexually explicit photos of children does not come within the purview of *Stanley.*)

86.   No. One may not be required to state in a loyalty oath that one has not performed a certain act (or that one will not perform it in the future) unless ***actual performance*** of that act would be grounds for discharge. One may not be discharged for membership in an organization advocating overthrow of the government or other illegality, unless one has ***knowledge*** of the organization's purpose and ***specific intent*** to further that purpose. Consequently, one may not be required to swear a blanket oath that one has not been a member of such an organization — language referring to the swearer's knowledge of the illegal purposes, and to her specific intent to further them, must be inserted into the oath. Since the oath here does not refer to Ramona's specific intent to use force to alter the Puerto Rican government, she cannot be penalized for refusing to sign it. See *Cole v. Richardson*.

87.   Yes, probably. When government attempts to deny a public job or benefit because of a person's speech- related activities, the level of judicial review depends on whether the speech related to matters of ***"public concern."*** If the speech did relate to matters of "public concern," then the Court gives something like strict scrutiny to the situation, striking a balance between the free speech rights of the employee and the state's interest as an employer in conducting its activities efficiently. *Connick v. Myers.* Here, the speech is clearly relating to a matter of public concern, i.e., whether the head of the department took a bribe. Since Sheryl was engaging in core political speech, her interest in being allowed to do so was a strong one. On the other side of the equation, Sheryl was a low-level clerk, not a policy-making official; therefore, her speech was unlikely to have created a severe additional threat to the department's efficiency, especially since other people inside and outside the department were undoubtedly discussing the same much-publicized issue anyway. *Rankin v. McPherson.* Consequently, a court would probably conclude that Sheryl's free speech interest outweighed the department's interest in maintaining smooth operations; if so, the court should order Sheryl reinstated.

By the way, it makes a difference that here, Sheryl's statement was ***not required as part of her job duties.*** *Garcetti v. Ceballos* establishes that where an employee speaks as part of her official duties, what she says ***gets no First Amendment protection at all.*** So if, say, Sheryl's official duties had included the obligation to make a report about any conflicts-of-interest she observed on the job, her statement, "Horace took money from Computer Systems in violation of our Department's conflict-of-interest rules," made in her officially-required report, would not get First Amendment protection, and Sheryl would now not be entitled to reinstatement. So it's only because Sheryl was speaking "as a citizen" (not as an employee) to her co-worker that she gets protection under *Connick v. Myers.*

Lastly, observe that because Sheryl was an at-will employee, she could be fired at any time for "no reason"; even so, under *Connick* she had a First Amendment right not to be fired for the ***particular*** reason that she was exercising her free speech rights.

88.   Yes, because the immigration condition is an unconstitutional condition. Government is free to set up a program subsidizing a particular private activity, and when government does so, it is free to prohibit the ***subsidy dollars themselves*** from being used for particular expressive activities opposed by government. *Rust v. Sullivan.* This right includes even the right to place viewpoint-based restrictions on the recipient's expressive activities conducted with the subsidy dollars. *Id.* So here, Calizona *would* have been free to say, for instance, "Receipt of the subsidy is conditioned on the recipient's promise that it will not use any of the grant monies to advocate for immigration reform." But this power of government to put conditions on how the subsidy funds will be used does ***not*** include the right to impose conditions that "seek to ***leverage funding*** to ***regulate speech outside the contours*** of the [government-subsidized] ***program itself.***" *Agency for Int'l Dev. v. Alliance for Open Soc'y Int'l, Inc.* (2013). When government tries to do such a "leveraging of funding" — by restricting recipients' expressive activities not carried out through use of the subsidy dollars — it violates the potential recipient's freedom of expression. *Id.*

This forbidden "leveraging" is what Calizona is trying to do here. The state is *not* saying, "The $100,000 can't be used for advocacy of immigration reform"; it's saying, "If you take the $100,000, then you must give up your right to use *even privately-raised funds* to advocate for immigration reform." Speech urging immigration reform is clearly "outside the contours" of the GOTVSA program, since the program's purpose is solely to increase in-state voter registration and turnout, not to influence national immigration policies. The case is therefore like *FCC v. League of Women Voters* (where the Court held that Congress couldn't condition funding to public broadcast stations on the stations' promise not to do editorializing even with private funds) and *A.I.D., supra* (where the Court held that Congress couldn't condition funding to combat HIV/AIDS on the recipient's promise to officially oppose prostitution).

90. Yes. The First Amendment is not violated when a reporter is required to testify before a grand jury concerning information obtained from confidential sources during newsgathering. In fact, reporters are not even entitled to a ***qualified privilege*** to refuse to identify their sources or information received from those sources — thus a reporter, like any other citizen, may be required to divulge information that could be obtained by police or prosecutors from other sources. *Branzburg v. Hayes.* (Over half of the states have enacted ***statutes*** that grant reporters a privilege against disclosure of confidential sources or information. If such a "shield law" existed here, it would prevent Roger from being held in contempt on these facts.)

91. (A) The Establishment Clause. The Establishment Clause of the First Amendment prohibits any law "respecting an establishment of religion." In a general sense, its purpose is to erect a wall between church and state.

(B) No, probably. The Establishment Clause prevents government from ***sponsoring*** or ***endorsing*** one religion over another, or religion over non-religion. A display of religiously-oriented materials at holiday time might indeed be found to constitute an implicit endorsement or sponsorship by the government of religion or of a religious message. In evaluating whether a particular display or ceremony violates the Establishment Clause, the Court generally uses a three-part test (derived from *Lemon v. Kurtzman*). Only if the action satisfies ***each*** of the following conditions will it be valid: (1) it must have a ***secular legislative purpose***; (2) its principal or ***primary effect*** must neither advance nor inhibit religion; and (3) it must not foster an ***excessive governmental entanglement*** with religion.

On facts very similar to these, the Court held by a 5-4 vote that the display did *not* violate any of these three tests. *Lynch v. Donnelly.* Here, a court would probably find a secular purpose (to celebrate the holiday, which is a secular government-observed holiday in addition to being one with religious significance). The primary effect of the display would probably not be found to benefit religion in general or Christianity specifically (since the non-religious "holiday spirit" was also being benefitted, and any advancement of religion was somewhat indirect). And there would probably not be found to be undue entanglement between government and religious institutions, since government basically left the space available and allowed citizens to do what they wished without further government intervention. The most important factor would probably be *context*: here, there were at least some non-religiously-oriented items in the display (e.g., the banner, and the reindeer), so that a reasonable observer would probably not conclude that the display was, overall, a government endorsement of religion. (Observe, however, that *Lynch* was a 5-4 decision, and even a small variation in the items displayed, or in how they came to be displayed, might have resulted in a shift of one vote and thus a change in result.)

92. Yes. The facts are similar to those in *Larson v. Valente*. The Court held that this type of scheme benefited one religion or group of religions over another. Therefore, the Court applied ***strict scrutiny***, not the *Lemon* three-prong test. Such a preference of one religious group over others could be sustained only if it was "justified by a compelling governmental interest and … closely fitted to further that interest." Although the state may have an interest in guarding against "abusive solicitation practices," the means selected here are not "closely fitted" to furthering that interest, since there is no reason to believe that the likelihood of solicitation abuse is closely related to the ratio of member contributions to total contributions.

The conclusion that the legislature has "played favorites" here is buttressed by the evidence that the legislature knew it was disfavoring Jehovah's Witnesses and other residential-door-bell-ringers. If there were evidence that the disfavoring of Jehovah's Witnesses was entirely *incidental*, perhaps strict scrutiny would not be called for.

93.   No, probably. The main issue is whether the program here has the "primary effect" of advancing religion (since if it does, it's a violation of the Establishment Clause). The facts here are quite similar to those in *Zelman v. Simmons-Harris*, where a bare majority of the Court held that the program was constitutional because any funding that went to religious education resulted from the "deliberate choices of numerous individual recipients," not from any legislative desire to aid religion. One difference between the facts here and those in *Zelman* is that in *Zelman*, there were other "alternative" educational programs paid for by the state that didn't even arguably aid religion (e.g., special public magnet schools and tutoring programs), and these alternative programs had more participants than the private-school-voucher program — so viewed in the aggregate, the total alternative programs didn't primarily advance religion. Therefore, it's possible that a court would rule that the absence of such alternatives here makes a difference. But probably, the result here would be the same as in *Zelman* — because (a) each parent is making her own decision about whether to use the voucher at a religious or non-religious school, (b) the voucher program is open to students and private-schools regardless of whether they do or don't have a religious affiliation; and (c) there's no evidence that the legislature was intending to advance religion, the program will probably pass muster.

94.   (A) The Free Exercise Clause. The First Amendment bars government from making any law "prohibiting the free exercise" of religion. The clause can apply to regulations that are directed at religious beliefs or, more commonly, directed at religiously-oriented *conduct*. Here, we have a regulation that is directed at conduct (the consumption of a particular beverage).

(B) Strict scrutiny. Where government takes an action whose *purpose* is to forbid or interfere with particular conduct *because* the conduct is dictated by a religious belief, the government action is strictly scrutinized and almost always struck down. Here, all the evidence is that the Pacifica Town Council was motivated principally by members' dislike of the Weejun religion and its practitioners, not by a generally-applicable dislike of drunkenness. The facts are roughly analogous to those of *Church of the Lukumi Babalu Aye, Inc. v. Hialeah*, where the Court struck down a ban on ritual animal sacrifice on the theory that the ban was motivated by hostility to practitioners of the Santeria religion. When the Court is deciding whether governmental regulation is designed for the purpose of interfering with a particular religious practice, the extent to which the ordinance is of "general applicability" will be considered; here, the ordinance speaks solely of nectaria, not other beverages of equal alcohol content, and the ordinance affects nobody but practitioners of Weejun. Therefore, a court would almost certainly conclude that there was an intent to interfere with the religious practice, not merely an unintended effect upon religion. Consequently, strict scrutiny must be used.

(C) No. Strict scrutiny in the free exercise context, as in other constitutional contexts, means that the regulation will be struck down unless it is *necessary* to achieve a *compelling* governmental interest. The government's interest here in cutting down on public drunkenness might be "compelling," but the means selected are certainly not "necessary" to achieving that end. For instance, the town could simply have banned public drunkenness, or banned all substances of sufficiently high alcohol content that were very likely to produce drunkenness. The ordinance here is extremely underinclusive (it deals with only one source of drunkenness), demonstrating that it is not "drawn in narrow terms" to accomplish the objective.

95. Yes, probably. The general rule today is as set forth in *Employment Div. v. Smith*: "the right of free exercise does not relieve an individual of the obligation to comply with a *valid and neutral law* of *general applicability* on the ground that the law proscribes (or prescribes) conduct that his religion prescribes (or proscribes)." Applying this principle would mean that Priscilla is not constitutionally entitled to an exemption. But a pre-*Smith* case that is somewhat on point has never been explicitly overruled post-*Smith*, and would probably be re-affirmed today. That case is *Wisconsin v. Yoder*, where the Court held that a state must exempt Amish teenage students from the requirement of attending school until the age of 16. If the case arose today, the Supreme Court would likely preserve *Yoder* by carving out a narrow exception to *Smith* to allow a free exercise claim by parents who want to home-school their children for religious reasons.

96. No. Where government enacts a generally-applicable ***criminal prohibition*** on a certain type of activity, and government does not intend to burden religious beliefs, government does not have to grant an exemption to those whose religious beliefs or practices are burdened by the prohibition. The facts are analogous to those of *Employment Division v. Smith*, where a state was allowed to refuse to grant American Indians an exemption from the ban on peyote, even though use of the drug was a central part of their religious rites. *Smith* establishes that government does not have to engage in any ***balancing*** of its interests in its prohibition against the burden on the individual's religious beliefs — so long as the ban is generally applicable, and not motivated by a governmental desire to affect religion, the law is fully enforceable no matter how large the burden on the plaintiff or how small the benefit to the state. Therefore, even though an exemption would not meaningfully interfere with the goal of safeguarding Great White Sharks, no exemption needs to be given.

98. (A) That Paul lacks standing.

(B) Yes. As a general matter, federal taxpayers do not have standing to assert that taxpayers' funds in general are being improperly spent. There is an extremely narrow exception if plaintiff is able to show: (1) that the federal action complained of is an exercise of Congress' power under the Taxing and Spending Clause; and (2) that the challenged action violates some specific constitutional limitation imposed on the Taxing and Spending power. *Flast v. Cohen.* It is highly unlikely that Paul can satisfy either of these requirements for the exception. The President's dispatch of troops presumably relies upon his Commander in Chief powers, and certainly does not rely upon Congress' Taxing and Spending power. Furthermore, the requirement that only Congress may declare war is not a specific constitutional limitation on the Taxing and Spending power, merely an unrelated constitutional limit. Therefore, the general rule that there is no taxpayer standing would apply.

99. No. The Supreme Court has never been willing to recognize standing on the part of individuals *as citizens* to object to unlawful or unconstitutional conduct. This refusal is based on the view that one citizen's interest in lawful government is no different from that of any other citizen, and that an individual litigant relying upon citizenship has not shown the ***"individualized"*** injury-in-fact required for standing. See, e.g., *Schlesinger v. Reservists to Stop the War.*

100. Yes, probably. A federal-court plaintiff must show some concrete, *"individuated,"* "injury in fact." But this harm need ***not*** be ***economic*** in nature; harms to a person's esthetic enjoyment of nature, for example, will suffice. See, e.g., *Sierra Club v. Morton* (giving people who use national forests standing to protest construction of recreation area in the national forest). The threatened harm must be "actual or imminent." Since Penzel asserts that he will walk within one of the affected areas within the next year, the "imminence" requirement is probably satisfied. The fact that there are a large number of people suffering or likely to suffer the same harm as alleged by the plaintiff does not by itself remove standing from the plaintiff.

101. Yes. An association or organization has standing not only where its own interests are at stake, but in some cases where it is suing solely as a ***representative*** of its members. An association has standing to sue on behalf of its members if three conditions are met: (1) its members would otherwise have standing to sue ***in their own right***; (2) the interests the association seeks to protect are ***germane*** to the organization's ***purpose***; and (3) neither the claim asserted nor the relief requested requires the participation of ***individual members*** in the lawsuit. *Hunt v. Washington Apple Advertising Comm.* Here, all three of these requirements seem to be met: the prior question illustrates that individual forest-lovers would have standing; protection of the forests certainly is the core purpose of the organization; and there seems to be no reason why individuals rather than the organization need to participate in the lawsuit.

102. Yes, probably. One of the requirements for standing is that the challenged action must be the *"cause-in-fact"* of the injury. A sub-aspect of the "cause in fact" requirement is that the litigant must show that the relief being sought, if granted, has a reasonable likelihood of ***redressing*** the injury. The problem here is that even if the EPA was completely wrong in the first instance, it is far from clear that a victory by the plaintiff will result in the stadium being built in Yonkers rather than Rutherford. The ultimate decision is up to Brensteiner. Since Brensteiner has already bought the property in Rutherford and commenced construction, it is very unlikely that a declaratory judgment that the EPA should not have required an EIS for Yonkers will cause Brensteiner to stop construction and start it instead in Yonkers. Therefore, even though the other requirements of standing are met (Steve's loss of the ability to watch Strikers games near his house is certainly an "injury-in-fact" that is sufficiently concrete, individuated and imminent), the fact that victory in the suit will not redress the harm is fatal to Steve's standing. See, e.g., *Simon v. Eastern Ky. Welfare Rights Organization* (where IRS rules reduced the amount of free medical care that hospitals must donate to the poor in order to get tax breaks, a suit by poor people attacking those rules does not have standing, because the hospitals might not give the free medical care even if the rules were struck down).

103. No, probably. As a general rule, a litigant may normally not assert the constitutional rights of ***third persons not now before the court***. This is the rule of constitutional *"jus tertii."* Fred may have been injured "in fact" by the absence of other blacks on the force. But the Equal Protection Clause protects only those applicants who would have been hired had there not been intentional discrimination. Since Fred was not part of this group, the fact that he may have suffered some incidental injury is not enough to give him standing — he must assert that the challenged governmental action violates ***his*** rights, not the rights of some other person not now before the court. (There are some important exceptions to the rule against third-party standing, such as where there is some legal restriction preventing the third party from exercising his own constitutional rights. But here, black applicants whom the department intentionally declined to hire because of their race clearly could bring their own suit, so neither this nor any of the other exceptions to the rule against third-party standing applies.)

104. (A) That the action is now moot. A case is moot if it raised a justiciable controversy at the time the complaint was filed, but ***events occurring after the filing*** have deprived the litigant of an ongoing stake in the controversy.

(B) Yes. Where the intervening event is the defendant's ***voluntary*** cessation of the conduct complained of, this may or may not be enough to render the case moot. If the facts show that the conduct claimed to be illegal is ***very unlikely*** to recur, then the voluntary cessation usually ***is*** enough to make the case moot. That is probably what the court would find to be the situation here. Therefore, the OCA's desire to obtain a favorable decision that it may use as precedent elsewhere will not be enough to give it an ongoing stake in the controversy, and the action will be dismissed.

105. (A) The Eleventh Amendment. The Eleventh Amendment excludes from the federal judicial power any suit "against any one of the States by Citizens of another State or by Citizens or Subjects of any Foreign State."

(B) Yes. Although on its face the Eleventh Amendment does not seem to prohibit federal-court suits against a state by a citizen of that state, the amendment has been interpreted to ban these suits as well as those by a citizen of one state against another state. See *Hans v. Louisiana.* The Eleventh Amendment applies only to suits for damages (as opposed to suits for injunctions), but the facts make it clear that money damage relief is what is sought here. Therefore, the Eleventh Amendment defense will be successful.

106. (A) The Eleventh Amendment.

(B) Yes. *Seminole Tribe v. Florida* holds that except with respect to suits brought under federal statutes supported by Congress' power to enforce the post-Civil War Amendments, Congress cannot remove the state immunity provided by the Eleventh Amendment. Therefore, even though Congress has clearly said that a state may be sued for damages for violating the copyright act, this statement of congressional intent is without effect, and the Eleventh Amendment applies to bar the suit. (But PC Word Corp. could get an *injunction* against the governor prohibiting further violations, since the Eleventh Amendment does not apply to injunction suits against state officials; see *Ex parte Young*.)

107. (A) That the issue posed here is a non-justiciable political question.

(B) Yes, probably. The Court will regard as a non-justiciable political question any issue whose determination is committed by the Constitution to ***another branch*** of government (i.e., the executive or the legislative). There is an excellent chance that the Court will conclude that the decision about whether a person elected to Congress meets the three standing requirements is committed by the Constitution to the House itself. The Court would point to Art. I, §5, which provides that "each House shall be the Judge of the Elections, Returns and Qualifications of its own members. ... " In *Powell v. McCormack*, the Court held that the issue of whether the House could refuse to seat a Congressman who met the three standing requirements but who had, in the House's opinion, committed other infractions, was ***not*** committed by the Constitution to the House, and could be heard by the Court. But it seems probable that a suit involving the narrow issue of whether a person met all of the three requirements expressly listed in Art. I, §2 is committed to the House and is thus non-justiciable (though the Court has never explicitly decided that question).

MULTIPLE-CHOICE QUESTIONS

Here are 30 multiple-choice questions, in a Multi-state-Bar-Exam style. These questions are taken from *"The Finz Multistate Method,"* a compendium of 1100 questions in the Multistate subjects (*Contracts*, *Torts*, *Property*, *Evidence*, *Criminal Law* and *Constitutional Law*) written by the late Professor Steven Finz and published by Wolters Kluwer Law & Business. To learn more about this book and other study aids, go to **www.aspenlaw.com** and click on "Education."

1. The feral tusker is an unusual species of wild pig which is found in the state of Tuscalona, having evolved from several strains of domestic swine which escaped from the farms of early Tuscalona settlers. A Tuscalona state law declares the feral tusker to be an endangered species, and prohibits the killing or shooting of any feral tusker within the state. The Tusker National Park was established by the federal government in order to preserve plants and animals native to the region, and is located entirely within the state of Tuscalona. The feral tusker is so hardy that it has begun to displace other wildlife in the Tusker National Park. Because the feral tusker is actually descended from European stock, the United States Department of the Interior has contracted with Termine, a resident of another state, to kill all feral tuskers living within Tusker National Park. The contract with Termine is specifically authorized by federal statutes regulating the operation of national parks.

   If Termine is prosecuted by the state of Tuscalona for violating the law which prohibits the killing of feral tuskers, which of the following is Termine's strongest argument in defense against that prosecution?

   (A) Only the federal government can declare a species to be endangered.
   (B) As applied, the Tuscalona statute unduly interferes with interstate commerce.
   (C) As applied, the Tuscalona statute violates the Obligation of Contracts Clause of the United States Constitution.
   (D) As applied, the Tuscalona statute violates the Supremacy Clause of the United States Constitution.

2. Congress passes a law regulating the wholesale and retail prices of "every purchase of an automobile in the United States." The strongest argument in support of the constitutionality of such a statute is that

   (A) taken as a whole, the domestic purchases and sales of such products affect interstate commerce.
   (B) the United States Constitution expressly authorizes Congress to pass laws for the general welfare.
   (C) Congress has the authority to regulate the prices of products purchased and sold because commerce includes buying and selling.
   (D) Congress has the right to regulate interstate transportation and the importation of products from abroad.

Questions 3-4 are based on the following fact situation.

A federal statute directs payment of federal funds to states for use in the improvement and expansion of state hospital facilities. The terms of the statute provide that "No state shall award a contract for hospital improvement or expansion financed in whole or in part by funds received under this section unless said contract requires that the contractor pay its employees a minimum wage of $12 per hour." The statute also says that any private individual who is not paid $12 per hour for work on such a hospital-improvement contract can bring suit in federal court against a state receiving funds under the statute, for any shortfall below $12 in the wages received by the worker from the contractor.

The state of Calizona contracted with Bilder for the construction of a new wing on the Calizona State Hospital, after receiving funds for that purpose under the federal statute. The contract did not require Bilder to pay its employees a minimum wage of $12 per hour.

3. For this question, assume that upon learning the above facts, federal officials demanded that the state of Calizona either modify its contract with Bilder or return the funds received under the statute. (All federal funds for hospital expansion represent less than 1% of total state expenditures for the year in question.) When Calizona refused, the federal government sued the state of Calizona in a federal court for return of the money. In the action by the United States against the state of Calizona, the court should find for

   (A) the state of Calizona, because fixing the minimum wage of employees is a traditional state function.
   (B) the state of Calizona, because the regulation of hospitals and of construction practices are traditional state functions.
   (C) the United States, because Congress has the power to regulate the way in which federal funds are spent.

(D) the United States, because some of the materials used in hospital construction are traded in interstate commerce.

4.   Assume for the purpose of this question that several employees of Bilder who received less than $12 per hour while working on the Calizona State Hospital expansion instituted an action for damages against the state of Calizona in a federal court, and that the state of Calizona moved to dismiss their cause of action. Which of the following is the best reason for dismissal of the suit?

(A) The state of Calizona is immune from such an action under the Eleventh Amendment to the United States Constitution.

(B) No federal question is involved.

(C) The state of Calizona did not employ the plaintiffs.

(D) The plaintiffs voluntarily accepted the wage which Bilder paid them.

5.   The zingbird is a rare species of quail found only in the state of Capricorn. Because its flesh is tasty, it was hunted nearly to extinction until thirty years ago. At that time, the state of Capricorn instituted conservation and game management programs designed to preserve the zingbird. These programs included the establishment of zingbird breeding preserves, the employment of ornithologists to study zingbird habits, the passage of laws restricting the hunting of zingbirds, and the employment of game wardens to enforce those laws. The expense of maintaining the programs was financed in part by the sale of hunting licenses. A recent statute passed by the Capricorn state legislature fixes the fee for a hunting license at $10 per year for Capricorn residents, and $20 per year for non-residents. Gunn, a hunter who resides outside the state of Capricorn, was arrested in Capricorn and prosecuted for hunting without a license in violation of the statute. He defended by asserting that the statute is unconstitutional because the hunting license fee for non-residents is higher than for residents.

Which of the following correctly identifies the clause or clauses of the United States Constitution violated by the Capricorn hunting license statute?

I.   The Privileges and Immunities Clause of Article IV.

II. The Privileges or Immunities Clause of the Fourteenth Amendment.

(A) I only.

(B) II only.

(C) I and II.

(D) Neither I nor II.

6.   An organization called the National Anarchist Party (NAP) asserts that government should be abolished. NAP's slogan is, "What if they made a law and nobody obeyed?" Its published literature urges all persons to violate laws, no matter how logical they might seem, and in this way to help bring about the abolition of government.

While in law school, Arthur joined the NAP for the purpose of acquiring material for a book which he was writing. Although he had heard that the NAP was a dangerous and subversive organization, Arthur thought its members to be fools, and believed their slogan and literature to be too ridiculous to ever convince anybody of anything. So that he could have access to NAP records, he volunteered to be Party Secretary. In his capacity as such, he frequently kept minutes of meetings, which he then distributed to all members. Arthur knew that others in the Party hierarchy frequently wrote and distributed handbills to members and non-members. All of these handbills contained the NAP slogan and urged the deliberate violation of laws. Arthur never intended to help convince anyone to believe in or act on the group's mission to abolish government. Eventually, Arthur wrote a book about the NAP entitled "The Lunatic Fringe." When he finished law school and applied for admission to the bar, his application was rejected. The state bar examiners stated that the only reason for the rejection of Arthur's application was a state law which provided that "No person shall be licensed to practice law who has belonged to any organization advocating unlawful activity." If Arthur brings an appropriate judicial proceeding for an order directing the state bar examiners to admit him to practice law, should Arthur win?

(A) Yes, because he joined the NAP for the purpose of gathering information for a book which he was writing.

(B) Yes, because he did not intend for the NAP to succeed in convincing people to violate laws.

(C) No, because he knew that the NAP advocated unlawful conduct when he joined the organization.

(D) No, because he played an active role in the NAP's activities.

7. A statute of the state of Mammoth requires pay television stations to set aside one hour of air time per week to be made available without charge for the broadcasting of spiritually uplifting programs produced by recognized religious organizations. The statute further provides that air time thereby made available shall be equally divided among Jewish, Roman Catholic, and Protestant organizations. A religious organization known as the American Buddhist League produced a spiritually uplifting program, but was advised by several pay television stations that it could not be broadcast under the statute. The American Buddhist League has instituted a proceeding in federal court challenging the constitutional validity of the Mammoth statute.

The clearest reason for finding that the statute is unconstitutional is that it violates

(A) the Free Exercise Clause, in that it treats religions unequally.

(B) the Establishment Clause, in that it is not closely fitted to furthering a compelling governmental interest.

(C) the Equal Protection Clause, in that it applies only to pay television stations.

(D) the Supremacy Clause, in that broadcasting is an area already subject to extensive federal regulation.

8. A federal statute prohibits male employees of the United States Census Bureau from wearing beards or moustaches, although no such prohibition exists for employees of other federal agencies. Parsons, an at-will employee of the Census Bureau, was discharged from his employment for violating the statute by refusing to remove his moustache. If Parsons asserts a claim on the ground that the statute was invalid, his most effective argument is that the law

    (A) denies him a privilege or immunity of national citizenship.
    (B) invidiously discriminates against him in violation of the Fifth Amendment to the United States Constitution.
    (C) invidiously discriminates against him in violation of the Fourteenth Amendment to the United States Constitution.
    (D) deprives him of a property right without just compensation.

9. Congress passes the Federal Humane Act prohibiting the interstate transportation of dogs for use in dogfighting competitions or exhibitions. Kennel is prosecuted in a federal court for violating the Federal Humane Act, and defends by asserting that the statute is not constitutionally valid because it was enacted for purposes which were entirely noncommercial. The most effective argument in support of the constitutionality of the statute is that

    (A) Congress is empowered to prohibit cruelty to animals under the federal police power.
    (B) the power to regulate interstate commerce includes the power to completely exclude specified items from interstate commerce without regard to congressional motives.
    (C) under the "Cooley Doctrine," the federal and state governments have concurrent power to prohibit cruelty to animals.
    (D) acts of Congress are presumptively constitutional.

10. Congress enacts the Truth in Selling Act, requiring that certain disclosures be made by sellers in interstate sales transactions, and fixing civil damages for failure to make the requisite disclosures. The Act authorizes parties allegedly damaged by violations of the Truth in Selling Act to sue in either state or federal courts. The act further provides that any decision of a lower state court construing a section of the Truth in Selling Act may be appealed directly to the United States Supreme Court.

    The provision of this statute which authorizes appeal of a lower state court decision directly to the United States Supreme Court, is

    (A) constitutional, because Congress has the power to regulate interstate commerce.
    (B) constitutional, because Congress may establish the manner in which the appellate jurisdiction of the United States Supreme Court is exercised.

(C) unconstitutional, because Article III of the United States Constitution does not authorize the United States Supreme Court to directly review the decisions of lower state courts.

(D) unconstitutional, because it infringes the sovereign right of a state to review decisions of its own lower courts.

11. A state statute provides that any married persons who engage in certain "unnatural" sex acts as described by the statute (e.g., contact between one person's mouth and the other's genitalia) are guilty of second degree sodomy, and that unmarried persons who engage in those acts are guilty of first degree sodomy. John and Mary Dalton, a married couple, were prosecuted for second degree sodomy after engaging in the prohibited acts with each other in a friend's home while at a party. In defense, they asserted that the statute was invalid under the United States Constitution.

The most effective argument in support of the assertion that the statute was unconstitutional is that it violated the Dalton's constitutional right to

(A) substantive due process.
(B) procedural due process.
(C) equal protection.
(D) freedom of expression.

12. The state of Ascaloosa requires persons applying for state welfare assistance, driving licenses, admission to the state university, or certain other state benefits to list their federal social security numbers as part of their applications. In this connection, Ascaloosa state agencies refer to an applicant's social security number as his or her "Central File Number." Lawrence, who has not applied for any such state benefits, has brought an action in a federal court against certain specified state officials for an order enjoining them from using social security numbers in this fashion. In support of his position, Lawrence argues that at some time almost all citizens of the state apply for some form of state benefit, and that the compilation of a central file on each citizen of the state is likely to have a chilling effect on the exercise of rights granted by the First Amendment to the United States Constitution.

The clearest reason for the dismissal of Lawrence's suit is that

(A) the action is unripe.
(B) the question presented is moot.
(C) under the Eleventh Amendment to the United States Constitution state officials are immune to lawsuits of this kind.
(D) the creation of a central file on each person applying for state benefits involves the resolution of political questions.

Questions 13 and 14 are based on the following fact situation.

Fraser City is located in the state of North Vellum, three miles from its border with the neighboring state of South Vellum. Fraser City hospitals recently treated several persons for food poisoning caused by the consumption of tainted meat. As a result, the Fraser City Council passed an ordinance prohibiting the sale in Fraser City of meat processed at a processing plant not certified by the Fraser City Health Department. Butch, who operated a retail grocery store in Fraser City, was arrested after selling meat to an undercover police officer. Because the meat had been processed at a plant in South Vellum which had not been inspected or certified by the Fraser City Health Department, Butch was charged with violating the ordinance and prosecuted in the Fraser City Municipal Court. Butch admitted violating the ordinance, but argued that the ordinance was not valid under the United States Constitution.

13. Does the Fraser City Municipal Court have jurisdiction to determine the constitutionality of the ordinance?

   (A) No, if determining the constitutionality of the ordinance requires interpretation of the United States Constitution.
   (B) No, because Butch will not have standing to challenge the constitutionality of the ordinance until he has been convicted of violating it.
   (C) Yes, because any court has the power to interpret the United States Constitution.
   (D) Yes, only if the Fraser City Municipal Court is a state court under the laws of North Vellum.

14. Assume for the purpose of this question only that a person with standing to do so sues in an appropriate federal court for an order enjoining enforcement of the Fraser City ordinance on the ground that it is invalid under the Commerce Clause of the United States Constitution. Which of the following is the best argument in support of granting the injunction?

   (A) As applied, the ordinance interferes with interstate commerce.
   (B) Regulation of the purity of food is not a matter which is of local concern.
   (C) The concurrent power to regulate commerce does not apply to municipalities.
   (D) There are ways of regulating the purity of food sold in Fraser City that are equally effective and less burdensome on commerce.

15. While trying to arrest an unarmed bank robber, Maple City police officer Orville fired a shot which killed an uninvolved bystander. When Orville returned to the police station, Captain, his supervisor, told him that he was suspended from duties without pay effective immediately, and took from him his gun and badge. Orville subsequently instituted an action for an order directing Captain to restore him to the job of police officer.

   Which of the following additional facts or inferences, if it were the only one true, would be most likely to result in a DENIAL of the relief sought by Orville?

(A) A Police Department hearing was scheduled for the following week to determine the propriety of Orville's conduct, and Orville would be restored to his position and compensated for lost pay if he was found to be without fault.

(B) Maple City Police Department policy prohibited police officers from firing their guns in attempting to arrest unarmed persons.

(C) Orville's killing of the bystander amounted to involuntary manslaughter.

(D) The Maple City Police Department Manual of Procedure called for immediate suspension of any police officer whose conduct while attempting to effect an arrest resulted in the death of an uninvolved bystander.

16. In which of the following fact situations has there most clearly been a violation of the plaintiff's rights under the Fourteenth Amendment to the United States Constitution?

(A) Plaintiff is a black person whose application for state employment was rejected because he failed to pass the state Civil Service examination. Statistics reveal that 10% of the black applicants and 60% of the white applicants who have taken the exam have passed it.

(B) Plaintiff is an American of Mexican descent who was denied admission to a privately-owned hospital solely because of her ethnic background, but who received competent professional treatment at a state hospital instead.

(C) Plaintiff is a Jewish person who resided in a federally operated housing project, and who was excluded from a prayer breakfast held by the federal agency which ran the project solely because of his religion.

(D) Plaintiff is a woman whose application for employment as a deputy sheriff was rejected by the county solely because of her sex.

Questions 17-18 are based on the following fact situation.

A state statute known as the Unlawful Assembly Law contains the following provisions:

Section I — it shall be a misdemeanor for any group of three or more persons to gather on a public sidewalk and to deliberately conduct themselves in a manner which is offensive to passersby.

Section II — it shall be a misdemeanor for any group of three or more persons to engage in a public demonstration on a public sidewalk in front of any state government office during regular business hours unless said demonstration is related to matters under consideration by officials employed in said government office.

When the governor of the state refused to grant a pardon to a college student who had been convicted of destroying state college property during a campus protest, members of a student organization decided to disrupt state government operations by conducting a loud and boisterous demonstration outside a state government office building which they selected at random. About thirty members gathered on the sidewalk outside the building with noisemakers and musical instruments, and began marching while making a loud and disturbing noise. Several persons who had business inside the building were unable to get past the crowd of demonstrators to enter. Demos, one of the participants, was arrested for marching and shouting obscene words which many passersby found offensive.

17. Assume that Demos is prosecuted for violating Section I of the Unlawful Assembly Law, and that he defends by asserting that the section is overbroad. The court should find him

(A) guilty, because his conduct was in fact offensive to passersby.

(B) guilty, only if the reasonable passerby would have been offended by Demos's conduct.

(C) guilty, only if the reasonable person in Demos's position would have known that his conduct would be offensive to passersby.

(D) not guilty, if some of the conduct which the law prohibited is constitutionally protected.

18. Assume that Demos is prosecuted for violating Section II of the Unlawful Assembly Law, and that he defends by asserting that the section violates the First Amendment to the United States Constitution. The court should find him

(A) not guilty, because the public sidewalk in front of a government building is traditionally regarded as a public forum.

(B) not guilty, because Section II unlawfully regulates the subject matter of demonstrations conducted outside government offices.

(C) guilty, because the state has a compelling interest in the orderly conduct of governmental affairs.

(D) guilty, because the demonstration in which Demos participated kept persons with lawful business from entering government offices to transact it.

19. Assume that the Hawk Party and the Dove Party are the major American political parties. In a certain presidential election, relations between the United States and the republic of Orinoco were the basis of a substantial disagreement between the candidates, each supporting the view of his political party. Bight, the Hawk Party candidate, had already served one term as president, but was defeated by Gentle, the Dove Party candidate. After taking office, President Gentle communicated with Henderson, who was serving as ambassador to Orinoco by appointment of President Bight with the advice and consent of the Senate. President Gentle demanded that Henderson either agree to support the foreign policy contained in the Dove Party platform or resign. When Henderson refused to do either, President Gentle told him that he was dismissed from the office of ambassador.

Given the facts, did President Gentle have the power to remove Henderson from office?

(A) Yes, because ideological differences constitute cause for dismissal from ambassadorial office.

(B) Yes, because the president has the power to dismiss ambassadors without cause.

(C) No, because an ambassador appointed with the advice and consent of the Senate cannot be dismissed from office without the advice and consent of the Senate.

(D) No, because removal of an ambassador is a *de facto* withdrawal of diplomatic relations with a foreign power.

Questions 20-21 are based on the following fact situation.

The Young Trailblazers is a youth organization with chapters and members in all fifty states. Concentrating on what it calls "the outdoor experience," the organization attempts to teach its members to love all forms of life. According to the bylaws of the Young Trailblazers, membership is open to all white children between the ages of eight and fourteen years. Penny, a twelve-year-old black child, applied for membership in the Young Trailblazers at the joint request of the Pintada state attorney general and the United States Department of Justice. The Young Trailblazers rejected her application solely on the basis of her race, advising her in writing that membership was open only to white children.

A federal statute makes it a crime for an organization with members in more than one state to deny membership to any person on the basis of that person's race. A statute of the state of Pintada makes it a crime to violate a right conferred on any person by the Fourteenth Amendment to the United States Constitution.

20. Is the Young Trailblazers guilty of violating the Pintada state statute?

(A) Yes, because the policy of The Young Trailblazers resulted in a denial of Penny's right to equal protection.

(B) Yes, because the policy of the Young Trailblazers resulted in a denial of Penny's right to the privileges and immunities of citizenship.

(C) Yes, because the policy of the Young Trailblazers resulted in a denial of Penny's right to substantive due process.

(D) No, because the Young Trailblazers is a private organization.

21. Assume that the Young Trailblazers is prosecuted in a federal court for violation of the federal statute, and the Young Trailblazers asserts that the statute is invalid under the United States Constitution. Which of the following would be the prosecutor's most effective argument in supporting the constitutional validity of the federal statute?

(A) The policy of The Young Trailblazers violates the spirit of the Commerce Clause.

(B) The policy of The Young Trailblazers establishes a badge of servitude in violation of the spirit of the Thirteenth Amendment.

(C) The United States Supreme Court has found racial discrimination to violate the United States Constitution.

(D) Racial discrimination is inimical to the general welfare of the citizens of the United States.

22. Mag was prosecuted in the Municipal Court of the city of New Morris for selling an obscene magazine. At his trial, the jury found the following by special verdict:

    (1) Applying standards of the average person residing in the city of New Morris, the magazine taken as a whole appealed to a prurient interest in sex.
    (2) Applying standards of the average person residing in the United States, the magazine taken as a whole did not appeal to a prurient interest in sex.
    (3) The magazine depicted sexual conduct in a way which was offensive to contemporary standards existing in the city of New Morris.
    (4) The magazine did not depict sexual conduct in a way which was offensive to contemporary standards existing in the United States in general.
    (5) Taken as a whole, the magazine had serious literary value.

    Based upon the jury's special verdict, Mag was found guilty. If Mag appeals his conviction on the ground that it violates the First Amendment to the United States Constitution, his conviction should be

    (A) reversed, because the magazine was found to have serious literary value.
    (B) reversed, because applying a national standard, the magazine did not appeal to a prurient interest in sex.
    (C) affirmed, because, applying a contemporary community standard, the magazine depicted sexual conduct in a manner which was offensive.
    (D) affirmed, because, applying a contemporary community standard, the magazine appealed to a prurient interest in sex.

23. After examining studies indicating that chewing gum was directly related to the incidence of tooth decay, the legislature of the state of Minnitonka enacted a law prohibiting the advertising of chewing gum in all media. Which of the following is the clearest reason for holding the law to be unconstitutional?

    (A) A state may not interfere with commercial speech.
    (B) The sale of chewing gum frequently involves interstate commerce.
    (C) The law imposes a prior restraint on publication.
    (D) There are substantially less restrictive ways of protecting the public against tooth decay which would be equally effective.

24. Assume that Congress enacted a statute making education through the 12th grade compulsory. Which one of the following facts or inferences, if it was the only one true, would be most likely to lead to finding that the statute is constitutionally valid?

    (A) The majority of people living in states which have inadequate compulsory education requirements are members of ethnic minorities.

(B) Educational levels in England, France, China, and the Russia are superior to those in several of the states of the United States.

(C) By its terms, the statute is applicable only to residents of the District of Columbia and of United States Military bases.

(D) The majority of American schoolchildren move from one state to another at some time during the first twelve years of their education.

25. In an attempt to improve air quality, several states pass laws providing that vehicles powered by diesel engines of more than a certain size must be equipped with a specified smog-elimination system in order to be driven on highways within the state. Ace Trucking Company challenges such a law in the state of Baxter on the ground that it unreasonably burdens interstate commerce. Which of the following is the state of Baxter's best argument in support of the law?

(A) The law applies to intra-state as well as interstate shipments.

(B) The law applies to all vehicles traveling through the state, including those which are garaged primarily in the state.

(C) The law is necessary to protect the health and safety of residents of the state.

(D) Other states have similar requirements.

26. In a case in which the constitutionality of a state law regulating the sale of birth control devices is in issue, which party will have the burden of persuasion?

(A) The state, because procreation involves a fundamental right, and the law may have a substantial impact on that right.

(B) The state, because the state law is more likely to have a substantial impact on women than on men.

(C) The person challenging the statute, since there is a rebuttable presumption that all state laws are constitutional.

(D) The person challenging the statute, since the regulation on non-expressive sexual conduct is reserved to the states by the Tenth Amendment.

27. After the state of Caledonia raised property taxes, Brown became active in an organization called Citizens Opposed to Soaring Taxes (COST). As part of a protest, Brown paraded nude in front of the tax collector's office, carrying a sign which read "Soaring taxes take the clothes off our backs." Brown was arrested under a statute that had been enacted the month before by the Caledonia state legislature, and that had not yet been judicially construed. The complete text of the law was, "No person shall behave in a shocking or offensive manner in a public place. Any violation of this section shall be punished by a term not to exceed six months in a county detention facility."

If Brown defends by asserting that the statute is unconstitutional, his most effective argument would be that

(A) under the First and Fourteenth Amendments, expressive conduct may not be punished by the state.
(B) the statute is vague.
(C) the reasonable person is not likely to have been shocked or offended by Brown's conduct.
(D) conviction under a newly enacted statute that has not yet been judicially construed is a violation of due process.

28. Durk was a member of an organization known as The Church of Twelve Gods. Members of this organization worship twelve different deities, each said to be in charge of a different field of worldly activity. Each month of the year, the organization conducts a festival dedicated to a different one of the deities. In March, the festival of Love was held to honor the goddess of love. As part of the festival, members met to engage in activities involving nudity and group sexual intercourse. Along with other members of the organization, Durk, who participated in the festival, was arrested by police from the county vice squad. He was convicted of violating a state law which made it a crime "for any adult to engage in sexual intercourse with another while any third person is present."

If Durk appeals, the conviction

(A) must be overturned, if the group sexual activity was required by a reasonable interpretation of the organization's religious beliefs.
(B) must be overturned, because the conduct was part of the free exercise of a religion.
(C) may be upheld, on the ground that an organization which worships multiple deities is not a "religion" for First Amendment purposes.
(D) may be upheld, even if the group sexual activity was required by Durk's sincere religious beliefs.

29. The White People's Socialist Party (WPSP) is a small political organization which advocates racial segregation and which occasionally runs a candidate for election to office in the state of Nevorado. The WPSP planned to hold a campaign rally at the state capitol two weeks prior to the last statewide election. Because anonymous threats of violence were received by the state police, however, a Nevorado court issued an injunction prohibiting the WPSP from conducting any public rallies until after the election. After the election was over, the WPSP sought United States Supreme Court review of the Nevorado court's decision.

The United States Supreme Court should

(A) review the state court's decision if the WPSP desires to hold future rallies in the state of Nevorado.
(B) review the state court's decision because any interference with the right to assemble violates the First Amendment to the United States Constitution.

(C) not review the state court's decision since the question presented has become moot.

(D) not review the state court's decision since the aims of the WPSP violate the Equal Protection Clause of the Fourteenth Amendment to the United States Constitution.

30. Congress passes a law requiring all females who are eighteen years of age to register for the draft. A non-profit organization known as Females Against Registration advertises that it will provide an attorney and defend without charge any female prosecuted for failing to register. If the Bar Association of the state of Tetonic sues to enjoin further publication of the advertisement in that state, the injunction should be

(A) granted, if Tetonic statutes prohibit advertising by attorneys.

(B) granted, since the advertisement could have the effect of encouraging young women to violate the law.

(C) denied, since the advertisement constitutes commercial speech.

(D) denied, as a violation of the First Amendment to the United States Constitution.

ANSWERS TO
MULTIPLE-CHOICE QUESTIONS

1 **D** Under the Supremacy Clause an otherwise valid state statute may be superseded by federal legislation to the extent that the two are inconsistent. The contract to kill feral tuskers in the national park was authorized by federal statutes. Since the Property clause gives Congress the power to control federal property, the federal statutes are valid, and so the state law which prohibits their killing is superseded, at least as to killings within the national park.

The power to protect the environment is held by both the federal and state governments, so states do have the power to declare a species to be endangered and to enact legislation protecting it. **A** is, therefore, incorrect. Since the Tuscalona statute prohibits the killing of feral tuskers only within the state, and since there is no indication that anyone other than Termine is interested in coming from outside the state to kill them or that killing them is commerce, the statute probably does not unduly interfere with interstate commerce. **B** is, therefore, incorrect. The Obligation of Contracts Clause prevents the state from interfering with rights acquired under existing contracts, but does not prevent the state from prohibiting activities which parties might otherwise contract to perform. **C** is, therefore, incorrect.

2. **A** Under the Commerce Clause, Congress has the power to regulate commerce among the states. The Necessary and Proper Clause permits Congress to do whatever is reasonably necessary to the exercise of its enumerated powers. The Supreme Court has held that if in the aggregate a particular industry has an impact on interstate commerce, Congress may regulate even those aspects of it which are completely intrastate. See, e.g., *Wickard v. Filburn* (1942): Congress can set quotas on how much wheat an individual farmer (P) may grow for consumption by his family, because such wheat-growing decisions by many individuals, each of whom is acting solely intra-state, cumulatively affect the interstate price of wheat.

B is incorrect because no provision of the United States Constitution gives Congress the power to legislate for the general welfare (i.e., federal police power). **C** is incorrect because the congressional power to regulate commerce is limited to interstate commerce, or at least to trade which has an impact on interstate commerce. **D** is a correct statement, but would not furnish an argument in support of the constitutionality of the statute in question since the statute regulates "every purchase of an automobile in the United States," and this may include those which are sold domestically and intrastate.

3. **C** Under the Necessary and Proper Clause, Congress has the power to make laws regulating the use of federal money disbursed pursuant to the spending power. This may enable Congress to control functions which are traditionally those of the state. (*N.F.I.B. v. Sebelius*, the health-care insurance case, says that Congress can't use its spending and Necessary-and-Proper powers to impose conditions on the payment of funds to states where the amount of federal funding that would be lost if the state didn't honor the conditions is so great that the states would be "coerced" by being left with no practical choice but to agree. However, the facts tell us that the total funds that might have to be returned if Calizona didn't follow the minimum-wage rule amount to less than 1% of Calizona's budget, so the federal government would not be found to have "coerced" the state into agreeing to the minimum-wage limits.)

Congress' general right to set conditions on a state's use of federal funds means that **A** and **B** are, therefore, incorrect, even though traditional state functions are at issue. An intrastate activity may be controlled by Congress under the Commerce Clause if its impact on interstate commerce justifies regulation to protect or promote interstate commerce. **D** is incorrect, however, because the fact that some of the materials used are traded in interstate commerce is not, alone, sufficient to establish such an impact.

4. **A** The Eleventh Amendment bars a private action against a state for money damages in a federal court by a resident or non-resident of the state if a judgment in the action would have to be paid out of the state's general treasury. The Amendment applies to the facts here unless Congress had power to nullify the Amendment, as Congress purported to do when it authorized a private action against the state. Congress *does* have power to nullify that Eleventh Amendment immunity, but *only if* (1) Congress is using its special enforcement powers under the post-Civil-War Amendments (13th, 14th and 15th) to prevent violations of those Amendments, and (2) Congress' response is "congruent and proportional" to the scope of past state violations of those Amendments, violations of the sort that Congress is now trying to prevent. *Boerne v. Flores*. (Congress cannot rely on any other power, such as the Commerce power, to nullify Eleventh Amendment immunity — only the 13th, 14th and 15th Amendment enforcement powers qualify. *Seminole Tribe of Florida v. Florida*.) Here, there is no evidence that Congress was attempting to prevent any state violation of the 13th, 14th or 15th Amendments; therefore, Congress did not have the power to overcome the state's Eleventh Amendment immunity.

B is incorrect because the suit arises under a federal statute. **C** is incorrect because this question does not depend on whom the plaintiff's employer was, since the action by employees of Bilder is for damages resulting from Calizona's failure to require Bilder to pay the $12.00 wage. Unless the employees were aware of their rights, they could not have waived them. **D** is incorrect because there is no indication that the employees knowingly waived their rights.

5. **D** The Privileges and Immunities Clause of Article 4 requires each state to treat non-residents in the same manner as it treats residents. However, the Clause has been interpreted to apply only to rights which are "fundamental to national unity," and only commercially-oriented rights qualify. Therefore, the right to use recreational resources is not protected by the Clause; *Baldwin v. Montana Fish & Game Comm'n*. Consequently, **I** is incorrect. The Privileges or Immunities Clause of the Fourteenth Amendment protects only those rights which persons enjoy as citizens of the United States (e.g., the right to travel from state to state, to vote for federal officials, to sue in federal courts, etc.). Since there is no federal right to hunt, **II** is also incorrect.

6. **B** Under *Scales v. U.S.*, mere membership in an organization advocating unlawful activity cannot be grounds for punishment or disqualification for a state benefit. Such punishment or disqualification may be imposed only if the person is an active member of the organization, knows that it advocates illegal conduct, and has the *specific intent* to bring about the accomplishment of its illegal goal. Although Arthur was an active member of NAP and knew that it advocated illegal conduct, he did not desire for it to succeed in accomplishing its illegal goal, and did not intend to help it so succeed. He therefore cannot constitutionally be punished for his membership in it. (A 2010 case, *Holder v. Humanitarian Law Project*, says that Congress may make it a crime to give "material support" to a foreign terrorist organization even where the supporter does not have a specific intent to further the organization's legal aims. But *Holder* is a narrow decision — applicable only to organizations designated as "foreign terrorist organizations" by Congress — and in any event, even *Holder* would require an intent to further *some* aim of the organization, legal or illegal, whereas here, Arthur had no intent to further even the NAP's legal aims.)

    C and **D** are, therefore, incorrect: C is wrong because it incorrectly asserts that mere membership while knowing of the organization's advocacy of illegality is sufficient, and D is wrong because it incorrectly asserts that playing an active role is sufficient even where the member has no desire to bring about the illegal aims.

    A is incorrect because freedom of the press applies only to the communication of ideas, and not to the conduct involved in acquiring the information to be communicated.

7. **B** A state law which intentionally favors some religions over others violates the Establishment Clause unless it is closely fitted to furthering a compelling governmental interest. It is unlikely that the statute in question would satisfy that stringent test, but, in any event, the argument contained in **B** is the only one listed which could possibly support the challenge. **B** is, therefore, correct.

A statute does not violate the Free Exercise Clause unless it interferes with a practice required by a religious belief. Since there is no indication that the religious beliefs of the American Buddhist League require the broadcasting of their program, **A** is incorrect. Although the statute's discrimination against pay television stations might violate the Equal Protection Clause, **C** is incorrect because only a victim of that discrimination (i.e., a pay television station) would have standing to assert that challenge. **D** is incorrect for two reasons: first, the power to regulate use of the airwaves is, to some extent, shared by the federal and state governments; and second, the Supremacy Clause makes a state law invalid only when it is inconsistent with some valid federal statute affecting the same subject matter. Since there is no indication that there is a federal statute which differs from the state law in question, **D** cannot be the correct answer.

8.   **B**   By the process of "reverse incorporation," the Due Process Clause of the Fifth Amendment has been held to require equal protection from the federal government similar to what the Fourteenth Amendment requires of state governments. Parsons may argue that since the statute applies only to employees of the Census Bureau and not to other federal employees who deal with the public, it arbitrarily discriminates against him. Parsons will probably lose on the merits: no suspect class or fundamental right is at issue, so the court will require only a rational relation between the ban and the achievement of a legitimate governmental objective, an easy-to-satisfy standard. But of the four choices, this is the only one that has even a theoretical chance of success, because it's the only one that relies on a constitutional provision that might possibly apply to the situation at hand.

A is incorrect because the Fourteenth Amendment prohibits *states* from abridging the privileges or immunities of national citizenship, but does not prohibit the federal government from doing so; also, the right to wear a moustache is probably not protected by the *Art. IV* Privileges and Immunities Clause because it is not "fundamental to national unity." **C** is incorrect because the Fourteenth Amendment prohibits invidious discrimination by the states, but not by the federal government. The Fifth Amendment prohibits the taking of private property for public use without just compensation, but is inapplicable since no property has been taken from Parsons for a public purpose. (Even if Parson had had some sort of "property" interest in his job — which he didn't, since he was an at-will employee — that interest was merely made subject to minor regulation, and was not "taken" for government use, which is the only thing that the Takings Clause protects against.) **D** is therefore, incorrect.

9.   **B**   The congressional power to regulate interstate commerce has been held to include the power to exclude whatever items Congress wants to exclude from commerce between the states. The courts generally do not examine congressional motives in determining the constitutionality of such a statute. Therefore, even though Congress probably wouldn't have power to outlaw *all* dogfighting

(this would be a ban on non-commercial conduct, and would run afoul of the holding in *U.S. v. Lopez* that Congress can't use its Commerce power to ban the possession of all guns near schools), it did have power under the Commerce Clause to ban just those instances of dogfighting that are directly dependent on interstate transportation of a dog, which is what it did here.

A is incorrect because there is no federal police power. The "Cooley Doctrine" provides that the Commerce power, at least in part, is held concurrently by the state and federal governments. **C** is incorrect because the "Cooley Doctrine" has nothing to do with the prohibition against cruelty to animals. Although acts of Congress are presumptively constitutional, **D** is not an effective argument because the presumption of constitutionality is a rebuttable one.

10. **B** Article III of the United States Constitution gives the Supreme Court appellate jurisdiction over all controversies arising under the laws of the United States, and authorizes Congress to determine the ways in which that jurisdiction shall be exercised. Since the Truth in Selling Act is a federal law, the court has jurisdiction to hear appeals from decisions construing it, and Congress may authorize appeals directly from lower state courts.

The power to regulate interstate commerce may empower Congress to authorize a statute requiring disclosures in interstate transactions, but **A** is incorrect because the power to regulate interstate commerce is separate from and unrelated to the power to regulate the exercise of appellate jurisdiction by the Supreme Court. **C** is incorrect because Article III gives the Supreme Court jurisdiction over the cases involving federal laws, and empowers Congress to determine how that jurisdiction should be exercised. Although a state has the right to review the decisions of its own courts, the United States Constitution gives the Supreme Court the power to review decisions relating to federal laws. Its exercise of that power is thus constitutionally valid, and not an infringement on the sovereignty of the states. **D** is, therefore, incorrect.

11. **A** The United States Supreme Court has held that the right of adults to engage in sexual activity is protected by the substantive Due Process requirement of the Fifth Amendment as extended to the states by the Fourteenth Amendment. See *Lawrence v. Texas* (2003), holding that Texas' ban on same-sex sodomy is so irrational as to constitute a due process violation even under the easy-to-satisfy rational-relation standard. Although *Lawrence* involved same-sex sodomy, the logic of the case — that adults have a substantive due process right to engage in private consensual acts of physical intimacy regardless of whether the majority morally approves of those acts — seems applicable to heterosexual sodomy as well. In any event, of all the arguments listed, **A** is the only one which could possibly support the Daltons' position.

B is incorrect because procedural Due Process refers to the receipt of notice and the opportunity to be heard before being deprived of life, liberty, or property. Although the statute appears to discriminate between married and unmarried persons, **C** is incorrect because the Daltons are not the victims of this discrimination and will not therefore benefit from a ruling which eliminates the discriminatory effect of the statute. Some public displays of sexual conduct have been held to be expression protected under the First Amendment. **D** is incorrect, however, because there is no indication that the Daltons' activity was intended to be a form of expression.

12. **A**   A controversy is not "ripe" for decision unless the issues are fully developed, clearly defined, and not merely speculative, conjectural, or premature. Usually, this requires a showing that objective harm will likely occur if the issues are not decided. Mere general allegations of a possible subjective "chill" are not sufficient to satisfy this requirement. See, e.g., *Clapper v. Amnesty Int'l* (2013) (where the Ps are afraid that federal intelligence officials will conduct electronic surveillance on them using a special statute, the Ps don't have standing to contest the statute's constitutionality, because they can't show that use of the statute against them is "certainly impending").

A case is "moot" when no unresolved contested questions essential to the effective disposition of the particular controversy remain for court decision. **B** is incorrect because all the issues raised by the action are unresolved. **C** is incorrect because the Eleventh Amendment does not prevent lawsuits to enjoin state officials from enforcing laws claimed to be invalid. A question is political if its resolution would unduly interfere with the operation of a co-equal branch of the federal government or with national policy. **D** is therefore incorrect.

13. **C**   Since the United States Constitution is the supreme law of the land, every court must determine whether the laws which it enforces violate the Constitution either by their terms or by the way in which they are applied. This necessarily involves interpretation of the Constitution. **A** is, therefore, incorrect.

B is incorrect for two reasons: first, the Fraser City Municipal Court determines who has standing to appear or make particular arguments before it; and, second, even if the Municipal Court's rules regarding standing were identical to the federal rules, Butch would have standing because the *possibility* of his conviction is sufficient to give him a personal stake in the outcome of the constitutional argument. **D** is incorrect because every court has the power to interpret the Constitution.

14. **D**   Under its police power, a state may enact laws to protect the welfare of its residents even though those laws impose a burden of some kind on interstate commerce, so long as there is no reasonable, less burdensome way of accomplishing that purpose. If, however, the burden which it imposes on interstate commerce is

an unreasonable one, the statute will be invalid under the Commerce Clause. Although it is not certain that the argument in **D** would succeed, it is the only one listed which could possibly support granting of the injunction.

A is incorrect because the fact that a statute interferes in some way with interstate commerce is not, alone, sufficient to make it invalid. Since the state's police power permits it to enact laws for the welfare of its residents, the purity of food is clearly a matter of local concern. **B** is, therefore, incorrect. Powers reserved to the states may be delegated by them to their municipalities and agencies. **C** is incorrect because the state's power to regulate commerce is concurrent with the federal Commerce power, and may thus be exercised by municipal governments within the state.

15. **A**   The concept of due process requires that a person be given a hearing before being deprived by government action of life, liberty, or property. Since termination of government employment is a deprivation of property, Orville is entitled to a hearing before his job, pay, gun, and badge are taken from him. If, however, delaying government action until a hearing would cause threat of serious harm, such emergency situation may justify acting first and holding the hearing as soon as practicable later. Since a police officer is armed and has much opportunity to do harm, it may successfully be argued that a suspension pending the hearing was necessary to avoid the obvious threat that would result from allowing an incompetent or unbalanced person to serve as a police officer. If a no-fault finding at the soon-to-be-held hearing will result in full restoration of job and pay, there has been no deprivation of property interest without Due Process.

Although the facts assumed in **B** and **C** might justify firing Orville, he is still entitled to due process (i.e., a hearing). **B** and **C** are, therefore, incorrect. **D** is incorrect for the same reason, since putting a procedure in the Procedure Manual does not exempt it from the due process requirement of the United States Constitution.

16. **D**   The Equal Protection Clause of the Fourteenth Amendment provides that "no state shall … deny to any person within its jurisdiction the equal protection of the laws." Actions of a county or other political subdivision of a state are regarded as state actions. While there may be valid reasons why certain women should not be employed as deputy sheriffs, the fact that plaintiff's application was rejected solely because of her sex would probably make that rejection invidious, and a violation of her Fourteenth Amendment rights.

In **A**, the disparity between the pass rates of black persons and white persons might be evidence that a law is being applied in a discriminatory manner, but does not establish it conclusively. **A** is therefore, incorrect. Although discrimination based solely on ethnic background may violate the Equal Protection Clause, **B** is incorrect because the Fourteenth Amendment prohibits state action only, and the discrimination in **B** was practiced by a privately-owned hospital. **C** is incorrect for the same reason, since the discrimination was practiced by a federal agency rather than a state one.

17. **D**   A statute is void for overbreadth if it punishes expression which is constitutionally protected along with expression which can validly be punished. Although certain types of offensive expression (including, perhaps, Demos') may be prohibited by statute, a law which prohibits all "offensive" conduct is so broad that it is likely to end up punishing substantial amounts of constitutionally protected speech (i.e., speech that offends only because of the message contained in it). Such a law is, therefore, overbroad. (And, even if the statute could constitutionally be applied to punish *Demos'* conduct, he has standing to assert the rights of others not before the court to whose conduct the statute could not constitutionally be applied — the First Amendment overbreadth doctrine supplies an exception to the usual rules of standing, which generally prohibit the litigant from raising the rights of absent third parties.)

A, **B,** and **C** are incorrect because, in First Amendment cases, a person whose conduct can be constitutionally punished under a statute has standing to assert the rights of persons whose conduct is unconstitutionally prohibited by the statute. (This is the overbreadth doctrine, as explained above.) Thus, although it might have been constitutional to punish Demos' conduct, the law is constitutionally invalid because of other conduct which it might reach, and if invalid, cannot be enforced even against Demos.

18. **B**   The state may impose "time, place and manner" restrictions on expression in protection of its interest in promoting free access to government buildings and the orderly conduct of governmental activities. But if such restrictions are "content based" (i.e., based on communicative content of the message), the restrictions will be *strictly scrutinized*, and almost inevitably struck down on the grounds that they are not necessary to achieve a compelling governmental objective. Cf. *Boos v. Barry.* Since Section II permits demonstrations involving one kind of message and prohibits demonstrations involving a different kind of message, it will be strictly scrutinized and found to violate the First Amendment: there's no compelling governmental interest that can only be satisfied by drawing this distinction between demonstrations concerning matters currently under consideration and other matters.

As to **A**, it is true that sidewalks in front of government buildings are a traditional public forum; but government may regulate the time, place and manner of expression even in traditional public fora (though not as extensively as where what's regulated is not a public forum). What makes the regulation impermissible here is its content-based nature, and the ban on content-based regulation applies whether the forum is public or not. Therefore, **A** is incorrect.

The state's interest in the orderly conduct of governmental affairs and in the protection of free access to government buildings might well be a compelling one, and would probably justify a content-*neutral* law prohibiting noise or demonstrations in front of government office buildings. But **C** is wrong because it doesn't include, as it would need to, the requirement that the means chosen be "necessary" for achieving the compelling governmental interest (a requirement that isn't met here, for the reason stated in the above discussion of why choice B is correct).

D is wrong because even if Demos kept persons with lawful business from entering government offices, he was entitled not to be prosecuted under a statute that discriminated against certain messages. To put it another way, D ignores the fact that the statute was *overbroad*: it unconstitutionally forbade a large swath of protected conduct (demonstrations relating to matters not under current consideration, in which the demonstrators didn't block anyone's access). Demos was entitled under the First Amendment overbreadth doctrine to assert the rights of persons not before the court; the court will find the statute overbroad and thus invalid on its face even though a differently-drafted statute (a content-neutral one that applied only to access-blockers) might constitutionally have been applied to him since he helped block access.

19. **B** Although the Constitution requires the advice and consent of the Senate for ambassadorial *appointments*, the Supreme Court has held that the president may *dismiss* an ambassador at will and without cause.

    A and **C** are, therefore, incorrect. Whether the removal of an ambassador constitutes a withdrawal of diplomatic relations depends on the reason for the ambassador's removal. **D** is incorrect for this reason, and because the president has the power to withdraw diplomatic relations with a foreign government.

20. **D** Although the Young Trailblazers may have violated a federal law, it did not violate the state statute. The Fourteenth Amendment provides that *no state* shall make or enforce a law which denies the privileges and immunities of citizenship, due process, or equal protection of the laws. Since The Young Trailblazers is not a state, the Fourteenth Amendment does not confer upon Penny a right to be protected against its action. Therefore, **A, B** and **C** are incorrect.

21. **B** The Thirteenth Amendment abolishes slavery, and gives Congress the power to make laws enforcing its provisions. Discrimination based solely on race has been held to involve a "badge" of slavery which the Thirteenth Amendment authorizes Congress to abolish; Congress' power under that Amendment includes the power to reach purely private racial discrimination that amounts to a badge of slavery.

The Commerce Clause gives Congress the power to regulate interstate commerce, but imposes no obligations on anyone. The Young Trailblazers' policy could not, therefore, violate "the spirit of the Commerce Clause," so **A** is incorrect. **C** is incorrect because racial discrimination violates the United States Constitution only when practiced by government. **D** is incorrect because there is no federal police power, and thus no congressional power to legislate for the general welfare.

22. **A**   In *Miller v California*, 413 U.S. 15 (1973), the United States Supreme Court held that no work may be found obscene unless it appeals to a prurient interest in sex (taken as a whole and applying contemporary community standards), *and* it depicts sexual conduct in a way which is patently offensive according to contemporary community standards, *and* it lacks serious literary, artistic, political, or scientific value. Since the jury found the magazine to have serious literary value, it does not meet all three parts of the definition, and cannot, therefore, be ruled obscene.

In determining whether material appeals to a prurient interest in sex, the standard of the local community (the judicial district or state) is applied. **B** is, therefore, incorrect. There is some question about whether a local or national standard should be applied in determining whether the material depicts sexual conduct in a way which is offensive according to contemporary community standards. **C** is incorrect, however, because no work can be obscene unless it meets all three criteria of the Supreme Courts's definition. **D** is incorrect for the same reason.

23. **D**   Although the state may interfere with commercial speech to serve a substantial governmental interest, it must not do so in a way which is substantially more restrictive than necessary. *Central Hudson Gas v. Public Serv. Comm.; Edenfield v. Fane.* Thus, even though the state may have a substantial interest in protecting the public against tooth decay, the law prohibiting the advertising of chewing gum would be constitutionally invalid if there are substantially less restrictive ways of accomplishing the same objective (e.g., by requiring a warning). See, e.g., *44 Liquormart v. Rhode Island* (state may not prohibit all advertising of liquor prices in order to discourage over-drinking; regulation of commercial speech must be "no more extensive than necessary," and here the state could have limited alcohol consumption by less restrictive means, such as increased taxation). Although it is not certain that the argument in **D** would result in a finding that the law is invalid, it is the only one listed which could possibly support such a finding.

A is an incorrect statement of law, since freedom of expression is not absolute and may be interfered with to serve a substantial government interest. The mere fact that a state law will have an effect on interstate commerce is not enough to make that law invalid, unless it imposes an unreasonable burden on interstate commerce. **B** is, therefore, incorrect. Although the Supreme Court is wary of laws which impose prior restraints on publication, it is far less concerned when those laws affect commercial speech only. **C** is incorrect because the speech involved is commercial, and the fact that the law imposes a prior restraint is, therefore, not alone sufficient to render it constitutionally invalid.

24. **C**   Congress has the power to make laws regulating conduct on federal property and in the District of Columbia, virtually without limitation.

A is incorrect because the police powers of the states include the power to regulate education. Although states must do so in a way which does not deny equal protection to persons within their jurisdiction, there is no constitutional requirement that each state do so in an identical way. Some highly imaginative argument might lead a court to conclude that if **B** were true the statute would be valid under the war and national defense powers of Congress, or that if **D** were true the statute would be valid under the Commerce Clause. No such stretch of the imagination is necessary in **C**, however, so **B** and **D** are incorrect.

25. **C**   Even if a state law burdens interstate commerce, the law will be valid so long as it neither: (1) discriminates against (i.e., intentionally disfavors) interstate commerce; and (2) does not impose burdens that are substantially greater than the benefits conferred by the law with respect to some legitimate state interest. Although not enough facts are given to allow a determination of whether both branches of this test are satisfied, the state has at least a plausible argument that they are. And in any event, **C** is the only argument which offers any support at all to the state's defense.

A and **B** are incorrect because the law is likely to discourage commerce from out of state, even though it applies equally to intra-state shipments and vehicles garaged within the state. If all or most other states have similar requirements, that fact might be relevant in determining that the burden on interstate commerce is not an unreasonable one. But the fact that some other states have such a requirement is not, alone, enough to establish that it is reasonable. **D** is therefore incorrect.

26. **A**   In an equal-protection challenge to a state interference with a "*fundamental right,*" or to a state law that allegedly discriminates against a "*suspect classification,*" *strict scrutiny* applies. In strict scrutiny cases, the state has the burden of establishing that the law is necessary to serve a compelling state interest. The United States Supreme Court has characterized opposite-sex marriage and procreation as fundamental rights for equal protection purposes. In particular, the Court held in *Griswold v. Connecticut* that a state ban on the use of contraceptives was invalid because it impaired the fundamental right of privacy. Therefore, choice A's emphasis on procreation as a fundamental right makes it the correct choice.

B is incorrect because although gender-based classification is subject to heightened security, the Supreme Court has not held gender to be a suspect classification. (Gender-based classifications merely get mid-level scrutiny; *Craig v. Boren*.) **C** is incorrect because interference with fundamental rights is presumed to be unconstitutional. **D** is incorrect for the same reason, and because state exercises of powers reserved under the Tenth Amendment must be consistent with other requirements of the federal constitution.

27. **B**   Statutory language which does not allow the person of ordinary intelligence to know what conduct is prohibited by the statute is vague and, therefore, unconstitutional. Language such as that given has frequently been held to be vague. Although it is not certain that a court would come to that conclusion, **B** is the only argument which could possibly support Brown's position.

Although it may be expressive, conduct like Brown's can be prohibited as part of "time, place and manner" regulations not aimed at the content of the symbolic speech. **A** is, therefore, incorrect. **C** is incorrect for two reasons: first, it may not be an accurate appraisal of the reasonable person's response to Brown's conduct; and, second, the constitutionality of a statute depends on how the person of ordinary intelligence would understand it without regard to any particular conduct. If the language of a statute can be understood by the person of ordinary intelligence, it is not vague and a conviction under it does not violate due process for the sole reason that the statute has been newly enacted and not yet judicially construed. **D** is, therefore, incorrect.

28. **D**   A state interference with the free exercise of a religious belief is constitutionally valid if it occurs as part of a religion-neutral generally-applicable law, no matter how great the burden on religious expression and now matter how small the state's interest in refusing an exemption for religious groups. *Employment Div. v. Smith*. Since the statute here is a generally-applicable provision, this rule makes it valid. Therefore, **D** is correct.

For the same reason, **A** and **B** are incorrect. **C** is incorrect because (even apart from the rule of *Employment Div. v. Smith*), in considering a challenge to the constitutionality of a state interference with religion, the court may not consider the validity of the religious beliefs in question.

29. **A**   The proper means of attacking an injunction is by judicial proceeding. Because of the short time period involved, however, it would have been impossible to obtain judicial review before the election. If the WPSP desires to hold rallies in the future, there is a likelihood that similarly issued injunctions will likewise evade review. Where a problem is capable of repetition, but likely to evade review — even though, as here, the injunction being challenged is no longer in effect — Supreme Court review is available.

B is incorrect because some state interference with the right to assemble is permitted, as in the case of valid "time, place and manner" regulations. **C** is incorrect because the possibility that similar future claims will evade review prevents the question from being regarded as moot. **D** is incorrect because the Fourteenth Amendment is not relevant to anything but *state* action, and the WPSP is a private organization.

30. **D** It has been held that the First Amendment protects the right of non-profit organizations who use litigation as an instrument of political expression to solicit prospective clients. *In Re Primus*.

A is incorrect, since the Supreme Court has held that non-deceptive advertising of legal services is protected by the First Amendment. **B** is incorrect because the fact that the advertisement "could have the effect" of inciting illegal conduct is not sufficient. In order for an interference with inciting expression to be valid there must be both an intention that the expression will cause illegal conduct and an imminent probability that such illegal conduct will occur. **C** is incorrect for two reasons: first, although commercial speech is entitled to First Amendment protection, the fact that speech is commercial does not alone mean that laws regulating it are invalid; and, second, the communication in this case is more likely to be regarded as political expression rather than commercial speech, since it does not relate solely to economic interests.

ESSAY EXAM
QUESTIONS & ANSWERS

The following Essay Questions are taken from the Constitutional Law volume of *Siegel's Essay & Multiple-Choice Questions & Answers*, a series developed by Brian Siegel and published by Wolters Kluwer Law & Business. The full volume contains 27 essays (with model answers), as well as 128 multiple choice questions. (Most of the essay questions were originally asked on the California Bar Exam, and are copyright the California Board of Bar Examiners, reprinted by permission.) The book is available from your bookstore, or by visiting **www.aspenlaw.com**.

QUESTION 1

City, a municipality of State X, has a permit ordinance that prohibits making speeches in the City-owned city park without first obtaining a permit from City's police chief. The ordinance authorizes the police chief to establish permit application procedures, and to grant or deny permits based upon the chief's "overall assessment of the good of the community." The ordinance also provides that denial of a permit may be appealed to the city council.

On Tuesday, Tom applied to Dan, City's police chief, for a permit to speak in the city park the following Saturday. Tom gave Dan his name and local address, but Dan denied Tom's application for a permit because Tom refused Dan's request for a summary of what he intended to say in his speech. When Tom told Dan that he intended to make his speech anyway, Dan immediately gave Tom's name and address to the city attorney of City.

The city attorney did nothing about the matter until Friday, when, without notice to Tom, he made application on behalf of City to a State X court of general jurisdiction for a temporary restraining order preventing Tom from speaking in the city park without a permit. The State X court issued an ex-parte temporary restraining order and an order to show cause, answerable in five days, directed to Tom. The orders were served on Tom in the city park on Saturday as he was about to speak. Despite the temporary restraining order, Tom spoke to about twenty mildly interested persons who were then in the park for various other reasons.

The essence of Tom's speech was that the federal government, "aided and abetted" by City's government, was "leading America to destruction," and that "those who would survive will eventually have to fight in the streets of City to regain their liberties." Tom urged the audience to "stockpile weapons" and to "start thinking about forming guerrilla units to take back freedom from the government."

Tom was arrested and charged in the State X court which had issued the temporary restraining order with **(a)** speaking in the city park without a permit, a misdemeanor, **(b)** contempt of court for violating the temporary restraining order, and **(c)** violation of the State X criminal advocacy statute prohibiting "advocating insurrection against local, state, or the federal governments," a felony.

Five years ago, the State X Supreme Court construed the criminal advocacy statute as applying only to advocacy that is not protected by the United States Constitution.

A week after Tom's speech, in a case unrelated to the charges against Tom, the State X Supreme Court construed City's permit ordinance as authorizing the City police chief to consider "only the time, place and manner of the proposed speech, and not its content" in passing upon permit applications.

What rights guaranteed by the United States Constitution should Tom assert in defense to the charges brought against him, and how should the court rule? Discuss.

ANSWER TO QUESTION 1

(a) The misdemeanor charge:

Tom ("T") could initially contend that the misdemeanor charge should be dismissed because it was based upon a statute which was overly broad on its face (i.e., the entity charged with enforcing the law had virtually total discretion in determining whether or not it should be applied to a particular situation). Such enactments cannot serve as the basis for governmental action; *Lovell v. Griffin*, 303 U.S. 444 (1938). Since the statutory standard to be utilized in granting licenses or not is highly subjective in nature (i.e., the "overall community good"), T would argue that it was constitutionally defective. While it would be difficult for City to argue that the test for determining if licenses should be granted or not is adequate, it could assert that where the defendant should have anticipated a constitutionally curative construction, an overly broad enactment may serve as the basis for governmental action; *Shuttlesworth v. Birmingham*, 394 U.S. 147 (1969). Since the State X Supreme Court had made a proper narrowing interpretation of the criminal advocacy statute five years earlier, T should have foreseen that a constitutionally proper interpretation of the misdemeanor statute would also be rendered when it was judicially reviewed.

T could respond, however, that he could ***not*** foresee a constitutionally curative interpretation of the licensing ordinance because it appeared to be plain on its face (i.e., it would have been very difficult to anticipate that the requirement for speaking would be almost completely repudiated and the factors of time, place and manner of speech substituted in lieu thereof).

Alternatively, T could argue that, even if a proper narrowing interpretation could have been anticipated, a law which is unconstitutionally applied (i.e., the permit was rejected for T's failure to disclose the content; not time, place or manner considerations) cannot serve as the basis for a criminal conviction where no adequate opportunity for review is available. T would assert that this standard was satisfied because (1) there was no provision for independent review by a judicial body (any appeal was to be heard by the city council, presumably the same entity which enacted the law), and (2) the facts are unclear as to how often the city council met (if it was not until after T's projected speaking date, no timely appeal to that body could possibly be taken). While City could contend in rebuttal that T waived any potential constitutional defect in the prescribed review procedure by neglecting to contest the police chief's decision to deny T's request for a permit before the city council, a procedure which requires appeal to a legislative branch of local government is probably inadequate.

In summary, the prosecution of T for violation of the licensing ordinance will probably **not** be successful.

(b) The contempt of court decree:

Ex-parte orders are ordinarily not appropriate unless there was a need to act immediately and there was no opportunity to give the opposing party notice. Since the attorney for City was apparently aware of T's prospective speech on Tuesday (the facts indicate that Dan "immediately" gave the City attorney T's name and address), T probably should have been given an opportunity to contest the issuance of an injunction. While even an improper court order must ordinarily be obeyed, where an ex-parte injunction is deliberately sought and served in such a manner as to preclude effective judicial review (as was the case in this instance since City's attorney served the order upon T just as he was beginning to speak), it may be attackable in a subsequent proceeding; *Walker v. Birmingham*, 388 U.S. 307 (1967). However, since T's speech had not been preceded by extensive publicity, it would not have greatly burdened him to have sought appellate review of the injunction. Thus, a conviction for contempt would appear to be proper.

(c) The felony charge:

While the advocacy of ideas is protected by the First Amendment (applicable to the states via the Fourteenth Amendment), speech made for the purpose of inciting immediate unlawful conduct and which is likely to incite such action may be proscribed; *Brandenburg v. Ohio*, 395 U.S. 444 (1969). T could contend that the felony charges must be dismissed because (1) the statute in question is too vague (i.e., a person of ordinary intelligence could not determine what words constituted "advocating insurrection"), and (2) alternatively, the above cited standard is not satisfied in this instance because (i) while he advocated that the listeners "stockpile weapons" be never suggested that this be done illegally (in most states, various types of firearms can be purchased in a lawful manner), (ii) even if his words could be construed as urging illegal conduct, it wouldn't be done imminently (i.e., it would take time to aggregate these weapons), and (iii) there was little likelihood that the listeners would respond to T's speech, since they were (a) in the park for "various other reasons," and (b) only mildly interested in T's speech. Finally, T's comment to "begin thinking about forming guerilla units" obviously does not contemplate immediate unlawful conduct.

While City could respond to T's vagueness assertion by pointing out that the statute had received a constitutionally curative interpretation, there appears to be no successful rebuttal to T's argument that the *Brandenburg* test is not met. Thus, the felony charge should be dismissed.

QUESTION 2

County School Board (Board) cancelled the remedial reading program in County's public schools. At the same time, Board increased funding for drama arts workshops provided for seniors in the public high schools of County. Such increased funding is about 15% of the cost of the remedial reading program.

Racial minorities comprise 10% of the County population and 50% of the students enrolled in the remedial reading program. "AB" is an organization consisting of the parents of these minority students.

Some students are enrolled in the remedial reading program because of learning disabilities or other handicaps adversely affecting reading skills. "CD" is an organization of the parents of these students.

AB objected to the cancellation of the remedial reading program on the ground that the program's termination would disproportionately affect their children adversely. CD objected to the program's termination on the ground that such action would effectively end public education for their children.

In recommending termination of the program, the Board's director had stated: "This action is a necessary economy measure. We have other educational programs, such as pre-college math, which are educationally more important. Handicapped students will simply have to be served sometime in the future when we again have sufficient financial resources. We will, even then, have to target the program so that it helps handicapped children, not children of racial minorities who just need to improve their skills in the English language." Board's actions were based on its director's recommendations.

AB and CD filed suit against Board in federal court, asserting that termination of the remedial reading program violated the constitutional right of the parents and the children represented by those organizations, and asking that Board be ordered to reinstate the program. While the suit was pending, Congress enacted a federal statute requiring school boards of all state political subdivisions to provide remedial reading courses. In passing this legislation, Congress relied upon findings derived through congressional hearings that adults without reading skills inhibit production, sales and travel in interstate commerce.

Assume that both AB and CD have standing to assert their claims.

1. Is the federal statute constitutional? Discuss.

2. If the court rules that the federal statute is unconstitutional:

A. What issues under the U.S. Constitution should AB raise against the actions of Board? How should they be decided? Discuss.

B. What issues under the U.S. Constitution should CD raise against the actions of Board? How should they be decided? Discuss.

ANSWER TO QUESTION 2

1. *Is the federal statute constitutional?*

Board's strongest argument is that the statute violates the Tenth Amendment, on the theory that Congress may not compel a local school board to provide remedial reading courses. Under *Printz v. U.S.*, 117 S. Ct. 2365 (1997), Congress may not compel a state or local government's executive branch (which includes local school boards) to perform tasks or functions, even doing background checks on gun purchasers. A court would probably conclude that requiring particular courses in public schools is a comparable overreaching of congressional power. Therefore, the statute will probably be held unconstitutional under *Printz*.

As a second argument, Board can contend that even if the statute was valid under the Tenth Amendment, it would be invalid under the Commerce Clause. Under Article I, Section 8 (Clause 3), of the Constitution, Congress has the right to regulate interstate commerce. There are three broad categories of activities that Congress can constitutionally regulate under its Commerce power: (1) "channels" of interstate commerce; (2) "instrumentalities" of interstate commerce; and (3) those activities having a "substantial effect" on interstate commerce. *U.S. v. Lopez*; 514 U.S. 549 (1995). The federal statute falls under the third category, since it has no effect on the channels or instrumentalities of interstate commerce. Since the activity being regulated (education) is non-commercial, there must be an *obvious connection* between the activity and interstate commerce. While Congress did make legislative findings linking the regulated activity to interstate commerce, the Court no longer finds this dispositive on the constitutionality of commerce clause regulations. *Lopez.* Here, there is no jurisdictional nexus between the regulations and interstate commerce; i.e., the regulation equally affects those people traveling in, and those not traveling in, interstate commerce. Therefore, there is no "obvious connection" between the regulation and interstate commerce, and it is likely that under *U.S. v. Lopez* the legislation will be held unconstitutional.

2A. *Assuming the federal statute is unconstitutional, what issues should the AB group raise against Board?*

The AB group would raise equal protection and due process objections to the Board's action.

In determining whether a law which is neutral on its face (such as the present legislation, which discontinues *all* remedial reading programs) has a discriminatory purpose, a court may consider any pertinent data (including the statements made by the Board's director). If purposeful discrimination could be shown, the County's actions would have to satisfy the strict scrutiny standard (i.e., a compelling state interest is furthered by the governmental conduct, and there is no less burdensome means of satisfying that objective). Since the termination of the program has a disproportionately adverse racial impact (while racial minorities comprise 10% of the County's population, they constitute 50% of the number of students enrolled in the program), Board would have the burden of proving that its actions were *not* racially motivated.

Board could argue that (1) its action was dictated by financial necessity, and (2) the effect of the program's termination also impacts upon non-minority students. In rebuttal, the AB group could contend that Board's purposeful discrimination is proven by the facts that (1) there were *increased* monies available for the drama arts workshops (however, the total of this amount was only 15% of the funds which had been available for the remedial reading program), and (2) the director indicated handicapped students would receive preference over minority students if adequate funding subsequently became available (although this could be defended by the fact that the latter group would completely fail to learn to read if their regular studies were not supplemented by the remedial program). Without data as to Board's financial situation, it is impossible to determine if the cessation of the program was "a necessary economy measure" or racially inspired. Assuming the court found that it was not, then County would only have to show that the program's termination had a reasonable relationship to a constitutional purpose to sustain its action. This would seem to be established by the County's showing that monetary pressures compelled cessation of the remedial reading program.

The AB group could alternatively contend that the program's closure violated their substantive due process rights. Under the Fourteenth Amendment, one cannot be deprived of fundamental "liberties" (i.e., rights recognized as essential to the orderly pursuit of happiness). The right to possess reasonably adequate reading skills is arguably "fundamental," since a failure to read proficiently inevitably results in lower paying jobs and an overall diminished ability to enjoy life. While the Supreme Court has held that there is no fundamental right to an equally financed education (i.e., all school districts within a particular county do not have to expend an equal dollar amount per child; *San Antonio School District v. Rodriguez*), it has never held that a school district can offer less than an adequate education.

Again, more facts are necessary to determine if, without the program, children of the AB group would be literate. If not, continuation of the program probably is a fundamental right, and therefore the strict scrutiny test would be applicable (i.e., Board would have to show that discontinuing the remedial reading program was virtually the only means of meeting its budgetary crisis). However, if the AB group would receive an adequate education without the program, Board's action would only have to have a reasonable relationship to a constitutional purpose. This would seem to be present in this case, since any good faith decision with respect to how a limited amount of education money is apportioned would be reasonable.

2B. *Assuming the federal statute is unconstitutional, what issues would the CD group raise against Board?*

The CD group would also raise the substantive due process argument described above (i.e., that the right to receive adequate reading skills is a "fundamental" one, and therefore cessation of the program is subject to a strict scrutiny analysis). The facts indicate that, given their innate learning disabilities, this group would not acquire adequate reading skills without the program. Since it is unlikely that Board could show that other programs are more important than minimal reading proficiency, it is highly doubtful that (1) cancellation of the program served a compelling state interest, and (2) there was no less burdensome means available to Board of satisfying its financial constraints. In summary, the substantive due process argument of the CD group should be successful.

Alternatively, the CD group would contend that their equal protection rights were violated. There is no case law supporting the proposition that educationally handicapped students are a "suspect" or "quasi-suspect" group. Since (1) there has probably been no history of purposeful unequal treatment with respect to educationally handicapped persons, and (2) their handicaps are (presumably) not unalterable, it appears to be doubtful that the CD group would be classified as "suspect" or "quasi-suspect." Since the program's cessation would probably meet the rational relationship test, CD's equal protection argument should be unsuccessful.

QUESTION 3

The legislature of State A recently passed a law requiring drivers of trucks carrying explosives on roads in State A to have "Special Driving Permits." These permits are to be issued only after rigorous physical examinations and driving tests. The State A law also provides that only permits issued by State A are acceptable for truck drivers; permits issued by certain other states, all of which have less stringent requirements, are not acceptable. Under the State A law, permits cannot be issued to persons under 30 or over 60 years of age, because statistical studies have shown that drivers in these categories have higher accident frequencies.

Assume that a federal law prohibits employers from discriminating against employees on the basis of age.

Ned, who is 62 years old, is a driver for Ajax, a truck company engaged in the interstate transportation of dynamite for construction projects in various states, including State A. Ned would normally be assigned to drive dynamite shipments from Ajax's headquarters in State B, into State A, but he cannot obtain a Special Driving Permit from State A. Ned would be able to satisfy both the physical examination and driving test requirements of the State A law, but is barred solely because of his age. Ned has a driver's permit issued by State B qualifying him to drive trucks carrying explosives. As a consequence of the State A law, Ajax has been obliged to revise its normal driver assignment policy to schedule Ned on routes which do not require ingress into State A.

Ajax and Ned have brought suit in the United States District Court in State A against the appropriate State A officials, seeking to have the State A law declared invalid. The defendants have moved to have the case dismissed on the grounds that (1) the plaintiffs lack standing, and (2) State A courts have not yet ruled upon the validity of the new law.

1. How should the court rule on the motion for dismissal? Discuss.

2. Assume the motion for dismissal is denied. What rights arising under the United States Constitution should Ajax and Ned urge in support of their claims that the State A law is invalid, and what result should follow? Discuss.

ANSWER TO QUESTION 3

1. The Motion for Dismissal:

Abstention:

A U.S. District Court may abstain from hearing a case which challenges the constitutionality of an ambiguous non-federal statute if the alleged defect might be cured by a narrowing interpretation by a state court. While State A might contend that abstention is appropriate in this instance because no state court has yet construed the statute in question, Ajax and Ned ("Plaintiffs") could probably successfully argue in rebuttal that a curative construction is unlikely since both the (1) 30-60 year parameters, and (2) specific testing requirements, leave virtually no room for a constitutionally valid interpretation.

2. The rights of the Constitution versus State A law:

Standing:

Article III of the Constitution requires that to have standing in federal court, a plaintiff must show a direct and immediate personal injury which is traceable to the challenged action; *Simon v. Eastern Kentucky Welfare Rights Organization*, 426 U.S 26 (1976). State X might contend that Ned has suffered no injury since he has not been terminated from his employment, nor is there any indication that he is receiving less compensation than he had made prior to the State A enactment. Ajax arguably lacks standing because it apparently has other drivers who are capable of obtaining the "Special Driving Permits." Assuming, however, (1) Ned's re-assignment (a) to other routes ultimately results in lessened compensation (of any amount) for him, or, (b) is disadvantageous for any other reason (i.e., the substituted routes are more physically demanding because they are longer and/or more dangerous), and (2) altering driving assignments to. comply with State A law could result in some drivers deciding to leave Ajax's employ, the Plaintiffs probably have standing.

The State A Statute:

Pursuant to the Tenth Amendment, a state may ordinarily enact legislation which is aimed at promoting the health, safety or welfare of its citizenry. Since the legislation in question is obviously aimed at decreasing the possibility of accidents involving explosive-carrying trucks, it would be constitutionally valid (unless it contravenes some federal interest).

Supremacy Clause:

Where a state statute conflicts with the language of, or purposes sought to be achieved by, a federal statute, the former enactment will be invalid under the Supremacy Clause.

Plaintiffs will contend that the State A statute is inconsistent with the purposes sought to be achieved by the federal law because it would induce age discrimination (i.e., to avoid being obliged to juggle schedules to circumvent State A, employers would (a) hire drivers within State A's age parameters, and (b) be more likely to terminate employees who could not travel within State A). However, State A could argue in rebuttal that (1) Plaintiffs' argument is premised on speculative secondary effects of its law, and (2) it is unlikely that Congress intended to preempt state legislation which was based upon bona fide occupational qualifications (statistical studies support State A's age restrictions). Unless there is clear legislative history that Congress intended to totally preclude age as a consideration for employment, Plaintiffs probably would not succeed on this argument.

Equal Protection Clause:

Since the elderly have not historically been subjected to purposeful unequal treatment or relegated to a position of political powerlessness, the strict scrutiny standard would probably not apply; *Massachusetts Board of Retirement v. Murgia*, 427 U.S. 307 (1976).

Plaintiffs might nevertheless contend that the rational relationship test (i.e., there must be a rational relationship between the classification drawn by the statute and the governmental object sought to be achieved) is not satisfied. This is because (1) the physical examination and driving test measure more accurately one's ability to drive safely than strict biological age, and (2) persons with perfect driving records could be excluded as a consequence of the statute, while others with negative driving histories might nevertheless qualify for a Special Driving Permit ("SDP"). However, since the classification (1) need only be rational (i.e., maybe drivers over 60 are more prone to heart attacks), and (2) is supported by empirical data, State A would probably prevail on this issue too.

Dormant Interstate Commerce Clause:

State legislation which unduly burdens interstate commerce (i.e., the interference with interstate commerce resulting from the local regulation outweighs the interest sought to be protected by the law) is invalid; *Bibb v. Navajo Freight Lines, Inc.*, 359 U.S. 520 (1959). Plaintiffs could contend that the State A statute imposes a substantial burden upon interstate commerce, since interstate trucking companies will now be obliged (probably at substantial inconvenience and expense) to avoid State A or be compelled to hire additional employees who can acquire a SDP. State A, however, could argue in rebuttal that it has a strong interest in the legislation (i.e., the desire to avoid catastrophic explosions which have a potential for causing great loss of lives and property).

Assuming State A could show that most truck companies have drivers within their employ who qualify for a SDP (and therefore the statute merely results in the inconvenience of having to alter job assignments), it would again prevail.

Due Process:

Where a state statute irrebuttably presumes that certain facts exist which result in an adverse classification, the denial of an opportunity to challenge that presumption violates an individual's Fourteenth Amendment's due process right to demonstrate that the fact presumed is not true in his/her case, some Supreme Court cases suggest. See, e.g., *Vlandis v. Kline*, 412 U.S. 441 (1973). Thus, Plaintiffs could argue that the irrebuttable presumption that persons over 60 are more prone to accidents than others is invalid (especially since Ned was capable of satisfying the physical examination and driving test requirements of State A). However, State A could probably successfully contend in rebuttal that (1) the irrebuttable-presumption cases like *Vlandis* are probably no longer good law; (2) there is no "property" interest in private employment, and (3) statistical studies (which were presumably methodologically sound) have established that drivers over 60 have a higher incidence of accidents than others, so the classification is certainly rational, which is all that is required by either due process or equal protection.

In summary, it is unlikely that Plaintiffs would be able to invalidate the State A statute.

TABLE OF CASES

This table includes references to cases cited everywhere in this book, including in the various Exam Q&A sections, except for references in the Flow Charts.

SUBJECT MATTER INDEX

This index includes references to the Capsule Summary
and to the Exam Tips, but not to Q&A or Flow Charts

ABORTION
Clinics, performance by, standards for, 82
Consent to, 81-82, 206
    By parents, 82, 206
    By spouse, 81
Counseling, restrictions on, 82
Immature, 82
Informed consent, 81-82
Mature or emancipated, 82
Minors, 82, 206
Notice and consultation, 81-82, 206
    By spouse, 81-82, 206
Parental consent, 206
Partial-birth method, 81, 82, 206
Planned Parenthood v. Casey, 81-82
    Informed consent, 81
    Parental consent, 82
    Significance, 81
    Spousal notification, 81-82
    Undue burden standard, 81
Public facilities, 82
    Ban on, 82
Public funding of, 82
Regulations discouraging abortion, 81
Right to privacy, 80
Significance, 206
Types of methods allowed, 82, 206
Undue burden standard, 81, 206

ADMISSIONS
Race-based admissions as equal protection
    violation, 216

ADULT SEXUAL RELATIONS
See EQUAL PROTECTION, SEXUALITY

ADVISORY OPINIONS
Generally, 172, 245

AFFIRMATIVE ACTION
See EQUAL PROTECTION

AFFORDABLE CARE ACT
Commerce power as basis for, 56-57
Spending power exceeded in, 60
Taxing power as basis for, 58-59

ALIENAGE
See EQUAL PROTECTION

APPOINTMENTS CLAUSE
Inferior (lower-level) officers and, 63-64

Meaning of, 63
Principal officers and, 63
Removal of officers, 64-65

BILL OF RIGHTS
Application to states, 76-77, 205
    Selective incorporation approach, 76
BILLS OF ATTAINDER
Generally, 122, 223
BIRTH CONTROL
Generally, 80
Regulation of following *Roe v. Wade*, 81, 206
Use by minors, 81, 206

CAMPAIGN FINANCE
Free speech and regulation of, 151-153
CIVIL RIGHTS LAWS
Congress' power to modify constitutional rights
    given by, 132
Congressional enforcement of, 125-129, 225-227
    Private conduct, Congress' power to
    reach, 126-127, 225
Repeal of as state action, 124
Thirteenth Amendment, laws passed under au-
    thority of, 126-127
Voting rights, 125
COMA
Rights of patient in, 85, 207
COMMERCE CLAUSE
See INTERSTATE COMMERCE
COMMERCIAL SPEECH
See FREEDOM OF SPEECH
CONGRESS' POWERS
Appointment and removal of federal officers, 63-
    66, 201
Commitment of the armed forces, 201
Enforcement of civil rights laws, 125-129, 225-
    227
Executive officers, right to remove, 203
Modification of constitutional rights, 129, 227
Removal of executive officers, 202
Removal of federal officers, 66, 202
Specific powers of, 52
Substantive scope of constitutional rights, modifi-

TION

RIGHT TO DIE
See also DUE PROCESS OF LAW, "Right to die"
"Clear and convincing" standard, 85, 208
Health-care proxy, 85, 207
Incompetent patient, 85, 207
Living well, 207
Suicide, 85, 208

RIGHT TO TRAVEL
See also EQUAL PROTECTION, 114
Protected under 14th Amendment Privileges or
  Immunities Clause, 116, 221

RIPENESS
Generally, 179, 248
Criminal statute, uncertain enforcement of, 180,
  248
Specific threatened harm, 180, 248

SAME-SEX MARRIAGE, 79, 83, 84, 94, 110-
111, 205, 207, 208, 214

SCHOOL SUSPENSION
Due process and, 90

SECOND AMENDMENT, 121-122

SEGREGATION
See EQUAL PROTECTION

SEPARATION OF POWERS
Generally, 61-67, 201-203
Appointment of federal officers, 201
Commitment of the armed forces, 201
Executive immunity, 66, 203
Executive privilege, 66, 203
Habeas corpus and, 62
Impeachment, 66, 202
President's power, *see* EXECUTIVE POWERS
President's veto power, 61, 201
Removal of appointees, 63-66, 202
  By Congress, 202
  By President, 63-66

SEXUALITY, 83, 207
See also DUE PROCESS OF LAW, GAY MAR-
  RIAGE, and HOMOSEXUALITY
Consensual sexual activity
  Constitutional protection for, 207
  Homosexual conduct, change in Court atti-
    tude towards, 206
  Rational relation "with bite" applied to, 84

SOVEREIGN IMMUNITY, 249
Of states before federal agencies, 181
Of states in their own courts, 181

SPEECH AND DEBATE CLAUSE, 66, 203

SPENDING POWER
Generally, 59

Coercion of states as limit on, 59-60
Conditions set on use of federal funds, 59-60
Distinct enumerated power, existence as, 59
"General welfare" requirement, 60-61
Regulation, attempt to use for, 61

STANDING
Generally, 173-178, 245-246
"Actual or imminent" requirement, 175, 246
Causation requirement, 176, 246
Citizenship suits, 174, 247
Federal taxpaper suits, 173
Federal taxpayer suits, 247
Harm suffered by many, 176
"Injury in fact" requirement, 174, 246
Non-economic harms, 174
Organizations and associations, 176, 246
Prudential standing, 178
Suits by states, 177
Suits not based on taxpayer or citizenship
  status, 174-177, 245
Third-party standing, 177-178, 247

STATE ACTION
Generally, 123-125, 223-225
Acquiescence by state, 125
Civil rights laws, repeal of, 124
Commandment by state, 124, 224
Company towns and shopping centers, 123
Electoral process as constituting, 123
Encouragement by state, 124, 224
Entanglement by state, 124
Involvement by state, 124, 224
Joint participation by state as a private actor, 125
Licensing by state, 125, 225
Modern approach to, 123, 224
"Nexus" doctrine, 124
Parks and recreation, operation of, 123, 224
"Public function" approach, 123-124, 224
Racially-restrictive covenants, 124, 224
State "exclusivity" requirement, 123, 224
"Symbiosis" between state and private actor, 124,
  224
Warehouseman's lien as, 124

STRICT SCRUTINY
See EQUAL PROTECTION

SUBSTANTIVE DUE PROCESS
See DUE PROCESS OF LAW

SUICIDE
See DUE PROCESS OF LAW, RIGHT TO DIE

SUPREMACY CLAUSE
See PREEMPTION

SUPREME COURT'S AUTHORITY
Generally, 49-50
Congress' control of, 50
Review of state court decisions, 49